Palgrave Studies in Prisons and Penology

Series Editors
Ben Crewe
Institute of Criminology
University of Cambridge
Cambridge, UK

Yvonne Jewkes
Social & Policy Sciences
University of Bath
Bath, UK

Thomas Ugelvik
Faculty of Law
University of Oslo
Oslo, Norway

This is a unique and innovative series, the first of its kind dedicated entirely to prison scholarship. At a historical point in which the prison population has reached an all-time high, the series seeks to analyse the form, nature and consequences of incarceration and related forms of punishment. Palgrave Studies in Prisons and Penology provides an important forum for burgeoning prison research across the world.

Series Advisory Board
Anna Eriksson (Monash University)
Andrew M. Jefferson (DIGNITY - Danish Institute Against Torture)
Shadd Maruna (Rutgers University)
Jonathon Simon (Berkeley Law, University of California)
Michael Welch (Rutgers University)

More information about this series at
http://www.palgrave.com/gp/series/14596

Alice Mills · Kathleen Kendall
Editors

Mental Health in Prisons

Critical Perspectives on Treatment and Confinement

Editors
Alice Mills
School of Social Sciences
University of Auckland
Auckland, New Zealand

Kathleen Kendall
Faculty of Medicine
University of Southampton
Southampton, UK

Palgrave Studies in Prisons and Penology
ISBN 978-3-319-94089-2   ISBN 978-3-319-94090-8   (eBook)
https://doi.org/10.1007/978-3-319-94090-8

Library of Congress Control Number: 2018946175

Cover credit: © Paul Doyle/Photofusion Picture Library/Alamy

This Palgrave Macmillan imprint is published by the registered company Springer Nature Switzerland AG
The registered company address is: Gewerbestrasse 11, 6330 Cham, Switzerland

To Kathy Biggar, founder of the Samaritans Listener scheme, which trains prisoners to provide compassionate emotional support to fellow prisoners in distress, and to all those prisoners who provide support to others.

Acknowledgements

We would like to thank our contributors for producing such innovative chapters, despite the pressures of their busy lives and usual jobs. Our thanks also go to Yvonne Jewkes and Ben Crewe, the series editors, and Josie Taylor at Palgrave for their considerable enthusiasm for the project and the patience they have shown whilst we have brought it to a conclusion. Our gratitude must also go to the Southampton prison mental health research team of Luke Birmingham, Judith Lathlean and David Morton, who were involved in the study which first sparked and maintained our interest in mental health in prisons, and who, along with Katey Thom and Susan Hatters-Friedman from Auckland, have provided tremendous support and encouragement.

Finally, our thanks go to Neil, Ella and Issy, and Clive, Pippin and MaryAnn and Allan Kendall for their love, support and patience.

Contents

Notes on Contributors

Bruce A. Arrigo, Ph.D. is Professor of Criminology, Law and Society, and of Public Policy in the Department of Criminal Justice and Criminology at UNC Charlotte, USA. He is a Fellow of the American Psychological Association and the Academy of Criminal Justice Sciences, and the recipient of Lifetime Achievement Awards from the Society for the Study of Social Problems and the American Society of Criminology. He has published more than 200 journal articles, law reviews, book chapters, and academic essays as well as 25 monographs, edited volumes, textbooks, and reference works. His most recent project is *The SAGE Encyclopedia of Surveillance, Security, and Privacy* (2018).

Eileen Baldry is Deputy Vice Chancellor, Diversity and Inclusion, and Professor of Criminology at UNSW Sydney. Her research focuses on social justice matters including social and criminal justice relating to women, Indigenous Australians, people with disabilities; homelessness, transition from prison and community development.

James Cavney, MBChB is a forensic psychiatrist with a background in anthropology and social psychology. Dr. Cavney is the Lead Clinician of the Kaupapa Māori and Pacifica Services at the Auckland Regional Forensic Psychiatry Services.

Catherine Cox is an Associate Professor in the School of History at University College Dublin and co-PI on the Wellcome Trust Investigator Award, 'Prisoners, Medical Care and Entitlement to Health in England and Ireland, 1850–2000'. Her past publications examine mental health and migration, institutionalisation and nineteenth-century medical practice.

Simon Cross is Senior Lecturer in Media and Cultural Studies at Nottingham Trent University, UK. He has published widely on historical and contemporary media reporting of sensitive public policy issues including mental health. His current work includes analysis of changes and continuities in UK press reporting on the insanity defence.

Andrea Daley is an Associate Professor and Director at the School of Social Work, Renison University College, Waterloo, Canada. She has published on social justice issues including those impacting sexual and gender-minority communities with a particular focus on access to equitable and good-quality health care; lesbian/queer women's experiences of psychiatric services; gender, sexuality, race, and class; and the interpretative nature of psychiatric chart documentation as it relates to psychiatric narratives of women's mental distress. She practises critical research methods to engage politics of knowledge building with communities towards the goal of social transformation. She teaches an undergraduate social work course at a provincial correctional faculty in Ontario, Canada that integrates university-enrolled students and incarcerated women.

Denise Edwards was incarcerated in a Canadian federal prison. She is currently working on an undergraduate degree in Caribbean Studies at the University of Toronto and has recently won the BMO Financial Access to Higher Education Award. She is a published fiction writer.

Susan Hatters Friedman, MD is Associate Professor in Psychological Medicine at the University of Auckland and a forensic and perinatal psychiatrist at the Auckland Regional Forensic Psychiatry Services. She is now also Professor of Psychiatry and Adjunct Professor of Law, Case Western Reserve University. Dr. Friedman has been part of the forensic prison team, providing mental health treatment at the Auckland Regional Women's Correctional Facility for several years.

Anastasia Jablonska is a Teaching and Research Fellow at Royal Holloway, University of London. Her research interests are primarily in the experiences of women in prison and the effects of imprisonment on their health and well-being. In her Ph.D. she explored themes such as food, physical activity and prison work to consider their impact on women's health during their incarceration.

Yvonne Jewkes is Professor of Criminology at the University of Bath and Visiting Professor in Criminology at the University of Melbourne. She is an expert on prison architecture and design and has published extensively in the area. She has also advised corrections departments and prison architects in several countries, including the UK, Ireland, Australia and New Zealand.

Kathleen Kendall is Associate Professor of Sociology as Applied to Medicine at the University of Southampton. The main focus of her research has been on criminalisation, imprisonment and mental health. Her labour of love has been researching Rockwood, the first stand-alone 'criminal lunatic' asylum in Canada.

Professor Hilary Marland is Professor of History at the University of Warwick and co-PI on the Wellcome Trust Investigator Award, 'Prisoners, Medical Care and Entitlement to Health in England and Ireland, 1850–2000'. Her past publications have focused on women and psychiatry, migration and mental illness, nineteenth-century medical practice, midwifery and obstetrics, and girls' health.

Ruth McCausland is Research Fellow in the School of Social Sciences at UNSW Sydney. Her research focuses on women, people with disabilities and Aboriginal people in the criminal justice system, with a particular interest in evaluation and cost-benefit analysis of alternatives to incarceration.

Elizabeth McEntyre is a Worimi and Wonnarua woman from Port Stephens, Great Lakes and Hunter Valley areas of New South Wales, Australia. Elizabeth is a Ph.D. scholar at UNSW Sydney and her research 'But-ton Kidn Doon-ga: Black Women Know', re-presents the lived experiences of Australian Indigenous women with mental and cognitive disability in Australian criminal justice systems. Elizabeth is an accredited Mental Health Social Worker, Aboriginal Statewide Official Visitor for NSW prisons and a Member of the NSW Mental Health Review Tribunal.

Rosie Meek is a Professor of Psychology at Royal Holloway, University of London. Her research is broadly concerned with prison regimes, interventions and evaluations, with a particular focus on prison education and health. Her most recent work has explored the use of sport in prison and (with Dr. Alice Mills) the role of the voluntary sector in criminal justice.

Alice Mills is a Senior Lecturer in Criminology at the University of Auckland, New Zealand. She has extensive experience of research into specialist courts, the role of the voluntary sector in criminal justice (with Rosie Meek), and prison mental health, including examining the effects of the prison environment and evaluating several mental health in-reach teams. Her current research examines the links between stable housing and re-offending amongst ex-prisoners, funded by the Royal Society of New Zealand.

Hattie Moyes (M.Sc., B.Sc. (Hons)) is the Research & Development Manager at Forward Trust. Hattie has written two award-winning papers on prisoners with substance dependence and mental health issues. As well as NPS, Hattie's research interests include the role of mindfulness in substance-misuse treatment and improving prisoner health and well-being.

Maureen Norton-Hawk is a Professor of Sociology at Suffolk University. Her research centres on women in conflict with the law and their pathway into and after prison. She recently co-authored a book *Can't Catch a Break: Gender, Jail, Drugs and the Limits of Personal Responsibility* which examined the life experiences of women for five years post-incarceration. She is currently analysing the costs of incarceration, prostitution and recidivism of women held in and released from MCI-Framingham.

Christian Perrin is a Lecturer in Criminology at the University of Liverpool. Christian's teaching and research takes a focus on imprisonment and he is enthusiastic about applied research and evidence-based practice. His Ph.D. explored the impact of prisoners doing personally meaningful work while serving time and the implications for policy and practice. Christian has published in many fields across Criminology, including desistance narrative, rehabilitative climate, and sexual offender treatment.

Shoshana Pollack is a Professor in the Faculty of Social Work at Wilfrid Laurier University, Canada. Shoshana has been working and conducting research with criminalised and imprisoned women for twenty-seven years. She is the Director of the Walls to Bridges programme in Canada.

Kim Radford is a radical social worker. Her lived experience of the psychiatric system informs her dedication to deconstructing the concept of 'mental health'. She is especially concerned with creating more ethical systems of care/support in partnership with Mad and psychiatric survivor communities.

Brian G. Sellers, Ph.D. is an Assistant Professor of Criminology and Criminal Justice at Eastern Michigan University. His research interests include juvenile justice policy, delinquency, restorative justice, school violence, homicide, psychology & law, and surveillance studies. He is the co-author of *Ethics of Total Confinement: A Critique of Madness, Citizenship, and Social Justice*. His work has recently been published in *Criminal Justice and Behavior, Behavioral Sciences & the Law, Journal of Forensic Psychology Research and Practice* and *Contemporary Justice Review*.

Susan Sered is Professor of Sociology at Suffolk University in Boston, Massachusetts. Her books include *Uninsured in America: Life and Death in the Land of Opportunity, Can't Catch a Break: Gender, Jail, Drugs, and the Limits of Personal Responsibility*, and *What Makes Women Sick: Maternity, Modesty, and Militarism in Israeli Society*.

Joe Sim is Professor of Criminology at Liverpool John Moores University. He is the author of a number of books on prisons and punishment including *Medical Power in Prisons* and *Punishment and Prisons*. He is also a trustee of the charity *INQUEST* which campaigns for truth, justice and accountability around deaths in custody.

Abbreviations

ABS	Australian Bureau of Statistics
ACCT	Assessment, Care in Custody and Teamwork
ADTP	Alcohol Dependency Treatment Programme
BHA	Boston Housing Authority
BJS	Bureau of Justice Statistics
CMCH	Corporate Manslaughter and Corporate Homicide Act 2007
CORI	Criminal Offender Record Information
CSC	Close Supervision Centre
DH/HMPS	Department of Health/HM Prison Service
DRWs	Drug Recovery Wings
DSM	Diagnostic and Statistical Manual of Mental Disorders
FPT	Forensic Prison Team
GLM	Good Lives Model
GP	General Practitioner
HMCIP	HM Chief Inspector of Prisons
HMIP	HM Inspectorate of Prisons
HMPPS	HM Prison and Probation Service
IAMHDCD	Indigenous Australians with Mental Health Disorders and Cognitive Disability in the Criminal Justice System Project
IEP	Incentive and Earned Privileges
IPA	Interpretative Phenomenological Analysis

IPP	Indeterminate Imprisonment for Public Protection
JCHR	Joint Committee on Human Rights
LBGTQ	Lesbian, Gay, Bisexual, Transgender and Queer
MDT	Mandatory Drug Testing
MFUs	Māori Focus Units
MHDCD	Mental Health Disorder and Cognitive Disability in the Criminal Justice System Project
MHIRT	Mental Health In-Reach Team
MHSU	Mental Health Screening Unit
MRC	Massachusetts Rehabilitation Commission
NAI	National Archives of Ireland
NAO	National Audit Office
NHS	National Health Service
NOMS	National Offender Management Service
NPS	New Psychoactive Substances
NSW	New South Wales
PHE	Public Health England
PIC	Prison Industrial Complex
PJ	Psychological Jurisprudence
PPO	Prisons and Probation Ombudsman
PSA	Psychoactive Substances Act 2016
PTSD	Post Traumatic Stress Disorder
RIDR	Report Illicit Drug Reaction
SC	Synthetic Cannabinoids
SDTP	Substance Dependence Treatment Programme
SLMC	See Life More Clearly
SMI	Serious Mental Illness
SSDI	Social Service Disability Insurance
SSI	Social Security Insurance
SUs	Service Users
THC	Tetrahydrocannabinol
VA	Veterans Administration
W2B	Walls to Bridges
WHO	World Health Organization
WSDTP	Women's Substance Dependence Treatment Programme

List of Figures

List of Tables

1

Introduction

Alice Mills and Kathleen Kendall

People with mental health problems have long been present in both prisons and other places of confinement. Seddon notes that throughout the eighteenth century 'it was increasingly becoming the case that the "natural repository for the lunatic who had committed a felony [...] was the local gaol or house of correction" (Walker and McCabe 1973, p. 1)' (Seddon 2007, p. 20, citation in original). Today, prison populations worldwide experience substantially higher levels of mental distress than the general population. In a systematic review of 81 studies from 24 countries, Fazel and Seewald (2012) found a prevalence of psychosis of 3.6% in male prisoners and 3.9% in females, with corresponding figures for major depression of 10.2 and 14.1%. In England and Wales, 90% of the prison population is said to experience one or more psychiatric

A. Mills (✉)
University of Auckland, Auckland, New Zealand
e-mail: a.mills@auckland.ac.nz

K. Kendall
University of Southampton, Southampton, UK
e-mail: K.A.Kendall@soton.ac.uk

© The Author(s) 2018
A. Mills and K. Kendall (eds.), *Mental Health in Prisons*, Palgrave Studies in Prisons and Penology, https://doi.org/10.1007/978-3-319-94090-8_1

1

disorders,[1] four times the corresponding rate in the wider community (Brooker et al. 2008). Women and young people in prison are particularly vulnerable to mental health problems (NHS Commissioning Board 2013; Fazel et al. 2008). In the US, the level of mental health problems in prisons is so high that carceral institutions have been seen as 'de facto' psychiatric hospitals (Daniel 2007). This can be at least partially attributed to the low tolerance shown towards disorderly public behaviour in the 1990s, which, as Young (2004) suggests, is likely to have been motivated by a desire to control people with mental health problems wandering the streets without proper facilities or treatment. Although in recent times various attempts have been made to divert or transfer those with mental health problems away from the prison system, such attempts have had a limited impact in practice. For Seddon (2007), this is because the very presence of those with mental health problems within prison is an intrinsic element of the whole confinement project. Institutional confinement is used as a method of punishment to exclude the 'deviant', the dangerous and the vulnerable and '[F]rom this perspective, the confinement of some of the mentally disordered within prisons is unsurprising' (Seddon 2007, p. 157).

Those with mental health issues are often criminalised, but imprisonment itself can create or exacerbate mental health problems. Prisons are hostile environments where people experience fear, intimidation, psychological and physical harm due to, amongst other issues, separation from family and friends, living at close quarters with other prisoners and a lack of constructive activity. The likelihood of self-inflicted death is 8.6 times greater in prison than in the community (Ministry of Justice 2017). This has been explicitly linked to the consequences of imprisonment including boredom, isolation, stressful events within prison such as intimidation and victimisation, and the increasing use of New Psychoactive Substances (NPS) (Dear 2008; National Audit Office [NAO] 2017).

The literature on mental health in prisons has grown exponentially in the last 20 years, and is currently somewhat dominated by mental health professionals, particularly from the 'psy' sciences (Mills and Kendall 2016), perhaps reflecting a substantial increase in the number of mental health staff working in prisons. More critical approaches such as those from sociology, criminology and gender studies have been neglected and little attention has therefore been paid to the constraints and impositions of the prison environment and the exercise of penal power on mental health and mental health treatment (Mills and Kendall 2016). This book seeks to overcome this deficit by presenting a variety of critical perspectives on mental health in prison from academics, practitioners and those who have been involved with the criminal justice system. It examines how the environment, regime, architecture and culture of a place designed for punishment can affect mental health and determine the type, delivery and effectiveness of mental health services. A range of different jurisdictions is discussed in order to demonstrate how mental health in prisons is affected by wider socio-economic and cultural factors, and how in recent years neo-liberalism has abandoned, criminalised and contained large numbers of the world's most marginalised and vulnerable populations. These jurisdictions include Australia, New Zealand and Canada, where due to the ongoing effects of colonialism, indigenous groups are substantially over-represented in the prison population, in addition to England and Wales, Ireland, and the United States. All are neo-liberal societies which have seen increasing structural inequalities. This book is therefore missing other, especially non-Western perspectives in low-income and middle-income countries, which, we would argue, should be the subject of further research and discussion. Overall, this collection challenges the dominant narratives of individualism and pathology and many contributors focus instead on the relationship between structural inequalities, suffering, survival and punishment.

In doing so, this book uses a broader conceptualisation of mental health than other literature in this area. Psychiatric studies such as those cited at the beginning of this book reveal high levels of diagnosed mental illness in prison populations; however, it should be remembered that these levels will be shaped by the instruments used to diagnose and measure them, which in turn are underpinned by a bio-medical framework (Busfield 2011). Many prisoners experience mental health difficulties which do not come to the attention of treatment services or fulfil the criteria for mental illness set by diagnostic manuals. The World Health Organization (WHO) (2014) defines mental disorders as comprising 'a broad range of problems [...] generally characterised by some combination of abnormal thoughts, emotions, behaviour and relation-ships with others'. However, it is difficult to judge what might be consid-ered 'abnormal' thoughts and behaviour in the abnormal environment of a prison, where mental and emotional distress may be considered intelligible responses to experiences of imprisonment, social exclusion and the histories of trauma, loss and abuse, which are considerably more likely to be present amongst incarcerated populations (Durcan 2006).

The terms 'mental illness', 'mental disorder' and 'mental health' are associated with narrow medicalised perspectives, limited in their ability to consider the causes of mental distress (Johnstone and Boyle 2018). Like Morrow and Malcoe (2017), we therefore also use terms such as 'mental distress', 'emotional distress' and 'psychological well-being', although the individual contributors to this volume may use the language of 'mental health' and 'mental illness' according to the aims of their work and their professional background.

Themes of This Book: Critical Approaches to Treatment in Confinement

This book aims primarily to (re)introduce a range of critical perspectives to scholarly work on mental health and penal institutions. Although each of the chapter authors brings their own unique critical approach to this topic, reflecting their varying focuses, academic and professional backgrounds and personal experiences, broadly, this volume is based upon four key themes which run throughout the chapters. Firstly, this collection acknowledges that prison is an unsuitable environment for those with mental health problems (Mills and Kendall 2016; Seddon 2007),[2] particularly as imprisonment, the prison environment, architecture and regime may create and/or exacerbate mental distress. Despite widespread recognition of this, the use of imprisonment for those with mental health issues persists. Although in England and Wales the 2010 Bradley report recommended the extension of police and court diversion services to direct those with serious mental disorder away from the criminal justice system, such schemes remain patchy, and only a small percentage of prisoners with mental health problems are transferred from prisons to outside psychiatric facilities. In the absence of alternative provision, many with mental health problems end up in prison as the 'default' institution (see McCausland et al., this volume) or a place of last resort, particularly if there is seemingly nowhere else for them to go.

In recent times, prison mental health has become a topic of heightened public interest due to the increasing incidence of suicide and self-harm in prisons. In England and Wales, incidents of self-harm increased by 73% between 2012 and 2016 and there were 120 self-inflicted deaths in prisons in 2016, the highest figure since records began (NAO 2017). As noted above, previous research into suicide and self-harm has demonstrated that whilst the prison population contains a high degree of 'imported vulnerability' to suicide and self-harm, the fear, boredom, isolation and other frustrations created by the prison environment strongly contribute to the risk of self-harming behaviours (Dear 2008; Liebling and Krarup 1993; Liebling 1992), alongside the continual failure of the state to learn the lessons from previous deaths in custody (Sim, this volume). The pains of imprisonment have been considerably extended since Sykes's seminal study (see, for example, Crewe 2011). Nevertheless, the deprivations of liberty, goods and services, heterosexual relationships,[3] autonomy and security remain salient as the basic premise, purpose and form of imprisonment endure. For Sykes (1958, p. 79), these pains represented considerable sources of frustration, boredom, discomfort and isolation but together also embody 'a set of threats or attacks which are directed against the very foundations of the prisoner's being'. Imprisonment therefore acts as an assault on the prisoner's sense of self, threatening their ontological security in addition to their physical safety. Moreover, the ability to take measures to ameliorate mental health difficulties, that might be recommended outside of carceral environments, such as constructive activity, support from family and friends, a healthy diet and exercise is highly limited by the prison environment and regime. In these circumstances, it is perhaps foreseeable that expressions of mental distress such as suicide and self-harm are likely to increase, particularly in the context of recent cuts to prison budgets such as in England and Wales.

Secondly, we explore the interface between correctional and psychiatric treatment and the tension between the competing priorities of care and custody. In prison, many mental health problems go undetected and untreated, even at the more serious end of the scale (Senior et al. 2013). In a US study, only one in three state prisoners and one in six jail inmates with a mental health problem received treatment in prison (James and Glaze 2006). Prisoners may not admit to having mental health problems at reception screening due to the shock of imprisonment (Sim 2002) or fear of being viewed as weak and/or vulnerable, and symptoms of mental distress may go ignored on prison wings (Birmingham 2003).

Even when prisoners do receive treatment, its value is likely to be limited by the fact of imprisonment, the priorities of treatment services and available resources. The extent and form of treatment, and quality of care may also be influenced by the degree to which treatment agencies and healthcare staff are bound to the prison authorities and their priorities of security and control. Psychiatric services may be provided by the prison itself, outside of the health departments responsible for public healthcare standards, such as in Belgium and Lithuania. In such instances, mental health services may be more concerned with control and custody, leading to substandard care and human rights violations (WHO/International Committee of the Red Cross 2005). For example, when the Prison Medical Service in England and Wales was responsible for the provision of mental health care, psychotropic medicine was administered to control recalcitrant prisoners and prisoners were thought to have been used as 'guinea pigs' for new forms of medication (Sim 1990, 2002; Woolf 1991; Coggan and Walker 1982). Healthcare professionals working in prison may be seen as part of the disciplinary structure of the prison, potentially constructing prisoners as 'less eligible subjects', undeserving of anything but poorer standards of care than non-prisoners (Sim 2002, p. 300).

Alternatively, mental health treatment in prison may be provided by external services including community mental health services, through commissioning either by the prison administration or justice department, such as in New Zealand (Wakem and McGee 2012), or by national or local health authorities, such as in England and Wales,

France, Italy, and most Nordic countries (Brooker and Webster 2017; Dressing and Salize 2009). In the case of the former, decisions regarding treatment may still be made in the interests of the institution and healthcare budgets may be used to supplement over-committed custody budgets (Wakem and McGee 2012). One example of the latter model are prison mental health in-reach teams (MHIRTs) introduced in Anglo-Welsh prisons in 2002. These multi-disciplinary teams, commissioned by local healthcare agencies, were designed to provide an equivalent range and quality of care to patients with severe mental illness in prison as they would receive in the community. Despite their relative independence from the prison authorities, their aim of providing equivalent mental health care can still be substantially hampered by the prison setting, the emphasis on punishment and security rather than well-being, and the sheer weight and complexity of demand for mental health services (Mills and Kendall 2016, this volume; Harvey and Smedley 2010). Mental health professionals may also be burdened with tasks associated with minimising harm to the institution rather than relieving the distress of the prisoner patient (see Cox and Marland, this volume), including assessing prisoners' suitability for administrative or punitive segregation and managing suicide and self-harm (Mills and Kendall 2010, this volume). The tendency to focus on managing risk and maintaining the public image of the prison, rather than providing appropriate care, was recently highlighted by the Ombudsman in New Zealand who examined several cases of prisoners accommodated in 'at risk units' due to self-harming behaviour. These units contain sparsely furnished isolation cells with no television or reading material and very little opportunity for contact with others. Prisoners kept there were subject to the use of tie down beds and waist restraints,[4] justified by the Department of Corrections as a legitimate response to the perceived risk of self-harm (Stanley 2017). In one case, a prisoner spent 37 nights on a tie-down bed from 4 p.m. to 8.30 a.m. ostensibly to prevent him from self-harming, a practice which the Ombudsman declared amounted to 'cruel, inhuman or degrading treatment or punishment for the purposes of Article 16 of the [UN] Convention against Torture' (Office of the Ombudsman 2017, p. 5).

Mental health services in prison have overwhelmingly focused on psychiatric treatment for prisoners with diagnosed serious mental illness, particularly medication, even though many prisoners have expressed an interest in wanting help with deep-rooted personal problems (Mills and Kendall 2010; Crewe 2009). Psychological treatment at least in UK prisons has become 'synonymous with reducing criminality' (Harvey and Smedley 2010, p. 10) through offending behaviour programmes rather than relieving emotional and mental distress, and psychologists may hold considerable power over prisoners, given their input into risk and security classifications and parole decisions (Crewe 2009), eroding the likelihood of a trusted therapeutic relationship.

Both the focus of mental health services in prisons and the punitive management of self-harm demonstrate how prisons tend to individualise and pathologise mental health problems rather than viewing them as a response to imprisonment, the prison environment, and structural violence outside the prison. In 1990 the then Chief Inspector of Prisons, Stephen Tumin, noted the danger of viewing suicide and self-harm in prison primarily as medical problems, as it may lead to the view 'that all the answers lie with the doctors' (HM Chief Inspector of Prisons 1990, p. 7). To counter this pathologising discourse, in this collection we also focus on non-medical approaches to alleviating mental and emotional distress. These include the use of peer supporters (see chapters by Moyes and Perrin, this volume), which may have substantial benefits for both peer supporters themselves and those whom they seek to help, and prison education programmes (Pollack and Edwards, this volume). Such approaches offer the possibility of inclusive transformative practice and support in prisons for all prisoners regardless of the level of symptoms or sources of their distress.

Thirdly, we argue that despite the individualising and pathologising discourses of much of the current policy and literature around mental health in prisons, mental health issues are likely to be strongly affected, if not created, by wider structural issues. As Johnstone and Boyle (2018, p. 8) assert, '[h]umans are fundamentally social beings whose experiences of distress and troubled or troubling behaviour are inseparable from their material, social, environmental, socioeconomic and cultural contexts'. In this regard, there is a well-established and growing body of scholarship demonstrating that poor mental health is more prevalent among individuals who are socially marginalised due to socio-economic disadvantage, gender, ethnicity, racialisation, colonialism, nationality, gender identity, sexual orientation, disability and age; and that persons who occupy several marginalised positions have an even greater likelihood of experiencing mental health problems (Macintyre et al. 2018; Silva et al. 2016; Rosenfield 2012). This is unsurprising since marginalisation is concomitant with numerous harms likely to cause mental and emotional distress including neglect, inequality, subordination, discrimination, oppression and violence (Pickett and Wilkinson 2010; Johnstone and Boyle 2018). Unfortunately, a diagnosis or label of mental illness can often lead to further marginalisation and harm (Pūras 2017).

This situation highlights the need to adopt policies and practices targeting social inequities and injustices. Yet, the current political and economic climates in the jurisdictions covered by this book are dominated by neoliberalism, which despite being diverse, complex and evolving, is fundamentally 'associated with increased inequality in income, power, and access to resources within countries and a dismantling of universal welfare provision' (Collins et al. 2016, p. 135). Under such a regime, marginalised individuals become even more vulnerable and are held entirely responsible for their circumstances. Rather than preventing and addressing the harms associated with inequalities through the establishment of fairer and caring communities, governments have instead embraced punitive responses through the expansion of prisons, community-based punishments and other spaces of confinement including immigration detention centres. Following their examination of imprisonment in ten nations across all five continents, Jacobson et al. (2017, p. vii) note that with well over 10 million people incarcerated worldwide, there has been a rapid and unrelenting growth in imprisonment, disproportionately harming marginalised groups. Thus, as many authors in this collection illustrate, socially excluded individuals are more likely to experience mental health problems, imprisonment or both (see, for example, chapters by McCausland et al.; Cavney and Friedman; Sim; Norton-Hawk and Sered, this volume). In such a way, imprisonment and patterns of mental health problems both serve as indices of inequality (Whitlock 2016).

Finally, given the above arguments, several contributors take an abolitionist stance, arguing that due to the punishing and debilitating effects of imprisonment, there is an urgent need to consider alternatives. Regardless of healthcare and other reforms that seek to humanise prisons or make them places of rehabilitation and/or treatment, prisons have failed to reduce crime and will only ever be likely to further damage mental health. Several jurisdictions such as England and Wales, Australia and New Zealand aim to provide health care to prisoners which is of a standard equivalent to that provided in the community (Mills and Kendall 2016). This is likely to be unrealistic and unachievable in an 'anti-therapeutic' environment designed for punishment and confinement where health care is not seen as a core business activity (Mills and Kendall 2010), and may be implicated in punishment and control (Seddon 2007). Additionally, if the presence of people with mental health problems in prison is an intrinsic element in the use of institutional confinement as punishment, as Seddon (2007) suggests, no matter how radically mental health care is improved, it will not address the problem. Seddon therefore urges 'a radical re-think of the whole confinement project' (2007, p. 166). Prisons remain expressions of state power which emphasise collective and individual punishment over collective support and empathy (Sim 2009). Security and control requirements will always be prioritised over therapeutic needs (Seddon 2007; Carlen and Tombs 2006) and the informal power held by unaccountable prison staff continually undermines more enlightened policies and practices (Ryan and Sim 2016).

Furthermore, given the socially excluded backgrounds of most prisoners, it is difficult to see how prison could be seen as rehabilitative (Carlen and Tombs 2006), particularly because as state institutions, prisons are 'intimately connected with the reproduction of an unequal and unjust social order divided by the social lacerations of class, gender, 'race', age and sexuality' (Sim 2009, p. 8; see also Ryan and Sim 2016). Despite criticisms of the abolitionist movement as unrealistic and idealistic, abolitionist campaigners in England and Wales have claimed success in abolishing the Prison Medical Service in the early 1990s, and the closure of the mentally torturous Control Units in the mid-1970s (Sim 2009). Resources that are used to provide ostensibly rehabilitative or ameliorative services in prisons such as mental health or drug treatment are likely to be more productive and cost-effective in non-carceral settings and several chapter authors therefore identify alternatives to imprisonment.

Structure of This Book

Mental Health in Prisons: Critical Perspectives on Treatment and Confinement is divided into four sections which cover different aspects of mental health in penal institutions. The first section, *Penal Power and the Psy Disciplines: Contextualising Mental Health and Imprisonment*, critically examines the context and development of mental health and imprisonment, with a particular emphasis on the role of the 'psy' disciplines. It establishes the historical and socio-legal context of mental health and imprisonment, and demonstrates the central role that these disciplines (e.g. psychiatry and psychology) and other professions have played, and continue to play, in governing individuals deemed to be both 'mad' and 'bad'. In their chapter, **Cox and Marland** explore the historical relationship between mental health and the prison system in England and Ireland. They note the persistently high rates of mental health problems in the prison population and the history of punitive confinement of those with mental illness. They discuss the system of separate cellular confinement, introduced in England in the mid nineteenth century as a method of reform, whereby prisoners were kept in their cells for 23 hours a day, isolated from others, and the disastrous effects the system had on the mental health of the prisoners confined within it. Cox and Marland then examine the inability of some prison medical officers to help those with mental health problems and the lack of alternative facilities which has hampered the removal of prisoners from the prison system.

Cross and Jewkes describe the intertwined history of the architecture of the asylum and the architecture of the prison and examine how these physical environments can affect not only the mental health of those incarcerated within but also public perceptions of asylums as being places of punishment. Although historically both asylums and prisons have been ostensibly designed to enhance the health of inmates, the introduction of the separate system (or silent system) led to prisons becoming enclosed and claustrophobic, with both this and contemporary experiences of solitary confinement leading to a deterioration in prisoners' mental health. Although in the mid twentieth century, prisons became heavily influenced by a range of clinical and treatment experts, asylums were to become more prison-like with increasingly restrictive regimes to maintain order and control, leading the American sociologist, Goffman (1961), to present the psychiatric hospital as a total institution, infantilising, de-individualising and wholly unsuited to mental health care. Cross and Jewkes also examine how fictional media accounts have emphasised the prison-like environment and effects of psychiatric hospitals. They argue that both types of building, in sharing a common disciplinary legacy, are symptomatic of punitive cultures which seek to 'other' their most vulnerable citizens.

Through the analytical framework of psychological jurisprudence, **Arrigo and Sellers** revisit and substantially build upon Gresham Sykes's classic 1958 study, *The Society of Captives* and Donald Clemmer's 1940 book, *The Prison Community*. Like their forebears, the authors draw our attention towards the social worlds and relational nature of incarceration. However, they focus upon contemporary deficit and desistance correctional mental health models and practices, and demonstrate how these technologies contribute to the pains of imprisonment. Weaving together a vast array of critical theories, the authors suggest that not only are prisoners embedded in processes of captivity, but so are those who keep, manage and treat them. They propose that to move forward, we must recognise our shared humanity and that therapeutic practices should address the relational dimensions of therapy, recovery and re-entry.

The chapters in the second section, *Care Versus Custody*, discuss different aspects of the contradictions and tensions between the goals of treatment and care, and confinement in an environment designed for punishment, and also consider in greater detail the effects of the prison regime on mental and emotional distress. Each chapter examines different aspects of these forces, including the strains between healthcare staff and custodial staff, the experience of users of New Psychoactive

Substances in prison and possible treatment for them, and the effect of the prison environment on the mental health of women in prison, particularly those with serious physical health conditions.

In their chapter, **Mills and Kendall** examine the tensions between care and custody through the experiences of a mental health in-reach team, staff and prisoners in an English prison. They suggest that the team was often engaged in practices and tasks that were integral to penal governance and the socio-legal apparatus of the criminal justice system which, along with the focus on security, left the team little opportunity to provide therapeutic treatments other than medication, strongly hindering their ability to provide care equivalent to that offered in the community. The low priority afforded to mental health care and the construction of prisoners as less eligible subjects, led to the team being treated with hostility and derision. Additionally, Mills and Kendall discuss the detrimental impact of the prison environment and regime, particularly the lack of purposeful activity, on prisoners' mental health, and argue that mental health professionals can do little to mitigate these harmful effects. They therefore question the concept of 'healthy prisons' which may deflect attention away from the systemic inequities that contribute to poor mental health amongst incarcerated populations, and suggest that rather than seeking to address the prison mental health crisis through prison reform, resources should be directed into the formation of socially just communities.

Hattie Moyes from the Forward Trust (previously known as RAPt) discusses the interface between mental health and addiction issues with particular reference to New Psychoactive Substances (NPS), most notably synthetic cannabis. She argues that NPS are more likely to be used in prisons than in the general community and are often taken by prisoners in order to cope with the pains of prison life, especially boredom, or to self-medicate for existing mental health problems. Yet, the use of NPS has contributed to increasing numbers of deaths, self-harm and victimisation in prison. The 'Spice Spiral' is used to demonstrate how NPS use can have a further detrimental effect on prisoner mental health and can have wider consequences including various punishments such as restricted regimes, which can lead to further isolation from peers and services, potentially exacerbating mental health difficulties. Moyes presents the results of a service evaluation which suggest that many prisoners would value interventions to tackle the challenges of prison life and vulnerability to using NPS, but also notes that such interventions may not be taken up by prisoners if they are fearful of being punished for identifying as NPS users.

Jablonska and Meek draw upon doctoral research on a houseblock in an English women's prison to explore how the prison regime and environment can affect women's mental health. They discuss how living in close proximity to others could lead women to feel both intimidated and lonely, particularly if they had little social support. Uncertainty about discipline and punishments under the Incentive and Earned Privileges Scheme, which could considerably restrict their time out of cell and access to constructive activities, led to considerable anxiety amongst the women. Yet, they often did not take up opportunities to leave the houseblock and engage in activities such as exercise in the gym or family visits which might ostensibly improve their mental well-being. Crucially, Jablonska and Meek examine the 'double punishment' experienced by women with serious physical health conditions and disabilities due to the lack of care and empathy from others and the unsuitability of the prison environment and regime, all of which could have a profound negative effect on their mental health. They argue that 'healthy prisons' are not possible, because women in prison do not have the freedom to make choices which may improve their mental health, and question the use of imprisonment for women, particularly for those who have committed less serious offences.

The third section, *Dividing Practices: Structural Violence, Mental Health and Imprisonment*, considers the intersection between mental health and imprisonment and structural violence, including poverty, heteronormativity, racialisation and colonisation. These chapters collectively consider how such structural violence intersects with mental health and imprisonment. They suggest that action could be taken to address oppressive structures and practices and that alternatives to imprisonment are necessary. **McCausland, McEntyre and Baldry** draw upon recent collaborative research with Aboriginal women with mental and cognitive disabilities in prisons in Australia. They note the gross over-representation of Aboriginal women in custodial settings and how

Aboriginal women have contact with the criminal justice agencies both earlier in their lives and more often throughout their lives. Informed by critical Indigenous, feminist, disability and criminological approaches, they argue that Aboriginal women in prison have experienced substantial trauma such as domestic violence and sexual assault but also structural violence and trauma resulting from ongoing colonisation, institutional racism and sexism. This is then compounded by prison which becomes the 'default' management institution for these women and their complex needs, and will remain so without appropriate, gender-specific, culturally- and trauma-informed, integrated services in the community for Aboriginal girls and women with mental and cognitive disabilities.

In their chapter, **Cavney and Friedman** examine the impact of colonisation on Māori, the indigenous population of New Zealand, noting the disproportionately high rates of imprisonment and mental health problems experienced by Māori. They argue that this can be attributed to socio-economic factors and racist stereotyping, but also cultural disenfranchisement, particularly dislocation from *whānau* (wider extended family networks) and the intergenerational transmission of cultural trauma, as a result of colonising practices. Cavney and Friedman therefore argue that there is a need to address cultural disenfranchisement to promote mental health recovery. They detail several ways of doing this including employing cultural advisers as part of prison mental health teams to assist with assessment and building relationships with service users and their whānau.

Joe Sim then discusses self-inflicted deaths in prisons in England and Wales. He argues that numerous inquests, reports, audits and investigations into these deaths have noted the poor standard of mental health care in prisons and the failure of prisons to follow procedures to identify and manage risk of self-harm. He contends that self-inflicted deaths, particularly those involving people with mental health problems, have been explained with recourse to positivist, pathologising discourses. This has shifted attention away from the role of the prison, and therefore the role of the state, in creating vulnerability to self-harm through its destructive, structural operationalising of power, systemic neglect and threat of violence, which torments, humiliates and traumatises prisoners, creating and exacerbating mental health problems. Sim suggests that a moratorium on prison building be introduced and existing prisons closed and the budget re-directed towards better mental health services, radical alternatives to custody and small group therapy. Furthermore, he argues that corporate manslaughter laws should be used to hold prisons to account where systemic failing and gross negligence have led to deaths in prison.

Norton-Hawk and Sered draw upon a five-year study of women released from prison to argue that many are caught up in 'institutional captivity', trapped in a circuit made up of a variety of institutions, including prisons, jails, homeless shelters, battered women's shelters, probation and parole offices, rehabilitation and detox facilities, welfare offices, child welfare services, public housing and parenting classes. Each institution dispossesses individuals of their 'outside' identities and obligates them to follow detailed rules, regulations and institutional norms and values. Despite the apparent diverse purposes of correctional and 'helping' institutions, these agencies preach and reinforce a cultural ethos that pathologises and individualises the suffering, victimisation and trauma experienced by these women rather than recognising the institutionalised, structural and gendered patterns of their life experiences. Disability payments given on the basis of mental illness keep women trapped in this circuit. With reference to the detailed stories of two women, Norton-Hawk and Sered contend that women are blamed for their own victimisation and suffering, and are locked into dependency on the institutional circuit. Rehabilitation is erroneously cast as a matter of individual choice, even though these women often return to poor, marginalised, urban neighbourhoods with few opportunities to escape.

Daley and Radford use a mad queer abolitionist framework to critically consider the mental and emotional distress experienced by incarcerated trans and queer people. They note the high levels of contact this population has with the criminal justice system, their racialised experiences, the greater prevalence of mental health problems amongst queer and trans persons and their heightened risk of harassment, discrimination and victimisation in the prison system. However, they reject the minority stress model which suggests that queer and trans mental and emotional distress is an outcome of stigma, discrimination and prejudice, as this individualises and pathologises reactions to structural violence and injustice, and validates strategies such as protective segregation which can cause further mental and emotional distress. They posit a mad queer abolitionist framework to (re) mobilise a prison justice analysis and reframe this distress as an expected and normal reaction to the unrelenting structural, gendered violence at the heart of the prison system. In so doing, the authors seek to unsettle heteronormativity and cisnormativity.

The final section, *Alternative Penal Practices and Communities* discusses initiatives to improve mental well-being in prison that go beyond narrow medical approaches and the use of psychotropic medication. Although alternatives to incarceration should be our long-term strategy, prisoners with mental health problems should not be neglected and it is therefore crucial to consider alternative forms of support. The chapters in this section examine two initiatives run by non-clinicians, including prisoners themselves, which consider that working with agencies and individuals from outside the prison to engage in education and peer support can be effective ways of improving mental health problems and re-thinking incarceration.

In their chapter, **Pollack and Edwards** discuss Walls to Bridges (W2B), an educational programme in which both incarcerated and non-incarcerated students study together for semester-long university courses in a correctional setting. In the first part of the chapter, Pollack, a W2B instructor, explains the philosophy behind W2B, including the destabilising of power relations between professors and students and between students themselves, and the development of a classroom climate which values different perspectives, lived experience, and an understanding of one's self as being situated within different contexts such as gender, race, class and culture. In this setting, non-judgemental reflective listening is fostered to dispel stigma and stereotypes. In the second part of the chapter, Edwards, a formerly incarcerated alumnus of W2B, discusses the powerful impact of the programme which helped her to feel valued, accepted and connected to a community, also ultimately improving her mental and emotional well-being and reducing her need for psychotropic medication.

Perrin then discusses the value of peer support schemes in prison in improving the mental well-being not only of service users but also of peer supporters themselves. A range of different peer support schemes operate in UK prisons, including the Listeners, which is run by the Samaritans, an emotional health charity. Peer support schemes are founded on the core tenets of shared problem-solving, empathy and experiential exchanges. They can reduce stress and anxiety amongst prisoners, for example, as service users have the opportunity to discuss negative feelings, or receive help to cope with the practicalities of prison life. Perrin suggests that supporting peers can strengthen individuals' social ties and counter the boredom of imprisonment through meaningful activity, in addition to enabling prisoners to develop a sense of agency, autonomy and normality, and gain a sense of perspective regarding their own lives.

Finally, in the conclusion, we bring together the different chapters by identifying the key messages and strategies running across them. We argue that in adopting a diversity of critical perspectives through which to revisit mental health in prison, this collection challenges the dominant narratives of individualism and pathology. Furthermore, it provides examples of strategies designed to address both the immediate pains of imprisonment and the longer term goal of creating equal, healthy and sustainable communities with improved mental health for all and imprisonment for none. Taken together, the critical analyses in this book suggest that we can best achieve this end by creating alliances among a diverse collection of academics, activists, prisoners and other criminalised persons, individuals with lived experience of mental health issues and practitioners.

Notes

1. Psychosis, neurosis, personality disorders, hazardous drinking and drug dependency. This is arguably a fairly broad definition of psychiatric disorder. This study also established that the prevalence of psychosis, usually deemed to be serious mental illness, was between 7 and 14% in prison compared to 0.4% in the general population (Singleton et al. 1998).
2. See, for example, the Trenčín Statement which states that acceptance is needed that 'penal institutions are seldom, if ever, able to treat and care

for seriously and acutely mentally ill prisoners' (WHO Regional Office for Europe 2008).

3. Homosexual and bisexual relationships may also be substantially constrained by imprisonment and should therefore be included on Sykes's list of 'deprivations'.

4. Waist restraints involve prisoners being placed in handcuffs which are then attached to a belt behind their backs.

Bibliography

Birmingham, L. (2003). The mental health of prisoners. *Advances in Psychiatric Treatment, 9,* 191–201.

Brooker, C., Duggan, S., Fox, C., Mills, A., & Parsonage, M. (2008). *Short changed: Spending on prison mental health care.* London: Sainsbury Centre for Mental Health.

Brooker, C., & Webster, R. (2017). Prison mental health in-reach teams, serious mental illness and the Care Programme Approach in England. *Journal of Forensic and Legal Medicine, 50,* 44–48.

Busfield, J. (2011). *Mental illness.* Cambridge: Polity Press.

Carlen, P., & Tombs, J. (2006). Reconfigurations of penality: The ongoing case of women's imprisonment and reintegration industries. *Theoretical Criminology, 10*(3), 337–360.

Coggan, G., & Walker, M. (1982). *Frightened for my life: An account of deaths in British prisons.* Glasgow: Fontana.

Collins, C., McCartney, G., & Garnham, L. (2016). Neoliberalism and health inequalities. In K. Smith, S. Hill, & C. Bambra (Eds.), *Health inequalities: Critical perspectives* (pp. 124–137). Oxford: Oxford University Press.

Crewe, B. (2009). *The prisoner society: Power, adaptation and social life in an English prison.* Oxford: Oxford University Press.

Crewe, B. (2011). Depth, weight, tightness: Revisiting the pains of imprisonment. *Punishment and Society, 13,* 509–529.

Daniel, A. E. (2007). Care of the mentally ill in prisons: Challenges and solutions. *Journal of the American Academy of Psychiatry and the Law Online, 35,* 406–410.

Dear, G. E. (2008). Ten years of research into self-harm in the Western Australian prisons system: Where to next? *Psychiatry, Psychology and the Law, 15*(3), 469–481.

Dressing, H., & Salize, H.-J. (2009). Pathways to psychiatric care in European prison systems. *Behavioral Sciences & the Law, 27,* 801–810.

Durcan, G. (2006). Equivalent to what? Mental health care in Britain's prisons. *Journal of Mental Health Workforce Development, 1,* 36–44.

Fazel, S., Doll, H., & Langstrom, N. (2008). Mental disorders among adolescents in juvenile detention and correctional facilities: A systematic review and metaregression analysis of 25 surveys. *Journal of American Academy of Child and Adolescent Psychiatry, 47,* 1010–1019.

Fazel, S., & Seewald, K. (2012). Severe mental illness in 33,588 prisoners worldwide: Systematic review and meta-regression analysis. *British Journal of Psychiatry, 2000,* 364–373.

Goffman, E. (1961). *Asylums: Essays on the social situation of mental patients and other inmates.* London: Penguin Books.

Harvey, J., & Smedley, K. (2010). Introduction. In J. Harvey & K. Smedley (Eds.), *Psychological therapy in prisons and other secure settings* (pp. 1–25). Abingdon: Willan Publishing.

HM Chief Inspector of Prisons. (1990). *Report of a review by her majesty's chief inspector of prisons for England and Wales of suicide and self-harm in prison service establishments in England and Wales.* London: HMSO.

Jacobson, J., Heard, C., & Fair, H. (2017). *Prison: Evidence of its use and overuse from around the world.* London: Institute for Criminal Policy Research.

James, D. J., & Glaze, L. E. (2006). *Mental health problems of prison and jail inmates.* US Department of Justice. Available at: https://www.bjs.gov/content/pub/pdf/mhppji.pdf. Accessed 2 Jan 2018.

Johnstone, L., & Boyle, M. with Cromby, J., Dillon, J., Harper, D., Kinderman, P., Longden, E., Pilgrim, D., & Read, J. (2018). *The power threat meaning framework: Overview.* Leicester: British Psychological Society.

Liebling, A. (1992). *Suicides in prison.* London: Routledge.

Liebling, A., & Krarup, H. (1993). *Suicide attempts and self-injury in male prisons.* London: Home Office.

Macintyre, A., Ferris, D., Gonçalves, B., & Quinn, N. (2018). What has economics got to do with it? The impact of socioeconomic factors on mental health and the case for collective action. *Palgrave Communications, 4*(10), 1–5.

Mills, A., & Kendall, K. (2010). Therapy and mental health in-reach teams. In J. Harvey & K. Smedley (Eds.), *Psychological therapy in prisons and other secure settings* (pp. 26–47). Abingdon: Routledge.

Mills, A., & Kendall, K. (2016). Mental health in prisons. In Y. Jewkes, B. Crewe, & J. Bennett (Eds.), *Handbook on prisons* (2nd ed., pp. 187–204). Abingdon: Routledge.

Ministry of Justice. (2017). *Safety in custody statistics bulletin, England and Wales: Deaths in prison custody to December 2016, assaults and self-harm to September 2016.* Available at: https://www.gov.uk/government/uploads/system/uploads/attachment_data/file/595797/safety-in-custody-quarterly-bulletin.pdf. Accessed 19 Sept 2017.

Morrow, M., & Malcoe, L. (Eds.). (2017). *Critical inquiries for social justice in mental health.* Toronto: University of Toronto Press.

National Audit Office (NAO). (2017). *Mental health in prisons.* London: National Audit Office.

NHS Commissioning Board. (2013). *Securing excellence in commissioning for offender health.* London: Department of Health.

Office of the Ombudsman. (2017). *A question of restraint. Care and management for prisoners considered to be at risk of suicide and self-harm: Observations and findings from OPCAT Inspectors.* Available at: http://www.ombudsman.parliament.nz/system/paperclip/document_files/document_files/1905/original/a_question_of_restraint_march_2017.pdf?1493174263. Accessed 15 Jan 2018.

Pickett, K. E., & Wilkinson, R. G. (2010). Inequality: An underacknowledged source of mental illness and distress. *British Journal of Psychiatry, 197*(6), 426–428.

Pūras, D. (2017). *Report of the special rapporteur on the right of everyone to the enjoyment of the highest attainable standard of physical and mental health.* United Nations General Assembly. A/HRC/35/21. Available at: http://ap.ohchr.org/documents/dpage_e.aspx?si=A/HRC/35/21. Accessed 2 Apr 2018.

Rosenfield, S. (2012). Triple Jeopardy? Mental health at the intersection of gender, race and class. *Social Science and Medicine, 74*(11), 1791–1801.

Ryan, M., & Sim, J. (2016). Campaigning for and campaigning against prisons: Excavating and reaffirming the case for prison abolition. In Y. Jewkes, J. Bennett, & B. Crewe (Eds.), *Handbook on prisons* (2nd ed., pp. 712–733). Abingdon: Oxford University Press.

Seddon, T. (2007). *Punishment and madness: Governing prisoners with mental health problems.* Abingdon: Glasshouse.

Senior, J., Birmingham, L., Harty, M. A., Hassan, L., Hayes, A. J., Kendall, K., et al. (2013). Identification and management of prisoners with severe psychiatric illness by specialist mental health services. *Psychological Medicine, 43,* 1511–1520.

Silva, M., Loureiro, A., & Cardoso, G. (2016). Social determinants of mental health: A review of the evidence. *European Journal of Psychiatry, 30*(4), 259–292.

Sim, J. (1990). *Medical power in prisons*. Milton Keynes: Open University Press.

Sim, J. (2002). The future of prison health care: A critical analysis. *Critical Social Policy, 22,* 300–323.

Sim, J. (2009). *Punishment and prisons*. London: Sage.

Singleton, N., Meltzer, H., & Gatward, R. (1998). *Psychiatric morbidity among prisoners*. London: Office for National Statistics.

Stanley, E. (2017, March 6). "Risk prevention" just won't wash: Torture in prisons is torture and we need to act now. *The Spinoff.* Available at: https://thespinoff.co.nz/society/06-03-2017/risk-prevention-just-wont-wash-torture-in-prisons-is-torture-and-we-need-to-act-now/. Accessed 16 Jan 2018.

Sykes, G. M. (1958). *The society of captives: A study of a maximum security prison*. Princeton, NJ: Princeton University Press.

Wakem, B., & McGee, D. (2012). *Investigation of the department of corrections in relation to the provision, access and availability of prisoner health services*. Wellington: Office of the Ombudsman.

Walker, N., & McCabe, S. (1973). *Crime and insanity in England: New solutions and new problems*. Edinburgh: Edinburgh University Press.

Whitlock, K. (2016). *Prison reform misdirection: 5 caveats about private prisons and mass incarceration*. Beacon Broadside. Available at: http://www.beaconbroadside.com/broadside/2016/09/prison-reform-misdirection-5-caveats-about-private-prisons-and-mass-incarceration.html. Accessed 2 Apr 2018.

WHO Regional Office for Europe. (2008). *Trenčín statement on prisons and mental health*. Copenhagen: World Health Organization.

World Health Organization (WHO)/International Committee of the Red Cross. (2005). *Information sheet on mental health and prisons*. Available at: http://www.euro.who.int/__data/assets/pdf_file/0007/98989/WHO_ICRC_InfoSht_MNH_Prisons.pdf. Accessed 14 Jan 2018.

World Health Organization (WHO). (2014). *Mental disorders*. Available at: http://www.who.int/topics/mental_disorders/en/. Accessed 6 July 2014.

Woolf, L. J. (1991). *Prison disturbances April 1990: Report of an inquiry by the Rt. Hon. Lord Justice Woolf (Parts I and II) and his honour Stephen Tumin (Part II)*. London: HMSO.

Young, J. (2004). Crime and the dialectics of inclusion/exclusion: Some comments on Yar and Penna. *British Journal of Criminology, 44,* 550–561.

Part I

Penal Power and the Psy Disciplines: Contextualising Mental Health and Imprisonment

2

'We Are Recreating Bedlam': A History of Mental Illness and Prison Systems in England and Ireland

Catherine Cox and Hilary Marland

In May 2014, the *Guardian* newspaper reported a number of shocking instances of homicide carried out by prison inmates suffering from mental health problems. The article went on to accuse the English prison system of 'recreating Bedlam', with a prison service poorly equipped to deal with the 10% of the prison population who were suffering from serious mental health disorders at any one time.[1] Unable to protect their mentally ill inmates from self-harm or from harming other prisoners, mental health support in some prisons was described as 'virtually non-existent' and mental health disorders were 'often viewed by management as a discipline problem rather than a health issue' (Sloan and Allison 2014). The Bradley Report of 2009, investigating the provision of mental health services in prison, had urged the

C. Cox (✉)
University College Dublin, Dublin, Ireland
e-mail: catherine.cox@ucd.ie

H. Marland
University of Warwick, Coventry, UK
e-mail: Hilary.Marland@warwick.ac.uk

© The Author(s) 2018   **25**
A. Mills and K. Kendall (eds.), *Mental Health in Prisons*, Palgrave Studies in Prisons and Penology, https://doi.org/10.1007/978-3-319-94090-8_2

'earliest possible diversion of offenders with mental disorders from the criminal justice system' (Bradley 2009, p. 53). Yet, little progress had been made by 2014 and mentally ill prisoners were still ending up in prison rather than hospital (Sloan and Allison 2014).

The issues identified by the *Guardian* are of long standing and have been reiterated time and again in recent inquires and in the press. In 2013, the *Irish Times* highlighted the damage caused by solitary confinement and described how reports over the past decade, conducted by Irish and international agencies, 'blamed prison conditions for incubating psychological problems that then spill over into self-harming or troubling behaviour' (Humphreys 2013). In 2005, the United Nation's special rapporteur observed that 'overcrowding, lack of privacy, enforced isolation and violence tend to exacerbate mental disabilities' and noted the limited access to basic mental healthcare and support services in Irish prisons (Humphreys 2013). Despite numerous initiatives to reform prisons and their regimes, prisons continue to confine large numbers of people with mental health problems who they are poorly equipped to care for.

Historically, prisons have consistently admitted large numbers of mentally ill people and have been charged with producing and exacerbating mental disorder amongst their inmates, and offering little in the way of treatment. Already by the sixteenth and seventeenth centuries, bridewells and houses of correction were confining 'more dangerous or troublesome lunatics' (Seddon 2007, p. 2) and prison reformer John Howard described how by the late eighteenth century, 'rooms which were designed for prisoners are occupied by lunatics', who were exposed to overcrowded and offensive conditions and denied treatment and proper care (Howard 1780, p. 10). Howard particularly singled out Irish prisons for their poor implementation of legislation intended to preserve the health of prisoners (Howard 1784, p. 205). Referring to the condition of 'lunatics' held at Lancaster Castle prison in the north of England in the first decade of the nineteenth century, penal reformer James Neild described how, violent and often dangerous, they posed a threat to prison order and put prison officers' lives at risk. Neild's suggestion that they be removed to a hospital or place of seclusion went unheeded, however, and in 1812, after one suicide attempt and a number of violent skirmishes with the prison warders, one of the 'lunatic' prisoners, James Rawlinson, was found hanged in his cell[2] (Neild 1812, p. 329; DeLacy 1986, pp. 116–119).

Since the mid-nineteenth century, government inquiries and the reports of prison reform organisations have urged change in the provision of mental health services in prison, while the appropriateness of prison for inmates suffering from mental health problems has been questioned time and again. Prisons have sought to improve their response to treating mentally ill inmates, but these efforts have been hampered by the tensions between the provision of care and need to manage and discipline, and more recently by a lack of viable alternatives in terms of psychiatric services outside the prison system. This essay explores the relationship between the prison and mental illness from the mid-nineteenth century onwards, as a new system of prison discipline was imposed across the British Isles. Our focus lies with England and Ireland, which enables us to trace the introduction of the system of separate confinement at Pentonville Prison in London and then within England, and efforts to respond to and modify the regime in Ireland.

In the first section, we examine the introduction of the system of separate confinement, which, even as it was being introduced, was strongly critiqued for its production of mental disorder. Yet, it endured and support for the separate system proved remarkably resilient. Moving to the late nineteenth century, we seek to explain the persistence of regimes that confined and failed to treat mentally ill prisoners. We also examine the ways in which prison staff dealt with such prisoners, bound as they were to enforcing the prison regime and discipline as well as attempting to ensure the health of their prisoner patients. We ask how far the management of mental illness in prison aimed to mitigate harm to the institution rather than relieving the prisoner patient. In the concluding section, we focus on continuities, examining how changing mental health policies and shortages in alternative provision of care contributed to the accumulation of large numbers of mentally ill people in prison. The challenging conditions that prevail in prisons—overcrowding, poor standards of psychiatric services and staffing issues—have enabled prisons to defend the continued use of solitary confinement and reproduced an environment damaging to prisoners' minds.

Creating Troubled Minds in Prison: The System of Separate Confinement

During the late 1830s, a new system of prison discipline was introduced to the British Isles, that of separate confinement or the 'Philadelphia system'. With the construction of Philadelphia's new prison, the Eastern State Penitentiary in 1829, its architects and supporters were able to isolate prisoners from each other in a way that had not been attempted before (Gray 1847; Rothman 1998). When William Crawford, founder of the Society for the Improvement of Prison Discipline, was commissioned by the British government to report on American prisons and systems of discipline in 1833, he returned entranced with the 'Philadelphia system'. An equally fervent advocate of separate confinement was Reverend William Whitworth Russell, who in 1830 was appointed Chaplain to Millbank Penitentiary that had opened in 1816 as a showcase government prison with separate cells. In this position, Russell established great power as he directed the prisoners' moral and religious education and undertook individual cell visits. In 1831 and again in 1835, Russell gave evidence to Select Committees on prison reform advocating single cellular confinement, and agreeing with Crawford on the superiority of the separate system as exemplified in Philadelphia.

What attracted both men to separate confinement was its apparent ability to produce genuine reform and repentance, based as it was on the rigorous separation of prisoners from each other, and its emphasis, through moral training, religious exhortation and individual cell visitations, on inspiring reflection and redemption. In addition to being spiritually and morally reformative, it was also penal and imposed a fierce discipline on both its inmates and the prison officers. Crawford and Russell, who were appointed prison officers for London in 1835, refuted warnings of the risks the regime posed to the mental health of prisoners. At Eastern State Penitentiary, not only did separation appear to produce higher rates of insanity but also increased mortality amongst the prison inmates (Charleroy and Marland 2016, p. 142). Following his visit to Eastern State Penitentiary, its most famous critic Charles

Dickens condemned the regime in his *American Notes*, published in 1842, describing the prisoners as 'dejected' and 'broken hearted' (Wilson 2009, p. 290). An editorial in the London *Times*, which ran a long-standing campaign against the importation of the separate system to England, predicted that insanity would be a 'probable', even 'inevitable', outcome of the Pentonville regime (*The Times*, 1 May 1841).

Despite such opposition, Pentonville Model Prison in London introduced separate cellular confinement in its most extreme form in 1842. Prisoners were confined in their cells alone and in silence for 23 hours out of 24, where they worked, ate and slept. Movement through the prison to attend chapel, where they sat in separate stalls, to take exercise and to attend classes, was rigorously controlled and prisoners were compelled to wear hoods to conceal their identity. Pentonville's carefully selected prisoners were to be first offenders in good health, aged between 18 and 35, fit and able to withstand the force of what was widely regarded as a testing regime and experiment. The prison chaplains, meanwhile, were 'central actors' in enforcing and superintending this system of discipline, through their sermons, management of the schoolmasters, and particularly their individual and frequent cell visitations (Forsythe 1987, p. 45). Prisoners were to endure this system of discipline for 18 months prior to transportation (Cox and Marland 2018, p. 84).

The predictions of Pentonville's critics proved accurate. Rather than producing the anticipated repentance, reform and improvement of the mind, in practice, Pentonville's early years were marked by high incidences of mental breakdown among the prisoners, alarming cases of delusion, hallucination, panic, depression, anxiety and morbid feelings. In 1851, eminent psychiatrist Dr. Forbes Winslow, explained that, despite aiming to exclude mentally ill prisoners, 1.4% of Pentonville's inmates were suffering from mental illness compared with 0.25% of the general population (Winslow 1851, p. 359). Peter Laurie, President of Bethlem Asylum, described Pentonville as a 'disgrace' and complained to *The Times* that 40 prisoners had been sent from Pentonville to Bethlem by 1847, 'the direct result of the separate system' (*The Times*, 11 January 1847).

The separate system was quickly adopted in other convict and local prisons in England and extended to most prisons in Ireland from 1850, even as it was being partly dismantled in Pentonville, where the length of separation was reduced after the sudden deaths of Crawford and Russell in 1847, to 12 months in 1848 and 9 months by 1853 (Henriques 1972, p. 86). Yet, responses varied in individual prisons. In 1856, a parliamentary review of the disciplinary systems in place in English and Irish prisons found that many prisons, including Reading, Bedford, Bath, Belfast, Kilkenny, Mountjoy and Pentonville, 'fully carried out' the separate system, while in others, implementation was partial or completely absent (Separate Confinement 1856 [163]). In 1853, Reverend John Field, Chaplain to Reading Gaol and a strong advocate of the separate system, declared to the Visiting Justices that 'I should... deeply lament both for the sake of Society and the Souls of Men that it should be subverted and abandoned, or even be modified as to impair its efficiency' (Berkshire Record Office, Q/S0 24, 17 October 1853, p. 143). Elsewhere, prison governors, medical officers and chaplains were more apprehensive about the impact of separation. Wakefield's prison officers expressed their reservations in 1847, its chaplain concluding that 'there appeared little doubt that cases of mental delusion might be attributed to the separate system'. Wakefield introduced modified dietary and exercise regimes, and allowed prisoners more outdoor exercise, which was claimed to reduce their mental stress (Wakefield Record Office Q/S 10/56, p. 98; Jebb 1852, p. 9). A number of other chaplains felt compelled to express doubt about the effectiveness of separate confinement. The chaplain of Spike Island Prison in Cork, Reverend Charles Gibson, described the cellular prison in 1863 as 'a delicate piece of machinery which no unskilful hand should touch. A few more turns of the screw, and you injure both the body and mind of the prisoners' (Gibson 1863, p. 69).

By the early 1850s, official reports were casting doubt on the initial evidence that had led to the advocacy of separate confinement. Though instrumental in extending the separate system to Mountjoy Convict Prison, Dublin, opened in 1850 and designed according to the Pentonville model, Surveyor-General of Prisons and Pentonville's architect, Col. Joshua Jebb, suggested in 1852 that Crawford's enthusiasm after his visit to the Eastern State Penitentiary had been based on 'slender data', and that Crawford's assertion that the discipline 'would have no unfavourable effect on the mind or health' might be unfounded (Carroll-Burke 2000, pp. 56–57; Jebb 1852, p. 5).

In preparation for the introduction of the separate system to the new 'model' prison at Mountjoy, Henry M. Hitchins, Inspector of Government Prisons in Ireland, had visited Pentonville in January 1850. Reporting back, Hitchins noted the almost 'universal rejection of the 'purest' form of the separate system as too severe, affecting both the mental and physical condition of the convict and tending to stupefy'. Long periods of separate confinement, he suggested, could 'produce a general debility of mind and body – this aggravating in the prisoners any previous predisposition which may have existed' (National Archives of Ireland (NAI) GPO/LB/12, pp. 35, 53). Hitchins advised the medical officer at Mountjoy, Dr. Francis Rynd, to extend the examination of prisoners on admission to include their 'mental' as well as their physical condition. Hitchins also commented on the 'dread' felt by the convict returning to his 'separate cell'. Nonetheless, he concluded that '"separation should be the principle" upon which Mountjoy prison is to be conducted, yet that many details of Pentonville which being extreme are necessarily futile, may be safely avoided' (NAI GPO/LB/12, pp. 35, 53). Rynd relaxed the 'strict prison discipline', by increasing the amount of time for exercise, and altering the diet and type of labour carried out in prisoners' cells. In 1851, he claimed that the absence of cases of mental disease in that year was a result of these modifications, in particular, his decision to provide 'sufficient occupation of the minds of prisoners' (Inspectors of Government Prisons in Ireland 1852, p. 54).

Managing Bedlam in the Late Nineteenth-Century Prison

Statements of this kind set the tone for the second half of the nineteenth century. Prison administrators, medical staff and the chaplains regularly voiced reservations about the separate system for its damaging effects on the mind and failure to reform. Yet, it prevailed. This is not to say that it was applied uniformly and with equal force in all prisons. Smaller prisons were ill adapted to implement separate confinement, while conditions of overcrowding hampered its imposition elsewhere. Some prisons would moderate or adapt separate confinement, and in Ireland more generally, the role of the chaplains as enforcers of moral reform was curtailed, as they exerted little control over the schoolmasters. Yet, the separate system would form the model and ideal for prison design and discipline throughout the nineteenth century. By 1850, Pentonville had inspired ten new English prisons to be built on the same model, and ten others had converted to the separate system, while in Ireland, by 1856, approximately one third of convict and local prisons, were either built or adapted for the separate system (Ignatieff 1978, p. 197; Separate Confinement 1856).[3]

Following the nationalisation of the prison system in England and Ireland in the late 1870s, prison regimes became harsher and support for cellular separation as a highly efficient and deterrent system strengthened (Forsythe 1991). Interest in imposing rigorous punishment and maximising control overrode the ideals of facilitating reflection and reformation amongst prisoners. As Miles Ogborn has argued, 'The terrors of solitude remained in place as a deterrent, alongside an increased emphasis on hard labour', once the system of transportation was dismantled and replaced by enforced labour (Ogborn 1995, p. 304).

During the second half of the nineteenth century, the presence of large numbers of mentally ill prisoners and the management of mental illness in prison were becoming a burdensome reality. It threatened the viability and success of separate confinement and hampered the smooth governance of prisons. Medical officers, chaplains and other prison officers were preoccupied on a daily basis with dealing with mentally ill prisoners, subduing their efforts to self-harm, commit suicide or to commit acts of destruction or violence. Already by the mid-1840s, Pentonville's medical officers and chaplains were reporting multiple cases of mental breakdown, some of whom were transferred to the infirmary for treatment, while others were retained under observation in their cells. While resisted by prison authorities keen to mask the extent of mental disorder in the prison, removals to Bethlem occurred on a regular basis (Cox and Marland 2018).

While many prison medical officers were reluctant to blame the system of separate confinement for cases of mental illness, they asserted that prisons were becoming repositories for inmates already suffering some form of 'mental weakness'. Dr. John Campbell noted that, by 1855, he was dealing with over 80 weak-minded prisoners at Dartmoor Prison's Invalid Depot, a figure that increased to 126 by 1860 (Hardy 1995, p. 71). In his 1857 review of medical officers' reports of convict prisons, Walter Crofton noted 'We have... in our prisons a class of prisoners in a state of mind verging between reckless viciousness and insanity, generally of deficient intellectual powers, of great irritability of temper and totally destitute of self-control ... they cannot be admitted with safety into association without proper treatment and in the lunatic cell they become confirmed and incurably insane' (Directors of Convict Prisons in Ireland 1858, p. 10). In 1873, the medical officer at Spike Island, Dr. Patrick O'Keeffe, estimated that there were 40 weak-minded inmates in the prison, many of whom had been transferred from Mountjoy (Royal Commission 1884–1885 [C.4233] [C.4233-I], p. 28). Their accumulation prompted debate within the General Prison Board as to whether a prison modelled on Woking Invalid Prison should be established in Ireland (NAI 1874). Towards the end of the century, the same situation in England prevailed with regard to the pressure of numbers. Brixton Prison's Medical Officer noted in 1882 that he did not have enough cell accommodation for troublesome mental cases (Hardy 1995, p. 74). By 1894, Holloway Prison, with a large turnover of inmates, including many on remand, was receiving between 3 and 13 cases of suspected mental illness daily; its medical officers noted this increased workload and their obligation to examine such prisoners several times to assess their mental condition (McConville 1995, p. 299).

As Martin Weiner has argued, 'penal Benthamism', that influenced much nineteenth-century policy and practice, incorporated the 'humanitarian' (that the 'ordinary condition' of convicted prisoners should not allow gratuitous physical suffering or danger to life and health) and the 'punitive', 'the rule of severity' and 'less eligibility'. The care of prisoners was measured against the 'scarce good' of health care for the general population, and produced an ongoing dilemma in prison healthcare provision (Weiner 1995, pp. 47–48). The constraints of 'dual loyalty', an effect of prison medical officers' complex role in both caring

and lobbying for prisoners' health and supporting the disciplinary procedures of the prison, produced particular tensions when dealing with
mentally ill prisoners (Sim 1990). While prison doctors certainly built
up a good deal of practical experience in dealing with insanity, they
normally had little in the way of specialist training. Their emphasis
remained on diagnosis—largely sorting out the mad from the sane—
rather than treatment, on minimising the impact of mentally ill inmates
on prison regimes, on damage limitation and preserving the reputation
of the prison.

Prison medical officers saw the challenge of weeding out prisoners who were 'malingering' or feigning in order to achieve an amelio-
ration of conditions as one of their principal duties, an aspect of their
work that highlights tensions between care and discipline. Prisoners
believed to be feigning could be harshly punished, beaten, deprived of
food or placed in punishment cells. Towards the end of the century,
prison medical officers also asserted that they were compelled to deal
with an overwhelming range of mental afflictions, from 'simple weakness of the intellect to well-marked lunacy' and to 'contend with aggra-
vated, chronic and intractable disease from hereditary disposition or
constitutional degeneracy, the result of intemperate and vicious hab-
its' (Campbell 1884, p. 73). Reporting on his experiences as Medical
Officer at Woking Invalid Prison, Campbell observed that some prisoners 'display a marked degree of dullness or stupor; others sharpness and
cunning more allied to the tricks of monkeys than the acts of reasonable
men' (Campbell 1884, p. 73). Even in what he describes as the 'more
favourable or hopeful cases', he pointed out that 'it must be remembered that we had to deal with lunatics that were also criminals, and it
was sometimes difficult to discriminate between these two elements of
character' (Campbell 1884, p. 86).

Dr. Robert McDonnell, Mountjoy's medical officer in the 1860s,
expressed similar opinions and several other prison medical officers
echoed these views during the hearings of the 1884 Royal Commission
on Irish Prisons. Dismissing allegations that the Irish local prison system was intentionally cruel or systematically harsh, the commissioners
justified instances of the excessive punishment of refractory prisoners on
the basis that their 'mental condition may be described as borderland

between sanity and insanity' (Royal Commission 1884–1885 [C.4233] [C.4233-I], p. 14).

While Campbell, O'Keeffe and others argued that some mentally ill prisoners were deserving of pity and that for some their illness had been caused by separate confinement, many prison officials denied this relationship. In 1896, Pentonville's medical officer, Dr. John Baker, argued that the number of insane in the prison system was exaggerated, and that '[T]he form of insanity in many cases is conclusive evidence that mental defect existed before reception into prison'. He, however, acknowledged that he had met with isolated cases where there was reason to believe that the prisoners' environment had adversely affected them, including cases of 'delusional insanity, probably due to the prolonged process of introspection, almost inseparable from cellular confinement'. 'These cases', he concluded, 'are few and far between' (Baker 1896, pp. 295, 301, 302).

Despite Baker's protestations, the number of cases of mental illness in prison continued to increase. In a memorandum on insanity in prisons in 1895, Dr. J. H. Bridges, acknowledged that 'among the prison population the ratio of insanity arising among persons apparently sane on admission is not less than three times as great as that amongst the general population of corresponding ages' (Gladstone Committee 1895, pp. 290–291). A year earlier, Reverend William Morrison, chaplain at Wandsworth Prison between 1887 and 1898, had argued that the severe and highly deterrent regime operating in prisons by the 1890s was responsible for driving prisoners mad and for further debilitating others who were constitutionally weak. He asserted that rates of insanity in local prisons had doubled between 1875–1877 and 1890–1892, as penal discipline became harsher, from 113 per 100,000 to 226 per 100,000 compared with 8 per 100,000 in the general population (Morrison 1894, p. 468).

Prisoner authors provide first-hand accounts of what they saw as the uselessness of many prison doctors, though a handful were positive about their own medical care or the efforts of the medical staff to improve the health of their prisoner patients more generally. Usually educated and more privileged than the majority of their fellow prisoners, these authors undertook to speak for them in many cases, and underlined the detrimental impact of a prison system that failed either to reform or treat. The nineteenth-century prison population was made up largely of impoverished men, with women accounting for around 20–25% of the prison population and those prosecuted by courts for minor offences (Johnston 2015, p. 122; Quinlan 2011, pp. 33–34). By the 1850s and 1860s, the label 'criminal class' had taken root, especially in urban areas and notably with regard to Irish communities, though social commentators, such as Henry Mayhew, asserted that many of the poor, while destitute, dirty and uneducated, were honest and industrious (Johnston 2015, pp. 26–27).

In particular, prisoner memoirs emphasised two issues related to mental breakdown. They described what they saw as the iniquity of the system of separate confinement, which was roundly condemned by almost all prison writers. They also highlighted the sluggishness of prison staff in responding to cases of mental illness and delays in receiving adequate treatment. While Dr. John Campbell claimed that he dealt with his patients with the greatest of consideration, one of his patients George Bidwell, referred to his 'inexpressible hatred and contempt' of all the prisoners he treated (Campbell 1884, p. 58; Bidwell 1895, p. 511). Oscar Wilde described prison doctors as 'ignorant men. The pathology of the mind is unknown to them. When a man grows insane, they treat him as shamming.' 'The production of insanity' was, he asserted, if not the object of separate confinement, 'certainly its result' (Wilde 1990). In correspondence with the Irish General Prisons Board, prisoners reported instances of medical officers' neglect and the inferior standard of treatment in prison hospitals, but these cases were often dismissed as malicious and unfounded.

Delays in treatment—and the frequent removal of prisoners between institutions—were also highlighted in prison records. Often, this was related to efforts to reach decisions on whether or not a prisoner was feigning, or to cases where the prison staff were uncertain as to whether a prisoner was mad or disruptive. Thomas Bourke was aged just 15 when in April 1853 he was convicted of burglary and robbery. He was first sent to Philipstown Prison, Co. Offaly, an invalid depot and associated labour prison, and then moved to Mountjoy in July 1855, where he was placed on the separate system. There, he repeatedly broke the rule of silence, assaulted wardens and his fellow prisoners, destroyed his cell, feigned suicide and refused to work. Frequent punishments—either by placing Bourke on a reduced diet, stopping his meals altogether, or confining him a dark cell—did not improve his behaviour. He was transferred to the associated labour prison at Spike Island, back to Mountjoy for a second period in separation, and then back again to Philipstown Prison. He was finally transferred to Dundrum Criminal Lunatic Asylum, Dublin, in 1860 after seven years in various prisons (NAI, GPO/PN/4 Reg. No. 1742.). The prison system revealed an inability to assess such prisoners and offer treatment and, in many cases, their responses are likely to have led to deterioration in the mental health of their charges. Yet more troubling, even when the damage caused by separate confinement was acknowledged, it was described as a form of collateral damage. As Dr. William Guy, Medical Superintendent of Millbank Prison (1859–1869), and a leading authority on prison medicine, observed:

> Our system of separate confinement does not appear to affect the mind injuriously. I do not mean to say that a prisoner who comes into prison upon the verge of unsoundness of mind, might not develop into full unsoundness in that time, partly because of the separation; but I am of opinion, also that a prisoner should expect that this may happen to him, and that the possibility of unsoundness must be taken into account as one of the results of his being in prison at all. (Select Committee 1863 (499), IX, p. 370)

Continuities and the Recreation of Bedlam

During the nineteenth century, the removal of prisoners to asylum care was frequently resisted, even though provisions were in place for such removals if a prisoner was certified insane after committal, and many prison doctors, like Campbell, urged the transfer of mentally ill prisoners from the prison estate, even when these were incarcerated in specialised invalid prisons like Woking. Such prisoners were difficult to deal with, impossible to help and disturbed the other inmates, according to

Campbell (1884). In the twentieth century, while taking very different routes in England and the Republic of Ireland, the reluctance to move mentally ill prisoners out of prisons was transformed into an inability to have prisoners moved on to specialist hospitals due to a lack of alternative provision.

Following the findings of the (1895) Gladstone Report on prisons, there were changes in responses to mentally ill prisoners; even though the Report's initial emphasis on insane prisoners was diluted and the relationship between criminality and mental illness left unresolved, the Report concluded that the separate system needed to be reformed. Toby Seddon (2007) has summarised changes in the twentieth-century English prison system with regard to mental health. Beginning in the early twentieth century, there were efforts to 'clear out' various categories of mentally ill prisoners, including the 'weak-minded', in order to focus on 'responsible prisoners'. During the 1920s and 1930s, psychological and psychoanalytical treatments impinged on approaches to mentally disordered offenders, with many doctors arguing that all crime had 'mental' origins. After the Second World War, psychiatric work in English prisons expanded, in what Seddon describes as 'the high-water mark of penal-welfarism and correctionalist crime control', though in effect most of the work with mentally ill prisoners was diagnostic (Seddon 2007, pp. 7, 34; Garland 2001, p. 34). Even at the start of the century, efforts to remove the 'weak-minded' from the prison system were limited by a lack of alternative institutional facilities, and, by the 1970s, shifts in mental health policy in England towards care in the community provision had led to the winding down of large Victorian asylums and to a steady decline in the number of psychiatric hospital beds. This lack of provision outside prisons was already observed in 1978, when J. H. Orr, Director of Prison Medical Services in England, described a situation where:

> mentally disordered offenders are entering prisons not because the net is insufficiently wide or discriminating but because hospital places are not forthcoming. It is an irony that under the Mental Health Act 1959... we imprison more mentally disordered offenders than under the old Lunacy and Mental Deficiency Acts. In 1931 (when the average prison

population was about 12,000) 105 sentenced prisoners were recognized as suffering from mental *illness* and transferred to hospital. In 1976 the number of sentenced prisoners recognized as suffering from mental illness was more than double this figure, but the number transferred…less than half. (Orr 1978, p. 195)

Those experiencing mental health problems in prison became more likely to circulate between hostels and homelessness, with short stays in hospital rather than long-term treatment in a mental hospital (Seddon 2007, p. 35).

Until the late 1960s, the prison estate and prison population in the Republic of Ireland was small. Penal policy had 'effectively calcified' (Kilcommins et al. 2004, p. 24) while prison psychiatric services were almost non-existent (O'Sullivan and O'Donnell 2012, p. 21). Provision outside the prison was also under severe pressure; there was a threefold increase in admissions to psychiatric hospitals between 1948 and 1960 (Walsh and Daly 2004, p. 31). Yet, prisons remained heavily dependent on these overcrowded hospitals as well as on the Central Mental Hospital, Dundrum, for psychiatric services. In 1965, there were 102 'patients in custody' in Dundrum and a further 95 in the District Mental Hospitals (Commission on Mental Illness 1966, p. 91). The late twentieth-century policy shift away from the institutional treatment of psychiatric patients coincided with the explosion in the Irish prison population. By the 1980s, as psychiatric facilities outside prison shrunk further, prisoners could only be accepted at Dundrum, while prisons continued to be criticised for failing to provide psychological and psychiatric services (O'Connor and O'Neill 1990, p. 118; 1991, p. 112). One of the striking features of late twentieth-century prisons has been the build-up of mentally disordered offenders; in 1993, it was estimated that 5% of prisoners in the Republic were mentally ill and there was a waiting list for admission to Dundrum (Hegarty 1993).

The problem of dual loyalty has persisted, as 'rather than operating within an independent set of discourses designed to care for the confined' prison doctors 'were integral to the control and disciplinary apparatus of the modern prison' (Sim 2002, p. 301; Reilly 2016, p. 14). In both England and Ireland, prison doctors continued to be criticised for their lack of training in psychiatry, particularly when they end up treating large numbers of prisoners with psychiatric disorders, while prisons have been censured for failing to provide access to psychiatric consultations and services on an in-patient basis (Crowley 2003, p. 47). In 1990—using a headline similar to the report cited at the start of this essay—the *Guardian* declared how 'Bedlam Lives On'. This was in response to Chief Inspector of Prisons Judge Stephen Tumin's report on Brixton Prison, which referred to the harsh conditions for mentally disturbed prisoners and the high number of suicides and asserted that the prison was failing in its duty to look after inmates with humanity. Judge Tumin was particularly critical about the crowded psychiatric wing at a time when Brixton housed more psychiatric prisoners than any other prison in the UK and possibly Europe. The proposed stop-gap in his view was the creation of specialist units in prison, but the solution lay with courts referring people with mental health problems for treatment in NHS hospitals. The 'quality of the medical treatment... has long been scandalously bad' with doctors part of the 'disciplinary structure of prison' (*Guardian* 14 December 1990; Ryan 1995, p. 72).

Specialist psychiatric units for prisoners within or outside prisons were slow to emerge in Ireland. A ten-bed high-support unit was opened at Mountjoy prison in 2010. However, Dundrum continued to be the only psychiatric hospital to accept prisoners[4] (Crowley 2003, p. 47). The potentially fatal consequences of the Irish Prison Service's over-reliance on Dundrum, alongside the gaps in in-patient psychiatric arrangement services, were revealed in July 2006 when Gary Douch, a prisoner in Mountjoy Prison, died following a brutal assault by fellow prisoner Stephen Egan. Both had been confined in a holding cell in the B-Base of the prison. In the preceding months Egan, who had a long history of psychiatric disorders and violent behaviour, was repeatedly transferred between Dundrum, Mountjoy and Cloverhill prisons, reproducing the movements of prisoners between institutions in the nineteenth century. The subsequent investigation highlighted serious failures in the management of prisoners with psychiatric disorders (McMorrow 2014).

While the separate system has been long abandoned, elements of it are still found today in solitary confinement, which, whether imposed for reasons of restraint or punishment, for the protection of prisoners, or, most likely in the UK context, because of a shortage of staff and facilities, causes or exacerbates mental breakdown in prisoners. A recent report on Wormwood Scrubs Prison in London revealed that many prisoners had less than two hours a day 'unlocked' and all had only 40 minutes of outdoor exercise a day, less than the time prescribed at Pentonville in 1842 (HM Prisons Inspectorate 2016). *Deep Custody*, produced by the English Prison Reform Trust, highlighted the 'toxic' effects of segregation, 'social isolation, reduced sensory input/ enforced idleness and increased control of prisoners' (Shalev and Edgar 2015, p. 91). Yet, solitary confinement continues to be used. Despite the Irish Prison Service's commitment to reduce solitary confinement and restricted regimes, in April 2017, 430 prisoners were on restricted regimes, defined as a minimum of 19 hours locked up in cells (Irish Penal Reform Trust 2017, p. 17).

Recent initiatives have attempted to improve poor psychiatric provision within prisons; in-reach psychiatric teams have been introduced to prisons in England and Ireland and a diversion scheme was developed at Cloverhill remand prison in Ireland. While often the subject of criticism, prison medical officers and prison medical services have over the last few decades become more open and engaged, joining in critiques of prison medical services and highlighting obstacles to the adequate provision of care for their prisoner/patients. In parliamentary inquiries undertaken in the mid-1980s in the UK, prison medical officers reflected openly on dual loyalty and expressed an eagerness to work more closely with rest of the medical profession (Duvall 2018).

This shift towards collaboration tended to replace, Duvall has argued, the assertions—similar to those of their nineteenth-century predecessors—that prison medical officers have a particular knowledge and special experience valuable in treating mentally ill prisoners (Duvall 2018). In England, in 2013, responsibility for commissioning all healthcare services for prisoners was transferred to the NHS, but as prison populations continue to grow, so too do the numbers of people in prison who report having mental health issues, and efforts to achieve an equivalent health service are hampered by the prison environment and lack of services outside of prison. This approach, however, has been accepted as a model for good practice and other jurisdictions have lobbied for the integration of prison medical services with general health systems. In 2016, Judge Michael Reilly, Inspector of Prisons, produced a report on prison health care in the Republic of Ireland, which strongly advocated for the incorporation of prison health care into the Irish Health Service Executive (Reilly 2016).

As the management of prisoners with mental disorders continues to attract regular reports, the attention of the media and the concern of prison reform organisations, history can be drawn on to highlight continuities in terms of the challenges facing prisons in dealing with mentally ill prisoners. It reveals the detrimental impact of solitary confinement and the negative and sometimes alarming consequences of leaving mentally ill prisoners to languish in prison. History provides examples and narratives of the impact of prison regimes on mental health and the obstacles in providing effective treatment, many resulting from ongoing tensions between care and discipline, and punishment and treatment. It also provides a final sobering conclusion that in the 175 years since the introduction of the modern prison system, little has changed in terms of the high rate of imprisonment of mentally ill people and the detrimental effects of prison on mental health.

Notes

1. Bedlam or Bethlem Hospital is London's oldest institution to specialise in treating mental illness, admitting insane patients from the fourteenth century onwards. Both famous and at times infamous, its popular designation, Bedlam, became synonymous with madness itself.
2. For a full account, see DeLacy (1986, chap. 5).
3. In 1854, the Directors of Convict Prisons for Ireland was established with Walter Crofton as Chair. Crofton implemented the 'mark' or 'Irish' system adapted from Alexander Maconochie's New South Wales system. At Mountjoy, convicts were initially placed on the separate system for 8 months. Then, convicts earned marks through work and good behavior and, if successful, were transferred to an intermediate, associated prison. Marks could also be removed and convicts demoted (Carroll-Burke 2000, pp. 103–104).

4. A national forensic hospital and intensive care units for Cork, Galway and Portrane is planned for Portrane, Co. Dublin to replace the Central Mental Hospital, Dundrum (Kelly 2017, pp. 266–267).

Bibliography

Baker, J. (1896). Insanity in English local prisons, 1894–95. *Journal of Mental Science, 42*(177), 294–302.

Berkshire Record Office Q/S0 24, Sessions Order Book, April 1853–July 1855, Chaplain's Report, General Quarter Sessions.

Bidwell, G. (1895). *From Wall Street to Newgate*. Hartford, CT: Bidwell Publishing.

Bradley, L. (2009). *The Bradley report. Lord Bradley's review of people with mental health problems or learning disabilities in the criminal justice system*. London: Department of Health.

Campbell, J. (1884). *Thirty years' experience of a medical officer in the English convict service*. London: T. Nelson and Sons.

Carroll-Burke, P. (2000). *Colonial discipline: The making of the Irish convict system*. Dublin: Four Courts Press.

Charleroy, M., & Marland, H. (2016). Prisoners of solitude: Bringing history to bear on prison health policy. *Endeavour, 40*(4), 141–147.

Commission of Inquiry on Mental Illness. (1966). *1966 Report*. Dublin: Stationary Office.

Cox, C., & Marland, H. (2018). "He must die or go mad in this place": Prisoners, insanity and the Pentonville model prison experiment, 1842–1852. *Bulletin of the History of Medicine, 92*(1), 78–104.

Crowley, F. (2003). *Mental illness: The neglected quarter*. Dublin: Amnesty International.

DeLacy, M. (1986). *Prison reform in Lancashire, 1700–1850: A study in local administration*. Stanford, CA: Stanford University Press.

Directors of Convict Prisons in Ireland. (1858). *Fourth annual report of the Directors of Convict Prisons in Ireland 1857*. Dublin: HMSO.

Duvall, N. (2018). "From defensive paranoia to ... openness to outside scrutiny": Prison medical officers in England and Wales in the 1970s and 1980s. *Medical History, 62*(1), 112–131.

Forsythe, W. J. (1987). *The reform of prisoners 1830–1900*. Sydney and London: Croom Helm.

Forsythe, W. J. (1991). Centralisation and autonomy: The experience of English prisons 1820–1877. *Journal of Historical Sociology, 4*(3), 317–345.

Garland, D. (2001). *The culture of control: Crime and social order in contemporary society.* Oxford: Oxford University Press.

Gibson, C. B. (1863). *Life among convicts* (Vol. 1). London: Henry Colburn.

Gladstone Committee. (1895). Report from the Departmental Committee on Prisons, 1895 [C.7702] [C.7702-I].

Gray, F. (1847). *Prison discipline in America.* Boston: Charles C. Little and James Brown.

Guardian. (1990, December 14). Bedlam lives on.

Hardy, A. (1995). Development of the prison medical service. In R. Creese, W. F. Bynum, & J. Bearn (Eds.), *The health of prisoners* (pp. 59–82). Amsterdam and Atlanta, GA: Rodopi.

Hegarty, T. (1993, March 24). Study finds 5% of prison inmates are mentally ill. *Irish Times.*

Henriques, U. R. Q. (1972). The rise and decline of the separate system of prison discipline. *Past and Present, 54*(1), 61–93.

HM Prisons Inspectorate. (2016). *Report of announced inspection of HMP Wormwood Scrubs 30 November–4 December 2015.* Available at: https://www.justiceinspectorates.gov.uk/hmiprisons/wp-content/uploads/sites/4/2016/04/Wormwood-Scrubs-web2015.pdf. Accessed 28 Nov 2017.

Howard, J. (1780/1784). *The state of the prisons in England and Wales.* Warrington: William Eyres.

Humphreys, J. (2013, September 16). The prison trap. *Irish Time.*

Ignatieff, M. (1978). *A just measure of pain: The penitentiary in the industrial revolution 1750–1850.* London and Basingstoke: Macmillan.

Inspectors of Government Prisons in Ireland. (1852). *Annual report for the year ended 31st December 1851,* 1852–1853.

Irish Penal Reform Trust. (2017). *Submission to the second periodic review of Ireland under the United Nations Convention against torture and other cruel, inhuman or degrading treatment or punishment.* Dublin: Irish Penal Reform Trust.

Jebb, J. (1852). *Report on the discipline and management of the convict prisons.* London: HMSO.

Johnston, H. (2015). *Crime in England 1815–1880.* London and New York: Routledge.

Kelly, B. (2017). *Hearing voices: The history of psychiatry in Ireland.* Dublin: Irish Academic Press.

Kilcommins, S., O'Donnell, I., O'Sullivan, E., & Vaughan, B. (2004). *Crime, punishment and the search for order in Ireland*. Dublin: Institute of Public Administration.

Laurie, P. (1847, May 1). Letter to Editor. *The Times*.

McConville, S. (1995). *English local prisons, 1860–1900: Next only to death*. London: Routledge.

McMorrow, G. (2014). *Report on commission of investigation into the death of Gary Douch*.

Morrison, W. D. (1894). Are our prisons a failure? *The Fortnightly Review, 61*(April), 459–469.

National Archives of Ireland (NAI). GPO/LB/12, Letter Book: Letter from Henry M. Hitchins to Francis Rynd, 14 February 1850.

National Archives of Ireland (NAI). GPO/PN/4, Philipstown Character Books, 1847–1862.

National Archives of Ireland (NAI). (1874). Chief Secretary's Office registered papers, 1874/4814.

Neild, J. (1812). *State of the prisons in England, Scotland and Wales*. London: John Nichols.

O'Connor, A., & O'Neill, H. (1990). Male prison transfers to the central mental hospital: A special hospital (1983–1988). *Irish Journal of Psychological Medicine, 7*(2), 118–120.

O'Connor, A., & O'Neill, H. (1991). Female prison transfers to the central mental hospital: A special hospital (1983–1988). *Irish Journal of Psychological Medicine, 8*(2), 122–123.

Ogborn, M. (1995). Discipline, government and law: Separate confinement in the prisons of England and Wales, 1830–1877. *Transactions of the Institute of British Geographers, 20*(3), 295–311.

Orr, J. H. (1978). The imprisonment of mentally disordered offenders. *British Journal of Psychiatry, 133*(3), 194–199.

O'Sullivan, E., & O'Donnell, I. (2012). *Coercive confinement in post-independence Ireland: Patients, prisoners and penitents*. Manchester: Manchester University Press.

Prisons (Separate Confinement). (1856). *Abstract of a 'Return of the prisons in England and Ireland; distinguishing those in which the system of separate confinement is fully carried out'*, 163.

Quinlan, C. M. (2011). *Inside: Ireland's women's prisons. Past and present*. Dublin: Irish Academic Press.

Reilly, M. (2016). *Healthcare in Irish prisons*. Nenagh: Inspector of Prisons.

Rothman, D. J. (1998). Perfecting the prison: United States 1789–1865. In N. Morris & D. J. Rothman (Eds.), *The Oxford history of the prison: The practice of punishment in Western society* (pp. 100–115). Oxford: Oxford University Press.

Royal Commission on Prisons in Ireland. Vols I and II, 1884–1885 [C.4233] [C.4233-I].

Ryan, M. (1995). *Lobbying from below: INQUEST in defence of civil liberties.* London: Routledge.

Seddon, T. (2007). *Punishment and madness: Governing prisoners with mental health problems.* Abingdon: Routledge.

Select Committee. (1863). Select committee of House of Lords on state of prison discipline in gaols and houses of correction [Carnarvon committee], 1863 (499).

Shalev, S., & Edgar, K. (2015). *Deep custody: Segregation units and close supervision centres in England and Wales.* London: Prison Reform Trust.

Sim, J. (1990). *Medical power in prisons: The Prison Medical Service in England 1774–1989.* Milton Keynes and Philadelphia: Open University Press.

Sim, J. (2002). The future of prison health care: A critical analysis. *Critical Social Policy, 22*(2), 300–323.

Sloan, A., & Allison, E. (2014, May 24). "We are recreating Bedlam": The crisis in prison mental health services. *Guardian.*

The Times. (1841, January 11). Editorial.

Wakefield Record Office Q/S 10/56, Quarter Sessions Order Book, October 1846–April 1850.

Walsh, D., & Daly, A. (2004). *Mental illness in Ireland, 1750–2002: Reflections on the rise and fall of institutional care.* Dublin: Health Research Board.

Weiner, M. J. (1995). The health of prisoners and two faces of Benthamism. In R. Creese, W. F. Bynum, & J. Bearn (Eds.), *The health of prisoners* (pp. 44–58). Amsterdam and Atlanta, GA: Rodopi.

Wilde, O. (1990). To the editor of the *Daily Chronicle*, 27 May [1897] and 23 March [1898]. In I. Murray (Ed.), *Oscar Wilde: The soul of man and prison writings.* Oxford: Oxford University Press.

Wilson, D. (2009). Testing a civilisation: Charles Dickens on the American penitentiary system. *The Howard Journal of Criminal Justice, 48*(3), 280–296.

Winslow, F. (1851, March). Medical society of London: Prison discipline. *Lancet*, 357–360.

3

The Architecture of Psychiatry and the Architecture of Incarceration

Simon Cross and Yvonne Jewkes

Introduction: Asylums, Architecture and Regimes of the Imagination

Many contemporary prison designers are inspired by progressive health-care facilities and increasingly employ concepts such as 'therapeutic spaces', 'healthy prisons' and 'trauma-informed' design to underpin their progressive models of incarceration. But it has only very recently been the case that prison architects have looked to facilities holding the mentally ill for humane and enlightened design inspiration.[1] On the surface, this may seem unsurprising because Victorian-built asylums appear designed to look and feel like places of severe punishment. Yet, Victorian lunacy campaigners proselytized the asylum as a haven

S. Cross (✉)
Nottingham Trent University, Nottingham, UK
e-mail: simon.cross@ntu.ac.uk

Y. Jewkes
University of Bath, Bath, UK
e-mail: y.jewkes@bath.ac.uk

© The Author(s) 2018
A. Mills and K. Kendall (eds.), *Mental Health in Prisons*, Palgrave Studies in Prisons and Penology, https://doi.org/10.1007/978-3-319-94090-8_3

of safety and refuge—asylum in the truest sense. That they became *popularly* associated with punishment, not therapy, reflected a prevailing uncertainty about what really went on behind the high walls and locked doors. Victorian reformists placed great faith in bricks-and-mortar solutions to social problems associated with the accelerating pace of modern life (Scull 1979; cf. Porter and Wright 2003), but both prisons and asylums remain 'hidden worlds' and are unusual in their ability to occlude (Fiddler 2007). Our gaze is thrown upon the impassive walls of their outer perimeters, leaving those of us who have not experienced at first-hand being confined within them to rely on images from popular culture and myth. And the problem that the psychiatric institution has never been able to shrug off is that its dark double—the penitentiary—casts a long shadow over the asylum story.

This chapter considers this intertwined history of the architecture of psychiatry and the architecture of incarceration. Since the establishment of the separate system of the Victorian penitentiary, which caused widespread insanity in its inmates (Cox and Marland, this volume; Johnston 2015), and its asylum counterpart, which imposed a brutal and uncompromising moral regime, the two institutions have shared a philosophy and aesthetic that is inseparable from their architecture and internal layout. Through the work of Goffman and Foucault, contemporary scholars are familiar with the shared characteristics of 'total institutions' and the relationship between space, meaning, power and discipline that operates within such institutions. Informed by a multidisciplinary approach combining cultural studies of madness, the history of prisons, architectural theory and media, our aim is to deepen our understanding of the contribution that the changing physical environment makes to the pains of confinement and to public perceptions of prisons and mental institutions.

Palaces and Prisons: Asylum Visions and Useful Architecture

In the summer of 1810, James Tilley Matthews entered a competition with a £200 prize awarded by the governors of London's Bethlem Hospital. The hospital, founded in 1247 and popularly known as

Bedlam, specialized in the care of insane paupers. The prize was for the best design of a new building to replace the one built 150 years earlier sited on the edge of the city (which had replaced the medieval original), but was now structurally unsound. Demolition of what had once been the only building that looked like a palace in London (and the butt of jokes about palaces and paupers) was an opportunity to reimagine the notorious madhouse. Matthews did not win the competition, though the judges awarded him a special prize for his plans to improve patients' living conditions. Matthews called his ideas 'useful architecture', a subject on which he felt suitably qualified to comment because for thirteen years, he had been a patient inside Bethlem's incurable ward.

Matthews' confinement in Bethlem had been brought about by his delusional belief that terrorists were controlling his mind using an 'influencing machine' (Jay 2003). Doctors who examined Matthews confirmed that he was insane and dangerous, yet his vision for the new Bethlem shows he was neither, at least on architectural grounds. His designs emphasize maximum security, ample ventilation, efficient drainage, and optimal visibility—architectural features held to be of cardinal importance by later asylum builders who conceived of psychiatric architecture as 'therapy in stone'. Matthews' architectural plans never came to fruition, but his legacy is long-lasting and extends beyond Bethlem because, for the first time ever, a design for a lunatic asylum was conceived from the perspective of the patient who has to live in it. The redoubtable Matthews promoted his ideas on asylum-building to a wider audience through a short-lived magazine, *Useful Architecture* but, as things turned out, the relationship between madness, architecture and the built environment was destined to rely on the visions of those not deemed to be insane.

A case in point concerns the York Retreat founded by William Tuke in 1796, which played a seminal role in humane designs for mental health in the nineteenth century, but which had double-edged consequences. The Tukes were Quakers and their Retreat was built following the unexplained death of a fellow Quaker in a private madhouse. Tuke insisted that bars sent the wrong moral-religious message to patients and banned them from his institution, though Tuke did retain use of certain 'material bonds' (i.e. chains) for the control of violent or dangerous inmates (Jones 1993). The Retreat adopted a 'moralized use of architecture' based on the God-fearing Puritan household (Digby 1985). In his effort to restore what had been weakened by insanity, Tuke replicated as far as possible the ideal Quaker home on the basis that by providing patients with a persuasive reproduction of the décor in which they had lived, they would return to the self-discipline from which they had lapsed. The ideas developed by Tuke formed the basis for the ideals of humane treatment in the Victorian asylum.

Tuke was not medically trained, but his ideas were taken up by a nascent psychiatric profession keen to establish a system of non-restraint to distinguish their work from prisons. Tuke's management of the York Retreat's sensory environment, such as door locks especially selected for their acoustic properties, and vaulting in the roofing and coverings on floors and walls, influenced later nineteenth-century asylum soundscapes (Fennelly 2014). The promotion of patients' sensory well-being by outlawing 'objectionable sounds' was complemented by the practice of building asylums in out-of-town locations guaranteeing fresh air and peace and quiet (and arguably keeping the 'mad' away from the general populace) (Jones 1993). The importance of internal design and external build and layout was set out in public statements by asylum pioneers. In his *Treatise on the Nature, Symptoms, Causes and Treatment of Insanity* (1838), Dr. William Ellis of the Middlesex Asylum included a detailed visual plan showing the main hospital surrounded by trees, gardens, cultivated grounds and on the periphery, a farm for purpose of agricultural employment. As patients' conditions improved, the idea was that they acquired freedom within the asylum boundary, a recognizably utopian principle, even if the whips, chains and prison bars that were used to control the insane were still fresh in popular memory.

The early history of English prisons (at least as we would recognize them today) was very similar. In an architectural competition for the first 'penitentiary', William Blackburn won the prize of £100 for a design that foreshadowed the later Panopticon, whereby radial geometry was used to exploit the principles of surveillance and inspection. In Blackburn's design, all the exterior parts of the prison were visible and the fences around the yards were made of wicket, so as not to obscure the gaoler's view. In a sense, Blackburn was responsible for turning prison design into a 'useful architecture', translating the emerging doctrine of reform into the practicalities of construction (Evans 1982). Ventilation was improved with the installation of bars instead of glass, circular iron gratings in passage floors, wicket turnstiles instead of solid wood doors, and double leaf cell doors with iron latticework (Jewkes and Johnston 2007). While good ventilation was (and is) regarded as a core component in the design of any building, it was a matter of life and death in the second half of the eighteenth century. 'Gaol fever' was a virulent disease that affected not only prisoners, but also the esteemed members of the legal and judicial professions with whom they came into contact. In 1750, over forty people died in one outbreak alone, when attendants at the Old Bailey were firstly struck by a 'noisome smell' in court and, a week later, became ill with a highly malignant fever (ibid.). Fatalities included the Lord Mayor of London, two judges, an alderman, a lawyer, an under-sheriff and several members of the jury (Evans 1982).

The most influential prison architect of the early to mid-eighteenth century was Stephen Hales, a Doctor of Divinity and a Fellow of the Royal Society, who pioneered technologies and methods to make prisons physically healthier, based on the idea that the building, like an animal, needed to breathe. Hales' ideas influenced celebrated prison reformer and 'architects' mentor', John Howard (1726–1790), who decreed that prisons should not be cramped among other buildings, but should be in open country—perhaps on the rise of a hill to get the full force of the wind, and close to running water (Jewkes and Johnston 2007). Shrewsbury prison, built on Castle Hill near the River Severn, and designed as a series of irregularly spaced pavilions, each raised off the ground on arcades to allow the air to circulate was, in effect, a 'model prison' according to Howard's vision of reform through purity.

John Howard was also the first prison reformer to note the high number of people with mental illnesses in prison, and the lack of care they received:

> many of the bridewells are crowded and offensive, because the rooms which were designed for prisoners are occupied by lunatics... No care is taken of them, although it is probable that by medicines, and proper regimen, some of them might be restored to their senses, and usefulness in life. (Howard 1784, p. 22)

However, the regime of solitary confinement implemented at both of the UK's first two national prisons, Millbank (1816) and Pentonville (1842), was a far cry from Howard's enlightened principles. Intended to prevent *moral* rather than viral contagion, the 'separate system', which had in practice, if not in name, already been adopted at Millbank and at various local prisons, was formally legislated into the Prison Act in 1839. It required prisoners to be kept apart at all times, and held alone in separate cells where they would work, sleep and take meals. The only time they could leave their cell was to attend chapel, when their faces would be masked, or for exercise during which they might be sent to separate exercise yards (Cox and Marland, this volume; Jewkes and Johnston 2007). While solitary confinement was nothing new, what was unique about 'new model prison' Pentonville was that, for the first time, the fabric of the prison became harmonized with the enforcement of the regime. Prison architecture and penal purpose were explicitly inter-linked as 'seclusion through architecture overcame the need for communication to be suppressed by naked force and intimidation' and good behaviour was maintained 'with the passive instrument of the building itself' (Evans 1982, p. 323).

As a result of separation, prison accommodation in the mid-nineteenth century became increasingly enclosed and cellularized and earlier design principles based on the need for air and ventilation were abandoned. Ironically, as holes were being filled and interior spaces were becoming more enclosed and claustrophobic, the exterior façade of the prison—like that of the asylum—was becoming more expansive and grandiose. Penal policy was taking a more ostentatious, dramatic and communicative turn, and prisons were being built to designs that communicated to the public a clear message about punishment from the 'carefully scripted' construction of their exterior architecture (Pratt 2002, pp. 39–40). The ornate symbolism that adorned early prisons in Anglophone nations was, then, intended to have a 'see and beware' function, warning the community at large to refrain from transgressing lest they too should end up within the monstrous institution's imposing walls, but some feared that prisons were too decorative to be a deterrent to crime. As early as 1789, John Howard wrote of the 'pompous fronts' of new prisons, which would 'appear like palaces' to the lower classes.

But, in a sense, the great architects of institutions in this era were simply doing what was expected of them. This was an 'evocative architecture' of cloisters, palazzos and the motifs of the medieval castle (Pevsner 1976, p. 293) and, in a sense, each successive architect was trying to outshine the 'magnificent but maleficent Pentonville Prison' (Jewkes and Moran 2017, p. 556).

In fact, the construction of Pentonville in 1842 precipitated a further 54 prisons, all constructed on the same panoptic template. This was truly the age of prison expansion. Meanwhile, a series of scandals in the 1840s involving mistreatment of lunatics led to public legislation requiring each county to provide their own asylum and so they too rapidly increased in number. Many lunatics lived in prison-like workhouses and when the rush to build asylums began they quickly filled, whereupon others followed (by 1914, the county of Surrey alone had fourteen asylums including a cluster of five along a two-mile corridor). Few architects designed more than one or two asylums and their legacy is an architectural mishmash of popular historic styles including 'Tudorbethan', popular in the 1840s and 1850s (Wells 1845–1848), Gothic (Lancaster, 1882 and the Royal Albert Institution for Idiots, 1866–1873) and Queen Anne style (Rauceby, Lincolnshire 1897–1992). Despite their many façades, however, Victorian psychiatric culture expressed through bricks and mortar, the idea of the asylum as 'intelligible regularity'; the assumption that by living in places that represented order and reason, inmates would repossess their own (Porter 1991).

Despite their architectural diversity, Victorian popular culture persisted in seeing asylums as pseudo-prisons with high walls, locked doors and chains, and a propaganda effort was mounted by the governors of London's St. Luke's Asylum to try to change public attitude. The doors were opened to no less a figure than Charles Dickens who reported on St. Luke's 1867 Boxing Day dance for his widely read *Household Words* magazine. Dickens documents the apparent harmony of staff, patients and the outside world coming together to show that this really was a healing institution, not a prison. From a twenty-first century perspective, however, we find it hard to understand how they were ever conceived as harmonious institutions given that, as Scull (2006, p. 82) puts it of late-Victorian psychiatric attitudes, 'asylums were silted up with the chronically crazy' unamenable to any sort of treatment. And, ironically, from the very first days of the national penitentiaries, many prisoners experienced insanity (Johnston 2015). At Millbank, a period of strict and severe seclusion was followed by a second, more moderate phase of confinement, by which time, the initial period of solitary confinement had already caused many prisoners to go mad. Indeed, the regime was so brutal that over 30 prisoners died in the first few years of its operation, leading to critical newspaper reports and political intervention, which testify to the lack of legitimacy of the prison in this early period (Johnston 2015). Even as the last bricks were being laid, social commentators of the day were expressing their views that the new prison would be 'unnecessarily cruel' and that 'madness will seize those whom death has spared' (*The Times* 20 May 1841, cited in Johnston 2015, p. 109).

Further Expansion of Institutions in the Twentieth Century

By the close of the nineteenth century, asylums had become mammoth, custodial institutions. One asylum, Colney Hatch Asylum in north London, held over 3000 patients. In a sense, asylums were victims of their own success: as more and more were built, more public money was spent, and more public hopes were invested in their success. These hopes were dashed when asylums became clogged up with chronic cases unamenable to therapy (Barham 1992). Historians point out that the Victorian's belief in the goodness of the asylum today appears curious, perverse even, but their optimism reflects faith in institutional solutions in general (schools, workhouses, prisons, hospitals, and asylums) to social problems spawned by demographic change, urbanization, and industrialization.

It is easy to forget, too, that prisons at this time were intended to be places of human(e) experimentation. Even Bentham's Panopticon, on which Pentonville's radial design was based (and which is still being replicated to this day), was essentially intended to be a benign attempt to ensure good behaviour without the need for bars and chains and, as the twentieth century unfolded, a new therapeutic discourse emerged. By mid-century, when the asylum system was beginning to look bloated and unsustainable, the 'treatment model' was transposed to criminal justice and prisons became influenced by a new raft of professional experts, including psychologists, health professionals, social workers and academics. This emphasis on treatment and therapy also permeated discussions about what prisons should look like. Following a Government announcement in 1958 that an ambitious prison building programme was to be undertaken, Prison Commissioner AW Peterson proclaimed in an early article in the *British Journal of Criminology*, 'Changes in treatment may bring with them changes in architecture, and research into treatment methods is developing rapidly' (1961, p. 375; see Jewkes and Moran 2017).

Paradoxically, though, as 'treatment' became the dominant aspiration within prisons, asylums were becoming more and more like penal regimes.[2] Keen attention was paid to a regime of labour, which would stimulate the mind and discipline the body (Porter 2002) and, despite new psychiatric techniques, over most of their existence, the daily grind in the asylum changed little. Work, plain food and conformity was the norm. Inmates were expected to display suitable gratitude for the care and shelter provided and there was considerable social distance between staff and inmates; an aroma of moral censure permeated the attitudes of many who worked there (Scull 1989). In the manner of penal establishments, committal to the asylum involved a sense of degradation as new patients learned their place in the pecking order. For many patients with limited family support, once they had been 'put away' it was unlikely they would ever assume their former place in society (Barham 1992). By the mid-1950s, Britain's asylum population had reached 150,000 (Jones 1993). As the mental health estate expanded and asylums became larger to take greater numbers of vulnerable people, individualized treatment was of necessity compromised, while the need for control and order became more prevalent.

It is not as if there was no warning. As early as mid-Victorian times, when the asylum-building programme was at its height, psychiatric reformers expressed their view that a gigantic asylum in which patients would become lost in the system was a gigantic evil (Scull 2006).

For instance, Dr. John Connolly in his (1847) book *The Construction and Government of Lunatic Asylums* proposed that only small asylums could make best use of non-restraint methods as well as occupational therapies, and he suggested that a gentle and kind psychiatric care and treatment were not guaranteed even with enlightened asylum management based on moral therapy (such as he was promoting in his book). It would take more than a century before Connolly's prophesy would be proven accurate as asylum conditions, especially in English-speaking countries, came under increasing public scrutiny.

Meanwhile, critics of the prison system were also rehearsing arguments about optimum size of custodial facilities that still rage today. For example, when the new prison expansion programme got underway in the early 1960s, architectural theorist Leslie Fairweather, writing at a time when a prison holding in excess of 400 prisoners was considered 'very large', could not have anticipated just how vast prisons would become when he wrote in 1961:

> The internal arrangement of a building can influence the degree and quality of personal relationships within it to a remarkable degree. These relationships will not develop healthily in huge impersonal blocks of cells where the individual is dwarfed by the overpowering size of the structure. They can only be attempted in buildings which respect the quality of the individual by being attractive, as normal in appearance as possible, and suitable in scale. (Fairweather 1961, p. 340)

Regrettably, since this time, Fairweather's argument that small prisons are more operationally effective and are more likely to result in rehabilitated prisoners has fallen on deaf ears. Despite a wealth of recent research that finds that smaller prisons are better than larger facilities at housing prisoners in safe and secure conditions, providing them with meaningful work, education and training, encouraging purposeful activity, and fostering healthy relationships between prisoners and prison staff (e.g. Liebling and Arnold 2004; Johnsen et al. 2011), the prison estate has grown exponentially both in number and in size. By way of illustration, HMP Berwyn (the newest prison in England & Wales, which opened in February 2017) has a capacity of 2106, making it the second largest publicly run prison in Europe. The move to such super-sized prisons is, in part, a response to the fact that prisoner population numbers have more than doubled since 1985 and currently stand at just below 86,000.

The prison shows no sign of disappearing, then. Indeed, Anglophone nations have persistently shown remarkable faith in and a deep cultural attachment to the institution of the prison despite all evidence that it does not 'work'. Only in the early years of the twentieth century was there widespread public discussion about the effects of imprisonment and that came largely because of reports in national newspapers about the conditions that Suffragettes[3] were held in at HMP Holloway. The asylum, however, has a rather different story at this juncture although, again, it was the confinement of women that alerted the public to the cruelties and dehumanization of institutions. In fact, it was in America, the home of the sensation-fuelled reportage known as 'New Journalism', where critics set a slow-burning fire underneath the asylum. In 1888, *New York World* reporter Nellie Bly (the pen name of Elizabeth Jane Cochrane) feigned insanity to breach the walls of New York's Blackwell's Island Asylum. Her first-person viewpoint exposed a prison-like exist-ence endured by inmates including a description of women roped together by chains pleading for help. Lingering concerns about mental hospitals in time led to other important journalist exposes of mental hospitals such Albert Q Maisel's *Life* magazine essay 'Bedlam 1946', a loaded title for man's inhumanity to man, followed two years by Albert Deutsch's expose, *Shame of the States*, documenting filthy conditions and abandoned patients inside state mental hospitals (Cross 2010). Maisel and Deutsch used photographs to show evidence that patients were treated akin to brute animals.

By the 1960s, the tide of American mental health policy was turn-ing against large-scale psychiatric facilities and towards deinstitutional-ization. In Britain, a similar 'open door' movement in psychiatry was occurring—not because of concerns about patients, but driven by fis-cal pressures (Jones 1993). Too expensive to run, the old rambling asy-lums were earmarked for closure. It was Conservative Health Minister Enoch Powell who delivered the news to the psychiatric profession that Victorian-built asylums had had their day. In his address to the 1961 conference of the National Association for Mental Health, Powell spoke in characteristically uncompromising terms:

> There they stand, isolated, majestic, imperious, brooded over by the gigantic water-tower and chimney combined, rising unmistakable and daunting out of the countryside – the asylums which our forefathers built with such immense solidity. Do not for a moment underestimate their power of resistance to our assault. (quoted in Jones 1993, p. 160)

Powell's 'water-tower' speech was part magnificent hyperbole, part wishful thinking, and his assumption that asylum closures would be resisted was correct. Many within the psychiatric profession opposed his policy, arguing that the asylum was successful in caring for vulnerable and friendless people and should not be allowed to close (ibid.).[4] It would be a further four decades before Britain's Victorian asylums finally closed for good. In the meantime, a slow process began of displacing those held in mental institutions back into society; some with family support, others housed in dilapidated privately run care homes or on the streets. More were destined to be mopped up by the prison system, as happened in the eighteenth century and remains the case today. But the chorus of critics who lined up to say asylums were like prisons did not foresee how one mode of confinement would be replaced by another.

The confinement of significant numbers of mentally disturbed offenders in the prison population has been the subject of debate that prison is a dumping ground for people who would otherwise be hospitalized. In Britain, the closure of Victorian-built asylums since the 1980s has led to lingering concern that mentally disturbed individuals are in prison because there are precious few psychiatric hospital beds available (Seddon 2006). To be sure, prison is not the best place for someone suffering from a mental disturbance, but we need to be careful lest we too readily align this debate with a version of 'Penrose's Law', namely that as prison populations rose mental hospitals declined, and vice versa. The distinguished criminologist Herschel Prins (1995, p. 48) cautions against 'the tendency to accept too readily the view that mentally disturbed offenders detained in prison are there because if they were not they would be in hospital'. Penrose's Law also provided support for now discredited ideas about 'transcarceration' with inmates redistributed across various sites of confinement. Asylum closures from the 1980s onwards affected mainly older institutionalized patients and the idea they took up a prison residency is hardly a convincing basis on which to understand the shifting politics and policies of either the prison or mental health systems. This is not to deny that there are good reasons for keeping the interconnected dimensions of asylums and prisons in twin view.

Asylums and Prisons Under Scrutiny: The Role of Sociology, Psychology and the Media

It was the power of scholarship and the written word, followed by the new media of mass communications, that led the final assault on the effects of protracted institutional living—collectively described as institutionalization (Crossely 2006). With the growth of university degree courses in the new '-ologies', hospital and prison environments became the subjects of powerful critiques on both sides of the Atlantic that identified long-term confinement as a cause of apathy, dehumanization and passive dependence which, in combination, rendered both prisoner and psychiatric patient far more damaged than when they were admitted to the institution. In 1959, a British psychiatrist, Russell Barton, medicalized the problem using the term 'institutional neurosis', describing a constellation of adverse effects on patients (Barton 1959). A year earlier, Gresham Sykes published his seminal work *The Society of Captives*, in which he described the dehumanizing architecture and layout of New Jersey State Prison ('compounded of naked electric lights, echoing corridors, walls encrusted with the paint of decades, and the stale air of rooms shut up too long' [1958, pp. 7–8]). Not only was this one of the first accounts that reported the blandness and lack of variation in penal architecture and design, but it also understood the relationship between the physical compression induced by such environments and the psychological compression experienced by inmates. However, the 'mental bed sores' described by Barton and 'Kafka-like atmosphere' evoked by Sykes quickly gave way to an even more damning insider account of institutional life that explicitly connected the architecture of incarceration and the architecture of madness. The American sociologist Erving Goffman's book *Asylums: Essays on the Social Situation of Mental Patients and Other Inmates* (1961) proved a memorable indictment of mental health patient care as prison-like in its social impact and consequences. Indeed, such is his influence in prison scholarship that it is sometimes almost forgotten that Goffman was writing about (and viscerally dissecting) a psychiatric hospital. Based on his participant-observations working as a physical therapy instructor at a Washington State mental hospital, Goffman revealed how the new inmate is 'shaped and coded into the kind of object that can be fed into the administrative machinery', before its rigid confines further 'stripped' people of their individuality, leading inevitably to social atrophy in this most bounded of locales (Goffman 1961, p. 23).

Goffman's descriptions of a separate staff and inmate existence where 'never the twain meet' drew a picture of the mental hospital as punitive and unsuitable to the promotion of mental health. Loss of liberty was compounded by a loss of individuality, whereby inmates were infantilized, unable to enact fully adult roles in the institution and made dependent on the very regime that was supposed to effect their cure. Above all, though, it is Goffman's description of the mental hospital as a 'total institution' with shared characteristics of prisons, borstals, and army life that killed off any lingering attachment that they may have been a happy home: as Scull (1989, p. 310) puts it, 'who in the circumstances would attempt to dispute the claim that "the worst home is better than the best mental hospital"?' Meanwhile, Goffman's descriptions of the 'abasements, degradations, humiliations and profanations of self' amounting to a kind of 'civil death' (1961, p. 25), followed by his further work on stigmatization (1963), have inspired countless scholars to write about the lack of a positive common social identity of both mentally ill patients and prisoners on which they can base a call for collective action. Both groups occupy the margins of visibility and social consciousness, both within institutions and in the wider political and cultural spheres. The assault on America's mental hospitals was joined by other critics, among them the Hungarian émigré psychiatrist Thomas Szasz (1974) and sociologist Thomas Scheff (1966) whose views on labelling mental illness included criticism that US mental hospitals are prisons and those who work in them jailers.

In the 1960s, as this trans-Atlantic assault by liberal thinkers continued, others looked backwards to psychiatric history and culture to point out the downsides of humane thinking. Michel Foucault's work on the history of madness and the history of reason came late to the ideological debates on psychiatric institutions because his work did not get translated from French until the 1970s. When his book *Madness and Civilization* (1967/2005) was published in English, his argument that psychiatric patients are locked within the disciplinary limits of psychiatric power/knowledge to which, and against which, madness has proven the 'grand transgressor' (Jenks 2003), had immediate global impact. For Foucault, the history of psychiatry is also a history of power relations. It could not be otherwise, because what he calls the 'great age' of institutionalizing—asylums, prisons, hospitals, factories, schools, etc.—embodied and assured the maintenance of bourgeois reason. In Foucault's estimation, 'reason' triumphed over unreason, silencing the voices of the insane in an age of rampant asylum building.

Foucault's work has implications for how we might reinterpret psychiatry's 'humane' enterprise—not least in the face of sustained attacks by the main creators of unreason and irrational thinking in the late-modern era—the popular press. It is easy to miss the contradictory history of British press reporting on mental health policies; from unalloyed support for tearing down institutions in the 1960s and 1970s, through their demands for an end to community care policy in the 1980s and 1990s, to more recent calls for prison-like punishment for mentally disordered offenders in the 2000s. Such mutations in tabloid logic on mental health reflect Britain's changing newspaper market (Cross 2014), but also underline confusion in the architecture of mental health policy itself: to cure or to punish?

Fictional accounts led the way in describing the debasing, prison-like effects of mental hospitals on individuals. They included Ken Kesey's *One Flew Over the Cuckoo's Nest* based on his observations of working as an orderly in a US state mental hospital (published in 1972) and Marge Piercy's (1976) story of asylum incarceration in *Woman on the Edge of Time*. A pioneering personal account of time spent locked up in mental hospital with no discernible means of securing release was Judi Chamberlain's *On Our Own* (1977). The image of the mental hospital as a prison-machine also took a controversial non-fictional turn. In 1967, Fred Wiseman made *Titicut Follies*, a disturbing documentary film about Bridgewater Hospital, a Massachusetts prison for the criminally insane. Taking its title from the annual musical revue performed by inmates and staff, Wiseman's fly-on-the-wall account visualized Bridgewater as a place where any identifiable distinction between normal and non-normal identities had collapsed: warders, patients, psychiatrists all seem equally insane (Cross 2004). So challenging was Wiseman's fly-on-wall depiction of the prison that it was banned from public exhibition even though Wiseman had permission to film there. Ironically, the film was censored on grounds that it *mis*represented the punishing realities of prison hospital life including naked, secluded inmates and a forced feeding regime (Cross 2004).

In Britain, media access to mental hospitals was restricted in this period and this perhaps explains why the 1975 Oscar winning film version of Kesey's *One Flew Over the Cuckoo's Nest* (dir. Milos Forman) became synonymous with the British asylum experience, despite its American setting. Nonetheless, the assault on the mental hospital was also fought on the European cultural front. The Scottish psychiatrist R.D. Laing (1965) wrote about mental illness as 'intelligible' and his ideas primed the counter-culture and set the scene for a cultural attack on the idea of the benign psychiatric hospital. To take one example, David Mercer's primetime TV drama *In Two Minds* (*BBC1* 1967) drew on Laing's ideas to portray familial conflict leading to the institutionalization of a young woman. Mercer's audience was left in no doubt that the mental hospital into which she is admitted is prison-like punishment for having an independent mind. In the 1970s, Laing established an anti-psychiatric community (the term 'hospital' was avoided), Kingsley Hall, where psychiatrists and patients lived together under the same roof in a manner reminiscent of the curative domesticity inherent in William Tuke's York Retreat. A 2017 feature film, *Mad To Be Normal* (dir. Robert Mullan) starring David Tennant, trades on the heroic image of Laing (a modern-day Tuke) taking a film crew on a tour of a mental hospital replete with prison bars, locked doors, padded cells and shock treatment: 'It's not a prison it's a hospital', says Tennant's Laing, 'It's meant to be a cure not a punishment'.

The perception that mental hospitals may not be what they seem has for two-and-a-half centuries fuelled public anxiety about what goes on behind the high walls and locked doors. From the eighteenth century, patient protest about mistreatment has been voiced, but was rarely taken seriously. It was only when ex-patients and (crucially) ex-nurses spoke on camera in the 1970s and 1980s that punitive conditions became impossible to ignore (Martin 1984). For instance, a TV documentary exposé of conditions inside Rampton high-security hospital, broadcast in 1979 (*The Secret Hospital: Rampton—The Big House*; dir. John Willis, Yorkshire Television), documented accounts of degradation and demoralization: nurses wearing prison officer uniform; stories of medication used as a 'liquid cosh'; and isolation used as a punishment, all of which smacked of punishment not cure. Ironically, when the mass murderer Peter Sutcliffe (the 'Yorkshire Ripper') was transferred in 1983 from prison to Broadmoor, newspaper headlines emphasized his 'cushy' life in a psychiatric hospital.

The documentary on Rampton bore remarkable similarities to the contemporaneous prison documentaries of British film-maker, Rex Bloomstein. Perhaps the most profoundly affecting of Bloomstein's subjects was Steve, who was interviewed twice; first for *Lifers*, a two-hour documentary made for ITV in 1982 and, 21 years later for the follow-up, *Lifer—Living With Murder*, which was broadcast on Channel 4. In the first film, Steve is twelve years into his life sentence and he is cocky, restless and resistant. Prone to responding violently to provocation, he describes how his anger has led him to trash his cell and cause damage to the prison wing on several occasions. He speaks contemptuously of the prison officers who restrain him physically and with drugs. But 21 years later, we see the effects that the 'liquid cosh' has had on Steve. Bloated, dulled and his speech so slurred that the interview has to be accompanied by subtitles, the effects of 32 years in custody are dramatically conveyed. Now held in the secure wing of a psychiatric hospital and reduced to a shell of his former self, there can be no more graphic or moving illustration of a life inside Britain's institutions in the twentieth century (Jewkes 2015).

Concluding Thoughts: Will Future Psychiatric Hospitals and Prisons Cure, Care or Inflict Further Harm?

Perhaps it should not surprise us to find similarities between the regimes of mental institutions and those of prisons, given their shared architectural vernacular over the last two hundred years. The historic buildings that hold criminals and the mentally ill are manifestations of punitive philosophies and a culture that is prone to 'othering' its most vulnerable citizens. Originally built in 1863 to house the criminally insane (and still used for this purpose), Broadmoor was designed by the architect of London's Pentonville Prison and Dublin's Mountjoy Prison, Joshua Jebb. Little wonder, they share a common disciplinary legacy as well as a common architectural legacy.

However, in very recent years, there has been another parallel move towards making both prisons and psychiatric hospitals less bleak and more imaginative in design, with a view to improving the long-term life chances of their occupants.[5] In 2016, then UK Prime Minister David Cameron promised the 'biggest shake-up of prisons since the Victorian era'. Conceiving of the new establishments as places of care, as well as punishment, he acknowledged the extent to which the buildings and spatial design of prisons are conducive to rehabilitating offenders and helping them 'find meaning in their lives' (Cameron 2016). At the same time, the parts of the estate deemed no longer fit-for-purpose would be closed. Such prisons, the PM commented, were barely fit for human habitation when they were built, and are 'much, much worse today'[6] (Cameron 2016; see Jewkes and Moran 2017 for further discussion).

At the time of writing, the design of the new prisons is still under discussion but it is hoped that, while larger in size than most prison experts would recommend, they will not be 'future-proofed' (i.e. over-securitized for the population they hold) or 'value-engineered' (stripped back to the most basic design in order to save money) to the degree that recent prison builds have been in England and Wales, and nor, hopefully, will they look like super-sized, sterile warehouses

(Jewkes and Moran 2017; Jewkes et al. 2017). They may actually more closely resemble the redeveloped Broadmoor psychiatric hospital, which is due to open as this volume goes to press in early 2018. At a cost of £242 million, the new Broadmoor will be built within the existing grounds and will provide accommodation for 210 patients.[7] The early indications are that the new Broadmoor makes imaginative use of light, colour and therapeutic gardens, but that it still has a rather traditional, institutional feel in its healthcare spaces and residential accommodation.[8] In short, it looks just like the kind of medium- or high-security prison that would be commissioned by a government that wished to convey a more enlightened and cautiously optimistic message about the potential of custodial institutions to rehabilitate, while remaining mindful of the mainstream media's tendency to criticize anything that smacks of giving offenders 'privileges' or 'perks'. To prison architects in many countries in northern Europe, and even in some states in Australia and the US, this 'new' style of institution—for all its pastel colours and relative freedom of movement—would seem woefully unambitious and unimaginative in its design, perhaps not entirely unsurprisingly given that the final-stage design and build contract was awarded to Kier who previously delivered the controversial 'prison warehouse' HMP Oakwood (Jewkes and Moran 2014).

However, at least the buildings that make up the new Broadmoor will probably not play 'tricks' on the minds of occupants, as famously described by Mayer Spivack in his (1967) work on 'sensory distortions'. Describing various optical illusions created by institutional corridors and tunnels, Spivack highlights the deleterious, hallucinatory effects that glare on gloss-painted walls, reflections on glass, contrasting material textures and deceptive finishes (e.g. a wood-grain façade on a metal door) can have on the mentally ill. Even these, however, are not as severe as the Erich Lindemann Mental Health Center in Boston, whose architect Paul Marvin Rudolph deliberately designed an 'insane' building to reflect the interior mental states of its occupants. Citing it as a 'notorious example of architecture's power to agitate, confuse and fatally overwhelm',[9] Michele Koh gives us her interpretation of Rudolph's intent:

He tried to recreate the hallucinogenic or exaggerated mental and emotional states of the insane with never ending inchoate corridors, a chapel with a dismal atmosphere and macabre twisting stairways, one of which, like an oubliette in a medieval keep, leads nowhere. The building's dramatic structures and subliminal imagery (there is a thinly veiled frog's head looking out from the building's facade) make the Lindemann Center very expressive, but also foreboding and dangerous. With a romanticized view of mental illness, Rudolph made the building "insane" in the hope that it would sooth those who dwell in it by reflecting the insanity they feel within. Unfortunately, the outcome is not what the architect had hoped for. (Koh 2010, p. 148)

The Lindemann Center provided the perfect location for the paranoia-inducing 2006 crime film *The Departed* (dir. Martin Scorsese), but Boston psychiatrist Matthew Dumont has documented his fears about sending patients to the Center, describing the 'perverse genius' in designing a building which itself evinced a kind of madness (Dumont 1992). Rudolph himself stated that his aim was to create a humanizing architecture, responsive to urban conditions and engaged with the 'psychological effect' of expressive and emotionally moving space (1973, p. 96). A 'useful architecture', then. We are left to wonder what James Tilly Matthews, from his cell in Bethlem, would have made of it.

Notes

1. Examples being Hopewood Park in Northumberland, UK http://www.buildingconstructiondesign.co.uk/news/an-enlightened-approach-to-mental-healthcare/ and the Southwest Centre for Forensic Mental Health Care in Ontario, Canada http://www.parkin.ca/projects/southwest-centre-for-forensic-mental-health-care/.
2. For instance, the so-called 'special hospitals' housing the criminally insane (Broadmoor, Rampton, and Moss Side (renamed Ashworth in 1983) employed disproportionally more male nurses wearing prison-officer uniform (until 1999) and, until 1996, special hospitals were managed by the Home Office (the department of state responsible for managing prisons) not the National Health Service.

3. Many Suffragettes were well educated and well connected and their stories about Holloway's harsh conditions and the brutal treatment they were subjected to (including force feeding when they went on hunger strike) were sympathetically reported, particularly by the *Guardian* newspaper (or *Manchester Guardian* as it was then).

4. Significantly, no one thought it necessary to seek the views of patients. Davies (2007) argues this omission obscures how psychiatric spaces and places held 'good' and 'bad' meanings for those whose lives were lived as recipients of *care*.

5. Of course, this is not uncontentious and there have been calls from many critical criminologists, abolitionists and prison reform groups for a moratorium on prison building. However, Jewkes and Moran (2017) argue that a focus on designing humanizing prison spaces that are focused on supporting rehabilitation and desistance could be a vital component in achieving radical justice reform, including decarceration.

6. Notably, while some archetypal prisons (including Reading, Gloucester, Shrewsbury and Holloway) have been closed down, others such as Pentonville (built 1842) and Wandsworth (1851) are still in operation.

7. Unusually, the redesign of the high-security hospital follows consultation with patients by an independent healthcare organization—this kind of consultation does not yet happen with prisoners.

8. See http://www.wlmht.nhs.uk/about-wlmht/redevelopment/broadmoor-hospital-redevelopment/ and http://www.bbc.co.uk/news/av/uk-england-berkshire-40597023/first-pictures-inside-the-new-242m-broadmoor-hospital.

9. By way of tragic illustration, the chapel at Lindemann was closed a year after it opened because a patient set fire to himself on the concrete slab altar. A psychiatrist working there claimed the man was simply following his environmental cues because the altar 'looks like a place that should be used for human sacrifice' (quoted in Ledford 2014).

Bibliography

Barham, P. (1992). *Closing the asylum*. London: Penguin Books.

Barton, W. R. (1959). *Institutional neurosis*. Bristol: Wright and Sons.

Cameron, D. (2016). *Speech to policy exchange*. Available at: http://www.politics.co.uk/comment-analysis/2016/02/08/cameron-prison-reform-speech-in-full. Accessed 28 Nov 2017.

Cross, S. (2004). Visualising madness: Mental illness and public representation. *Television and New Media, 5*(1), 197–216.

Cross, S. (2010). *Mediating madness: Mental distress and cultural representation.* London: Palgrave Macmillan.

Cross, S. (2014). Mad and bad media: Populism and pathology in the British tabloids. *European Journal of Communication, 20*(4), 460–483.

Crossley, N. (2006). *Contesting psychiatry: Social movements in mental health.* London: Routledge.

Davies, K. (2007). "A small corner that's for myself": Space, place, and patients' experiences of mental health care, 1948–98. In L. Topp, J. Moran, & J. Andrews (Eds.), *Madness, architecture and the built environment: Psychiatric spaces in historical context* (pp. 305–320). London: Routledge.

Digby, A. (1985). *Madness, morality and medicine: A study of the York Retreat, 1796–1914.* Cambridge: Cambridge University Press.

Dumont, M. (1992). *Treating the poor: A personal sojourn through the rise and fall of community mental health.* Belmont, MA: Dymphna Press.

Evans, R. (1982). *The fabrication of virtue: English prison architecture, 1750–1840.* Cambridge: Cambridge University Press.

Fairweather, L. (1961). Prison architecture in England [special issue on 'Prison Architecture']. *British Journal of Criminology, 1*(4), 339–361.

Fennelly, K. (2014). Out of sound, out of mind: Noise control in early nineteenth-century lunatic asylums in England and Ireland. *World Archaeology, 46*(3), 416–430.

Fiddler, M. (2007). Projecting the prison: The depiction of the uncanny in The Shawshank Redemption. *Crime, Media, Culture: An International Journal, 3*(2), 192–206.

Fiddler, M. (2010). Four walls and what lies within: The meaning of space and place in prisons. *Prison Service Journal, 187,* 3–8.

Foucault, M. (2005). *Madness and civilization: A history of insanity in the age of reason.* London: Tavistock (Original English publication 1967).

Goffman, E. (1961). *Asylums: Essays on the social situation of mental patients and other inmates.* Harmondsworth: Penguin Books.

Goffman, E. (1963). *Stigma: Notes on the management of spoiled identity.* Princeton, NJ: Prentice Hall.

Howard, J. (1784). *The state of the prisons in England and Wales.* Warrington. Available at: https://archive.org/details/stateofprisonsin00howa. Accessed 10 July 2017.

Jay, M. (2003). *The Air Loom Gang. The strange and true story of the James Tilly Matthews and his visionary madness.* London: Bantam Press.

Jenks, C. (2003). *Transgression*. London: Routledge.

Jewkes, Y. (2015). *Media and crime* (revised 3rd ed.). London: Sage.

Jewkes, Y., & Johnston, H. (2007). The evolution of prison architecture. In Y. Jewkes (Ed.), *Handbook on prisons* (pp. 174–196). Cullompton: Willan.

Jewkes, Y., & Moran, D. (2014). Bad design breeds violence in sterile mega-prisons. *The Conversation*. Available at: https://theconversation.com/bad-design-breeds-violence-in-sterile-megaprisons-22424. Accessed 27 July 2017.

Jewkes, Y., & Moran, D. (2017). Prison architecture and design: Perspectives from criminology and carceral geography. In A. Liebling, S. Maruna, & L. McAra (Eds.), *Oxford handbook of criminology* (6th ed., pp. 541–561). Oxford: Oxford University Press.

Jewkes, Y., Slee, E., & Moran, D. (2017). The visual retreat of the prison: Non-places for non-people. In M. Brown & E. Carrabine (Eds.), *The routledge handbook of visual criminology*. Abingdon: Routledge.

Johnsen, B., Granheim, P. K., & Helgesen, J. (2011). Exceptional prison conditions and the quality of prison life: Prison size and prison culture in Norwegian closed prisons. *European Journal of Criminology, 8*(6), 515–529.

Johnston, H. (2015). *Crime in England, 1815–1880: Experiencing the criminal justice system*. Abingdon: Routledge.

Jones, K. (1993). *Asylums and after: A revised history of the mental health services: From the early 18th century to the 1990s*. London: The Athlone Press.

Koh, M. (2010, April). Architecture of insanity: Boston Government Services Center. *Singapore Architect*, pp. 148–153.

Laing, R. D. (1965). *The divided self*. London: Pelican.

Ledford, D. L. (2014). *"Psychology of space": The psycho-spatial architecture of Paul Rudolph* (Yale Divinity School dissertation). Available at: https://www.academia.edu/10200011/Psychology_of_Space_The_Psycho-Spatial_Architecture_of_Paul_Rudolph. Accessed 27 July 2017.

Liebling, A., & Arnold, H. (2004). *Prisons and their moral performance: A study of values, quality, and prison life*. Oxford: Oxford University Press.

Martin, J. P. (1984). *Hospitals in trouble*. Oxford: Blackwell.

Peterson, A. W. (1961). The prison building programme. *British Journal of Criminology, 1*(4), 307–316.

Pevsner, N. (1976). *A history of building types*. Thames & Hudson Ltd.

Porter, R. (1987). *Mind-forg'd manacles: A history of madness in England from the restoration to the regency*. London: Weidenfeld and Nicholson.

Porter, R. (Ed.). (1991). *The Faber book of madness*. London: Faber and Faber.

Porter, R. (2002). *Madness. A brief history*. Oxford: Oxford University Press.

Porter, R., & Wright, D. (Eds.). (2003). *The confinement of the insane, 1800–1965: International perspectives*. Cambridge: Cambridge University Press.

Pratt, J. (2002). *Punishment and civilization*. London: Sage.

Prins, H. (1995). *Offenders, deviants or patients?* London: Routledge.

Scheff, T. (1966). *Being mentally ill: A sociological theory*. New York: Aldine de Gruyter.

Scull, A. (1979). *Museums of madness: The social organisation of insanity in nineteenth century England*. London: Allen Lane/Penguin Books.

Scull, A. (1989). *Social order/mental disorder: Anglo American psychiatry in historical context*. London: Routledge.

Scull, A. (2006). *The insanity of place/the place of insanity: Essays on the history of psychiatry*. London: Routledge.

Seddon, T. (2006). *Punishment and madness: Governing prisoners with mental health problems*. Abingdon: Routledge-Cavendish.

Spens, I. (1994). *Architecture of incarceration*. London: Academy.

Spivack, M. (1967). Sensory distortions in tunnels and corridors. *Psychiatric Services, 18*(1), 12–18.

Sykes, G. (1958). *The society of captives: A study of a maximum security prison*. Princeton, NJ: Princeton University Press.

Szasz, T. (1974). *The myth of mental illness*. New York: Harper and Row.

4

Psychological Jurisprudence and the Relational Problems of De-vitalisation and Finalisation: Revisiting the Society of Captives Thesis

Bruce A. Arrigo and Brian G. Sellers

Introduction

The role of Psychological Jurisprudence (PJ)[1] as a relevant analytical framework with which to diagnose contemporary social issues and to investigate enduring human problems is well documented in the extant mental health, law and society, and offender treatment literatures (Birgden 2014; Fox 1993). The insights of PJ have been used to further a critical psychology of law (Arrigo and Fox 2009), to advance doctrinal and/or empirical legal analysis (Bersot and Arrigo 2015; Arrigo and Waldman 2015), to develop clinical taxonomies (Arrigo 2013, 2015), and to propose justice-based public policy reform (Arrigo and Acheson

B. A. Arrigo (✉)
University of North Carolina at Charlotte, Charlotte, NC, USA
e-mail: barrigo@uncc.edu

B. G. Sellers
Eastern Michigan University, Ypsilanti, MI, USA
e-mail: bseller3@emich.edu

© The Author(s) 2018   **73**
A. Mills and K. Kendall (eds.), *Mental Health in Prisons*, Palgrave Studies in Prisons
and Penology, https://doi.org/10.1007/978-3-319-94090-8_4

2015; Sellers and Arrigo 2009; Trull and Arrigo 2015). Recently, Ward (2013) noted the following when summarising PJ's general acumen:

> [It is composed of] significant epistemological, economic, social, cultural, psychological, and ethical strands [reminding us] that we are under the spell of…contestable, and specific [renditions of reality]… The crucial issue is [one of diagnosing] the relationship [among those cultural forces]…that reinforce, and in a sense constitute [finite depictions of subjectivity]. By understanding how these factors dynamically interact… it may be possible to open up a conceptual space for considering alternative ways of dealing with atypical human behavior. (p. 704)

Notwithstanding its apparent analytical efficacy, one facet of PJ that remains mostly underdeveloped is the radical philosophy that informs its interdisciplinary and humanistic approach to research and practice. Counted among these under-examined features of philosophy are PJ's operating assumptions. These assumptions inform PJ's position on why reciprocal consciousness, inter-subjectivity, and mutual power are so important to the processes of offender treatment, recovery, and re-entry. As we subsequently explain, when these associational components of human experience (consciousness, subjectivity, and power) are iteratively neutralised (i.e. recursively forestalled and/or foreclosed), then forms of ontological and epistemological captivity (e.g. the reduction of relational being, the repression of relational becoming) can emerge as the normalised, healthy, and inevitable conditions of coexistence. Moreover, to the extent that the conditions of relationality are in excess states of neutralisation, then the captivity-generating forms of reciprocal ontology and epistemology become totalising (i.e. socio-culturally harm-generating and injury-producing). In the extreme, these 'relations of humanness' engender a 'society of captives' (Arrigo 2015, p. 9; Arrigo and Milovanovic 2009; see also Clemmer 1940; Sykes 1958). This is the captivity of the kept *and* those who work within the systems of offender treatment, recovery and re-entry. When recurring states of excess neutralisation populate this society, then reciprocal ontology is de-vitalised and mutual epistemology is finalised.[2] Sustaining these neutralisations signals the demise of authentically lived human experience (e.g. Heidegger 2008; Leder 1991; Levinas 2004) in spaces of coexistence.

At issue in this chapter, then, is the chronicling of an under-examined dimension of mass incarceration itself. This is the imprisonment of human relatedness within a society of captives, and the de-vitalising and finalising ways in which this carceral reality is destructively re-enacted (ceremonialised) and dangerously reproduced (ritualised) by its members.

In the first part of this chapter, we offer several summary observations on PJ's radical philosophy. This includes commentary on PJ's object of theoretical and methodological inquiry (i.e. relational humanity), the socio-cultural roots of such investigations, and the core operating assumptions that inform such inquiries. In part two, we explain why an assessment of the symbols, discourses, and technologies of coexistence matter with respect to diagnosing and responding to the associational problems of de-vitalisation and finalisation. We also identify and elaborate on the excess forms of de-vitalisation and finalisation. The forms of de-vitalisation include limits on relational being, harms of reduction, and bad faith. The forms of finalisation include denials of relational becoming, harms of repression, and negative freedom. We assert that the excesses of both sets of forms, as habituated neutralisations, nurture the mass imprisonment of human relatedness. In the third section of the chapter, we summarily, and thus tentatively, critique the deficit and desistance models of correctional treatment, recovery, and re-entry. We also explain how the interpersonal symbols, discourses, and technologies of these models re-enact and reproduce relations of humanness that are totalising in their iterative effects on reciprocal consciousness, subjectivity and power. As we assert, maintaining or cultivating the de-vitalising and finalising forms of relatedness engendered by these models is an exercise in co-productive madness (Arrigo et al. 2011). Indeed, the human project of shared struggle and the human experience of collective overcoming are forfeited within this repetitive coexistence. As PJ maintains, both this project and these experiences are necessary ontological and epistemological conditions for interdependent human flourishing to occur, including the becoming of justice (as restorative and transformative) for a people yet to be (Deleuze and Guattari 1994). We use illustrations from the mental health and prison literatures throughout the commentary to amplify the chapter's overall thesis and to illuminate its central analytics.

Psychological Jurisprudence as Radical Philosophy: An Overview

As radical philosophy, PJ acknowledges that the shaping and remaking of one's human existence (e.g. who each of us is, how each of us knows, the way each of us lives) consists of a dynamic set of reciprocal experiences. These experiences are constructed from and contribute to multiple expressions of meaning-making, including those meanings that depict the human experience of coexistence. There are many social worlds that are inhabited relationally. The prison milieu is one such sphere and it contains many examples of relationality. To illustrate, solitary confinement functions as a space for ritualising death-in-life socially (Guenther 2013), death row represents a deviant site for reconceiving the psychology of community (Arrigo and Fowler 2001), and offender therapy denotes the setting and moment in which the 'rehabilitative machine' all too frequently guarantees 'fabricated selves' for treatment provider and convict in recovery alike (Polizzi et al. 2014b, p. 231). Even the mutuality of recovery for offenders lived through 'narrative lifelines' over time (Weaver and McNeill 2015, p. 95) is revealing of human experience and the struggle to make and take shared meaning from it. In each instance, important questions persist about the ontic nature of relationship and the epistemic problem of coexistence that both the kept and their collective keepers confront. Indeed, as Polizzi et al. (2014a) noted when summarising the dysfunctional relations of humanness that populate the prison environment's landscape of coexistence:

> Current attitudes in corrections and offender treatment and the policy initiatives these evoke, reveal an underlying set of negatively defined socially constructed meanings about offenders that effectively contradict and undercut any superficial [let alone detailed] discussion about the benefits of rehabilitation, reentry, or restorative justice practices. It is very difficult to envision what successful work in corrections, offender psychotherapy, or rehabilitation would actually look like in such an environment. Successful work with offender populations will be difficult to achieve without first thoroughly addressing the way in which these

socially-generated definitions, concerning who and what the offender is, both restrict and actually prevent the type of success the criminal justice [and mental health] system[s] appear willing to pursue. (p. 4)

The radical philosophy of PJ, including its analytical framework, was developed as a partial response to such totalising and destructive environments (Arrigo 2013; Arrigo and Bersot 2016). In this important respect, then, PJ offers both a clinical diagnosis of, and proposes a set of therapeutic correctives for, such relational states of captivity-generating coexistence.

PJ is rooted in the continental rather than the analytic tradition.[3] The continental tradition of philosophy rejects reliance on the empirics of positivism as the legitimate basis by which to explain the complexities and contradictions of human experience (Bargdill and Broome 2016; Crewe 2013). Moreover, continental thought emphasises historicism (i.e. the importance of symbols and signs, languages and codes, practices and customs) as a preferred method by which to account for forms of identity-claiming, knowledge production, and meaning-making (Lacan 1977; Derrida 1978). Still further, it locates prospects for human social change (e.g. shared restoration and collective transformation) within the unconscious and its libidinal and political-economic liberation and production (i.e. de-territorialisaion and re-territorialisation, Arrigo and Milovanovic 2009; Deleuze and Guattari 1994). Finally, this tradition recognises the socio-cultural embeddedness of medicine, law, education, and other disciplinary domains as sites of discursive contestation and dynamic normalisation (Foucault 1977), especially within systems of institutional governance and organisational decision-making (Hardie-Bick and Lippens 2011; Polizzi et al. 2014a). We note, therefore, that the radical philosophy of PJ concerns itself with macro-level questions applied to micro-level interactions, ceremonially re-enacted and ritually reproduced through system-level forces. These are the questions of consciousness, subjectivity, and power. These are the interactions of relational being and associational meaning. These are the system-level forces that populate spaces of coexistence.

The analytical framework of PJ contains several core operating assumptions, and these suppositions function to guide the investigation and/or diagnosis of relational humanity. Inquiries that examine our relations of humanness reveal both the ontological complexion and epistemological composition of shared human experience in various domains of coexistence, including the manifold settings of offender therapy, recovery, and re-entry (Arrigo and Bersot 2016). In brief, these suppositions state that: (1) the unconscious is structured like a language; (2) subjectivity (e.g. the criminal defendant, the psychiatric patient) is always politicised (e.g. standpoint epistemologies), given that a 'master discourse' (a language system) pre-codes and pre-figures conscious thought; and (3) power functions through these politics (through standpoints) and these languages (through symbolic representations), producing 'technologies' (i.e. bodies of knowledge, and correspondingly, bodies of being). As we subsequently explain in the chapter's next section, in order to assess the complexion and composition of human relatedness found within the sphere of prison coexistence, it is important to examine how reciprocal consciousness, inter-subjectivity, and mutual power fill this space of cohabitation. This analysis depends on the ways in which shared human experience is both constrained by and contributes to the symbols, discourses, and technologies of everyday (penal) life. In what follows, however, we further elaborate upon PJ's operating assumptions. These suppositions suggest why the relations of humanness are so important to the processes of offender treatment, recovery, and re-entry.

The first assumption maintains that our conscious human experiences are mediated by unconscious (and therefore pre-reflective) 'laws'. According to Lacan (1977), these laws indicate that the unconscious is structured like a language. Stated differently, our conscious sense of self (who we claim to be) and our conscious sense of society (what we claim to know) are both source and product of an unspoken discourse that is itself a master code or a coordinated language system of preferred meaning-making. For Lacan, this code spoke the subject. It pre-figured (symbolised) consciousness and the manifold depictions of conscious human experience. Lacan (1981) further maintained that this unconscious code, that spoke the subject, communicated 'lack' (i.e. the incompleteness in being; the absence in knowing) or awaiting yet-to-be symbolisation. These symbolisations are the unimagined codes and registers of meaning that pre-form the presently 'un-representable' (Cornell 1991, p. 169). The un-representable signifies more of what could be (human production) rather than the subjectivity of lack (human incompleteness) in consciousness (e.g. Deleuze and Guattari 1987).

The second assumption asserts that subjectivity is always politicised. If the laws of the unconscious symbolise human experience through a master discourse that pre-figures consciousness as lack (in being and in knowing), then entire registers of meaning-making are made present in consciousness while others are suspended, silenced, and even rendered absent. But, how does this 'metaphysical' process of meaning-making occur in consciousness whose source is the unconscious and its symbolisations? For Derrida (1973), the answer to this question was found in deconstructionist philosophy. Deconstruction maintains that spoken utterances and written phrases are always and already composed of embedded binaries or terms in opposition ('law-abider' defers 'law-violator', 'healthy' postpones 'unhealthy', 'competent' obscures 'incompetent'). These unstated binaries both reveal and conceal the logocentric conditions (e.g. the presumed unambiguous meanings, the taken-for-granted preferred hierarchies) of Western thought (Derrida 1977). These conditions consist of the hidden presuppositions, covert values, and implicit truth-claims on which the relations of humanness depend if shared meaning-making is to occur, and from which the experiences of reciprocal consciousness, inter-subjectivity, and mutual power are correspondingly deferred if shared meaning-stabilisation is to occur. What is problematic about such dependencies and deferrals, is that alternative and fuller meaning resides within the unexamined *interdependencies* of such binaries (Derrida 1977, 1978), and by extension, the novel and awaiting forms of social relating to which they (these interdependent meanings) would otherwise direct human choice and collective action (Donati 2012). The postponement of untapped and nascent relational meaning further explains how inter-subjectivity is both ritually scripted and ceremonially politicised *within the unconscious*, consistent with status quo systems-level forces and the socio-cultural conditions that are their tangible support.

The third assumption contends that power's diffusion is located through these politics (these standpoints) and languages (these symbolisations), producing 'technologies' (i.e. bodies of knowledge, and correspondingly, bodies of being) (Foucault 1973). The proliferation of these technologies yields disciplinary/disciplining truths (e.g. in community psychology, in correctional psychiatry, in clinical criminology) and regimes of comportment (for the kept and their collective keepers). This is what Foucault (1977, p. 194) meant when he reasoned that 'power produces; it produces reality; it produces domains of objects and rituals of truth'. In this important respect, then, power's diffusion guarantees a type of micro-physics and a form of bio-politics (Foucault 1980). The former reduces the relations of humanness to the panoptics of suspicion; the latter represses the relations of humanness through the hermeneutics of governmentality. Both of these surveillance mechanisms re-enact and reproduce technologies of the marketplace (as truth) and subjugate those of the self (as freedom). Indeed, as Foucault (1980, p. 39) observed, 'in thinking of the mechanisms of power, I am thinking rather of its capillary forms of existence, the point where power reaches into the very grain of individuals, touches their bodies, and inserts itself into their actions and attitudes, their discourse, learning processes, and everyday lives'. This is how power manufactures bodies (of knowing and of being) that are themselves 'docile', that are bodies of 'abject utility', in which the subject becomes nothing more than a 'mere functionary of the State' (Foucault 1977, p. 210). Under these conditions, the possibilities of co-habiting the space of relational growth and change (i.e. the space of emergent human restoration and dynamic human transformation) are reduced to finite processes of inter-relating and fixed methods of coexisting.

Given these three operating assumptions, PJ considers how reciprocal consciousness is bounded, how inter-subjectivity is held in check, and how mutual power is constrained in spaces of coexistence. This includes the shared human experience of offender treatment, recovery, and re-entry in which relational ontology and epistemology are co-constituted. Thus, we pose the following queries. First, what are the conscious depictions (mental representations) of human relatedness in confinement settings (e.g. forensic hospitals, county jails or rehabilitation centres) and how do their unconscious symbolisations speak the subject? Second, what are the scripts or narratives on which human relatedness depends within prisons, jails, and other total institutions, and how do these codes of meaning-making defer inter-subjectivity? Third, what are the bodies of human relatedness in knowing and in being that are ceremonialised and ritualised within total institutions, and what type of microphysics of reciprocal power do these bodies engender? These questions are the source of examination in the section addressing the deficit-correcting and desistance-managing models of correctional mental health. Before moving to these concerns, however, it is important to provide additional commentary on the relational problems of de-vitalisation and finalisation.

The Relational Problems of De-vitalisation and Finalisation

In the lexicon of PJ, de-vitalisation and finalisation represent destructive conditions of human relatedness in which reciprocal consciousness, inter-subjectivity, and shared power are neutralised (i.e. forestalled and/or foreclosed).[4] De-vitalisation occurs when the symbols, discourses, and technologies of coexistence preclude the project of mutual (i.e. dialectical) struggle (Adorno 1970).[5] Finalisation occurs when the symbols, discourses, and technologies of social reality exclude the experiences of collective (i.e. dialogical) overcoming (Bahktin 1982).[6] This project of mutual struggle and these experiences of collective overcoming are necessary ontological and epistemological conditions for interdependent human flourishing to occur, including the possibilities of justice (as restorative and transformative) for a 'people yet to come' (Deleuze and Guattari 1994, p. 108).

The relational problems of de-vitalisation and finalisation cannot be underestimated, especially when the forms that these conditions assume are in states of excess neutralisation (i.e. states that forestall and preclude human relatedness, states that foreclose and exclude human relatedness). De-vitalisation assumes three forms, including limits of relational being, harms of reduction, and bad faith. Finalisation assumes three forms, including denials of relational becoming, harms of repression, and negative freedom. We maintain that the ontic complexion and epistemic composition of shared human experience in spaces of coexistence is made evident by assessing the unconscious symbols (the mind's laws), the unspoken discourses (subjectivity's politics), and the inhabited technologies of truth (power's microphysics) that are ceremonially re-enacted and ritually reproduced in settings of human relatedness. The shared humanity to which we refer is mutual struggle and collective overcoming in the manifold sites of penal coexistence. Thus, an examination of de-vitalisation and finalisation represents a clinical analysis of mass captivity and the recurring socio-cultural forces that nurture its ubiquity.

The Space of Relational Coexistence is schematised in Fig. 4.1. The specific 'space' to which we refer includes multiple sites of offender treatment, recovery, and re-entry. Relations of humanness populate these sites. The ontic complexion and epistemic composition of shared humanity within these manifold sites are co-produced by and interconnected to three socio-cultural domains or spheres of co-constituted human relatedness. These spheres of co-shaped relationality include the mind's laws, subjectivity's politics, and power's microphysics. Figure 4.1 identifies the essential features of each domain. To reiterate, the shared humanity under consideration is mutual struggle and collective overcoming. De-vitalisation and finalisation (including their respective forms, states of excess and neutralisations) are constrained by, and contribute to, the symbols, discourses, and technologies that fill the various settings of (penal) cohabitation.

We note further that bi-directional arrows extend beyond the Relational Space of Coexistence. These arrows signify that the possibilities of emergent ontology and novel epistemology presently remain un-representable (Cornell 1991). These awaiting possibilities and potentials are associational, co-productive, and mutually supporting in their iterative effects. The various bi-directional arrows located within the Relational Space of Coexistence signify the constitutive forces that dynamically operate within a given (carceral) setting. The interactive and interdependent stabilisation of these forces (in consciousness, through subjectivity, and by way of power) reveals the ontological complexion and epistemological composition of shared humanity within

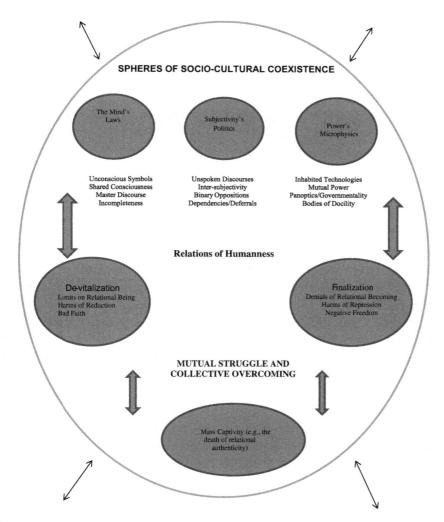

Fig. 4.1 The relational space of coexistence

that cohabited site. When the set of de-vitalising and finalising forms of human relatedness are in recurring states of excess neutralisation, then mass captivity ensues. This includes the death of shared authenticity (e.g. restoring and transforming justice for a people yet to be) and its un-representable forms. These forms of human relatedness await symbolic representation, discursive articulation, and their technologies of the self (i.e. of truth and of freedom).

How does de-vitalisation manifest itself? When relational being is limited, then the symbols for and about reciprocal consciousness are precluded from consciousness. These preclusions encompass the bounds (i.e. aversions, side-steps, and postponements) of mutual struggle that populate shared human experience (e.g. the processes of offender treatment, recovery, and re-entry) in spaces of coexistence (e.g. confinement settings). This boundedness is unspoken, but it makes its presence felt.[7] These impediments to reciprocal consciousness are unconsciously symbolised through the relatedness of master statuses and/or spoiled identities (e.g. as correctional psychologist, as forensic patient, as recovering addict (Goffman 1963). These statuses and identities (including their ideological content) pre-figure conscious thought and they pre-code (i.e. speak) the subject (Lacan 1981).

When reciprocal consciousness is iteratively forestalled, then harms of reduction occur (Henry and Milovanovic 1996). These harms hold in check the relatedness of inter-subjectivity, of experiencing life relationally. Harms of reduction confine mutual struggle to the dialectics of master statuses and identity categories that then narratively configure (pre-reflexively delimit and script) relatedness in spaces of coexistence. These statuses and categories are the oppositional binaries on which human experience (e.g. the processes of offender treatment, recovery, and re-entry) depends if shared meaning-making is to occur, and from which the horizon of possible interdependent human relatedness is deferred (Derrida 1977) if shared meaning-stabilisation is to occur. The politics of such harms reduce the relations of humanness to the taken-for-granted hierarchies of and presumed unambiguous meanings for inter-subjectivity (e.g. Weaver and McNeill 2015).

When harms of reduction are embodied as the natural, healthy, and inevitable conditions of human relating, then they (these harms) inscribe (discipline, govern) shared human experience through technologies of truth (systems of thought; bodies of knowledge) (Foucault 1980). These truths represent power's diffusion and they inhabit bodies (i.e. subjectivity, inter-subjectivity). This habitation is the power to constrain (rather than to unleash) knowing (as in, how to think relationally) and being (as in, who to be reciprocally) in spaces of coexistence such that interrelatedness is itself rendered docile. The maintenance of this docility constitutes bad faith (Sartre 1956). Bad faith is the reduction of one's humanity (and the humanity of another) to the stifling choices that master statuses and spoiled identities will permit within ritual settings and ceremonial sites (see also Goffman 1961). The microphysics of such choice-making forecloses power's mutuality.

How does finalisation manifest itself? When relational becoming is denied, then the symbols for reciprocal consciousness are altogether excluded from conscious perception, thought, and action. They are unimaginable, unthinkable, and uninhabitable in consciousness. They (these images, scripts, and bodies of knowledge/self) are finalised (Bahktin 1982). These finalisations represent harms of repression (Henry and Milovanovic 1996). What is repressed is inter-subjectivity. When inter-subjectivity is foreclosed, then the co-constitution of shared humanity in spaces of coexistence has no meaning dialogically and it holds no purchase relationally. This exclusion extends to all within the space of (penal) coexistence. Under these conditions of human relatedness, power's diffusion reproduces negative freedom. Negative freedom is a state of neutralisation in which technologies of docility (e.g. panopticism, governmentality, and suspicion) are embodied as if they (re)produce technologies of positive freedom (i.e. dynamism, becoming, *élan vital*), and technologies of positive freedom are deferred because technologies of docility territorialise and vanquish such human possibilities. Negative freedom is disciplined by predictability and routinisation and it is captivated by stasis and normalisation. The human experience of collective overcoming (ontologically, epistemologically, and dialogically) is anathema to negative freedom's biopolitics. Mass captivity ensues.[8]

On the Deficit and Desistance Models of Correctional Mental Health: Rethinking the Society of Captives

What is the ontological complexion and epistemological composition of human relatedness within the remit of correctional mental health (i.e. offender treatment, recovery, and re-entry), and how do this complexion and composition further the project of mutual struggle and the experiences of collective overcoming for the kept and their keepers? As we have intimated, both this project of mutual struggle and these experiences of collective overcoming are necessary conditions for interdependent human flourishing to occur, including the becoming (or the metamorphosis) of justice as restorative and transformative for a people yet to be. In order to address these matters, it is essential to examine the various artefacts (i.e. symbols, discourses, and technologies) of relational humanity that populate the deficit model of institutional recovery and the desistance model of community re-entry. We posit that these models (and their respective relations of humanness) are the recurring source and product of penal coexistence and they (these relations) territorialise the communal experience of carceral reality. Indeed, the relationality of being and knowing emerges from the socio-cultural artefacts of these models, and they (these artefacts) are shared, shaped, and inhabited by their human producers (Arrigo and Milovanovic 2009; Crewe 2013).

Thus far, we have relied on PJ's analytical framework (especially its core operating assumptions) to explain how reciprocal consciousness, inter-subjectivity, and mutual power function in spaces of coexistence. Additionally, we have examined how de-vitalisation and finalisation operate, especially when their forms are in states of excess neutralisation. In what follows, we suggestively explore the relevance of PJ's clinical diagnostics and fit them to the systems-level force that is the 'rehabilitative machine' (Polizzi et al. 2014b, p. 233). Institutional recovery derived from a deficit-correcting model and community re-entry derived from a desistance-managing model represent two of this machine's essentialising artefacts. We speculatively consider what these artefacts ceremonially re-enact (ontologically, dialectically, and relationally) and what they ritually reproduce (epistemologically, dialogically, and relationally) in spaces of penal coexistence. These considerations emphasise the ceremonies and rituals of reciprocal consciousness, inter-subjectivity, and mutual power.

The Pains of Imprisonment: On the Deficit and Desistance Models of Human Relatedness

What are the conscious depictions (mental representations) of human relatedness in confinement settings (e.g. forensic hospitals, county jails, or rehabilitation centres) and how do their unconscious symbolisations speak the subject of reciprocal consciousness?

Figure 4.2 schematises The Relational Spaces of Penal Coexistence: Deficit and Desistance Models of Human Relatedness. This schematisation incorporates and illustrates the central components of PJ's analytical framework as depicted in Fig. 4.1. When coexisting within the Relational Spaces of Penal Coexistence, the mindfulness of deficit-correcting and desistance-managing is unconsciously symbolised. These symbolisations speak the subject of 'lack' in relational being and knowing. This is the incomplete meaning (awaiting symbolisation in the unconscious) that follows when experiencing relatedness through the summary representations of bounded (i.e. forestalled/foreclosed) humanity that master statuses and identity categories can only summon or ever register in consciousness. The preclusions to reciprocal consciousness within the deficit-correcting model of recovery are made evident in its emphasis 'on failures, on punishing transgressors, on 'going straight,' on the singularity of the event, on unilaterally constructed plans (operative while incarcerated and in release plans), [and] on the behavioral surface of bodies' (Arrigo and Milovanovic 2009, p. 119). These are the symbolisations into which the kept and their keepers are inserted and out of which human relatedness (e.g. the shared struggle over treatment and for recovery) dialectically unfolds.

The exclusions to reciprocal consciousness within the desistance-managing model of re-entry are made evident given the model's emphasis on re-socialisation (Farrall and Calverley 2006); on the duality of the 'deviant or conforming citizen' (Uggen et al. 2004, p. 287); and on the 'good lives' philosophy of establishing 'stable' employment, maintaining 'healthy' family relationships, and promoting 'collective' aspirations or hopes (e.g. the American dream) (Ward and Maruna 2007).[9] These are the symbolisations into which the kept and their keepers are inserted

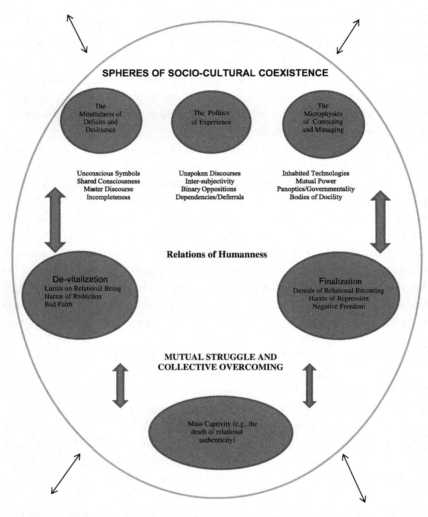

Fig. 4.2 The relational spaces of penal coexistence: deficit and desistance models of human relatedness

and out of which human relatedness (e.g. the communal and collective experience of re-entry) dialogically unfolds.

What are the scripts or narratives on which human relatedness depends within prisons, jails and other total institutions, and how do these codes of meaning-making defer inter-subjectivity?

The pains of imprisonment (Sykes 1958) that recursively follow from the deficit and desistance models are the 'prison rules [themselves that] place people [including the kept and their collective keepers] under an institutional routine [a regime of comportment] that virtually suspends their power' (Farrall and Calverley 2006, p. 181). These rules function as the fixed associational scripts on which the relations of humanness (mutual struggle, collective overcoming) depend, and these dependencies function to legitimise finite ontic and fixed epistemic categories of inter-subjective meaning-making (Crewe 2013). Interestingly, however, it is this deferred or suspended meaning-making that has the nearest potential to restore and to transform shared struggle and collective overcoming in spaces of penal coexistence. Indeed, what remain suspended are the images, texts, practices, and emergent representations of each that could reterritorialise the politics of human experience, thereby signifying an inter-subjective revolution-in-the-making. It is this untapped and unharnessed associational productivity that awaits symbolisation and activation as will that is mobilised to power. This awaiting humanity is the unconscious lack that is a deferred narrative (an absent body of knowledge) in offender treatment, institutional recovery, and community re-entry. The dialectical and dialogical silencing of this relationality extends throughout correctional policy.[10]

Consider the case of the custodial subject (the convict) whose conditional release is contemplated wherein offender treatment and re-entry curatives (desistance management) must be specified and hurdled. What follows, then, is a 'master' plan, a discourse (Lacan 1977) that focuses not only on creating 'bodies of docility and utility (Foucault 1977) but tend[s] toward the stabilisation of reactive forces—the separation of the body from what it can potentially do' (Arrigo and Milovanovic 2009, p. 98). As Taxman et al. (2004, p. 244) noted, '[d]uring structured re-entry, offenders sign behavioral contracts that set priorities, specify supervision requirements and service participation, and detail sanctions for not complying with the contract'.[11] However, in this repetitively uninspired process of constructing reductive/repressive relations of humanness for the society of captives (i.e. the kept, as well as their keepers), 'opportunities for disruption' must nonetheless occur (Halsey 2007, p. 1230). These opportunities are the critical situations themselves in which a more humanistic approach to inter-subjectivity can (and should) be envisioned. This approach 'demands that...educators, penitentiary administrators, correctional officers, and psychotherapists examine the way[s] in which policies, theories, and ideological proclivities have helped to perpetuate the status quo and [have] insure[d] a consistent record of failure' (Polizzi et al. 2014a, pp. 8–9).

What are the bodies of human relatedness in knowing and in being that are ceremonialised and ritualised within total institutions, and what type of microphysics of reciprocal power do these bodies engender?

When human relatedness is managed through static rules, procedures, codes of conduct, and evidentiary outlets that support fixed, axiomatic categories, then limits to and denials of relationality most assuredly follow. Employment based on the capitalist mode of production; intimacy and fellowship governed by the nuclear family model; hoping and dreaming defined by collectivist aspirations; violence, victimisation, and recidivism regulated on the terms of actuarial science; offender treatment, institutional recovery, and community re-entry as categories to classify, record and compartmentalise all illustrate this point. What is resisted through reliance on this ordering of things is their harm-generating and injury-producing tendency towards closure and to barrier-obliging configurations for human relatedness. When these configurations are ceremonially re-enacted and ritually reproduced, then associational identities within spaces of penal coexistence are increasingly de-vitalised and finalised. This is how inter-subjectivity is reduced in being dialectically and repressed in knowing dialogically. When the harm-generating and injury-producing process of de-vitalisation and finalisation is cyclically sustained, then its excess neutralisations foster a totalising madness, a systemic pathology. This is the ontological and epistemological imprisonment of human experience, mutual struggle, and collective overcoming.

The problem of docility and utility is particularly prescient in offender therapy. The locus of change is often externalised and dependent on the use of a range of industry apparatuses. These include devices, instruments, and mechanisms that represent the standard for promoting best treatment practices and evidence-based therapeutics. These assembled technologies (and the discourse and reasoning that breathe meaning and vitality into them), then, produce a body of knowledge, a regime of truth. As methods for and measures of co-habitable change, these industry apparatuses fill the space in which the social person (e.g. the mental health therapist, the correctional officer, and the criminal offender) dwells, makes meaning, chooses to act, and exists. As a practical matter, however, these technologies and their bio-power can only further status quo dynamics (customs) or equilibrium conditions (practices) such that the norms of utility, efficiency, and obedience prevail (Arrigo 2013). This ordering of human existence follows as such because the methods for and measures of change ceremonially empiricise the prediction of dangerousness, the management of disease, and the treatment of disorder. Thus, making and then developing technologies of the self (i.e. the industries of human capital) remain inactive and undone while technologies of the marketplace (i.e. the rehabilitative machine) prevail uninterrupted. When the imperatives of evidence-based corrections and solution-focused change increasingly depend on apparatuses that manufacture engineered selves derived largely from habitualised inventories and checklists to further, at best, fabricated relations of humanness, then prospects for ritualising ever more authentic recovery and for co-habiting ever more mutual transformation are regrettably thwarted (Polizzi et al. 2014b). Indeed, excessive reliance on these marketplace technologies can only ritualise customs and ceremonialise practices that undo personal, institutional, and even structural change for the society of captives.[12] This, then, is the ruin of human potential; the fall of being more vital in moments of our shared existences. To be clear, this absent or deferred body of knowledge signifies the yet-to-be inhabited space of creative, innovative, and experimental human relatedness.

Summary and Conclusions

This chapter described the relational problems of de-vitalisation and finalisation guided by the socio-cultural insights of Psychological Jurisprudence (PJ). As we explained, de-vitalisation and finalisation are non-reflexive states of human relatedness in which reciprocal consciousness, inter-subjectivity, and mutual power are neutralised. Problematically, these neutralisations function to limit and/or to deny the project of shared struggle and the experiences of collective overcoming in spaces of (penal) coexistence. As the chapter proposed, both this project of mutual struggle and these experiences of collective overcoming are necessary ontological and epistemological conditions for interdependent human flourishing to occur, including the becoming of human justice (as restorative and transformative) for a people yet to be.

The chapter explained how the excess forms of de-vitalisation (e.g. limits on relational being, harms of reduction, and bad faith) and the excess forms of finalisation (e.g. denials of relational becoming, harms of repression, and negative freedom) nurture a society of captives. This is the ontological and epistemological captivity of the kept *and* those who keep, manage, observe, treat, and/or inspect them. As we argued, the ubiquity of this captivity is made evident in the relations of humanness that populate this society.

The chapter tentatively proposed how these relations—derived mostly from the deficit-correcting and desistance-managing models of offender therapy, recovery, and re-entry—are totalising (i.e. socioculturally harm-generating and injury-producing) in their iterative effects on reciprocal consciousness, subjectivity, and power. Stated differently, the ontological complexion and epistemological composition of human relatedness within the remit of correctional mental health forestalls and forecloses reciprocal consciousness, inter-subjectivity, and reciprocal power. As such, this complexion and composition limit the project of mutual struggle and it denies the experiences of collective overcoming. We argued that maintaining or cultivating these de-vitalising and finalising relations of humanness is an exercise in co-productive madness. Mass captivity or the death of relational authenticity ensues uninterrupted. Illustrations from the mental health and prison literatures were used to highlight the chapter's core thesis.

Given the depth and expanse of the thesis explored in this chapter, provocative questions surface about the future direction of mental health in prisons and the critical approach to confinement and treatment that most assuredly must follow. While detailed commentary on these matters is clearly beyond the scope of inclusion here, overall, we recommend that citizen safety professionals, health-system practitioners, and public policy experts rethink the embedded and under-examined relational problems posed by sustaining a society of captives. De-vitalisation and finalisation are both dangerous for and destructive to the experience of shared humanity, especially in spaces of penal coexistence. What this means, therefore, is that prison reform, alternatives to incarceration, and even prison abolition must all be revisited. In instances where therapeutic interventions are proposed, these correctives and curatives must emphasise healing that attends to the associational dimensions of offender therapy, recovery, and re-entry. To reiterate, the ontological and epistemological experiences of reciprocal consciousness, inter-subjectivity, and mutual power implicate the kept as well as their keepers. Finally, to the extent that solution-focused change strategies are pursued, a care ethic of relational virtue must inform the reformist agenda. Indeed, if justice is to have the nearest possibility of emerging for a people yet to be, then restoration (the possibilities of human emancipation, flourishing, or excellence) and transformation (the possibilities of human interdependence, flourishing, or excellence) must drive the programme-setting decision-making. Here, too, what is at stake is the management of risk (i.e. coping with mutual struggle and striving for collective overcoming) as a way to obviate clinical captivity and its corresponding forces of totalising carceral coexistence.

Notes

1. Psychological Jurisprudence (PJ) is not a fully formed clinical model; rather, it is a paradigm that radicalises human relatedness culled from its own theory development, method of inquiry, and approach to therapeutic practice. PJ's conceptualisation of the social person or the self-in-society argues that reciprocal consciousness, inter-subjectivity, and mutual power are the evolving, interactive, and co-productive forces of (correctional) coexistence. PJ's Aristotelian-inspired methodology demonstrates that human justice as restorative (i.e. the possibilities of emancipated being, flourishing or excellence) and human justice as transformative (i.e. the possibilities of interdependent becoming,

flourishing or excellence) hinge on one's capacity and willingness to inhabit the space of relational virtue. PJ's framework for practice asserts that the management of risk (i.e. coping with mutual struggle and striving for collective overcoming) is an existential circumstance of (penal) coexistence and that this circumstance extends to the kept as well as to their keepers (i.e. the society of captives). Consequently, ongoing associational efforts at virtue-based risk management function to avoid clinical captivity or the imprisonment of human relatedness and its corresponding forces of (carceral) coexistence.

2. Among other things, de-vitalisation and finalisation are temporal and spatial phenomena of coexistence in complexion, composition and effect. The former term refers to harms of reduction in which (un)conscious thought, spoken/written language, and direct/indirect action limit human relatedness by imposing some immediate loss or injury. The latter term refers to harms of repression in which (un)conscious thought, spoken/written language, and direct/indirect action deny human relatedness by negating its future development or potential (Arrigo and Milovanovic 2009; Henry and Milovanovic 1996).

3. The relevance of symbolic interactionism (Goffman 1961, 1963); constitutive thought (Giddens 1986, 1991), including its criminological elaborations (Henry and Milovanoivc 1996); and reflexive sociology (Bourdieu 1977; Bourdieu and Wacquant 1992) are acknowledged as additional dimensions of PJ's overarching analytics and specialised diagnostics (e.g. Arrigo 2013; Arrigo and Bersot 2016). For purposes of this chapter, however, we emphasise how PJ's philosophical origins in continental thought radicalise the critique regarding the relational problems of de-vitalisation and finalisation.

4. Our use of the terms de-vitalisation and finalisation is inspired by Bergson (1911) and his notion of *élan vital*. This is the force of self-organisation, the current of life, and the plane of imminent consciousness (see generally, Deleuze and Guattari 1994). The 'biophilosophy' of *élan vital* is "becoming as creative involution" (Hansen 2000, p. 1; see also De Landa 2011). De-vitalisation constitutes the limits imposed on such vitality; finalisation constitutes the denials of such vitality.

5. Unlike Hegel's dialectic in which the negation of the negation produces the unification of opposites (i.e. new knowledge about objects external to it), Adorno's negative dialectics argues that new knowledge emerges from specifying the limits of knowledge itself. Thus, thought processes can (and should) be subject to recurring dialectical critique.

6. Dialogic expression is 'unfinalisable', in that it is always incomplete, in-process, and productive of further response sequences. In this respect, then, dialogical meaning is never static or closed, and its teleology is directed towards each moment's awaiting humanity (Bahktin 1982, pp. 279–280).

7. Civil commitment hearings, pre-trial competency evaluations, custody classification reviews, parole board hearings, and post-sentencing planning panels are spaces of coexistence. These settings and contexts exemplify how human relatedness is dialectically forestalled through rituals and ceremonies that neutralise the reciprocity of shared experience (i.e. including the project of mutual struggle). The reach of these limits extends to the kept as well as to their collective keepers.

8. The clinical anecdote of Amy Johnson (an incest survivor) exemplifies the problem of mass captivity for the kept as well as for their keepers (Johnson 2013). The law enforcement and mental health systems into which she was inserted and out of which police intervention, psychiatric treatment, and personal recovery occurred, reveal the ontic limits to and epistemic denials of reciprocal consciousness, inter-subjectivity, and mutual power. In Amy's case, these forces of coexistence were reduced to a quality of risk management (i.e. coping with mutual struggle, striving for collective overcoming) that repressed (i.e. marginalised) her identity, and correspondingly, those with whom she interacted (see also Arrigo 2013). As Johnson (2013) noted:

> To be raped and tortured by your parents is bad enough... [But] when I told on my dad, told [the police] what awful things he had done to me...[these] men in position, men in power, [said] 'No, your father would never do something like that'... [What they] roughly told me [was that they] had a job to do, that [they] didn't care about my story. [What they] basically told me [was that] I had no say... Today, I am in therapy recounting and reliving the abuses I went through at the hands of my parents and the subsequent abuses I went through at the hands of the hospital staff. The term for what the hospital staff did to me is called *retraumatization*. I fe[lt] like a prisoner in my own home, and I definitely was held captive by the mental hospitals... Wittingly or unwittingly, the 'treatment' I received inside those mental hospitals succeeded only in *cementing* the crippling fear I now live with every day... Both

home and hospital obliterated my human dignity and self-esteem by humiliating me bodily with forced nakedness and physical restraint, and my will was affected. This fear affects everything I think and everything I do... I am acutely aware of how small I am... (pp. 669–670)

As Amy's case makes evident, the human project of shared struggle was (and remains) forestalled and the human experience of collective over-coming was (and remains) forfeited, given the de-vitalising and finalis-ing nature of her repetitive coexistence.

9. In the Good Lives Model (GLM), the treatment goal is 'optimal personal fulfillment' as a way to address 'basic human needs' other-wise expressed anti-socially and/or criminally (Andrews et al. 2011, p. 736). These basic needs or goods include a quality of rehabilitation that makes possible 'friendship, enjoyable work, loving relationships, creative pursuits, sexual satisfaction, positive self-regard, and an intel-lectually challenging environment' (Ward and Stewart 2003, p. 142). While GLM's rehabilitative focus promotes restoration (recovery) *categories*, GLM's desistance-management does not consider how the ideological content that pre-figures these categories is itself ritually encoded within the unconscious. Indeed, 'in the desistance model, it is not the imagery of 'going straight' but of 'going crooked'... that pervades the social consciousness' (Arrigo and Milovanovic 2009, p. 120).

10. For example, commenting on the programming of institutional recov-ery for the custodial subject, Halsey (2007, p. 1222) observed that:

young men in custody generally are not permitted, let alone expected, to show initiative or to take anything approaching a mean-ingful degree of responsibility for their daily lives. Instead things are done to them and for them and only very rarely with them (and/or with their consent). In this sense, [the kept] are taught to react rather than to act. They are taught to respond rather than to initiate. They are taught what to think rather than how to (un)reason.

11. Given the rigidity of such release plans, the deadening of dynamic pro-ductivity, and the finalisation of human potential, it is no surprise that

some custodial subjects refuse structured re-entry on occasion and opt, instead, to remain physically behind bars (Arrigo 2013; Halsey 2007).

12. Elsewhere (Arrigo 2013, 2015; Sellers and Arrigo 2018), we have referred to these excessive investments as the phenomenon of 'hyper-securitisation' or the informationalising of risky behaviour ad infinitum and ad nauseam. Following hyper-securitisation, 'freedom, privacy, and sovereignty are all illusions because people, events, objects, and spaces are all sites of information to be processed and policed' (Sellers and Arrigo 2018, p. 133). Consequently, 'under these normalising conditions, subjectivity (humanity) is reduced to the cyber-laws of passwords, and subjectivity (humanness) is repressed through the cyber-logics of profiles' (Sellers and Arrigo 2018, p. 136). Hyper-securitisation is the digitally encoded manifestation of clinical captivity for the kept and their collective keepers.

Bibliography

Adorno, T. (1970). *Negative dialectics*. New York, NY: Continuum Press.

Althusser, L. (1971). *Lenin and philosophy and other essays*. New York: Monthly Review Press.

Andrews, D. A., Bonta, J., & Wormith, J. S. (2011). The risk-need-responsivity model: Does adding the Good Lives Model contribute to effective crime prevention? *Criminal Justice and Behavior, 38*, 735–755.

Arrigo, B. A. (2013). Managing risk and marginalizing identities: On the society-of-captives thesis and the harm of social dis-ease. *International Journal of Offender Therapy and Comparative Criminology, 57*, 672–693.

Arrigo, B. A. (2015). Responding to crime: Psychological jurisprudence, normative philosophy, and trans-desistance theory. *Criminal Justice and Behavior: An International Journal, 42*, 7–18.

Arrigo, B. A., & Acheson, A. (2015). Concealed carry bans and the American college campus: A law, social sciences, and policy perspective. *Contemporary Justice Review: Issues in Criminal, Social, and Restorative Justice, 19*, 120–141.

Arrigo, B. A., & Bersot, H. Y. (2016). Psychological jurisprudence: Problems with and prospects for mental health and justice system reform. In J. Winstone (Ed.), *Mental health, crime, and criminal justice: Responses and reforms* (pp. 266–283). Basingstoke: Palgrave Macmillan.

Arrigo, B. A., Bersot, H. Y., & Sellers, B. G. (2011). *The ethics of total confinement: A critique of madness, citizenship, and social justice.* New York, NY: Oxford University Press.

Arrigo, B. A., & Fowler, C. R. (2001). The 'death row community': A community psychology perspective. *Deviant Behavior: An Interdisciplinary Journal, 22,* 43–71.

Arrigo, B. A., & Fox, D. (2009). Psychology and law: The crime of policy and the search for justice. In D. Fox, I. Prilleltensky, & S. Austin (Eds.), *Critical psychology: An introduction* (2nd ed., pp. 159–175). London, UK: Sage.

Arrigo, B. A., & Milovanovic, D. (2009). *Revolution in penology: Rethinking the society of captives.* New York: Rowman and Littlefield.

Arrigo, B. A., & Waldman, J. L. (2015). Psychological jurisprudence and the power of law: A critique of North Carolina's Woman's Right to Know Act. *Duke Journal of Gender, Law, and Policy, 22,* 55–88.

Bakhtin, M. (1982). *The dialogic imagination: Four essays.* Austin: University of Texas Press.

Bargdill, R., & Broome, R. (2016). *Humanistic contributions for psychology 101: Growth, choice, and responsibility.* Colorado Springs, CO: University Professors Press.

Bergson, H. (1911). *Creative evolution* (Vol. 231). Lanham, MD: University Press of America.

Bersot, H. Y., & Arrigo, B. A. (2015). Responding to sex offenders: Empirical findings, judicial decision-making, and virtue jurisprudence. *Criminal Justice and Behavior: An International Journal, 42,* 32–44.

Birgden, A. (2014). Psychological jurisprudence. In B. A. Arrigo (Ed.), *The encyclopedia of criminal justice ethics* (pp. 748–752). Thousand Oaks, CA: Sage.

Bourdieu, P. (1977). *Outline of a theory of practice.* Cambridge: Cambridge University Press.

Bourdieu, P., & Wacquant, L. (1992). *Invitation to reflexive sociology.* Chicago: University of Chicago Press.

Clemmer, D. (1940). *The prison community.* New York: Christopher Publishing House.

Cornell, D. (1991). *Beyond accommodation: Ethical feminism, deconstruction, and the law.* New York, NY: Routledge.

Crewe, D. (2013). *Becoming criminal: The socio-cultural origins of law, transgression, and deviance.* Basingstoke: Palgrave Macmillan.

De Landa, M. (2011). *Philosophy and simulation: The emergence of synthetic reason.* London: Continuum International Publishing Group.

Deleuze, G., & Guattari, F. (1987). *A thousand plateaus.* Minneapolis: University of Minnesota Press.

Deleuze, G., & Guattari, F. (1994). *What is philosophy?* New York: Columbia University Press.

Derrida, J. (1973). *Speech and other phenomena.* Evanston, IL: Northwestern University Press.

Derrida, J. (1977). *Of grammatology.* Baltimore: Johns Hopkins University Press.

Derrida, J. (1978). *Writing and difference.* Chicago: University of Chicago Press.

Donati, P. (2012). *Relational sociology: A new paradigm for the social sciences.* New York: Routledge.

Farrall, S., & Calverley, A. (2006). *Understanding desistance from crime.* Berkshire: Open University Press.

Foucault, M. (1973). *The order of things.* New York: Vintage.

Foucault, M. (1977). *Discipline and punish: The birth of a prison.* New York: Pantheon.

Foucault, M. (1980). *Power/knowledge: Selected interviews and other writings.* London: Harvester.

Fox, D. (1993). Psychological jurisprudence and radical social change. *American Psychologist, 48,* 234–251.

Giddens, A. (1986). *The constitution of society: Outline of the theory of structuration.* Berkeley: University of California Press.

Giddens, A. (1991). *The consequences of modernity.* Stanford, CA: University of Stanford Press.

Goffman, E. (1961). *Asylums: Essays on the social situation of mental patients and other inmates.* Garden City, NY: Anchor Books.

Goffman, E. (1963). *Stigma: Notes on the management of spoiled identity.* New York: Simon and Schuster.

Guenther, L. (2013). *Solitary confinement: Social death and its afterlives.* Minnesota: University of Minnesota Press.

Halsey, M. (2007). Assembling recidivism: The promise and contingencies of post-release life. *Journal of Criminal Law and Criminology, 97*(4), 1209–1260.

Hansen, M. (2000). Becoming as creative involution? Contextualizing Deleuze and Guattari's biophilosophy. *Postmodern Culture, 11*(1), 3.

Hardie-Bick, J., & Lippens, R. (Eds.). (2011). *Crime, governance, and existential predicaments.* London, UK: Palgrave Macmillan.

Heidegger, M. (2008). *Ontology—The hermeneutics of facticity.* Bloomington, ID: Indiana University Press.

Henry, S., & Milovanovic, D. (1996). *Constitutive criminology: Beyond post-modernism*. London: Sage.

Johnson, A. (2013). Clinical anecdote: I should be dead. *International Journal of Offender Therapy and Comparative Criminology, 57*(4), 666–671.

Lacan, J. (1977). *Ecrits: A selection*. New York: W. W. Norton.

Lacan, J. (1981). *The four fundamental concepts of psychoanalysis*. New York, NY: W. W. Norton.

Leder, D. (1991). *The absent body*. Chicago: University of Chicago Press.

Levinas, E. (2004). *Otherwise than being*. Pittsburgh: Duquesne University Press.

Polizzi, D., Braswell, M., & Draper, M. (Eds.). (2014a). *Transforming corrections: Humanistic approaches to corrections and offender treatment* (2nd ed.). Durham, NC: Carolina Academic Press.

Polizzi, D., Draper, M., & Andersen, M. (2014b). Fabricated selves and the rehabilitative machine: Toward a phenomenology of the social construction of offender treatment. In B. A. Arrigo & H. Y. Bersot (Eds.), *The Routledge handbook of international crime and justice studies* (pp. 231–255). UK: Taylor and Francis.

Sartre, J. P. (1956). *Being and nothingness: An essay on phenomenological ontology*. New York: Philosophical Library Press.

Sellers, B. G., & Arrigo, B. A. (2009). Adolescent transfer, developmental maturity, and adjudicative competence: An ethical and justice policy inquiry. *Journal of Criminal Law and Criminology, 99*, 435–488.

Sellers, B. G., & Arrigo, B. A. (2018). Postmodern criminology and technocrime. In K. F. Steinmetz & M. R. Nobles (Eds.), *Technocrime and criminological theory* (pp. 133–146). Boca Raton, FL: CRC Press.

Sykes, G. (1958). *Society of captives: A study of a maximum security prison*. Princeton: Princeton University Press.

Taxman, F., Young, D., & Byrne, J. (2004). With eyes wide open: Formalizing community and social control intervention in offender reintegration programmes. In S. Maruna & R. Immarigeon (Eds.), *After crime and punishment: Pathways to offender reintegration* (pp. 233–260). Cullumpton, UK: Willan Publishing.

Trull, L., & Arrigo, B. A. (2015). US immigration policy and the 21st century conundrum of 'child saving': A human rights, law and social science, political, economic, and philosophical inquiry. *Studies in Law, Politics, and Society, 66*, 179–225.

Uggen, C., Manza, J., & Behrens, A. (2004). Less than the average citizen. In S. Maruna & R. Immarigeon (Eds.), *After crime and punishment: Pathways to offender reintegration* (pp. 261–293). Cullumpton, UK: Willan Publishing.

Ward, T. (2013). Moral strangers and moral acquaintances: How to conduct professional relationships in a society of captives: A commentary on Arrigo. *International Journal of Offender Therapy and Comparative Criminology, 57*(6), 703–711.

Ward, T., & Maruna, S. (2007). *Rehabilitation: Beyond the risk paradigm.* London: Routledge.

Ward, T., & Stewart, C. (2003). Criminogenic needs and human needs: A theoretical model. *Psychology, Law, and Crime, 9,* 125–143.

Weaver, B., & McNeill, F. (2015). Lifelines: Desistance, social relations, and reciprocity. *Criminal Justice and Behavior, 42*(1), 95–107.

Part II

Care Versus Custody

5

Care Versus Custody: Challenges in the Provision of Prison Mental Health Care

Alice Mills and Kathleen Kendall

Introduction

In the early 2000s, mental health in-reach teams were introduced into prisons in England and Wales. Initially, these multi-disciplinary teams of community-employed mental health professionals were intended to provide the same range and quality of services to prisoners as is available to the general population (the principle of 'equivalence of care'). However, little thought was given to how such teams might operate in the closed prison environment where security and control take precedence over more therapeutic goals and where cultural clashes and differences in working practices between prison and National Health Service (NHS)[1] healthcare staff may affect the delivery and extent

A. Mills (✉)
University of Auckland, Auckland, New Zealand
e-mail: a.mills@auckland.ac.nz

K. Kendall
University of Southampton, Southampton, UK
e-mail: K.A.Kendall@soton.ac.uk

© The Author(s) 2018
A. Mills and K. Kendall (eds.), *Mental Health in Prisons*, Palgrave Studies in Prisons and Penology, https://doi.org/10.1007/978-3-319-94090-8_5

105

of mental health care. In this chapter, we draw upon on a qualitative study of a mental health in-reach team at an English local prison to highlight the enduring conflict between care and custody. We challenge the goal of providing equivalent care within prison structures and the notion of 'healthy prisons', as the prison imposed numerous harms to mental health and the work of the mental health team was dominated by risk management-related activities. We therefore argue that mental health services can neither rehabilitate prisoners nor mitigate the harmful effects of imprisonment. Rather, we suggest that resources currently invested in the prison system be redirected into the creation of compassionate and socially just communities.

Mental Health[2] Demand and Services in Prisons in England and Wales

Amongst the prison population in England and Wales, there is a high demand for mental healthcare services. Despite calls for an up-to-date study (House of Commons Committee of Public Accounts 2017; Prisons and Probation Ombudsman [PPO] 2016; Bradley 2009), the most recent national prevalence study of mental illness in prison dates from 1998. It found that over 90% of prisoners had one or more mental disorders from psychosis, affective disorder, personality disorder, hazardous drinking and drug dependence (Singleton et al. 1998), four times the corresponding rate in the wider community (Brooker et al. 2008). A more recent study of two large remand prisons in London found that 12% of prisoners met the criteria for psychosis, 54% for depressive disorders, 27% for anxiety disorders and 34% for personality disorders (Bebbington et al. 2017). Thirty-three per cent were dependent on alcohol and 57% on illegal drugs, and nearly 70% had two disorders or more (Bebbington et al. 2017). However, these rates may be unrepresentative of the prison population in England and Wales as a whole as remand prisoners, along with other groups including women, young prisoners and elderly prisoners, are at higher risk of mental health problems than others (Bebbington et al. 2017; Fazel et al. 2001; O'Brien et al. 2001; Lader et al. 2000).

Critical scholars have argued that statistics on mental illness are not value-free objective facts but rather social constructions underpinned by a bio-medical framework and the social and cultural context within which they are situated, and are shaped by the instruments used to diagnose and measure them (Busfield 2011). Nonetheless, many incarcerated individuals experience mental distress (Rembis 2014). This can be 'connected to oppression, social disparity and conflict' (Fabris and Aubrecht 2014, p. 188) as opposed to merely individual pathologies. Prisoners identified as having mental health problems tend to have backgrounds of complex multiple disadvantage, trauma and social exclusion (HM Chief Inspector of Prisons [HMCIP] 2007). Women are particularly likely to have histories of domestic violence, sexual assault, child abuse and bereavement (Norton-Hawk and Sered, this volume; Corston 2007; Medlicott 2007).

The difficulty of living with mental health problems while incarcerated has been highlighted by the high incidence of suicide and self-harm in prisons, where the likelihood of self-inflicted death is 8.6 times greater than in the community (Ministry of Justice 2017). In 2016 the number of self-inflicted deaths reached a record high of 119, up 32% on the previous year, and self-harm incidents in prison increased 23% from the previous year (Ministry of Justice 2017). The rate of self-inflicted death has increased to twice that of 2012 at 1.4 per 1000 prisoners. Such increases have largely been attributed to substantial budget and staffing cuts which have greatly curtailed already restrictive prison regimes. Funding for prisons and probation in England and Wales fell by 13% between 2009–2010 and 2016–2017 and prison staff numbers were cut by 30% (National Audit Office [NAO] 2017). Around two-thirds of the prisoners who died in custody between 2012 and 2014 had been seen by mental health in-reach services (PPO 2016).

Until the late 1990s, healthcare services in prisons in England and Wales were the sole responsibility of HM Prison Service[3] and were frequently criticised for being substandard in comparison to those provided by the NHS in the community (Birmingham et al. 1996), and more concerned with caring for the order of the prison rather than for prisoners (Sim 1990, 2002; Woolf 1991). Penal reformers, professional associations, academics and agencies such as HM Inspectorate of Prisons had long argued that prison healthcare services should be integrated with the NHS in order to raise standards and ensure equivalence of care with the general population (Reed and Lyne 1997; HMCIP 1996; Gostin and Staunton 1985). In response to such demands, in 1999 a partnership between HM Prison Service and the NHS was formed with HM Prison Service remaining responsible for primary care and the NHS becoming responsible for secondary care, including community mental health services. The idea that responsibility for *all* prison health care should move to the NHS was rejected on the basis of concerns over existing tensions between custody and care and the fear that healthcare staff working in prisons might become marginalised due to management and cultural differences. Instead, it was hoped that a partnership approach would help foster a nurturing environment in which both sides could cultivate successful working relationships (Department of Health/HM Prison Service [DH/HMPS] 1999).

A subsequent prison mental health strategy published in 2001 introduced multi-disciplinary mental health in-reach teams (MHIRTs), funded by local Primary Care Trusts, to provide specialist mental health services to prisoners with severe and enduring mental illness in the same way as Community Mental Health Teams (CMHTs) do for individuals in the community. In most establishments, in-reach services are provided by the NHS, with a small, but increasing number of independent providers (Forrester et al. 2013).

Central to the MHIRT programme is the concept of 'equivalence of care', the idea that:

> prisoners should have access to the same range and quality of services appropriate to their needs as are available to the general population through the NHS. (DH/HMPS 2001, p. 5)

The introduction of MHIRTs has undoubtedly led to some improvements in mental health care in prisons (Mills and Kendall 2010; HMCIP 2007). However, MHIRTs have faced several difficulties implementing NHS standards and models of care in a secure setting with its attendant restrictions and limitations (Brooker and Webster 2017; HMCIP 2007), some of which we discuss in detail below. Far from

MHIRTs being a panacea, many prisoners with mental health problems continue to go unidentified and untreated (NAO 2017). One evaluation of MHIRTs found that they assessed only 25% of prisoners with severe and enduring mental illness and accepted just 13% onto their caseloads (Senior et al. 2013). Moreover, despite the initial intention that MHIRTs should be multi-disciplinary, the majority of staff are psychiatric nurses with variable and often limited input from other disciplines (HMCIP 2007), whilst psychological therapies and other services offered in the community have remained considerably underdeveloped (Mills and Kendall 2010; Brooker and Gojkovic 2009).

MHIRTs have also struggled to live up to the promise of providing care equivalent to that in the community, partly due to the high demand for their services. In 2009 Brooker and Gojkovic suggested that to provide equivalent care, given the prevalence and severity of mental ill-health in prisons, MHIRTs would require over double the then level of mental health practitioners (see also Brooker et al. 2008). Although the average number of mental health in-reach practitioners per team has since grown (Brooker and Webster 2017), many prisoners continue to go untreated. Jakobowitz et al. (2017) estimate that half the needs of prisoners with treatable mental health conditions were unmet in two London remand prisons.

Despite the recent considerable expansion of healthcare research in prisons, the research literature has been slow to address the role played by the punitive prison culture and the restrictive prison setting in mediating the quality of care that can be provided by MHIRTs in the custodial context. Sim (1990) has long raised questions about the role of medicine and healthcare professionals 'in controlling the behaviour of the ill-disciplined and recalcitrant' (1990, p. 5). The degree to which equivalence of care is realistic in the prison environment where the dominant discourse of discipline and control can conflict with notions of care and treatment therefore requires further examination.

Drawing on a qualitative study of the MHIRT at a remand prison in southern England, the remainder of this chapter will highlight the enduring conflict and tension between care and custody. In particular, we demonstrate how NHS staff can be hindered in providing mental health care to prisoners by the priorities of the prison to confine, control and punish, and the sensibilities of prison staff cultures. We argue that the goal of equivalent care is unrealistic and inappropriate and question whether prison can ever be a suitable place for mental health care and treatment, given the capacity of the prison to dehumanise, deprive and degrade. Fundamentally, our findings suggest that rather than offering mental health treatment in prison, we could adopt alternatives which instead foster the creation of compassionate and socially just communities.

Study Aims and Methodology

The qualitative study on which this chapter is based aimed to evaluate the operation and effectiveness of the MHIRT, and to examine the processes which aided and/or hindered the team's success. It was funded by HOPE (Wessex Medical Trust), and the fieldwork was conducted between 2005 and 2006. Despite the historical nature of the research data, they illuminate many of the fundamental challenges faced by MHIRTs working in the custodial environment which are unlikely to have been resolved in the interim due to the unchanging essential nature of imprisonment. Indeed, many of these difficulties are likely to have worsened due to recent financial and staffing cuts in addition to overcrowding. The research findings are therefore discussed here as a challenge to current calls to expand mental health care and recruit additional prison staff as a means of addressing the current penal mental health 'crisis'.

Research Setting

The research site was a local remand prison with an operational capacity of approximately 550 remand and sentenced male prisoners, and a turnover of approximately 5000 prisoners each year. The MHIRT was established in the first wave of in-reach teams in 2002 and initially consisted of six mental health practitioners, including four psychiatric nurses (one of whom acted as a team leader), a part-time consultant psychiatrist and an occupational therapist, with additional sessional input from other consultant psychiatrists from the local medium secure unit. Throughout the fieldwork period, the make-up of the team changed considerably due to staff retention and recruitment difficulties.

The stated aim of the MHIRT was to give prisoners with severe and enduring mental illness the opportunity to engage in secondary mental health services equivalent to those in the community. This involved providing 'speedy' assessments and appropriate short-term treatments, arranging safe and 'speedy' transfers to NHS secure facilities, and liaising with various groups to ensure continuity of care between the prison and the community.

Methods and Methodology

The study adopted a qualitative research design employing three methods. Firstly, documentary analysis of background information, including the service specification and service user case files, was employed to explore the development, operation and use of the services. Secondly, six focus groups were held with three sets of participants: MHIRT staff, service users and prisoners who did not use MHIRT services. The focus groups consisted of three to six participants, and were utilised to generate concepts and themes for further exploration in interviews. Through the focus groups with non-service users, general awareness of MHIRT services in the prison and any additional benefits that the team may have brought to the prison could be identified. Finally, semi-structured interviews were undertaken with all eight members of the MHIRT who worked in the prison during the course of the study, 15 service users and 24 staff from various parts of the prison (e.g. health care, Safer Custody, substance misuse, Care and Separation). A semi-structured interview format was used, as it ensured that certain topics were covered but also allowed respondents the latitude and flexibility to bring up issues of importance to them (May 2001).

All focus groups and interviews were audio-recorded with the permission of respondents, and were transcribed verbatim. Transcripts were analysed by both researchers through the iterative approach of the constant comparative method (Maykut and Morehouse 1994), and by using Strauss and Corbin's (1990) three types of grounded theory coding practice—open coding, axial coding and selective coding. Primary themes and categories, and the connections between them, were identified and crosschecked, and then theoretically elaborated upon in order to conceptualise perceptions and experiences of the MHIRT.

Care Versus Custody

Risk Management and Institutional Convenience

MHIRT members faced various barriers to their aim of providing equivalent care due to the disciplinary nature of the prison and its key priorities of maintaining security and control. Over thirty years ago, Carlen (1986, p. 247) argued that the 'majority of prisoners who come into contact with psychiatrists in prison do so only for the purposes of assessment, categorization and the prescription of drugs'. This largely continues to be true as the MHIRT under study was predominantly engaged in practices which were integral to the control and disciplinary regime of the prison and to the larger socio-legal apparatus (Carlen 1986; see also Sim 1990, 2002). The high demand for MHIRT involvement in activities associated with penal governance and risk management, such as court reports, suitability assessments for the segregation unit, and suicide prevention, meant that in a prison with a high turnover, the MHIRT operated more as a crisis resolution team, with little time to engage in therapeutic services as they typically would in the community. In common with other research in this area (Durcan 2008), prisoners were generally very positive about the MHIRT and identified 'having someone to talk to' as one of the key benefits of their interactions with them. The ability to speak and be listened to with kindness and care is fundamental to a good therapeutic relationship leading to better outcomes (Ballatt and Campling 2011). However, the MHIRT was often unable to help in this way. One member of the team stated:

Often all the inmates need is somebody to listen and talk to [...] but our case loads don't enable us to do that...they then become more depressed and end up needing more input than they would have initially. (MHIRT Staff Member 3)

Short-term cognitive behavioural therapy and anxiety management sessions offered by the nurses were halted due to staff shortages. The emphasis on security also exacerbated the challenges of providing any treatment other than medication and contributed to staff retention difficulties. At the beginning of the research period, the team included a full-time occupational therapist, who planned to establish regular group work activities such as anxiety management, but there was little suitable space for these groups to run. Even when such space was secured, staff shortages and the prison's primary functions of security and control overrode mental health concerns:

You plan to do something but then there's not enough staff to let them out of the cells in Health Care. They may say someone needs three [prison officers] to actually let them out of their cell...those who are more seriously more mentally ill, who are deemed to be more of a security risk, are not able to get out... (MHIRT Staff Member 4)

Even the range of prescribed medication the team could offer was restricted, due to security protocols governing the prescription of drugs that are open to abuse, clearly affecting their ability to provide equivalent care, and this was noted by prisoners in addition to mental health staff:

The Health Care Centre in prison...even their formulary for prescribing was <u>different</u> from that what would be happening in the community. (MHIRT Staff Member 5)

They're very limited to what they can do. Apparently they are not allowed to prescribe sleeping drugs here [...] Outside I was prescribed something...for about four weeks to help me sleep. (Prisoner F)

Despite a general acceptance of the need for mental health services, both mental health and prison staff in the research suggested that mental health was of low priority in the prison. Mental health services were perceived to be at the mercy of 'institutional convenience' (Owers 2010), in that they were only offered if it was convenient to the regime, or 'institutional thoughtlessness' (Crawley 2005), whereby the prison demonstrated a degree of indifference to the MHIRT which negatively affected the individuals they worked with. This was amply demonstrated by the difficulties faced by the team in simply meeting prisoners for assessments and consultations. Visiting prisoners in their cells was discouraged by the prison due to security considerations. The few available consulting rooms on the main prison wings were frequently occupied by other services, and the alternative was to see prisoners in private interview rooms in the healthcare centre. However, this required prison officers to escort them to appointments; a service which was highly dependent on the availability of uniformed staff and competing demands:

> The problem is, and it sounds like a cop out, but I don't think you can appreciate how difficult it is to just <u>see</u> somebody…you're at the officer's mercy. You'd be waiting there in Health Care and at half ten they haven't been brought over…they'll say 'Oh we're not bringing him. It's too late now'. (MHIRT Staff Member 5)

Many hours of professional consultation time were wasted in this way as MHIRT staff regularly waited in vain to see prisoners who were prevented from attending due to staff shortages, security lockdowns or other issues which took priority. Crucially, difficulties seeing service users could be further detrimental to their psychological well-being:

> If you're seeing somebody who's having great difficulties and they're just not called up for any reason…it can have an adverse affect on their mental health. That they're sat in their cell for yet another 24 hours. (MHIRT Staff Member 1)

Consequently, the MHIRT felt considerable frustration at being hindered from providing care, let alone equivalent care, due to the restrictions of the prison setting. One team member summed up this sentiment:

> It's the environment we moan about, it's not the prisoners... It's just that on a daily basis yeah, it does grind you down. It's not the prisoners that are the problem, it's the system. (MHIRT Staff Member 2)

Culture Clashes

Members of the MHIRT also experienced open hostility and animosity from prison staff, highlighting further tensions between care and custody. At the time of the research, the prison was renowned for having a strong adherence to the traditional prison officer culture (Liebling et al. 2005), characterised by machismo, negative attitudes towards management and prisoners, and hostility towards and lack of cooperation with those who seek to help prisoners (Bennett 2016; Crawley and Crawley 2008). Despite some prison officers on the wings being grateful for the support provided by the team, others, notably those working in the healthcare setting, saw them as 'do-gooders' or 'care bears' and their clients as prisoners to be controlled and managed, rather than as people in need of health care. The MHIRT and other health staff working in the prison suggested that this punitive attitude meant that officers were often keen to interpret behaviour and symptoms caused by mental illness as discipline issues:

> I think the officers don't understand about mental health nursing because there is a chap down there [care and separation unit] who can be aggressive...he's hearing voices and things. [...] And immediately if he does anything, 'right, you're locked in and you've lost all your benefits and everything...you're staying in, you're not coming out for education', and so that kind of really upsets him even more. So he becomes more angry, starts kicking his door, and they'll go, 'see!'. (Prison Staff Member 8)

Prisoners' ill-health may be interpreted by prison staff as 'malingering' or 'attention seeking' particularly in the case of mental health problems which may have no obvious symptoms. A punitive response may worsen the underlying mental health issues (PPO 2016), particularly if prisoners are placed in segregation with little contact with others (Haney 2017; Shalev and Edgar 2015) or on a basic regime with few constructive activities and opportunities to exercise (see Jablonska and Meek, this volume). Unsurprisingly, in prisons where high proportions of staff adhere to traditional cultural attitudes, levels of prisoner distress have been found to be higher (Liebling 2008), potentially increasing demands on mental health services in prison. The stress of the prison officer culture on the punitive degradation of prisoners (Sim 2009) can lead them to be constructed as 'less eligible subjects whose criminality has placed them beyond the contractual pale of respectable society' (Sim 2002, p. 317). Any attempts to provide care to prisoners may thus be viewed as 'disturbing the normative equilibrium of the punitive culture' (Sim 2002, p. 316).

Much of the hostility and suspicion faced by the MHIRT was from staff that worked in the healthcare centre, both officers and healthcare workers, who at the time were employed and managed by the prison.[4] For Sim (1990, 2002, 2009), healthcare culture within prisons is also permeated with custodial and masculinist discursive practices, and within this, staff who want to help prisoners can be seen in pejorative terms (Sim 2002). In the case of the MHIRT, such tension may also have been a reaction to the fact that they were NHS staff coming into the prison domain, challenging established ways of working, and potentially opening up the closed world of the prison. The MHIRT highlighted several examples of poor practice in the healthcare centre which contravened community healthcare standards, such as unqualified staff giving out medication and taking blood samples:

> They've [the prisons] ruled their own domain for many, many years […] suddenly they've got these people coming in who are professionals as well, who are identifying poor practice, and questioning them. It's kind of made them look at perhaps how they function, how they practice and made them feel very vulnerable. (MHIRT Staff Member 1)

Prison management similarly responded defensively to the MHIRT, with one team member being threatened with being banned from the premises, if she continued to complain about poor healthcare standards. This incident raises important questions about safeguards for people employed by outside agencies working in the prison environment, particularly as non-operational staff such as mental health professionals may carry little authority in the eyes of the general staff group and may find their expertise undervalued (Bennett 2016). Since the research fieldwork was conducted, other research has indicated that the mental health staff remain marginalised even in their areas of expertise. For example, the Prison and Probation Ombudsman (2016) found that views of mental health professionals were not given sufficient weight when decisions are made about the management of suicidal prisoners.

The formal and informal networks of power in the prison created such high levels of stress and dissatisfaction among team members that within the first six months of our study, three had left and one had taken extended sick leave. When faced with so much conflict and stress in their work, NHS staff working in prisons may be tempted to adopt the practices and attitudes of the custodial culture in order to survive (Ross et al. 2011; DH/HMPS 1999). Although MHIRT members admitted to accepting some of the banter from prison officers, they also felt able to resist becoming acculturated into the prison climate, and suggested that they at least respected the service users in prison in the same way they would those in the community:

> [Interviewer: And you mentioned about how you were very keen on the notion of equivalence. Do you feel that has been achieved?]
>
> If we were looking at it in terms of people being treated with respect, value… I think we've done that…it would have been easy to have actually gone and actually joined that culture where they're nothing but a load of, bunch of, bloody scallies. (MHIRT Staff Member 5)

Even though mental health in prisons may be a low priority for the NHS (HMCIP 2007), the team was proactive in aligning themselves and their work with the NHS, its culture and standards of care, including clinical governance tools used by CMHTs, in order to maintain their professionalism and distinctive ways of working.

Anti-therapeutic: Can Prisons Really Be Mentally 'Healthy'?

The degree to which the prison environment and regime can create or exacerbate mental health problems has been the subject of considerable debate in recent years. Some commentators have suggested that prison may act as a 'stabilising' factor in otherwise chaotic lives characterised by substance misuse and poor physical health (Goomany and Dickinson 2015; Durcan 2008) and may represent an opportunity to engage prisoners with services that they may not have had access to in the community. However, imprisonment and the 'pains' or deprivations it entails are also likely to have a negative impact on mental health (Jordan 2011; Durcan 2008), making prison an unsuitable place to carry out mental health treatment. The lack of understanding of mental health problems by staff and other prisoners, and worries about family and life outside as well as the uncertainty of life inside could exacerbate prisoners' mental health difficulties (see also Goomany and Dickinson 2015), and potentially further aggravate pre-prison experiences of traumatisation (Armour 2012).

One of the key issues raised by prisoner respondents in our research was the lack of purposeful activity in the prison. Purposeful activity has been defined as the ability and expectation for prisoners to engage in activity that is likely to benefit them such as work and education (HM Inspectorate of Prisons 2017). Within the research prison, such opportunities were highly limited. The amount of time prisoners spent 'banged up' in their cells was the most frequently mentioned aspect of prison life thought to be detrimental to mental health:

> You are just existing, just for the sake of existing… In here you've got nothing to do. Time plays on your mind and you think when are you going to get out. You're counting the days down and you just get more and more depressed… (Prisoner C)

> It hasn't been easy, especially when you're doing a lot of bangup and you are just getting messages after messages [hearing voices] and you're not sleeping a lot. (Prisoner M)

How tough must it be to be really quite depressed in a twelve foot by six foot cell for the vast majority of the day? Since I've been here we've had one successful [sic] suicide and a couple of attempted. I guess that goes to show that it is a tough time. (Prison Staff Member 20)

Being locked up in a cell for hours at a time can create feelings of anger, frustration, anxiety, stress and boredom, exacerbating the likelihood of substance misuse (Moyes, this volume; Nurse et al. 2003) and/or the risk of suicide and self-harm (Liebling 1992). The impoverishment of the prison regime due to recent public service spending cuts, leading to prisoners spending substantially more time locked up in their cells, has been noted as a factor in the increase in self-inflicted deaths and self-harm (NAO 2017).

Safety concerns could also impact on prisoners' mental health and daily routines, exacerbating a sense of isolation and anxiety:

People who are paranoid have a very hard time in prison because there is such a high concentration of bodies around them that they find very difficult to deal with. (MHIRT Staff Member 3)

I don't go out on association because I'm frightened of other prisoners… Yesterday I didn't actually eat all day because I was too frightened to go down for a meal so I am virtually just locked up in the cell. (Prisoner H)

Prisoners in receipt of treatment for mental health issues report higher rates of physical victimisation (Blitz et al. 2008). Since the research was conducted, the incidence of violence in prisons has increased considerably (Ministry of Justice 2017), suggesting that those with mental health problems may be at considerable risk of being harmed by other prisoners. However, caution should be exercised when considering violence within prisons since the dominant discourse neglects the institutional, organisational and structural violence inflicted upon prisoners (Sim 2018). Despite the substantial efforts of the MHIRT to improve prisoners' mental health, they were unable to mitigate the harmful effects of the anti-therapeutic prison environment.

Discussion

Notwithstanding initial intentions, MHIRT services were introduced with little thought as to how they might realistically be implemented in a restrictive, punitive and essentially 'anti-therapeutic' prison environment. Whilst some prisoners may benefit from the health care they receive while incarcerated, prisons do not exist to provide health care but rather to impose custody (Sim 2002; Hannah-Moffat 2000). Imprisonment is first and foremost a punishment for those convicted of breaking the law (Coyle 2005), which, as participants in our study confirmed, can exacerbate and/or create mental health problems (Armour 2012; World Health Organization [WHO] 2005). The prison environment is therefore 'not and never will be conducive to mental well-being, despite the commitment of medical and prison staff' (Bebbington et al. 2017, p. 228). Prisoners are unlikely to be able to take steps towards mental well-being in prison such as connecting with people, being listened to with kindness, keeping active, seeking support, and learning new skills, when isolated from family and friends, locked up with little or no constructive activity and when most aspects of their daily life such as sleep and diet are controlled by the prison (NAO 2017, p. 5). Such difficulties may be exacerbated by the current substantial prison overcrowding in England and Wales (Bulman 2017), which is likely to fuel tension and restrict access to services and activities (Goomany and Dickinson 2015; Appelbaum 2011). Recent cuts in public expenditure and the resulting prison staff shortages have drastically restricted time out of cell, reduced the already tenuous safety of prisons, and led to an increase in the use of illicit psychoactive substances in prison (Ministry of Justice 2017; see also Moyes, this volume). These are all likely to worsen prisoners' mental health, and have further compromised the provision of mental health services (Brooker and Webster 2017). Although Goomany and Dickinson (2015) and others argue that healthcare professionals should demonstrate innovation and imagination in their application of interventions to minimise the harmful impact of prison environment on individuals, this research shows the very real difficulties that MHIRTs may face in seeking to do so. As Haney (2017, p. 211) argues, we would be hard pressed to design anything worse than prisons for people who are emotionally distressed and vulnerable since they 'are fraught with danger, dehumanization, and deprivation...the very antithesis of a treatment-oriented milieu that promotes openness, caring and mutual concern'.

In such circumstances, the aim of providing mental health care equivalent to that provided in the community is clearly problematic. Equivalence does not 'take account of the adaptations necessary for the organization of care in a correctional setting' (Niveau 2007, p. 610) or the high, multiple and complex, interrelated needs of prisoners (Durcan 2008). Furthermore, our research indicates that the 'formal and informal networks of penal power' (Sim 2002, p. 300) ensure that mental health care and treatment could be not only practically difficult to administer but also degraded in their significance unless co-opted into tasks of security, control and risk management. The MHIRT studied had good intentions, attempted to treat individual prisoners with decency and respect, and saw themselves as sitting outside of and resisting the prison machinery and its culture. Nonetheless, they remained marginalised in the prison with their expertise undervalued, and much of the work they did remained integral to penal governance and the smooth running of the prison.

The question must therefore be raised as to whether 'healthy prisons' can ever be possible. Schemes to establish 'healthy prisons' (Gatherer et al. 2014; Department of Health [DH] 2002; WHO 1996) could potentially establish holistic interventions which address upstream social determinants of prison health. However, Woodall (2016) notes that health promotion policies purporting to do this have instead drifted downstream to focus on 'lifestyle' interventions such as smoking cessation and healthy eating, which hold individuals entirely responsible for their mental and physical health as the consequence of having made poor choices (Mills and Kendall 2016). While certain prisoners may benefit from some of the health care they receive, the healthy prison movement may deflect attention away from systemic inequities contributing to the poor mental and physical health of criminalised individuals. Furthermore, prison health care may reconfigure social problems contributing to imprisonment and mental distress as health issues. This process, described as 'healthification' by Morrow (2013), individualises and depoliticises inequities such as poverty, racism, sexism and ableism, directing resources towards psychiatric rather than social care. It additionally serves to obscure how imprisonment has become a means of addressing social problems created by fierce and oppressive neo-liberal regimes that also gives the illusion of solving them. As Davis (1998) notes, '[P]risons do not disappear social problems, they disappear human beings'.

Conclusion

As we were writing this chapter, a series of headline-grabbing articles on suicide and self-harm declared that prisons in England and Wales were being plagued by a 'mental health crisis'. These news reports called for an expansion of prison mental healthcare services, the recruitment of more prison staff and the creation of more psychiatric facilities in the community (see, for example, Allison 2017; Bulman 2017). As Cox and Marland (this volume), Sim (2018), and Seddon (2007) demonstrate, such a crisis is not new. Rather, mental distress, self-harm and suicide have been present since prisons first appeared. The research discussed here, and the continuity of crises across the years while under different penal philosophies and regimes, suggests that attempts to reform prisons in the hope of establishing 'therapunitive' (Carlen and Tombs 2006, p. 339) establishments which make their captives and staff healthier are unrealistic. Even with comprehensive mental health services and the extra 2500 prison officers who are in the process of being recruited (Travis 2016), prisons are ultimately damaging; a steady simmering of multiple harms and indifference feeding into what eventually becomes labelled a prison mental health crisis.

The concept of 'slow violence' was coined by Rob Nixon (2011) to refer to the temporal and visual dimensions of environmental violence, highlighting how it can be incremental, accretive, and invisible rather than abrupt and spectacular. As such, it does not engage public concern which could foster efforts to stop it before spilling over into calamity. In the context of imprisonment, 'slow violence' can help us recognise the cumulative harmful and often catastrophic emotional and physical effects of everyday practices highlighted in our study such as 'bang up', the inability for prisoners to simply be heard by a compassionate listener, and the hostility expressed not only towards prisoners but also towards the MHIRT. These routine events are built into the very fabric of prisons but remain largely hidden from the public eye until they erupt into something explosive. Rather than continue to invest in prisons and subject society's poorest and most oppressed populations to the violence of imprisonment, alternatives to prison must be considered, not just for individuals experiencing mental distress, but for everyone. Mad studies scholars and activists urge us towards solutions that strive towards the creation of compassionate and socially just communities (Ben-Moshe et al. 2014; LeFrancois et al. 2013). Such a vision requires us to first recognise our shared humanity and to understand that our liberty is bound together.

Acknowledgements The authors would like to thank Luke Birmingham and David Morton for their contribution to the research on which this chapter is based.

Notes

1. The NHS is the public body which provides comprehensive health services in Great Britain.
2. Although the term 'mental health' is used here as a more holistic alternative to the biomedical language of 'mental illness' or 'mental disorder', we recognise that it is nonetheless problematic because it still reflects a medical model and often serves to individualise human struggle (Morrow and Malcoe 2017).
3. Now known as HM Prisons and Probation Service.
4. In 2006, responsibility for funding and contracting prison health services in public sector prisons in England was transferred from the Home Office to the Department of Health. Although this might be expected

to challenge some of these working practices, in the case of the research prison, the local NHS Primary Care Trust simply re-commissioned the prison to provide primary healthcare services meaning that many of the existing staff were re-employed.

Bibliography

Allison, E. (2017, December 20). There's a mental health crisis in our prisons, yet the justice secretary is silent. *The Guardian*. Available at: https://www.theguardian.com/commentisfree/2017/dec/20/prisoners-mental-health-self-harm-deaths-jails-liverpool. Accessed 7 Jan 2018.

Appelbaum, P. (2011). Lost in the crowd: Prison mental health care, overcrowding and the courts. *Psychiatric Services, 62*(10), 1121–1123.

Armour, C. (2012). Mental in prison: A trauma perspective on importation and deprivation. *International Journal of Criminology and Sociological Theory, 5*(2), 886–894.

Ballatt, J., & Campling, P. (2011). *Intelligent kindness: Reforming the culture of healthcare*. London: RCPsych Publications.

Bebbington, P., Jakobowitz, S., McKenzie, N., Killaspy, H., Iveson, R., Duffield, G., & Kerr, M. (2017). Assessing needs for psychiatric treatment in prisoners: 1. Prevalence of disorder. *Social Psychiatry and Psychiatric Epidemiology, 52*, 221–229.

Ben-Moshe, L., Chapman, C., & Carey, A. (Eds.). (2014). *Disability incarcerated*. Basingstoke, Hampshire: Palgrave Macmillan.

Bennett, J. (2016). *The working lives of prison managers*. London: Palgrave Macmillan.

Birmingham, L., Mason, D., & Grubin, D. (1996). Prevalence of mental disorder in remand prisoners. *British Medical Journal, 313*, 1521–1524.

Blitz, C. L., Wolff, N., & Shi, J. (2008). Physical victimization in prison: The role of mental illness. *International Journal of Law and Psychiatry, 31*, 385–393.

Bradley, L. (2009). *The Bradley report*. London: Department of Health.

Brooker, C., Duggan, S., Fox, C., Mills, A., & Parsonage, M. (2008). *Short changed: Spending on prison mental health care*. London: Sainsbury Centre for Mental Health.

Brooker, C., & Gojkovic, D. (2009). The second national survey of mental health in-reach services in prisons. *Journal of Forensic Psychiatry and Psychology, 20,* S11–S28.

Brooker, C., & Webster, R. (2017). Prison mental health in-reach teams, serious mental illness and the care programme approach in England. *Journal of Forensic and Legal Medicine, 50,* 44–48.

Bulman, M. (2017, December 13). Record high levels of prisoner self-harm a "damning indictment" of failures in mental health provision in jails. *The Independent.* Available at: http://www.independent.co.uk/news/uk/home-news/record-high-prisoner-self-harm-mental-health-prisons-public-accounts-committee-ministry-justice-a8106766.html. Accessed 7 Jan 2017.

Busfield, J. (2011). *Mental illness.* Cambridge: Polity Press.

Carlen, P. (1986). Psychiatry in prisons: Promises, premises, practices and politics. In P. Miller & N. Rose (Eds.), *The power of psychiatry* (pp. 241–266). Cambridge: Cambridge University Press.

Carlen, P., & Tombs, J. (2006). Reconfigurations of penality: The ongoing case of women's imprisonment and reintegration industries. *Theoretical Criminology, 10*(3), 337–360.

Corston, J. (2007). *The Corston report: A review of women with particular vulnerabilities in the criminal justice system.* London: Home Office.

Coyle, A. (2005). *Understanding prisons.* Buckingham: Open University Press.

Crawley, E. (2005). Institutional thoughtlessness and its impacts on the day to day prison lives of elderly men. *Journal of Contemporary Criminal Justice, 21*(4), 350–363.

Crawley, E., & Crawley, P. (2008). Understanding prison officers: Culture, cohesion and conflict. In J. Bennett, B. Crewe, & A. Wahidin (Eds.), *Understanding prison staff* (pp. 134–152). Cullompton: Willan.

Davis, A. (1998). Masked racism: Reflections on the prison industrial complex. *Colorlines.* Available at: https://www.colorlines.com/articles/masked-racism-reflections-prison-industrial-complex. Accessed 5 Jan 2017.

Department of Health (DH). (2002). *Health promoting prisons: A shared approach.* London: Department of Health.

Department of Health/HM Prison Service (DH/HMPS). (1999). *The future organisation of prison healthcare.* London: Department of Health.

Department of Health/HM Prison Service (DH/HMPS). (2001). *Changing the outlook: A strategy for developing and modernising mental health services in prisons.* London: Department of Health.

Durcan, G. (2008). *From the inside: Experiences of prison mental health care.* London: Sainsbury Centre for Mental Health.

Fabris, E., & Aubrecht, K. (2014). Chemical constraint: Experiences of psychiatric coercion, restraint and detention as carceratory techniques. In L. Ben-Mosche, C. Chapman, & A. Carey (Eds.), *Disability incarcerated* (pp. 139–159). Houndmills, Basingstoke: Palgrave Macmillan.

Fazel, S., Hope, T., O'Donnell, I., & Jacoby, R. (2001). Hidden psychiatric morbidity in elderly prisoners. *British Journal of Psychiatry, 179,* 535–539.

Forrester, A., Exworthy, T., Olumoroti, O., Sessay, M., Parrott, J., Spencer, S.-J., & Whyte, S. (2013). Variations in prison mental health services in England and Wales. *International Journal of Law and Psychiatry, 36,* 326–332.

Gatherer, A., Enggist, S., & Moller, L. (2014). The essentials about prison and health. In S. Enggist, L. Moller, G. Galea, & C. Udeson (Eds.), *Prisons and health* (pp. 1–5). Copenhagen: WHO Regional Office for Europe.

Goomany, A., & Dickinson, T. (2015). The influence of prison climate on the mental health of adult prisoners: A literature review. *Journal of Psychiatric and Mental Health Nursing, 22,* 413–422.

Gostin, L., & Staunton, M. (1985). The case for prison standards: Conditions of confinement, segregation, and medical treatment. In J. Vagg, R. Morgan, & M. Maguire (Eds.), *Accountability and prisons: Opening up a closed world* (pp. 81–96). London: Tavistock.

Haney, C. (2017). "Madness" and penal confinement: Some observations on mental illness and prison pain. *Punishment and Society, 19*(3), 310–326.

Hannah-Moffat, K. (2000). Prisons that empower: Neoliberal governance in Canadian women's prisons. *British Journal of Criminology, 40*(3), 510–531.

HM Chief Inspector of Prisons (HMCIP). (1996). *Patient or prisoner? A new strategy for healthcare in prisons.* London: Home Office.

HM Chief Inspector of Prisons (HMCIP). (2007). *The mental health of prisoners: A thematic review of the care and support of prisoners with mental health needs.* London: HM Inspectorate of Prisons.

HM Inspectorate of Prisons. (2017). *Our expectations: Purposeful activity.* Available at: https://www.justiceinspectorates.gov.uk/hmiprisons/our-expectations/prison-expectations/purposeful-activity/. Accessed 23 Jan 2018.

House of Commons Committee of Public Accounts. (2017). *Mental health in prisons.* Eighth Report of Session 2017–19. London: House of Commons.

Jakobowitz, S., Bebbington, P., McKenzie, N., Iveson, R., Duffield, G., Kerr, M., & Killaspy, H. (2017). Assessing needs for psychiatric treatment in prisoners: 2. Met and unmet need. *Social Psychiatry and Psychiatric Epidemiology, 52,* 231–240.

Jordan, M. (2011). Embracing the notion that context is crucial in prison mental health care. *British Journal of Forensic Practice, 12*(4), 26–35.

Lader, D., Singleton, N., & Meltzer, H. (2000). *Psychiatric morbidity among young offenders in England and Wales.* London: Office for National Statistics.

LeFrancois, B., Menzies, R., & Reaume, G. (Eds.). (2013). *Mad matters: A critical reader in Canadian mad studies.* Toronto: Canadian Scholars' Press Inc.

Liebling, A. (1992). *Suicides in prison.* London: Routledge.

Liebling, A. (2008). Why prison staff culture matters. In J. M. Byrne, D. Hummer, & F. S. Taxman (Eds.), *The culture of prison violence* (pp. 105–122). New York: Pearson.

Liebling, A., Tait, S., Stiles, A., Durie, L., Harvey, J., & Rose, G. (2005). *An evaluation of the safer locals programme.* Report submitted to the Home Office.

May, T. (2001). *Social research: Issues, methods and process.* Buckingham: Open University Press.

Maykut, P., & Morehouse, R. (1994). Qualitative data analysis: Using the constant comparative method. In P. Maykut & R. Morehouse (Eds.), *Beginning qualitative research: A philosophic and practical guide* (pp. 116–137). London: Falmer Press.

Medlicott, D. (2007). Women in prison. In Y. Jewkes (Ed.), *Handbook on prisons* (1st ed., pp. 245–267). Cullompton: Willan.

Mills, A., & Kendall, K. (2010). Therapy and mental health in-reach teams. In J. Harvey & K. Smedley (Eds.), *Psychological therapy in prisons and other secure settings* (pp. 26–47). Abingdon: Routledge.

Mills, A., & Kendall, K. (2016). Mental health in prisons. In Y. Jewkes, B. Crewe, & J. Bennett (Eds.), *Handbook on prisons* (2nd ed., pp. 187–204). Abingdon: Routledge.

Ministry of Justice. (2017). *Safety in custody statistics bulletin, England and Wales: Deaths in prison custody to December 2016, assaults and self-harm to September 2016.* Available at: https://www.gov.uk/government/uploads/system/uploads/attachment_data/file/595797/safety-in-custody-quarterly-bulletin.pdf. Accessed 19 Sept 2017.

Morrow, M. (2013). Recovery: Progressive paradigm or neoliberal smokescreen? In B. LeFrancois, R. Menzies, & G. Reaume (Eds.), *Mad matters: A critical reader in Canadian mad studies* (pp. 323–333). Toronto: Canadian Scholars' Press Inc.

Morrow, M., & Malcoe, L. H. (2017). Preface. In M. Morrow & L. H. Malcoe (Eds.), *Critical inquiries for social justice in mental health* (pp. ix–xv). Toronto: University of Toronto Press.

National Audit Office (NAO). (2017). *Mental health in prisons*. London: National Audit Office.

Niveau, G. (2007). Relevance and limits of the principle of "equivalence of care" in prison medicine. *Journal of Medical Ethics, 33,* 610–613.

Nixon, R. (2011). *Slow violence and the environmentalism of the poor*. London: Harvard University Press.

Nurse, J., Woodcock, P., & Ormsby, J. (2003). Influence of environmental factors on mental health within prisons: Focus group study. *British Medical Journal, 327*(7413), 480–483.

O'Brien, M., Mortimer, L., Singleton, N., & Meltzer, H. (2001). *Psychiatric morbidity amongst women prisoners in England and Wales*. London: Office for National Statistics.

Owers, A. (2010, July 13). *Inside out: Reflections on nine years as HM Chief Inspector of Prisons*. Prison Reform Trust lecture.

Prisons and Probation Ombudsman (PPO). (2016). *Prisoner mental health: Learning from PPO investigations*. London: Prisons and Probation Ombudsman.

Reed, J., & Lyne, M. (1997). The quality of health care in prison: Results of a year's programme of semi structured inspections. *British Medical Journal, 315,* 1420–1424.

Rembis, M. (2014). The new asylums: Madness and mass incarceration. In L. Ben-Mosche, C. Chapman, & A. Carey (Eds.), *Disability incarcerated* (pp. 139–159). Houndmills, Basingstoke: Palgrave Macmillan.

Ross, M. W., Liebling, A., & Tait, S. (2011). The relationships of prison climate to health service in correctional environments: Inmate health care measurement, satisfaction and access in prisons. *Howard Journal of Criminal Justice, 50,* 262–274.

Seddon, T. (2007). *Punishment and madness: Governing prisoners with mental health problems*. Abingdon: Glasshouse.

Senior, J., Birmingham, L., Harty, M. A., Hassan, L., Hayes, A. J., Kendall, K., et al. (2013). Identification and management of prisoners with severe psychiatric illness by specialist mental health services. *Psychological Medicine, 43,* 1511–1520.

Shalev, S., & Edgar, K. (2015). *Deep custody: Segregation units and close supervision centres in England and Wales*. London: Prison Reform Trust.

Sim, J. (1990). *Medical power in prisons*. Milton Keynes: Open University Press.

Sim, J. (2002). The future of prison health care: A critical analysis. *Critical Social Policy, 22*, 300–323.

Sim, J. (2009). *Punishment and prisons*. London: Sage.

Sim, J. (2018). We are all (neo) liberals now: Reform and the prison crisis in England and Wales. *Justice, Power and Resistance, 2*(1), 165–188.

Singleton, N., Meltzer, H., & Gatward, R. (1998). *Psychiatric morbidity among prisoners*. London: Office for National Statistics.

Strauss, A., & Corbin, J. (1990). *Basics of qualitative research: Grounded theory procedures and techniques*. Newbury Park, CA: Sage.

Travis, A. (2016, November 3). Prisons in England and Wales to get 2,500 extra staff to tackle violence. *The Guardian*. Available at: https://www.theguardian.com/society/2016/nov/02/prisons-in-england-and-wales-given-boost-of-2500-new-staff-to-tackle-violence. Accessed 3 Jan 2018.

World Health Organization (WHO). (1996). *Health in prisons. Health promotion in the prison setting: Summary report on a WHO meeting*, London, 15–17 October 1995. Copenhagen: WHO Regional Office for Europe.

World Health Organization (WHO). (2005). *Information sheet on mental health and prisons*. Available at: http://www.euro.who.int/__data/assets/pdf_file/0007/98989/WHO_ICRC_InfoSht_MNH_Prisons.pdf. Accessed 14 Jan 2018.

Woodall, J. (2016). A critical examination of the health promoting prison two decades on. *Critical Public Health, 26*(5), 615–621.

Woolf, L. J. (1991). *Prison disturbances April 1990: Report of an inquiry by the Rt. Hon. Lord Justice Woolf (Parts I and II) and his Honour Stephen Tumin (Part II)*. London: HMSO.

6

How Do New Psychoactive Substances Affect the Mental Health of Prisoners?

Hattie Moyes

'If you have mental health problems, do not use NPS, it's a definite no-no.' (Prisoner)

The influx of New Psychoactive Substances (NPS) into Her Majesty's Prison Estate has contributed to record levels of self-harm, deaths and violence in prisons in England and Wales (HM Inspectorate of Prisons [HMIP] 2016; Prisons and Probation Ombudsman [PPO] 2015). A high proportion of the English and Welsh prison population has pre-existing mental health problems (Singleton et al. 1998) and being imprisoned can cause psychological distress (Birmingham 2003). Therefore, the widespread availability of NPS is likely to exacerbate the already high levels of mental health problems amongst prisoners, as well as having a detrimental effect on the prison regime and the safety of prisoners and prison staff (Ralphs et al. 2017).

H. Moyes (✉)
The Forward Trust, London, UK
e-mail: Hattie.Moyes@forwardtrust.org.uk

© The Author(s) 2018   **131**
A. Mills and K. Kendall (eds.), *Mental Health in Prisons*, Palgrave Studies in Prisons and Penology, https://doi.org/10.1007/978-3-319-94090-8_6

NPS are naturally occurring and synthetic mood-enhancing substances intended to mimic the effects of 'traditional' drugs such as cannabis, cocaine and heroin, among others (Pirona et al. 2017). Drugs that are not new, but are increasingly abused, such as MDMA, ecstasy and methamphetamine are also classified as NPS (Public Health England [PHE] 2014). NPS were often called 'legal highs' which was misleading as many of these substances such as synthetic cannabinoids and mephedrone were already controlled under the Misuse of Drugs Act 1971, prior to the Psychoactive Substances Act (PSA) 2016 coming into effect. The PSA was introduced to make it illegal to produce or supply any substance with a psychoactive effect (except alcohol, caffeine, nicotine and medicinal products) to prevent suppliers changing chemical compositions to make substances that were technically 'legal' and with unpredictable effects (Drugwatch 2016).

Public Health England (2015) has grouped NPS into five different categories based on their composition and effects: depressants (e.g. GBL, GHB); synthetic stimulants such as mephedrone; hallucinogens including lysergamides (e.g. LSD), tryptamines (e.g. magic mushrooms) and phenethylamines (e.g. N-Bomb); and dissociatives (e.g. ketamine and methoxetamine).

The most commonly used NPS are synthetic cannabinoids (SC) (PHE 2015). Prisoners often refer to these substances as 'Spice' or 'Mamba'—brand names under which SC were first sold on the market. Synthetic cannabinoids are typically sold as smoking mixtures of dried vegetable matter sprayed with cannabinoids which are dissolved in a solvent such as acetone or methanol using cement mixers, leading to uneven distribution of the cannabinoids. This can result in some potent SC batches, where cannabinoid doses are higher than intended and put users at risk of adverse mental and physical health effects (European Monitoring Centre for Drugs and Drug Addiction 2013). Synthetic cannabinoids mimic the effects of Tetrahydrocannabinol (THC)—the main psychoactive substance found in cannabis—and attach to CB1 cannabinoid receptors in the brain (United Nations Office on Drugs and Crime 2011). Users desire the same effects from SC as with cannabis such as disinhibition, euphoria and altered consciousness (Vandrey et al. 2012). However, the adverse effects of SC are stronger than cannabis—this may be due to their different pharmacological structures. Synthetic cannabinoids are full agonists of CB1 receptors, whereas THC is a partial agonist (Brents and Pather 2013). Cannabis also contains cannabidiol, which can block the psychotic effects (e.g. hallucinations and paranoia) of THC. Synthetic cannabinoids do not contain cannabidiol, thereby increasing the risk to mental health for users (Murray 2017).

Less than 1 in 100 of the general population had used NPS in the last year (HMIP 2015a). Conversely, it has been estimated that 60 to 90% of prisoners in England and Wales—which equates to at least 51,000 prisoners—have used SC while incarcerated (Centre for Social Justice 2015). Therefore, there are likely to be more users of SC in prisons than in the general population (Ralphs et al. 2017). Additionally, more prisoners reported using SC whilst incarcerated, compared to the two months before going into prison (HMIP 2015b). Why do so many prisoners use SC compared to the general population?

The popularity of SC is partially due to their widespread availability (User Voice 2016). The low cost of manufacturing and buying large quantities of SC has meant there is a larger difference in the price of SC between community and prison, whereas the price of opiates and cannabis does not differ so dramatically due to the higher risk of detection and penalties associated with these substances. Although SC are still relatively cheap in prisons, those selling it make a much larger profit than with other drugs (HMIP 2015a). Due to the availability of SC in prisons, over a third (34%) of prisoners with existing drug/alcohol addiction use them instead of their primary substance of choice (User Voice 2016).

Furthermore, until September 2016, NPS were not detectable by Mandatory Drug Testing (MDT) in English and Welsh prisons (National Offender Management Service [NOMS] 2016). Now that tests have been developed to detect NPS commonly used by prisoners including many SC, prisoners are more likely to test positive for using these substances and risk adjudication (Ryan 2017).

The increase in SC use has contributed to increasingly dangerous prison environments. In 2016, there were 40,161 incidents of self-harm and 120 suicides, almost double the number in 2012 (National Audit

Office 2017); between June 2013 and April 2016, there were 64 NPS-related deaths in prison. Forty-four of these deaths were self-inflicted, either due to psychotic episodes, or NPS-related debts exacerbating vulnerability and triggering self-harm/suicide. Two homicides resulted from a punch from another prisoner; nine natural-cause deaths involved NPS triggering a physiological effect e.g. a heart attack; six deaths were due to drug toxicity linked with NPS use and the cause of three deaths was unascertained, but NPS could not be ruled out (PPO 2016).

This situation has coincided with staff cuts across prisons in England and Wales; there are not enough prison officers to deal with NPS and the problems they can cause (User Voice 2016). Consequently, dealing with the impact of NPS stops prison officers from doing their regular work, resulting in prisoners spending increasing amounts of time locked in their cells (Howard League for Penal Reform 2017; Ralphs et al. 2017).

Prisoners get bored spending extended periods of time in their cells; SC have mind-numbing effects and can alleviate this boredom (Crewe 2009; HMIP 2015a). In a national survey of prisoners, over half of respondents said that boredom was the reason they used SC. Many prisoners also have poor coping mechanisms, so prolonged boredom and reduced access to support services can trigger psychological distress, for which they turn to SC to cope (User Voice 2016). The SC are also used to self-medicate for existing mental health problems (User Voice 2016). For some, using SC may be an informed, rational choice if it helps prisoners to cope with problems they cannot deal with (Blackman and Bradley 2017). In a BBC News (2017) report, one former SC user said, 'I think you need to up the mental health [support] and that, there's a reason why people are wanting to smoke it…There's a problem with that person, they can't deal with their thoughts'.

This chapter will assess the scale of the problem of NPS in UK prisons and the impact of NPS use on prisoner mental health. Firstly, findings from existing literature will be presented to improve understanding of the direct and indirect effects NPS and SC can have on the mental health of prisoners, as currently not much is known (Gray et al. 2016).

There is little specific guidance on what to do when someone presents with NPS-related problems (Drugwise 2016). This chapter also presents findings from a multi-site, service evaluation of NPS interventions in prisons. Capturing the perspectives of prisoners and those working with them will provide a comprehensive picture of the problem of NPS and prisoner mental health, what is currently being done to tackle it and what more can be done to improve the situation.

The Direct and Indirect Effects of SC on Prisoner Mental Health

NPS can have serious and unpredictable effects on prisoner mental health (PPO 2016). Due to the variety of synthetic cannabinoid compounds and the different dosages consumed, the effects experienced by users can differ wildly. The reported effects on mental health include: anxiety, paranoia, hallucinations, psychosis and psychotic symptoms, delusions, depression, panic attacks, aggression, agitation, depersonalisation, violent behaviour, suicidal ideation and self-harm (HMIP 2015a; MacFarlane and Christie 2015; NEPTUNE 2015; Gray et al. 2016; PPO 2016; User Voice 2016; PHE 2017a; Ralphs et al. 2017). Self-harming behaviour can be exacerbated or triggered by SC use and can lead to fatalities (PPO 2016; User Voice 2016). Additionally, NPS can affect the physical health of prisoners. Frequently reported effects include: weight loss, convulsions, temporary paralysis, rapid heart rate, loss of appetite, nausea, vomiting, sweating, stomach cramps, twitching limbs, high blood pressure, seizures and hyperthermia (MacFarlane and Christie 2015; NEPTUNE 2015; PHE 2015; PHE 2017a; Ralphs et al. 2017).

The duration of effects caused by using NPS can vary. In their systematic review of the effects of NPS on people with serious mental illness (SMI), Gray and colleagues (2016) found that some individuals recovered from psychotic symptoms within two to twelve hours of initial use, others took 3–4 days and some were still unwell one month later. Psychosis, depression, anxiety and paranoia can be long-lasting, resulting in healthcare and custodial staff having to manage these for months after initial SC use (PHE 2015; Drugwise 2016).

Many SC users in prisons are likely to have existing mental health problems and histories of substance misuse and dependence (Ralphs et al. 2017). Data from over 6500 substance-misusing prisoners found that this group presented with an average of at least three mental health problems each (Forward 2015). NPS can have potentially serious effects on the mental health of individuals with SMI (Gray et al. 2016). An inpatient study found that four hospitalised patients who had used NPS experienced new psychotic symptoms, but their previous symptoms were not exacerbated (Celofiga et al. 2014). However, as this study has limited generalisability, conclusions cannot be made about whether psychotic symptoms manifest before or after SC use. In a study of 804 prisoners, 60% said that mental health issues were a consequence of smoking SC (User Voice 2016).

SC use can have numerous indirect effects on prisoner mental health. Regular SC use can lead to dependence and consequently, debt, bullying and violence (MacFarlane and Christie 2015; Van Hout and Hearne 2017). Debt can easily spiral out of control if users have to pay back double the amount they borrowed to pay for SC. This debt can be passed onto friends, cellmates or new prisoners who move into their cells, putting all these people—plus the user—at risk of bullying, violence, psychological distress and consequently, self-harm (HMIP 2015a; User Voice 2016; PHE 2017a).

Some prisoners with mental health problems are at risk of bullying and violence whilst under the influence of SC (User Voice 2016). For example, they may be given a spiked joint or made to become 'Spice pigs' for other prisoners' entertainment (HMIP 2015a; PHE 2017a). Spice pigs test batches of SC before they are disseminated across the prison; new batches will only be sold based on how Spice pigs react to them. There have also been reports of SC spiked with cannabis, so individuals test positive on MDTs and lose privileges, get time added onto their sentence and miss out on getting parole (PHE 2017a).

Despite knowing that using SC puts their mental and physical health at risk, prisoners continue to take these substances for several reasons. SC can be highly addictive—users can easily become dependent on these substances. Almost three-quarters (73%) of prisoners surveyed reported being addicted to SC (User Voice 2016). This may be because SC affect dopamine and opioid peptide neurotransmitters in the brain; the same neurotransmitters that are affected by opioids and are involved in physical dependence (Newcombe 2016). Furthermore, NPS withdrawal has been reported to be harder than withdrawing from heroin (PHE 2017a). Psychological symptoms such as suicidal thoughts, depression and anxiety are associated with SC withdrawal (MacFarlane and Christie 2015; PHE 2017a). There is a dearth of information about the duration of SC withdrawal symptoms; however a small-scale, retrospective case file examination study of SC users found that the intensity of withdrawal symptoms peaked on day two and remained high until day five (MacFarlane and Christie 2015). Therefore, despite the adverse effects they experience, without significant psychosocial and clinical support, prisoners are likely to find it difficult to stop using SC (PHE 2017a).

NPS use can lead to uncharacteristic aggressive and violent behaviour, which can put the user, other prisoners and staff at risk (PPO 2016). Between 2014–2015 and 2015–2016, there was a 27% increase in the number of assaults in prison, which have been mainly attributed to NPS use (HMIP 2016). This may be due to prisoners acting violently whilst under the influence of NPS or NPS-related debt, leading to increased bullying and violence (HMIP 2015b). Violence can also lead to being put in segregation and/or on a basic regime, resulting in reduced contact with other prisoners, the outside world and loss of incentives such as a television. Reduced access to peers and services can cause more problems, particularly for prisoners with poor coping skills, and they may turn to SC to cope (User Voice 2016), thereby reinforcing this vicious cycle, or 'Spice Spiral' as shown in Fig. 6.1.

The Spice Spiral and aforementioned literature show that NPS can have a detrimental effect on prisoner mental health and wide-reaching consequences. Despite the expanding research on the effects that NPS can have, there is a scarce amount of robust evidence on the harms and clinical management of NPS use, and on psychosocial interventions to address NPS use (NEPTUNE 2015).

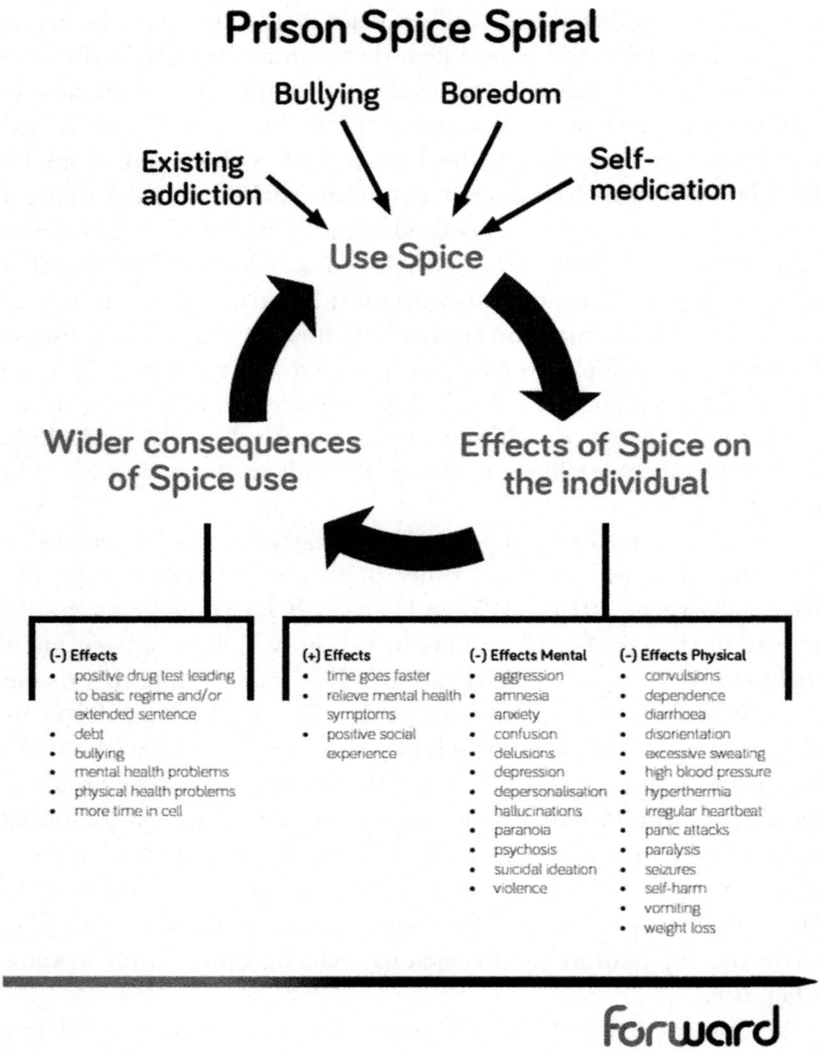

Prison Spice Spiral

Bullying   Boredom

Existing addiction   Self-medication

Use Spice

Wider consequences of Spice use

Effects of Spice on the individual

(-) Effects	(+) Effects	(-) Effects Mental	(-) Effects Physical
• positive drug test leading to basic regime and/or extended sentence	• time goes faster	• aggression	• convulsions
• debt	• relieve mental health symptoms	• amnesia	• dependence
• bullying	• positive social experience	• anxiety	• diarrhoea
• mental health problems		• confusion	• disorientation
• physical health problems		• delusions	• excessive sweating
• more time in cell		• depression	• high blood pressure
		• depersonalisation	• hyperthermia
		• hallucinations	• irregular heartbeat
		• paranoia	• panic attacks
		• psychosis	• paralysis
		• suicidal ideation	• seizures
		• violence	• self-harm
			• vomiting
			• weight loss

forward

Fig. 6.1 Prison Spice Spiral 1

Service Evaluation

A service evaluation was conducted on the NPS interventions delivered by The Forward Trust (Forward) to investigate what could be done to stop SC use following a vicious cycle—as shown in the Spice Spiral—and reduce the impact it has on prisoner mental health. Forward (formerly known as RAPt) is one of the largest providers of prison-based substance misuse services in England (Forward 2017). At the time of the evaluation, Forward were operating in 19 prisons. There were three strands to the service evaluation:

(1) Feedback from 166 service users (SUs) was obtained via a survey and focus groups. Table 6.1 provides a breakdown of participating SUs by age and ethnicity. Twenty-six (16%) respondents were female.

A six-question survey was disseminated to SUs at all 19 prisons where Forward were delivering services throughout May and June 2017 by Forward staff members and peer supporters, and returned by post to Forward's Research team for analysis. In total, 148 surveys were received from prisoners in Hertfordshire, Kent, London, Norfolk, Shropshire, Surrey and Sussex.

Three focus groups were conducted with SUs in two prisons in Kent (14 participants) and one prison in Hertfordshire (4 participants). Participants were asked questions in a semi-structured format, to provide context to the survey results and gain more detailed qualitative data (Morgan 1996). The questions focused on the impact of NPS on prisoner mental health; awareness of NPS interventions, e.g. 'What support is available for prisoners seeking help for NPS use?'; and what SUs learnt from this support and improvements that could be made.

(2) Semi-structured interviews were conducted with Forward staff working with NPS-using prisoners. Of the 15 individuals invited to interview, 11 agreed to participate. Participating staff included Drug and Alcohol Practitioners, Service Managers and Director of Services. The interviews ranged in length from 30 minutes to 1 hour and 10 minutes. Each interviewee was asked nine questions which covered mental health; services provided to address NPS use; and ideas on how to reduce NPS use and its effects, e.g. 'What can be done to moderate the negative effects of NPS use?'.

Table 6.1 Age and ethnicity of participating service users

	Number	Percentage
Age group		
20–24	15	9
25–29	29	18
30–34	34	20
35–39	29	17
40–44	12	7
45–49	16	10
50–54	7	4
55–59	3	2
60–64	0	0
65+	1	1
Did not state	20	12
Ethnicity		
White British	93	56
White Irish	6	4
Other White	6	4
White and Black Caribbean	12	7
White and Black African	2	1
White and Asian	2	1
Other mixed	3	2
Pakistani	0	0
Bangladeshi	3	2
Other Asian	2	1
Caribbean	11	7
African	8	5
Other Black	2	1
Chinese	2	1
Other	5	3
Did not state	7	4

(3) Quantitative data analysis was carried out of Forward's accredited substance misuse programmes and 'See Life More Clearly' (SLMC) pilot to investigate whether these programmes can help prisoners stop using SC. Forward deliver four substance misuse interventions accredited by the Ministry of Justice's Correctional Services Accreditation and Advice Panel that combine cognitive behavioural therapy, motivational enhancement therapy and Twelve-Step approaches. The Substance Dependence Treatment Programme (SDTP) and Women's Substance Dependence Treatment Programme (WSDTP) target the dynamic or

potentially changeable risk factors, such as deficient social support networks and emotion management of male and female prisoners, respectively, over a 16- to 21-week period. Two six-week programmes—The Bridge and Alcohol Dependence Treatment Programme (ADTP)—are designed for short-sentenced prisoners. Mental health profiles and completion rates of NPS users on these programmes were analysed.

The SLMC programme was developed by Forward and HM Prison and Probation Service (HMPPS) at a Kent prison to engage more NPS users in treatment. The SLMC programme has been piloted in this prison since February 2017. It is a holistic six-week programme that includes yoga, mindfulness and Tai Chi practice; creative writing; designated gym sessions; a healthcare clinic; and peer support sessions. Completion rates and qualitative feedback from prisoners who engaged with SLMC were analysed.

The results from the service evaluation will be presented in line with the four stages of the Spice Spiral: reducing reasons to use SC; moderating the negative effects of SC use; reducing the appeal of 'positive' SC effects; limiting the long-lasting and wider consequences of SC use.

Reducing Reasons to Use SC

Respondents explained in detail how each potential reason can act as a pathway to using SC and had numerous ideas on how to stop these pathways inevitably leading to SC use.

- *Boredom*

Boredom often resulted in a desire to kill time; however, many prisoners did not have the skills or resources to fill their time with meaningful activity: 'Unless you're creative and know how to occupy yourself, you just go round in circles' (Prisoner). Many respondents said that routine was essential to helping time pass without using SC and purposeful activity could help prisoners pass the time and alleviate boredom: 'they need relevant and meaningful activity, like SLMC. They need to be kept occupied' (Staff).

Prisoners with a job were less likely to report using drugs in prison (17%) compared to prisoners with no job (20%; HMIP 2015a). However, with prison staff shortages, only 36% of prisons were providing purposeful activity (HMIP 2015b). Even within these prisons, it is unclear how purposeful the activities provided are.

If prisoners are locked in their cells for extended periods of time, what can be done to help them cope with boredom? Respondents had a number of ideas, including a greater emphasis on well-being and in-cell activities. In-cell packs are Forward's interactive workbooks on substance misuse and well-being topics that SUs (including those with low literacy levels) can work through whilst locked in their cells. They contain quizzes, tasks and techniques to practise and can help prisoners pass time meaningfully. However, more needs to be done at a prison-wide level. Service providers can offer interim measures, but boredom-related SC use will continue unless prisoners are let out of their cells for longer and have access to meaningful, purposeful activity.

- *Self-medication*

As can be seen in Table 6.2, a high proportion of NPS users reported experiencing symptoms of anxiety, depression and trauma, comparable with prisoners who use other substances.

Table 6.2 Mental health symptoms experienced by participants on Forward's accredited programmes (2012–2017)

	NPS user ($n = 216$) (%)	Non-NPS user ($n = 3598$) (%)
Depression		
Episodes of depression	52	54
Symptoms of depression	18	15
No symptoms	23	26
Missing data	7	5
Anxiety		
Symptoms of anxiety	74	69
No symptoms	23	30
Missing data	3	1
Trauma		
Symptoms of trauma	70	67
No symptoms	27	32
Missing data	3	1

Prisoners' desire to self-medicate often results from their inability to cope with the mental health symptoms they experience: 'It stops your thoughts, stops you caring about things' (Prisoner). Despite knowing the risks that SC can pose to their mental health, prisoners were willing to use SC to help them deal with their adverse mental health symptoms.

According to research participants, identifying mental health needs and providing appropriate support should be the first step in preventing self-medication. However, due to reduced funding, only 25% of people with a mental health issue received treatment whilst in prison (NAO 2017), reinforcing the temptation to self-medicate: 'If they'd [mental health team] come seen me and given me my meds, I wouldn't have picked up Spice' (Prisoner).

Those who cannot access support from prison mental health teams could access low-level support from substance misuse and other support services. Light touch interventions such as mindfulness have been shown to be effective at targeting the mental health symptoms of prisoners (Bowen et al. 2006). Respondents were extremely positive about mindfulness: 'Mindfulness actually gets you talking and sharing. And teaches you how to cope with different situations. It really helped me a lot' (Prisoner). Furthermore, mindfulness can be practised anywhere—including a prison cell—which makes it a feasible intervention for those who do not require intensive mental health treatment (Moyes et al. 2016).

- *Existing addiction*

As with mental health, prisoners with an identified drug/alcohol addiction need to access substance misuse support as soon as possible. However, some may not want to engage and want to continue using their primary substance of choice. If this substance is unavailable, they will use whatever they can obtain. To reduce the likelihood of substance-misusing prisoners from trying SC, staff suggested: 'We need to raise awareness, have a transparent campaign, and talk about the risks of NPS, particularly since the Act [PSA 2016]' (Staff).

All of Forward's prison services delivered NPS awareness sessions with many prisoners attending. The effectiveness of these interventions was unclear, however, with some respondents reporting that they learnt a great deal, whereas others felt that more was needed. Several staff felt that a different approach was necessary for prisoners to realise the risks of SC use.

Moderating the Negative Effects of SC Use

Respondents described a number of clinical, psychosocial and integrated approaches that could be implemented to limit the impact of the negative effects of SC use. Firstly, SUs felt that there was currently no way out from SC use, as no detox or substitute was available for it: 'We need a substitute for Spice, like they have with heroin. The physical effects of Spice and the withdrawal are just so strong' (Prisoner).

No specific pharmacological treatments exist for the negative effects of NPS use (PHE 2015). In light of this and the absence of any formal harm reduction approaches, Forward staff in one Hertfordshire prison provide harm minimisation advice about NPS to all new SUs including information about NPS and SC; the PSA; the different effects they can experience; testing; and harm reduction techniques, for example, matchhead-size doses and not mixing with other substances.

Some establishments have developed protocols for treating prisoners withdrawing from NPS. For example, one Immigration Removal Centre puts those who stop using NPS on mental health watch for seven days. On days three to five after stopping, staff are vigilant for suicidal ideation (PHE 2017a). Best practice between clinical teams should be shared more widely, as knowledge on how to respond to NPS use was not common: 'Clinically we should symptomatically treat them. We should train our clinical nurses better so they have better understanding' (Staff). Staff and SUs also suggested that NPS-specific roles would help address the problem: 'A dedicated Spice worker would be good, and a Spice recovery wing' (Prisoner).

Drug Recovery Wings (DRWs) are specialist prison wings focused on abstinence-based substance misuse treatment. Successful DRWs are those that are exclusively for prisoners engaged in substance misuse treatment, have good staff–prisoner relationships, a strong sense of community and are separate from other prison wings. DRWs with these characteristics have been linked with reduced drug/alcohol use and improved quality of life for prisoners. However, many DRWs have difficulties maintaining a therapeutic regime in the current prison environment, suggesting that prisons may not be the most suitable environment for substance misuse treatment. Alternatives such as specialist drug recovery prisons may be more appropriate (Lloyd et al. 2017). The Ministry of Justice has recognised this and is piloting a drug recovery prison at HMP Holme House from 2018 (Independent Monitoring Board 2016).

In the absence of DRWs and drug recovery prisons, SUs talked at length about 'Spice reps', peer supporters with experience of SC. Some prisoners found it easier to seek support from their peers than staff: 'People are sometimes scared of RAPt. They need to know…they can get support from their peers. Peer mentors or Spice reps could have notes on their cell door, so everyone knows they can come in for a chat' (Prisoner). It was believed by many that having: '…someone they can relate to, who has been through it, mentors and Spice reps could work to bridge the gap between treatment' (Prisoner). Furthermore, peer supporters are often more flexible than staff at adapting support based on emerging trends amongst drug users (Marshall et al. 2015).

In addition to Spice reps, SUs recommended that there should be an ongoing awareness campaign on the support available; specific interventions delivered by NPS-specialist roles; incentives such as extra visits or phone calls; and ongoing awareness of the negative mental and physical effects of SC use: 'There needs to be focus on symptoms of Spice use, e.g. paranoia, stomach cramps, we need to help them cope with those. Teach them coping skills and raise awareness of these negative effects' (Prisoner).

There were limited ideas on how to support those who were at risk of being bullied/vulnerable prisoners. All staff interviewed felt that HMPPS needed to improve their management of bullying across the prison estate. Some felt that officers needed to respond better with greater education and supervision to tackle bullying more effectively.

The overwhelming response from all who participated in this evaluation was that ending supply was essential to stop prisoners using

SC, regardless of their reasons for wanting to use: 'It's about reducing supply into the prison' (Staff). SC and other drugs enter prisons via drones, visitors, staff, mail and being thrown over prison walls. One rural prison had 'blocked the road to the car park at night, so people can't drive down and throw over, or fly drones in' (Staff). This seemed to be reducing supply somewhat, though it was unclear as to what extent. Numerous suggestions for stopping supply have been made previously, such as better scanning and detection methods, drug dogs, working with the police, technology and intelligence-led searching (HMIP 2015a; PHE 2017a). However, many respondents and staff across the prison estate felt that these suggestions would not be implemented due to current financial pressures (PHE 2017a).

At the time of the evaluation, the SLMC pilot had been delivered to three cohorts, totalling 36 prisoners. Referrals to SLMC were targeted at prisoners identified through positive MDT tests and information shared at cross-departmental daily briefings. SLMC was popular with participants, as evidenced by the average completion rate of 78%. The feedback received from SLMC completers was overwhelmingly positive, especially in terms of improving well-being and coping skills: 'I have learnt new techniques to deal with my thoughts and feelings' (Prisoner).

Despite these encouraging results, SLMC is 'quite resource intensive' (Staff). If the resources to deliver a programme such as SLMC are not available across all prisons, can existing psychosocial support—as suggested by previous literature (e.g. NEPTUNE 2015)—be effective for SC users? Analysis of Forward's accredited prison-based substance misuse programmes found that many NPS users were able to successfully complete these programmes and achieve abstinence.

Although these results are promising, further work is needed to establish why fewer NPS users complete these programmes than non-NPS substance users. As can be seen in Table 6.3, far fewer NPS users than non-NPS users engaged with these interventions, this is comparable to the low numbers (<1%) of NPS users accessing substance misuse treatment across the prison estate (HMIP 2015a). This emphasises the need to promote the support available for NPS users to access.

Many staff believed that more integration with mental health and healthcare teams would help tackle the negative effects of SC use.

Table 6.3 Completion rates of NPS users and non-NPS users on Forward's accredited prison-based substance-misuse programmes, 2012–2017

| | Completion rate | |
	NPS user (n = 216) (%)	Non-NPS user (n = 3598) (%)
ADTP	59	75
The Bridge	69	78
SDTP	50	60
WSDTP	60	71

The quality of partnership working between these teams and substance misuse services varied across prisons. Some staff identified that integration may have been restricted by a lack of understanding about SC: 'We go to weekly meetings with in-reach—they're usually quite good at co-working but there's still some confusion about Spice' (Staff). That is, mental health in-reach teams do not know what impact SC have on prisoner mental health and response to treatment. If everyone is to have the responsibility for addressing NPS (and promoting well-being), everyone needs the right level of support and training to do so (Howard League for Penal Reform 2017).

Forward have delivered NPS training to prison officers in every institution they operate in; HMPPS have delivered training to 650 prison-based staff (PHE 2017a), though it appears that more is needed. In March 2017, PHE launched an online system called 'Report Illicit Drug Reaction' (RIDR) to improve healthcare professionals' knowledge of the harmful effects of NPS. The aim of this national system is to improve the monitoring of the negative effects of NPS, share best practice across prisons (and other frontline services), therefore helping staff to respond better to the emerging challenges of NPS (PHE 2017b). It remains to be seen whether RIDR will prove to be a useful resource for staff.

Reducing the Appeal of 'Positive' Effects of SC Use

Many staff were of the view that most prisoners were willing to risk the negative effects of NPS to enjoy the perceived positive effects. Staff discussed counteracting the perceived positives of SC use with awareness of negatives and risks: 'The positive effects are about short-term instant gratification and benefit. We need to be transparent and make people aware, especially of long-term risks' (Staff).

As highlighted in previous studies (e.g. Ward and Maruna 2007), looking at positive reasons to stop SC use may increase the likelihood of change. Once again, it was suggested that utilising peer support, particularly from those who had overcome SC use, could be relatable for SC users: 'Other prisoners could highlight the effects... [and provide] a visible solution...that people can understand and follow' (Staff).

All respondents felt that having something to do would help prisoners pass the time, increase positive social experiences and ultimately result in them using SC less often. Increasing exercise and access to the gym were desired by many SUs. Other, creative options—which in some cases could be peer-led and require little input from prison staff—were also proposed: 'I would like to see a book club, art therapy' (Staff).

Limiting the Long-Lasting and Wider Consequences of SC Use

Joint working with security and in-reach staff was again deemed to be essential to limit the wider and long-term consequences of SC use on the prison population and environment. Since September 2016, MDT has been capable of detecting many types of NPS including SC. Although HMPPS guidance states that adjudication should not be the automatic response to a positive test result (NOMS 2016), numerous prisoners experienced punishment rather than support to stop using SC which could be a barrier to seeking help: 'Being able to talk to staff without...being punished, that's why we don't ask for help' (Prisoner). Some described how even suspicion of use could lead to more time in cell and losing earned privileges: 'putting people on basic [regime] is not a good idea. As people will no longer ask for help. I witnessed a man ask for help for his cell-mate only to be put on basic for suspicion of using Spice' (Prisoner).

This situation illustrates the tension between care and punishment. If rehabilitation is the aim of prisons, then more supportive responses to asking for help with substance-related issues are needed. In the prisons where positive test results led to punishment, many staff felt that this approach was not working. Interlinked with this was the quality of prisoner and prison officer relationships. If these were improved, prisoners may be more likely to seek help: 'I'm a great believer in good relationships between prison officers and prisoners...really powerful to put a badge on a [supportive] prison officer so prisoners know they can speak to them' (Staff).

This was echoed by SUs: 'Officers...should promote the SLMC programme, wear badges or something. That would also increase the amount of people they can get help from, make support more visible' (Prisoner). Improving prisoner and prison officer relationships may also encourage more prisoners to seek help for SC-related debt: 'It's about... raising the support level, especially around debt—developing trust, trying to reduce use' (Staff).

Currently, it appears little is done about debt and respondents suggested that there could be interventions focusing on money management and holding peer-led Debtors Anonymous meetings. These self-help meetings could provide support that is not resource-intensive; however, running these meetings again comes down to prison officer and prisoner relationships: 'about re-education of prison staff, so they trust they [prisoners] won't automatically barricade themselves in' (Staff).

Some prisons do use positive test results to encourage SC users into treatment. For example, one Category B prison uses positive MDT results as an automatic referral to the weekly Spice drop-in session. At this drop-in, all attendees are given harm reduction advice and a 'Spice pack' with information on SC and other NPS; a quiz; case studies on SUs who have overcome their SC use; and interactive tasks on the mental and physical effects of SC. If prisoners referred to the drop-in did not attend, Forward staff would follow them up with an appointment to provide this information and advice. From March to May 2017, using this approach, Forward reached 143 SC users. Unfortunately, data on how many subsequently engaged with substance misuse services was not available.

The findings from this service evaluation demonstrate what is currently being done to tackle NPS use amongst prisoners plus a range of ideas on how to improve this situation and limit the impact of NPS—and SC in particular—can have on prisoner mental health. Much more can be done to improve outcomes for prisoners who use NPS. Substance misuse, mental health and healthcare teams, prison officers and governors can work closer together and more efficiently to reduce the likelihood of prisoners using NPS and entering the Spice Spiral.

Figure 6.2 provides an overview of the targeted support that can be offered to limit the effects that NPS can have on prisoner mental and physical health. It also demonstrates what can be done to limit the impact of wider-reaching consequences such as debt and increased amount of time in cell.

Many respondents in the evaluation felt that there was no support for SC use—that there was no way out of the Spice Spiral. The findings from the evaluation—represented in Fig. 6.2—show that there are multiple ways to escape the Spice Spiral, as long as prison support services work with the prison estate and are funded by commissioners to provide them. On a broader scale, SC use is predominantly a prison problem, as a result of the boredom, bullying, addiction and mental health problems that prisoners experience. If the findings from the evaluation and the Spice Spiral were implemented in a more rehabilitative environment—such as a drug recovery prison—there could perhaps be a greater reduction in SC use and its associated harms.

Limitations and Future Research

The biggest limitation to this evaluation is that almost everything suggested by respondents were ideas. Although many of these suggestions mirror proposals made in existing literature, none of them (except for completion of Forward's accredited programmes) has been shown to help prisoners stop using NPS, nor effectively tackle the negative consequences for prisoner mental health. As highlighted by NEPTUNE (2015), there is limited research evidence on the harms and

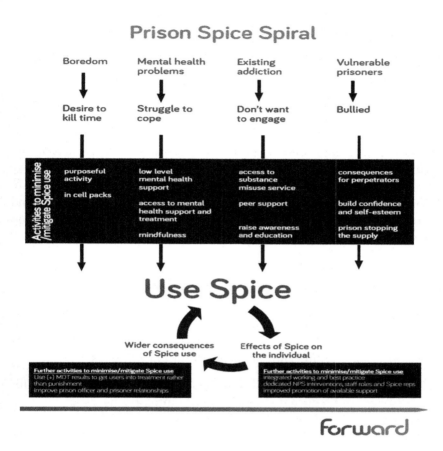

Fig. 6.2   Prison Spice Spiral 2

management of SC. Future research into NPS and SC use should investigate which existing and new interventions can reduce use of these substances and their associated negative consequences.

SUs who participated in this service evaluation may not have been representative of all prisoners accessing substance misuse treatment.

Surveys were given out to existing Forward SUs by staff and peer supporters on an opportunity basis over a two-month period. Participation in the survey and focus groups was voluntary and, in some instances, SUs were given surveys to fill out in their own time and return to staff when completed. If the survey was distributed over a longer time period, and SUs were chased up to return their completed surveys, then a more representative sample may have been achieved.

Participating staff almost exclusively worked in prisons in London and the South East of England. Therefore, they are not representative of staff working in prisons nationally where there may be variations in SC use. Staff delivering substance misuse services in other locations and prison governors and commissioners were invited to interview, but no response was received.

Recommendations and Conclusions

Notwithstanding the limitations identified above, the findings point to a number of recommendations that, if implemented, could have a positive impact on NPS use and the mental health of prisoners:

1. Providing more prison staff to facilitate more purposeful activity for prisoners and reduce the supply of NPS into prisons
2. More (low-level) support for mental health problems
3. Better promotion and awareness of NPS harms and the support available
4. Improved bullying management strategies
5. Sharing best practice on how to manage the negative effects of NPS use
6. The creation of specialist NPS roles
7. An increase in the number of peer supporters and Spice reps
8. Providing funding to pilot innovative interventions and/or research into the effectiveness of existing interventions to support NPS users
9. The development of joint working protocols between substance misuse services, mental health, healthcare and prison departments

10. Providing training to all staff working in prisons on NPS and their harmful effects

In addition to the above, the UK's first drug recovery prison is to be piloted from 2018. It is recommended that the model and interventions adopted in this prison be thoroughly evaluated so that best practice can be shared with other prisons to target NPS use and improve prisoner mental health. In order for these recommendations to make a difference, buy-in is needed from commissioners, prison governors, prison officers, substance misuse, mental health and healthcare teams to implement and monitor them effectively. Without this buy-in and shared responsibility, it is unlikely that the epidemic of NPS use and poor prisoner mental health will end anytime soon.

Bibliography

BBC News. (2017, May 19). *BBC news at ten* (Television broadcast). London: British Broadcasting Corporation.

Birmingham, L. (2003). The mental health of prisoners. *Advances in Psychiatric Treatment, 9*(3), 191–201.

Blackman, S., & Bradley, R. (2017). From niche to stigma—Headshops to prison: Exploring the rise and fall of synthetic cannabinoid use among young adults. *International Journal of Drug Policy, 40*, 70–77.

Bowen, S., Witkiewitz, K., Dillworth, T. M., Chawla, N., Simpson, T. L., Ostafin, B. D., et al. (2006). Mindfulness meditation and substance use in an incarcerated population. *Psychology of Addictive Behaviors, 20*(3), 343–347.

Brents, L. K., & Pather, P. L. (2013). The K2/Spice phenomenon: Emergence, identification, legislation and metabolic characterisation of synthetic cannabinoids in herbal incense products. *Drug Metabolism Reviews, 46*(1), 72–85.

Celofiga, A., Koprivsek, J., & Klavz, J. (2014). Use of synthetic cannabinoids in patients with psychotic disorders. *Journal of Dual Diagnosis, 10*(3), 168–173.

Centre for Social Justice. (2015). *Drugs in prison*. Available at: http://www. centreforsocialjustice.org.uk/core/wp-content/uploads/2016/08/CSJJ3090_ Drugs_in_Prison.pdf. Accessed 16 Mar 2015.

Crewe, B. (2009). *The prisoner society: Power, adaptation and social life in an English prison*. Oxford: Oxford University Press.

Drugwatch. (2016a). *A simple (ish) guide to the Psychoactive Substances Act*. Available at: www.drugwise.org.uk/wp-content/uploads/Psychoactive-Substances-Act.pdf. Accessed 1 Mar 2016.

Drugwise. (2016b). *NPS come of age: A UK overview*. Available at: http://www. drugwise.org.uk/wp-content/uploads/NPSComeofAge.pdf. Accessed 25 Jan 2017.

European Monitoring Centre for Drugs and Drug Addiction. (2013). *European drug report 2013: Trends and developments*. Available at: http:// www.emcdda.europa.eu/publications/edr/trends-developments/2013. Accessed 23 Apr 2015.

Forward. (2015). *Tackling the issue of new psychoactive substances in prisons* (Forward research and policy briefings). London: Forward.

Forward. (2017). *Introducing The Forward Trust: The new name for RAPt and Blue Sky*. Available at: https://www.forwardtrust.org.uk/media/1413/00044-for-web.pdf. Accessed 17 July 2017.

Gray, R., Bressington, D., Hughes, E., & Ivanecka, A. (2016). A systematic review of the effects of novel psychoactive substances "legal highs" on people with severe mental illness. *Journal of Psychiatric and Mental Health Nursing, 23*(5), 267–281.

HM Inspectorate of Prisons (HMIP). (2015a). *Changing patterns of substance misuse in adult prisons and service responses: A thematic review*. London: HMIP.

HM Inspectorate of Prisons (HMIP). (2015b). *HM chief inspector of prisons for England and Wales: Annual report 2014–15*. London: HMIP.

HM Inspectorate of Prisons (HMIP). (2016). *HM chief inspector of prisons for England and Wales: Annual report 2015–16*. London: HMIP.

Howard League for Penal Reform. (2017). *Preventing prison suicide: Staff perspectives*. Available at: http://howardleague.org/publications/preventing-prison-suicide-staff-perspectives/. Accessed 17 July 2017.

Independent Monitoring Board. (2016). *Holme House annual report 2016*. Available at: https://s3-eu-west-2.amazonaws.com/imb-prod-storage-1oc-od6bqky0vo/uploads/2017/04/Holme-House-2016.pdf. Accessed 19 May 2017.

Lloyd, C., Page, G., McKeganey, N., Russell, C., & Liebling, A. (2017). *The evaluation of the drug recovery wing pilots: Final report.* Available at: https://www.york.ac.uk/media/healthsciences/documents/research/mentalhealthresearch/DRWsFinalPublishedReport.pdf. Accessed 30 Oct 2017.

MacFarlane, V., & Christie, G. (2015). Synthetic cannabinoid withdrawal: A new demand on detoxification services. *Drug and Alcohol Review, 34,* 147–153.

Marshall, Z., Dechman, M. K., Minichiello, A., Alcock, L., & Harris, G. E. (2015). Peering into the literature: A systematic review of the roles of people who inject drugs in harm reduction initiatives. *Drug and Alcohol Dependence, 151,* 1–14.

Morgan, D. L. (1996). Focus groups. *Annual Review of Sociology, 22,* 129–152. Available at: https://www.researchgate.net/profile/David_Morgan19/publication/261773532_Focus_Groups/links/0deec5314d8bd0836c000000.pdf. Accessed 17 July 2017.

Moyes, H. C. A., Heath, J. J., & Dean, L. V. (2016). What can be done to improve outcomes for prisoners with a dual diagnosis? *Advances in Dual Diagnosis, 9*(1), 14–25.

Murray, R. (2017, October 23–24). Use of old and new recreational drugs and risk of psychosis. *The V international conference on Novel Psychoactive Substances at the United Nations.* Vienna.

National Audit Office (NAO). (2017). *Mental health in prisons.* London: NAO. Available at: https://www.nao.org.uk/wp-content/uploads/2017/06/Mental-health-in-prisons.pdf. Accessed 29 June 2017.

National Offender Management Service (NOMS). (2016, September 22). *Psychoactive substance testing as part of MDT* (Letter to all prison service Governors and Directors).

NEPTUNE (Novel Psychoactive Treatment UK Network). (2015). *Guidance on the clinical management of acute and chronic harms of club drugs and novel psychoactive substances.* Available at: http://www.neptune-clinical-guidance.co.uk/wp-content/uploads/2015/03/NEPTUNE-Guidance-March-2015.pdf. Accessed 22 Apr 2015.

Newcombe, R. (2016, November). *The bird killer: A study of the outbreak of Spice (SCRA) use among men in English prisons in 2016.* London: The QNPMHS Special Interest Day, Managing Dual Diagnosis and New Psychoactive Substances (NPS) in Prisons, Royal College of Psychiatrists.

Pirona, A., Bo, A., Hedrich, D., Ferri, M., van Gelder, N., Giraudon, I., et al. (2017). New psychoactive substances: Current health-related practices and challenges in responding to use and harms in Europe. *International Journal of Drug Policy, 40,* 80–88.

Prisons and Probation Ombudsman (PPO). (2015). *Learning lessons bulletin: Fatal incident investigations issue 9.* Available at: http://www.ppo.gov.uk/wp-content/uploads/2015/07/LLB_FII-Issue-9_NPS_Final.pdf. Accessed 25 Jan 2017.

Prisons and Probation Ombudsman (PPO). (2016, November 28). *Speech by the prisons and probation ombudsman, Nigel Newcomen CBE at Royal College of Psychiatrists learning day on new psychoactive substances.* Available at: www.ppo.gov.uk/document/ombudsman-speeches/. Accessed 25 Jan 2017.

Public Health England (PHE). (2014). *New psychoactive substances: A toolkit for substance misuse commissioners.* London: Public Health England.

Public Health England (PHE). (2015). *New psychoactive substances (NPS) in prisons: A toolkit for prison staff.* London: Public Health England.

Public Health England (PHE) (2017a) *Thematic analysis of training for prison staff on new psychoactive substances: November 2015 to May 2016.* London: Public Health England.

Public Health England (PHE). (2017b, March 22). *Online system launched to tackle harms from new psychoactive substances* (Press Release). Available at: https://www.gov.uk/government/news/system-launched-to-help-tackle-harms-from-new-psychoactive-substances. Accessed 24 Mar 2017.

Ralphs, R., Williams, L., Askew, R., & Norton, A. (2017). Adding spice to the porridge: The development of a synthetic cannabinoid market in an English prison. *International Journal of Drug Policy, 40,* 57–69.

Ryan, G. (2017). *Novel psychoactive substances: Synthetic cannabinoids—Best practice treatment approaches.* Available at: http://smmgp.org.uk/news-events/2017/novel-psychoactive-substances-synthetic-cannabinoids/. Accessed 17 July 2017.

Singleton, N., Meltzer, H., & Gatward, R. (1998). *Psychiatric morbidity among prisoners.* London: The Stationery Office.

United Nations Office on Drugs and Crime. (2011). *Synthetic cannabinoids in herbal products.* Available at: http://www.unodc.org/documents/scientific/Synthetic_Cannabinoids.pdf. Accessed 15 July 2017.

User Voice. (2016). *Spice: The bird killer. What prisoners think about the use of spice and other legal highs in prison.* London: User Voice.

Van Hout, M., & Hearne, E. (2017). User experiences of development of dependence on the synthetic cannabinoids, 5F-AKB48 and 5F-PB-22, and subsequent withdrawal syndromes. *International Journal of Mental Health & Addiction, 15*(3), 565–579.

Vandrey, R., Dunn, K. E., Fry, J. A., & Girling, E. R. (2012). A survey study to characterize use of Spice products (synthetic cannabinoids). *Drug and Alcohol Dependence, 20*(1–3), 238–241.

Ward, T., & Maruna, S. (2007). *Rehabilitation: Beyond the risk paradigm.* London: Routledge.

7

'There Was No Understanding, There Was No Care, There Was No Looking After Me': The Impact of the Prison Environment on the Mental Health of Female Prisoners

Anastasia Jablonska and Rosie Meek

Introduction

The mental health status of incarcerated individuals is consistently reported to be lower than that of the general population (de Viggiani 2007, 2012; Fazel et al. 2001; Baillargeon et al. 2000). Treatment of the mental health problems of prisoners is complex and usually requires a multimodal approach to address co-occurring substance misuse and communicable diseases (Herbert et al. 2012; Plugge and Fitzpatrick 2005; Social Exclusion Unit 2002). Despite the requirement in England and Wales for an equivalence of healthcare services in prisons with those of the local community (Penal Reform International 2012; Hayton and Boyington 2006), it is widely argued that prison further harms the mental health of prisoners through situations such as overcrowding,

A. Jablonska (✉) · R. Meek
Royal Holloway, University of London, Egham, UK
e-mail: Anastasia.Jablonska@rhul.ac.uk

R. Meek
e-mail: R.Meek@rhul.ac.uk

© The Author(s) 2018
A. Mills and K. Kendall (eds.), *Mental Health in Prisons*, Palgrave Studies in Prisons and Penology, https://doi.org/10.1007/978-3-319-94090-8_7

separation from family, violence and boredom (Mills and Kendall, this volume; Baybutt et al. 2014; Cheliotis 2012; Douglas et al. 2009; Levenson 2002; World Health Organization 1998).

Compared with the general population and men in prison, female prisoners are said to experience higher rates of mental illness (Ministry of Justice 2013; Plugge et al. 2006; Plugge and Fitzpatrick 2005). Over 80% of women in prison have a long-standing health condition, compared with 32% of the general female population (Plugge et al. 2006), and the most prominent long-standing illness overall reported by women in prison is depression, followed by anxiety and/or panic attacks (Plugge et al. 2006). Over 40% of women in prison are reported to have some form of drug dependence, compared with less than 5% and just under 10% of the general female and male population respectively (Plugge et al. 2009; Singleton et al. 1998, 2001). Over half of women in prison report hazardous drinking. This is higher than the reported rate for both men and women in the general population (Singleton et al. 1998, 2001).

Women prisoners also have pathways into criminality which are often a result of physical or sexual abuse, substance misuse, or mental health-care needs (Penal Reform International 2012; Covington and Bloom 2008; Pollock 1998). Women are more likely to be primary caregivers for children than men (Sheehan et al. 2013; HM Chief Inspector of Prisons [HMCIP] 1997) and to commit non-violent crimes for monetary gain (Hedderman and Jolliffe 2015; Steffensmeier and Allen 1998). The existing research has tended to focus on how men in prison interact in the environment, paying close attention to how control is negotiated, and how masculine identities are forged, maintained and interact with the 'prison code' (Woodall 2012; Hua-Fu 2005; Sabo et al. 2001). However, much less is known about how women in prison interact with the regime and their lived environment (Rowe 2016). In order to understand further how the environment of the prison can impact mental health, this chapter will explore women's experiences of living on the main housing block in an English prison. The need for a specific focus on women's mental health in prison is demonstrated through research identifying distinct and unmet needs across the female prison estate (Corston 2007, 2011). Furthermore, exploring the experience of women in custody presents an opportunity to target interventions to promote better mental health outcomes for the individual. There is also the potential benefit to the individual and society as an individual who is released from custody physical and mentally well is more likely to gain employment, and actively participate in society, and overall is less likely to reoffend (Meek et al. 2012; Social Exclusion Unit 2002).

Research studies on the impact of initial imprisonment on health provide a potentially valuable insight into how the environment of the prison can impact women's mental health. Douglas et al. (2009) revealed the shock and fear that women felt on entry to the prison, their emotional distress at being separated from their children and families, and their concerns about living with women who were withdrawing from drugs or had serious mental health problems. Other research has focused on women's roles as primary care givers to children and the distress caused by the loss of this role during imprisonment (Ward and Kassebaum 1965). Furthermore, social relationships and coping mechanisms have been found to be shaped by the prison environment (Kruttschnitt and Gartner 2005).

More broadly, the importance of considering the environment when researching matters related to mental health is supported through health promotion policies which advocate empowerment, agency, and 'settings based' principles (Woodall 2012, 2016; Woodall et al. 2014; Caraher et al. 2002). These 'settings based' principles recognise health, including mental health, as a complex notion, driven and sustained through experiences of everyday life—in the workplace, schools, hospitals, and prisons (Woodall et al. 2014). Interaction with these sites, their environment and conditions, need to be considered when developing and understanding health promotion strategies (Dooris 2009). However, despite an understanding and acceptance of the benefits of this approach in penal policy (see HM Prison Service 2003), little practical change has occurred in prisons to promote prisoner health (Frater and Tan 2016; Woodall 2016; Caraher et al. 2002). The lived environment of the prison continues to be an important consideration in the potential of the prison to promote mental health (Jewkes and Moran 2015; Lindemuth 2007; Bradley and Davino 2002), and is thus the focus of this research.

Methodology

As noted earlier, the broad aim of this chapter is to explore how women in prison perceive and manage the impact of incarceration on their mental health, and in doing so, to consider the role of the environment in women's mental health. To achieve this, we draw upon a study of the main housing block in a women's prison in England, consisting of three wings housing 118 sentenced women.

Design

To develop a better understanding of the complexities of living on the main housing block, a qualitative approach was employed through individual, semi-structured interviews, which lasted between 45 and 80 minutes. The interviews were conducted predominantly in the association room on the first floor of the housing block, as this offered privacy, but was also a comfortable, familiar space. With participants' permission, the interviews were audio recorded, then transcribed verbatim with all identifiable information removed.

Sampling and Participants

Purposive sampling was used to recruit participants who spent the majority of their time within the housing block environment. The age of the ten participants ranged between 25 and 55 years. The majority were of White ethnicity ($n = 7$), together with two women of Black ethnicity and one Asian woman. Two participants were serving life sentences and one had a sentence of indeterminate imprisonment for public protection, with a tariff of five years. The sentence length of the remaining seven participants ranged from two years to 15 years, with an average of six years. The length of incarceration in the prison ranged from one week to 17 years, with an average of three years.

Analysis

In order to reach a better understanding of women's daily lives on the main housing block and how this impacted their mental health, the research was grounded in the participants' own accounts of their experiences. Interpretative Phenomenological Analysis (IPA) was employed to explore the particular meanings their experiences in this environment had on their mental health. This was considered an appropriate technique as IPA has been demonstrated to work particularly well in analysing the meanings a particular group of individuals ascribe to a particular topic or lived experience (Fade 2004). While most commonly used in the discipline of health psychology (Smith 2011; Biggerstaff and Thompson 2008), IPA has been used to understand well-being (Dunne and Quayle 2001), exercise (Pridgeon and Grogan 2012), in addition to experiences of prison (Kennedy 2014; Aresti et al. 2010; Meek 2007, 2008) and women's experiences of a particular social or cultural context (Wingood et al. 2000). However, this research is the first of its kind to apply IPA to understand how experiences in the particular environment of a prison can impact women's mental health.

The interview transcripts were analysed using IPA in accordance with the process described by Smith (1996). Notes were made during close reading and re-reading of the transcripts and were later organised into clusters, which after further reading of the text were developed into themes. The following findings section is organised according to four themes: forced community; discipline and punishment; lack of comfort and care; and physical activity, family and mental health. Examples of verbatim extracts from interview transcripts are used to ground each theme in the participants' accounts.

Findings

The main housing block represented an environment where multiple activities occurred, in addition to being the place where women resided and could socialise with one another. Each of the three wings housed approximately 40 women in single occupancy rooms. The wings were joined together by corridors and had a communal association room, which could be accessed during association time. An office for staff was located at the end of the wing. Down a long corridor, about three metres wide, there were ten rooms on either side with a small window at the end. Next to the wing office was a set of stairs that went up to the next floor with the same layout.

Forced Community

Women on the houseblock had no choice but to be around one another, which could place a strain on their mental health in a variety of ways. Even if they remained in their rooms, the sounds of voices, music, and doors slamming could still be heard. For some women, this could be especially difficult. There seemed to be a 'collective conscious', or a shared belief that this houseblock was a difficult part of the prison to be in, particularly C wing which was described as 'bad girls' wing', where the 'riffraff' was and a place to put the 'trouble makers' and 'no hopers'. Issues of loud music, general noise, bullying, gossiping, and intimidation emerged in the interviews. Illustrating this, Janet talked about not being able to do basic things such as watching television because of the noise levels:

> It's like being a constant youth club... My ears started ringing about a week after I moved onto C1... I love music...but when it's constant drum and bass [laughs], when all you're trying to do...is watch something as basic as Eastenders and the DUM-PER DUM-PER DUM-PER DUM-PER DUM- PER DUM- PER DUM! FUCK YOUR MUM-BOM BER DUM! And it just, it drives you insane. [Janet]

The close proximity to other women in the prison made it a difficult place to be when experiencing mental ill health. Becky recalled that when she was having a psychotic breakdown, despite being around the women on the wing who she may have called her friends, there was no support from them:

At the time... I couldn't be around people because I couldn't bear the thought of being the topic of conversation but I wasn't presenting very well. I was unkept [sic]...looking back now it was awful, AWFUL!. It teaches you a lot about people...you find out who your fucking friends are...because I stood alone, no one was there really'. [Becky]

Despite being in an environment where there are many staff and fellow prisoners around, Becky's accounts suggest the main housing block can be a lonely place where women may go through difficult times alone, with little or no support. This can be likened to the attitude of male prisoners described in Crewe et al. (2014) research where difficult emotions, other than bereavements or close family matters, were considered subjects with which others should not be burdened and therefore needed to be dealt with alone without overt expression. The rationale for some women not getting involved in the problems of others was to avoid investing their emotional energy elsewhere, thus facilitating their own mental health.

From Tamara's perspective, coming to prison meant that she was amongst women she had never come across before. In this new environment, her heteronormativity was challenged, and this represented a threat to her. Tamara explained how some of her fellow prisoners scared her to the point where she felt she would have to retreat to her room for safety, while maintaining an element of politeness to ensure that she did not cause conflict:

I've never seen so many women who look like men. Being butch with a beard... They go to the gym and they look like men! They dress up like men, they wear their pants half way down (laughing). They scare me... I've had a few approach me saying 'oh your eyes are so beautiful', this and that. And I said 'oh thank you, but I just need to let you know I'm not that way inclined'...they will leave you, but one or two do pester you. [Tamara]

There were clear signs of Tamara feeling intimidated, stressed, anxious and worried about being outside of her room on the open wing. Her way of coping with these emotions was to forcibly remove herself from the shared environment and to isolate herself in her cell. Such self-segregation is of concern due to the level of self-harm that occurs in the female estate, which is most likely to occur during periods of isolation (Ministry of Justice 2017; Hawton et al. 2014; Völlm and Dolan 2009). Isolation and lack of social support in prison have also both been linked to increased vulnerability to suicide (Liebling 1992).

Not all the participants described living closely with other women as negative. Danny had made friends on the wing, particularly Becky, who had introduced her to new and more positive ways of thinking. Although she had only known Becky seven months, their friendship was strong, having worked together and been around each other for most of that time, and Danny talked about her intention to come back and see Becky and stay friends with her after release:

> I've proper changed. I've only been here seven months. I think it's I've bothered with people I wouldn't have bothered with, like my friends like Becky and that they've changed my views on things a bit differently, maybe widened me up to people a bit more. My outlook on life is a bit different now. I'm coming back to visit Becky. [Danny]

In essence, what these extracts have shown is that the forced community that prison creates can affect the women's mental health. As noted by one of the prisoners' in Sykes's (1958) seminal study, the worse thing about prison is having to live with other people. However, this can be positive through developing close social bonds with other women. Forming relationships with others has been characterised as a way to pass the time (Bosworth and Carrabine 2001) and aid coping with imprisonment (Kruttschnitt and Gartner 2005), particularly the loneliness of imprisonment as a consequence of being separated from family and friends (Beer et al. 2007). Relationships with others can provide vital social support, which can help to cope with stress and emotional adjustment after experiencing a life crisis (see Kessler et al. 1985). Furthermore, Ward and Kassebaum (1965) discuss the psychological need that women in prison have for relationships and how such relationships can provide a mechanism for them to develop a social role, potentially allowing the mirroring of roles they may have had prior to imprisonment. Yet, for some women, the environment of the main housing block was a negative experience leading to isolation and withdrawal. Drawing on Irwin and Cressey's (1962) importation model, it is possible to understand that these women may have used isolation prior to custody as a strategy to lessen physical or emotional abuse experienced in previous relationships (DeHart 2008). These behaviours are then employed during imprisonment to protect them from any further abuse on the prison wing.

Discipline and Punishment

English and Welsh prisons maintain a complex system of prescribed rules and regulations, and violations can result in reprimands and punishments. The Incentive and Earned Privileges (IEP) scheme sets out the expectations of prisoners in England and Wales (see National Offender Management Service [NOMS] 2015). In the research prison, all prisoners were allocated to 'standard' level on entry to prison. Following compliance with protocols and regulations, in addition to engagement in work or purposeful activity, a prisoner can be promoted to 'enhanced' status. This raised position entitles them to longer visits and increased spending in the prison shop if they have the funds in their private account. Failure to adhere to the protocols and regulations, however, can result in demotion to 'basic' status. In the main housing block, women on 'basic' regime would only be allowed out of their cell for small amounts of association time (usually around thirty minutes a day), and for fifteen minutes to have dinner in the dining hall. This lasted for a period of twenty-eight days before a review was held to consider progression to 'standard' regime. For some participants, therefore, the wing was also a site of punishment in the prison environment. Women could be demoted onto 'basic' regime for what was considered by them to be minor wrongdoing, as Angela describes:

> For wearing flip flops... You're not allowed to wear them on the landing but they give you prison issue flip flops so you assume you you'd be allowed to wear them...you're only allowed them in your room... It's ridiculous, for really silly things. [Angela]

Being on basic regime could result in women being forcibly isolated from prison life, and from the outside world through having no access to in cell television and/or radio. Experiencing this for extended periods of time could create emotional distress and frustration as Sarah describes:

> On Saturday I was locked up at quarter to five in the evening and they didn't unlock my door till quarter to one, dinner time the next day. It's like twenty hours solidly behind my door with no radio, no TV, that done my head in. [Sarah]

The participants in this study also demonstrated considerable emotional distress from anticipating reprimands that could result in demotion to basic level. In his reworking of the pains of imprisonment, Crewe (2011) similarly discussed the uncertainty and insecurity that prisoners experience as a result of the discretionary use of power and its unpredictable application. Uncertainty can impact mental health and create feelings of fear, anxiety and stress (see, for example, Grupe and Nitschke 2013). From the prisoners' perspectives, what they are entitled to under the rules of the IEP scheme could change due to the unfair and inconsistent application of the scheme by staff. According to Crewe's (2011) reassessment of the 'pains of uncertainty and indeterminacy', prisoners' uncertainty in the prison environment is not only shaped by the inconsistent timing of discipline, but also the form and length of the punishment. Such arguments have been made in other previous research, particularly since the inception of new rules to the IEP scheme in November 2013, which most notably banned books being sent into prisoners (Prison Reform Trust 2014; Prison and Probation Ombudsman 2013; Liebling 2008). The Prison and Probation Ombudsman (2013) and the Prison Reform Trust (2014) both called into question the effect that these new rules had on prisoners' wellbeing. From the current research, it seems that there has been a lack of progress towards a consistent approach to applying the scheme.

The uncertainty surrounding the enforcement of prison rules and regulations additionally relates to Crewe's (2011) work on the 'pains of self governance'. He argues that modern prisons have shifted away from intense oversight of prisoners to encouraging prisoners to take responsibility for their own actions. While prisoners have to watch their own conduct, it is also evident that they may watch the conduct of others. The lack of clarity as to what behaviours are acceptable and what is punishable, along with the individual discretion exercised by staff when enforcing the rules, creates frustration within the environment for both those receiving punishment and those apparently adhering to the rules.

> Here, they call work, here right. People are just getting out of bed when they call work and then when free flow ceases, that's when they're walking down – 'Miss can you unlock the door I need to go to work'- and the staff say 'Okay'. So how are we supposed to learn? You can't do that. If they're missing you should punish them. [Wendy]

Lack of Comfort and Care

While in prison some of the women had experienced the trauma of being diagnosed with serious physical health conditions that would alter their well-being for the rest of their lives. These accounts provide an insight into coming to terms with such a diagnosis, treatment and aftercare while being in prison and the subsequent impact on the women's mental health. What stood out from the women's accounts was a profound lack of care, empathy and comfort from both staff and other prisoners while going through such a difficult time in prison:

> I had to have a hysterectomy in prison. The care afterwards wasn't there, my mental health deteriorated last year. The staff didn't know what to do...so long as you're getting up every day and you're not dead they don't really give a shit (laughs)... The choice [to undergo a hysterectomy] was taken away from me but I suppose lifer, drug user, like it was quite easy for them to make that decision in this environment... It was hard afterwards cause it was so final and there was no real care there... There was no empathy ...there was no understanding, there was no care, there was no looking after me. I was just put back on normal location and made to do all the things that everybody else does. I was off work for a little while... I declared that I was using drugs so I was taken back down to

detox and at that point I still wasn't supposed to be manoeuvring any heavy objects, but I was made to carry my full kit down to the detox wing because then they were like 'oh well, fuck her' type thing. [Becky]

Becky questioned if the option of a hysterectomy would have been considered if she were not in prison. Through her narrative, it appears as though she felt she did not have a choice. This provides a grave example of deprivation of autonomy (Sykes 1958) and how medical care can be a mechanism of control in prison. As she was in prison, Becky felt that others believed that the hysterectomy should not have affected her, when she needed to emotionally come to terms with the procedure she underwent. She also discussed the difference between 'presenting well' and 'being well'. In prison, if you carry on as normal, everyone around you assumes that there is no need to question feelings or emotions. Becky suggests that the prison environment is a superficial one where women are 'presenting well', and that is interpreted as things are well, when in actual fact, they are not. The lack of comfort, support or empathy from staff in the prison environment was demonstrated by Becky having to carry her belongings despite recently having had major surgery. Rather than her use of drugs being seen as a reaction to her diagnosis and helping her to cope, staff punished her further.

Many women in prison experience long-term health conditions, which can be exacerbated by the prison environment. Long-term health conditions and mental health problems can interact to have a strong negative impact on quality of life and ability to function (Moussavi et al. 2007). Poor mental health can also result in poor self-management including lack of motivation and energy to adhere to treatment plans or appointments (DiMatteo et al. 2000), and thus poorer clinical outcomes in dealing with health problems (Moussavi et al. 2007). Sue's account of her experiences of having Parkinson's disease while being in prison highlighted how lack of care and support by the prison exacerbated not only her physical condition, but also substantially affected her mental health:

They [prison officers] don't understand that with Parkinson's you have to have the medication exactly on time. So where I'm [supposed to take my medication] every 12 hours, I'm not getting the morning dose till after about 15 hours and I have to go and get it. But with Parkinson's it takes a long time to get going until you've had that medication. Without that medication I can't get up to go and get my medication...so I'm only getting one lot of medication once a day... Nobody will help me... Three weeks ago I tried to commit suicide, and all I've done since then is get worse and worse, and worse. [Sue]

Sue's access to medication was limited because of her condition, and the prison staff were not facilitating her access to the required dose of medication twice daily. Sue was exceptionally vulnerable as a prisoner with a long-term disabling health condition and was not being given by staff the care and support she clearly needed. She also did not have many women around her that she could ask for help, or to advocate on her behalf, as she was living in the disabled room on an induction wing where it was difficult to form relationships due to the short time women usually spent there. It was an wholly inappropriate environment for her and this exemplified the marginalisation that prisoners with disabilities can face due to prisons not being designed for their needs (Baum 1983; HMCIP 2009), perpetuating the 'double punishment' they experience, as they are not only imprisoned for committing a crime, but also subjected to physical and social isolation and discrimination by staff and fellow prisoners due to their disability (Haualand 2015; Kelly 2017). This in turn can affect their mental health due to the consequent lack of social contact, and may impact the likelihood of them being able to engage with the regime to enhance their IEP status (Mann 2016; Cunniffe et al. 2012; HMCIP 2009; Crawley and Sparks 2005). Sue's account provides insight into how she felt completely disempowered, disinhibited and disregarded by the prison.

Accounts from participants in this study demonstrate that the prison environment offers little care or comfort and that the purpose of imprisonment is principally to punish and detain rather than rehabilitate or care for individuals. Parker et al. (2009) argue that this emphasis on punishment undermines efforts to promote rehabilitation within the prison. The findings presented here suggest that imprisonment also serves to undermine women's mental health and emotional well-being.

The research also sheds light on practices by prison staff who lack empathy and do not attempt to understand the experiences of women who are extremely unwell. Although healthcare professionals have ethical obligations to advocate for their patients in prison settings (Willmott 2009), there is a need to extend this ethical obligation to all staff working within prisons, as the failure to provide appropriate support can ultimately contribute to a substantial deterioration in prisoners' mental health.

Physical Activity, Family and Mental Health

The study also considered activities outside of the main housing block environment that might affect the women's mental health. One activity that was available was going to the prison gym. Prior research has highlighted the potential benefits of physical activity in prison to both mental and physical health, as well as coping with imprisonment (Meek 2014; Meek and Lewis 2014; Buckaloo et al. 2009; Cooper and Berwick 2001). Participants in this study had the opportunity to use the gym, but more frequently provided reasons why they did not want to go, including session times being too long and the atmosphere not being something they enjoyed:

> I don't go like regularly… Too many people sometimes. I like to go in there when it's a time when you can go in for twenty minutes and come back out. I don't like that you have to go in there at three o'clock and you have to stay there till half past four. [Kate]

Furthermore, Janet highlighted that the activities on offer were not ones she would enjoy. A particular barrier was wanting to engage in activities such as rowing, that in the community would be surrounded by nature and fresh air, creating a sense of pleasure and well-being, whereas the corresponding activity in the prison gym did not offer this or was not seen as providing an environment that offered health-promoting benefits.

Visits from family or friends represented another way to temporarily leave the main housing block. However, participants recalled very difficult emotive experiences of talking to, or receiving visits from, their children and families while they had been in prison. Many women had played central roles in their children's or families' lives, but were now unable to due to their imprisonment. Relationships with children and family impacted women's emotions and consequently their mental health. Many participants on standard or enhanced regimes made use of the biannual extended family visits, but the feelings of loss afterwards had the potential to devastate them. To prevent these feelings, participants developed coping strategies such as shutting down their emotions or simply refusing visits:

> The last time I had a children's visit was in Holloway and my daughter was crying for me and I can't deal with it. What it shows you is to shut down your feelings, to shut down your emotions. That's what it teaches you. [Tamara]

The emotional difficulty of being separated from loved ones echoes previous research studies which document the initial stress of separation and the uncertainty of care for dependent children, and the long-term strain of attempting to remain their mother whilst being in custody (Celinska 2013; Sheehan et al. 2013; Rowe 2011). It is therefore perhaps unsurprising that when revisiting the pains of imprisonment through the paradigm of gender and the complexity of long-term imprisonment, Crewe et al. (2017, p. 1365) note that the pains of imprisonment 'were experienced with significantly greater severity by the women than the men'.

Conclusion

The findings presented in this chapter provide insight into the complex and varied experiences of women in prison. They demonstrate that the experience of imprisonment can have grave consequences for mental health due to the forced community of prison, lack of social support, the uncertainty of punishment and the lack of care for those with serious and/or long-term health conditions. Perhaps the most notable finding from this research is that female prisoners with disabilities experience 'double punishment' (Kelly 2017), in that they are punished for committing a crime, but also punished through marginalisation and being held in an environment that is not appropriately designed or adapted for their needs (HMCIP 2009; Baum 1983). This research demonstrates that such circumstances can lead to suicide attempts, low self-esteem and feelings of being completely disregarded by the prison and prison staff.

Despite the push towards 'healthy prisons' over the past twenty years, it is clear that the central tenets of settings-based health promotion strategies such as choice, control and empowerment (Woodall et al. 2014) are hardly possible in the setting of a women's prison. Where there are choices, such as to isolate oneself to avoid bullying, to go on visits or to the gym, they are constrained and appear ineffective in improving participants' mental health. These findings refute the possibility of a 'healthy prison setting' and would suggest that a fundamental shift is needed to better promote the mental health of women in prison. Smith (2000) has argued that there is a fundamental need to account for and tackle the wider structural determinants that result in poor health prior to imprisonment. Without changes to these structural determinants and opportunities to promote one's mental health during imprisonment, women face returning to the same or worse conditions on release, heightened by limited support available in the community and the additional difficulties of how to adjust to life in the community following the trauma of imprisonment (Carlton and Segrave 2011).

In her report, Baroness Corston (2007) advocated for the use of women centres to provide a 'one stop shop' for women released from custody and those at risk of offending or going to prison. Here, the support provided for housing, mental health and relationships, to name a few services, offered the potential to tackle the root causes of offending with the aim of reducing the number of women sent to prison (Women in Prison 2017). Despite emerging findings on the effectiveness of women's centres to meet the needs of women released from custody (Hedderman et al. 2008), the uncertainty of funding has led to the closure of some of these facilities around the United Kingdom (Gelsthorpe 2017). The loss of these centres signifies a reduction in the provision of support for women on release from custody and under supervision in the community, and for those women who are at risk of offending or going to prison, thus potentially further compromising their mental health.

The need for women's prisons has been strongly contested, given women's lower and less serious rates of offending and the damage inflicted on women's lives by imprisonment (Moore et al. 2017; Carlen 1998). The findings presented here question whether women's prisons are the appropriate facility to detain women who have committed less serious crimes, and suggest that we must question the ethical implications of imprisonment on the lives of women detained. Given the broader context of public discussions of victimisation and trauma that have occurred recently, in terms of child sex abuse (Greer and McLaughlin 2013) and female actors sexually abused by powerful men in the film industry, as part of the 'Time's Up' movement, perhaps the scales have tilted to allow for societal change and acknowledgement that for many women in prison, their crimes are as a result of victimisation and trauma and therefore prison is not the appropriate place for them, but more should be done to protect women and girls from these experiences.

While it is argued that prison is not the appropriate place for less serious offenders, it must be improved for the smaller numbers of serious offenders who are imprisoned due to the danger they present to the public. The White Paper, *Prison Safety and Reform* announced a new strategy for working with female offenders and plans to develop five new community prisons for women offenders, which would help to facilitate preparation for release and would allow women to be incarcerated closer to home (Ministry of Justice 2016). This resonates with Corston's (2007) recommendation for small geographically dispersed custodial centres, which was dismissed by the Labour government at the time. While the full government report on plans for women's imprisonment is still outstanding at the time of writing, these suggestions would indicate that there is at least the possibility of penal reform to meet the needs of those women who are imprisoned to protect the public from harm.

Overall, the findings highlight that further work is needed to improve the mental health of incarcerated women. Further qualitative investigation is therefore needed to understand how other areas of the prison impact mental health, in order to develop spaces that can promote better mental health outcomes for women in prison.

Bibliography

Aresti, A., Eatough, V., & Brooks-Gordon, B. (2010). Doing time after time: An interpretative phenomenological analysis of reformed ex-prisoners' experiences of self-change, identity and career opportunities. *Psychology, Crime and Law, 16*, 169–190.

Baillargeon, J., Black, S. A., Pulvino, J., & Dunn, K. (2000). The disease profile of Texas prison inmates. *Annals of Epidemiology, 10*, 74–80.

Baum, E. M. (1983). Handicapped prisoners: An ignored minority. *Columbia Journal of Law and Social Problems, 18*, 349–379.

Baybutt, M., Acin, E., Hayton, P., & Dooris, M. (2014). Promoting health in prisons: A settings approach. In E. Enngist, L. Møller, G. Galea, & C. Udesen (Eds.), *Prisons and health* (pp. 180–184). Copenhagen: WHO Regional Office for Europe.

Beer, A. M., Morgan, R. D., Garland, J. T., & Spanierman, L. B. (2007). The role of romantic/intimate relationships in the well-being of incarcerated females. *Psychological Services, 4*, 250–261.

Biggerstaff, D., & Thompson, A. R. (2008). Interpretative phenomenological analysis (IPA): A qualitative methodology of choice in healthcare research. *Qualitative Research in Psychology, 5*, 214–224.

Bosworth, M., & Carrabine, E. (2001). Reassessing resistance: Race, gender and sexuality in prison. *Punishment and Society, 3*, 501–515.

Bradley, R. G., & Davino, K. M. (2002). Women's perceptions of the prison environment: When prison is "the safest place I've ever been". *Psychology of Women Quarterly, 26*, 351–359.

Buckaloo, B. J., Krug, K. S., & Nelson, K. B. (2009). Exercise and the low-security inmate: Changes in depression, stress, and anxiety. *The Prison Journal, 89*, 328–343.

Caraher, M., Dixon, P., Carr-Hill, R., Hayton, P., McGough, H., & Bird, L. (2002). Are health-promoting prisons an impossibility? Lessons from England and Wales. *Health Education, 102*, 219–229.

Carlen, P. (1998). *Sledgehammer: Women's imprisonment at the millennium.* Basingstoke: Palgrave Macmillan.

Carlton, B., & Segrave, M. (2011). Women's survival post-imprisonment: Connecting imprisonment with pains past and present. *Punishment and Society, 13,* 551–570.

Celinska, K. (2013). The role of family in the lives of incarcerated women. *Prison Service Journal, 207,* 23–26.

Cheliotis, L. K. (2012). Suffering at the hands of the state: Conditions of imprisonment and prisoner health in contemporary Greece. *European Journal of Criminology, 9,* 183–190.

Cooper, C., & Berwick, S. (2001). Factors affecting psychological well-being of three groups of suicide-prone prisoners. *Current Psychology, 20,* 169–182.

Corston, J. (2007). *The Corston report: A report by Baroness Jean Corston of a review of women with particular vulnerabilities in the criminal justice system.* London: Home Office.

Corston, J. (2011). *Women in the penal system: Second report on women with particular vulnerabilities in the criminal justice system.* London: The Howard League for Penal Reform.

Covington, S., & Bloom, B. (2008). *Gender-responsive treatment and services in correctional settings.* Available at: http://stephaniecovington.com/assets/files/FINALC.pdf. Accessed 16 Jan 2018.

Crawley, E., & Sparks, R. (2005). Surviving the prison experience? Imprisonment and the elderly men. *Prison Service Journal, 160,* 3–8.

Crewe, B. (2011). Depth, weight, tightness: Revisiting the pains of imprisonment. *Punishment and Society, 13,* 509–529.

Crewe, B., Hulley, S., & Wright, S. (2017). The gendered pains of life imprisonment. *British Journal of Criminology, 57,* 1359–1378.

Crewe, B., Warr, J., Bennett, P., & Smith, A. (2014). The emotional geography of prison life. *Theoretical Criminology, 18,* 56–74.

Cunniffe, C., Van de Kerckhove, R., Williams, K., & Hopkins, K. (2012). *Estimating the prevalence of disability amongst prisoners: Results from the surveying prisoner crime reduction (SPCR) survey.* London: Ministry of Justice.

DeHart, D. D. (2008). Pathways to prison: Impact of victimization in the lives of incarcerated women. *Violence Against Women, 14,* 1362–1381.

de Viggiani, N. (2007). Unhealthy prisons: Exploring structural determinants of prison health. *Sociology of Health & Illness, 29,* 115–135.

de Viggiani, N. (2012). Creating a healthy prison: Developing a system wide approach to public health within an English prison. *Prison Service Journal, 202,* 12–19.

DiMatteo, M., Lepper, H., & Croghan, T. (2000). Depression is a risk factor for noncompliance with medical treatment: Meta-analysis of the effects of anxiety and depression on patient adherence. *Archives of Internal Medicine, 160*, 2101–2107.

Dooris, M. (2009). Holistic and sustainable health improvement: The contribution of the settings-based approach to health promotion. *Perspectives in Public Health, 129*, 29–36.

Douglas, N., Plugge, E., & Fitzpatrick, R. (2009). The impact of imprisonment on health: What do women prisoners say? *Journal of Epidemiology and Community Health, 63*, 749–754.

Dunne, E. A., & Quayle, E. (2001). The impact of iatrogenically acquired Hepatitis C infection on the well-being and relationships of a group of Irish women. *Journal of Health Psychology, 6*, 679–692.

Fade, S. (2004). Using interpretative phenomenological analysis for public health nutrition and dietetic research: A practical guide. *The Proceedings of the Nutrition Society, 63*, 647–653.

Fazel, S., Hope, T., O'Donnell, I., Piper, M., & Jacoby, R. (2001). Health of elderly male prisoners: Worse than the general population, worse than younger prisoners. *Age and Ageing, 30*, 403–407.

Frater, A., & Tan, H. (2016). *Women in the criminal justice system in London: A health strategy—Recommendations for action*. London: London Health in Justice and Other Vulnerable Adults London Clinical Network (HiJOVA LCN).

Gelsthorpe, L. (2017). After Corston: Community, challenge and challenges. In L. Moore, P. Scraton, & A. Wahidin (Eds.), *Women's imprisonment and the case for abolition: Critical reflections on Corston ten years on* (pp. 31–50). London: Routledge.

Greer, C., & McLaughlin, E. (2013). The Sir Jimmy Savile scandal: Child sexual abuse and institutional denial at the BBC. *Crime, Media, Culture, 9*, 243–263.

Grupe, D. W., & Nitschke, J. B. (2013). Uncertainty and anticipation in anxiety. *Nature Reviews Neuroscience, 14*, 488–501.

Haualand, H. (2015). Punished and isolated: Disabled prisoners in Norway. *Scandinavian Journal of Disability Research, 17*, 74–87.

Hawton, K., Linsell, L., Adeniji, T., Sariaslan, A., & Fazel, S. (2014). Self-harm in prisons in England and Wales: An epidemiological study of prevalence, risk factors, clustering, and subsequent suicide. *Lancet, 383*, 1147–1154.

Hayton, P., & Boyington, J. (2006). Prisons and health reforms in England and Wales. *American Journal of Public Health, 96*, 1730–1733.

Hedderman, C., & Jolliffe, D. (2015). The impact of prison for women on the edge: Paying the price for wrong decisions. *Victims and Offenders, 10*, 152–178.

Hedderman, C., Palmer, E., & Hollin, C. (2008). *Implementing services for women offenders and those 'at risk' of offending: Action research with together women* (Ministry of Justice Research Series 12/08). London: Ministry of Justice.

Herbert, K., Plugge, E., Foster, C., & Doll, H. (2012). Prevalence of risk factors for non-communicable diseases in prison populations worldwide: A systematic review. *Lancet, 379*, 1975–1982.

HM Chief Inspector of Prisons (HMCIP). (1997). *Women in prison: A thematic review by HM chief inspector of prisons.* London: Home Office.

HM Chief Inspector of Prisons (HMCIP). (2009). *Disabled prisoners: A short thematic review on the care and support prisoners with a disability.* London: HM Inspectorate of Prisons.

HM Prison Service. (2003). *Prison service order 3200: Health promotion.* London: Ministry of Justice.

Hua-Fu, H. (2005). The patterns of masculinity in prison. *Critical Criminology, 13*, 1–16.

Irwin, J., & Cressey, D. R. (1962). Thieves, convicts and the inmate culture. *Social Problems, 10*, 142–155.

Jewkes, Y., & Moran, D. (2015). The paradox of the 'green' prison: Sustaining the environment or sustaining the penal complex? *Theoretical Criminology, 19*, 451–469.

Kelly, L. (2017). Suffering in silence: The unmet needs of d/Deaf prisoners. *Prison Service Journal, 234*, 3–15.

Kennedy, N. (2014). An interpretative phenomenological analysis of prisoners' experience of riotous behaviour in an adult male prison. *Journal of Forensic Practice, 16*, 203–215.

Kessler, R. C., Price, R. H., & Wortman, C. B. (1985). Social factors in psychopathology: Stress, social support, and coping processes. *Annual Review of Psychology, 36*, 531–572.

Kruttschnitt, C., & Gartner, R. (2005). *Marking time in the golden state: Women's imprisonment in California.* Cambridge: Cambridge University Press.

Levenson, J. (2002). *Prison overcrowding: The inside story.* London: Prison Reform Trust.

Liebling, A. (1992). *Suicides in prison.* London: Routledge.

Liebling, A. (2008). Incentives and earned privileges revisited: Fairness, discretion, and the quality of prison life. *Journal of Scandinavian Studies in Criminology and Crime Prevention, 9*, 25–41.

Lindemuth, A. L. (2007). Designing therapeutic environments for inmates and prison staff in the United States: Precedents and contemporary applications. *Journal of Mediterranean Ecology, 8*, 87–97.

Mann, N. (2016). Older age, harder time: Ageing and imprisonment. In Y. Jewkes, J. Bennett, & B. Crewe (Eds.), *Handbook on prisons* (2nd ed., pp. 514–528). London: Routledge.

Meek, R. (2007). The experiences of a young Gypsy-traveller in the transition from custody to community: An interpretative phenomenological analysis. *Legal and Criminological Psychology, 12,* 133–147.

Meek, R. (2008). Experiences of younger siblings of young men in prison. *Children and Society, 22,* 265–277.

Meek, R. (2014). *Sport in prison: Exploring the role of physical activity in correctional settings.* London: Routledge.

Meek, R., Champion, N., & Klier, S. (2012). *Fit for release: How sports-based learning can help prisoners engage in education, gain employment and desist from crime.* London: Prison Education Trust.

Meek, R., & Lewis, G. E. (2014). Promoting well-being and desistance through sport and physical activity: The opportunities and barriers experienced by women in English prisons. *Women and Criminal Justice, 24,* 151–172.

Ministry of Justice. (2013). *Gendered differences in substance misuse and mental health amongst prisoners: Results from Surveying Prisoner Crime Reduction (SPCR) longitudinal cohort study of prisoners.* London: Ministry of Justice. Available at: https://www.gov.uk/government/uploads/system/uploads/attachment_data/file/220060/gender-substance-misuse-mental-health-prisoners.pdf. Accessed 16 Jan 2018.

Ministry of Justice. (2016). *Prison safety and reform.* London: Ministry of Justice.

Ministry of Justice. (2017). *Safety in custody statistics bulletin, England and Wales. Deaths in prison custody to March 2017, assaults and self-harm to December 2016.* London: Ministry of Justice. Available at: https://www.gov.uk/government/uploads/system/uploads/attachment_data/file/611187/safety-in-custody-statistics-q4-2016.pdf. Accessed 16 Jan 2018.

Moore, L., Scraton, P., & Wahidin, A. (2017). Introduction. In L. Moore, P. Scraton, & A. Wahidin (Eds.), *Women's imprisonment and the case for abolition: Critical reflections on Corston ten years on* (pp. 1–9). London: Routledge.

Moussavi, S., Chatterji, S., Verdes, E., Tandon, A., Patel, V., & Ustun, B. (2007). Depression, chronic diseases, and decrements in health: Results from the World Health Surveys. *Lancet, 370,* 851–858.

National Offender Management Service. (2015). *Incentives and earned privileges, PSI 30/2013.* London: National Offender Management Service.

Parker, J., Kilroy, D., & Hirst, J. (2009). Women, health and prisons in Australia. In D. C. Hatton & A. A. Fisher (Eds.), *Women prisoners and health justice* (pp. 45–54). Abingdon: Radcliffe Publishing Ltd.

Penal Reform International. (2012). *United Nations rules in the treatment of women prisoners and non-custodial measures for women offenders* (The Bangkok Rules). Available at: https://www.penalreform.org/priorities/women-in-the-criminal-justice-system/bangkok-rules-2/. Accessed 16 Jan 2018.

Plugge, E., Douglas, N., & Fitzpatrick, R. (2006). *The health of women in prison: Study findings*. Oxford: Department of Public Health, University of Oxford.

Plugge, E., & Fitzpatrick, R. (2005). Assessing the health of women in prison: A study from the United Kingdom. *Health Care for Women International, 26,* 62–68.

Plugge, E., Yudkin, P., & Douglas, N. (2009). Changes in women's use of illicit drugs following imprisonment. *Addiction, 104,* 215–222.

Pollock, J. M. (1998). *Counselling women in prison*. Thousand Oaks, CA: Sage.

Pridgeon, L., & Grogan, S. (2012). Understanding exercise adherence and dropout: An interpretative phenomenological analysis of men and women's accounts of gym attendance and non-attendance. *Qualitative Research in Sport, Exercise and Health, 4,* 382–399.

Prison and Probation Ombudsman. (2013). *Learning lessons bulletin: Fatal incidents investigation issue 4*. London: Prison and Probation Ombudsman.

Prison Reform Trust. (2014). *Punishment without purpose: The Incentives and Earned Privileges (IEP) scheme and its impact on fairness, decency and rehabilitation behind bars*. London: Prison Reform Trust.

Rowe, A. (2011). Narratives of self and identity in women's prisons: Stigma and the struggle for self-definition in penal regimes. *Punishment and Society, 13,* 571–591.

Rowe, A. (2016). "Tactics", agency and power in women's prisons. *British Journal of Criminology, 56,* 332–349.

Sabo, D. F., Kupers, T. A., & London, W. J. (Eds.). (2001). *Prison masculinities*. Philadelphia, PA: Temple University Press.

Sheehan, R., McIvor, G., & Trotter, C. (2013). Women prisoners and their children. In R. Sheehan, G. McIvor, & C. Trotter (Eds.), *What works with women offenders* (pp. 214–239). London: Routledge.

Singleton, N., Bumpstead, R., O'Brien, M., Lee, A., & Meltzer, H. (2001). *Psychiatric morbidity among adults living in private households*. London: HMSO.

Singleton, N., Meltzer, H., & Gatward, R. (1998). *Psychiatric morbidity among prisoners in England and Wales*. London: Office for National Statistics.

Smith, C. (2000). 'Healthy prisons': A contradiction in terms? *The Howard Journal of Criminal Justice, 39,* 339–353.

Smith, J. A. (1996). Beyond the divide between cognition and discourse: Using interpretative phenomenological analysis in health psychology. *Psychology and Health, 11,* 261–271.

Smith, J. A. (2011). Evaluating the contribution of interpretative phenomenological analysis. *Health Psychology Review, 5,* 9–27.

Social Exclusion Unit. (2002). *Reducing reoffending by ex-prisoners*. London: Cabinet Office.

Steffensmeier, D., & Allen, E. (1998). The nature of female offending: Patterns and explanations. In R. Zaplin (Ed.), *Female offenders: Critical perspectives and effective interventions* (pp. 5–29). Gaithersburg, MD: Aspen Publishing.

Sykes, G. M. (1958). *The society of captives: A study of a maximum security prison*. Princeton, NJ: Princeton University Press.

Völlm, B. A., & Dolan, M. C. (2009). Self-harm among UK female prisoners: A cross-sectional study. *Journal of Forensic Psychiatry and Psychology, 20,* 741–751.

Ward, D. A., & Kassebaum, G. G. (1965). *Women's prison: Sex and social structure*. New Brunswick, NJ: Transaction Publishers.

Willmott, D. (2009). Advocacy. In D. C. Hatton & A. A. Fisher (Eds.), *Women prisoners and health justice* (pp. 117–126). Abingdon: Radcliffe Publishing Ltd.

Wingood, G. M., DiClemente, R. J., & Raj, A. (2000). Adverse consequences of intimate partner abuse among women in non-urban domestic violence shelters. *American Journal of Preventive Medicine, 19,* 270–275.

Women in Prison. (2017). *The Corston report 10 years on: How far have we come on the road to reform for women affected by the criminal justice system?* London: Women in Prison.

Woodall, J. (2012). Health promoting prisons: An overview and critique of the concept. *Prison Service Journal, 202,* 6–12.

Woodall, J. (2016). A critical examination of the health promoting prison two decades on. *Critical Public Health, 26,* 615–621.

Woodall, J., Dixey, R., & South, J. (2014). Control and choice in English prisons: Developing health-promoting prisons. *Health Promotion International, 29,* 474–482.

World Health Organization. (1998). *Report of the third meeting of the European health in prisons project*. Geneva: World Health Organisation.

Part III

Dividing Practices: Structural Violence,
Mental Health and Imprisonment

8

Institutions of Default and Management: Aboriginal Women with Mental and Cognitive Disability in Prison

Ruth McCausland, Elizabeth McEntyre and Eileen Baldry

Introduction

Aboriginal and Torres Strait Islander women are grossly over-represented in Australian prisons, making up 2% of the Australian women's population but around a third of all women in prison. Indigenous women in custody experience poorer mental health, with common collateral histories of violence, abuse and trauma. Yet, there is a dearth of empirical research on the perspectives and needs of Indigenous women detained in custody, in particular those with multiple diagnoses and disability, which our research seeks to address. The research reported in this chapter was part of a larger Australian

R. McCausland (✉) · E. McEntyre · E. Baldry
University of New South Wales, Sydney, Australia
e-mail: ruth.mccausland@unsw.edu.au

E. McEntyre
e-mail: e.mcentyre@unsw.edu.au

E. Baldry
e-mail: e.baldry@unsw.edu.au

© The Author(s) 2018
A. Mills and K. Kendall (eds.), *Mental Health in Prisons*, Palgrave Studies in Prisons and Penology, https://doi.org/10.1007/978-3-319-94090-8_8

Research Council grant on Indigenous Australians with mental and cognitive disability in the criminal justice system (IAMHDCD Project). This particular aspect of the study explored for the first time the lived realities of Australian Aboriginal women with mental and cognitive disability who are involved in criminal justice systems in New South Wales (NSW) and the Northern Territory. This chapter first sets out the available data on Indigenous[1] women imprisoned in Australia. It then details the critical research framework engaged for our study, drawing on Indigenous, feminist, disability and criminology studies. We then report on our quantitative and qualitative research focusing on Aboriginal women with mental and cognitive disability,[2] which found that Aboriginal women are significantly more disadvantaged, with greater complex support needs and ongoing criminal justice involvement, than either non-Aboriginal women or non-Aboriginal and Aboriginal men. Aboriginal women face structural disadvantage and discrimination, becoming entrenched in a cycle of imprisonment by the absence of coherent frameworks for holistic supports in the community. We conclude that prisons will remain the response without Aboriginal community-based culture, disability- and gender-centred policy and practice, a trauma-specific approach and integrated services in the community for Aboriginal girls and women with mental and cognitive disability.

Aboriginal and Torres Strait Islander Women in Prison

Aboriginal and Torres Strait Islander women are imprisoned at 21 times the rate of non-Indigenous women (Australian Bureau of Statistics [ABS] 2016). Although Indigenous Australian men and Indigenous young people are also grossly over-incarcerated, from 2000 to 2016, the Indigenous women's imprisonment rate increased at more than double the rate of Indigenous men (Productivity Commission 2016). Indigenous women enter the justice system at an earlier age and are almost twice as likely to return to prison after release compared to non-Indigenous women (ABS 2016). Indigenous girls and young women on average make up more than half of the female youth detention population in Australia, and are nearly 20 times more likely to be incarcerated than their non-Indigenous counterparts (Australian Institute of Health and Welfare 2017).

While available Australian data on the offending patterns of Indigenous women are limited and inconsistent, it appears that Indigenous women are most commonly prosecuted for driving and traffic offences, assault, theft and offences against justice procedures (such as breach of community orders or bail conditions) (MacGillivray and Baldry 2015). Studies have indicated that Indigenous women are far more likely to be sentenced to imprisonment than non-Indigenous women across a range of offences (McCausland 2014), and that Indigenous women generally serve shorter sentences than their non-Indigenous counterparts, suggesting that they are being imprisoned for more trivial offences (Bartels 2012). Indigenous women serving short sentences have their family responsibilities and housing arrangements disrupted, often with devastating consequences, but are not in custody long enough to access counselling, therapeutic treatment or rehabilitative courses (McCausland 2014).

Indigenous women in custody experience particularly poor mental health, with common histories of multiple traumatic events (Heffernan et al. 2015; Baldry and McEntyre 2011; Indig et al. 2009). The majority of Indigenous women in prison have experienced sexual assault, domestic and family violence, and post-traumatic stress disorder, and their needs are poorly understood and not supported either in the community or in prison (Heffernan et al. 2015; Baldry and McEntyre 2011; Lawrie 2003). The therapeutic needs of Indigenous women are significantly different from non-Indigenous women, as the trauma resulting from ongoing colonisation and living each day in the colonial realm and routine must be understood and addressed (Atkinson 2002; Sherwood 2009). Despite this, system and agency responses are often poorly integrated and inappropriate, resulting in inadequate service and support across the life course for Indigenous women (Baldry et al. 2015; Baldry and McEntyre 2011; Aboriginal and Torres Strait Islander Social Justice Commissioner 2002, 2004, 2008).

Although Indigenous Australian women are the fastest growing group in custody, they make up a relatively small proportion of the overall prison population in Australia (Productivity Commission 2016). Compounded by institutional racism and sexism and poor understanding of mental and cognitive disability, this manifests as scant attention paid to the perspectives, distinct pathways and unmet needs of Indigenous women in Australian state and territory criminal justice systems who are mentally unwell and with lower cognitive functioning. This chapter aims to respond to this by reporting on innovative qualitative and quantitative research on the specific experiences and needs of Indigenous women with mental and cognitive disability in NSW. This research is a nested study in a larger research project—*Indigenous Australians with Mental Health Disorders and Cognitive Disability in the Criminal Justice System* (IAMHDCD Project) funded by the Australian Research Council and completed in 2016. The IAMHDCD Project used data gathered in a previous ARC project (People with Mental Health Disorder and Cognitive Disability in the Criminal Justice System—MHDCD Project) that analysed life course data from all criminal justice and human service agencies in NSW on 2731 persons who had been in prison in NSW. Twenty-five per cent of this cohort was Indigenous Australian. It also partnered with four Indigenous Australian communities (three in NSW and one in the Northern Territory) to explore how Indigenous Australians with mental and cognitive disability and their family, community and service supporters experienced criminal justice involvement and what their suggestions were to prevent criminalisation as well as improve support (see Baldry et al. 2015 for the full report of this project).

Critical Framework

The methodology and analysis of the qualitative and quantitative research reported in this article were developed as part of the IAMHDCD Project and are informed by critical Indigenous, feminist, disability and criminology studies (Baldry et al. 2015). A critical perspective offers a structural lens on the complex interactions of individual, social and systemic factors and compounding disadvantages that operate to make prisons the institutions of default for disadvantaged Indigenous women and men with mental health disorders and cognitive disabilities. This meant establishing mutual and respectful partnerships with Indigenous peoples and communities; recognising their self-determining ownership and control of their knowledges; and understanding that disability is constructed and maintained by society's attitudes to and structural arrangements affecting persons with an impairment: that is, that social and structural arrangements disable. The IAMHDCD Project provided a touchstone for the protocols and practices used in this nested study. Its objectives were to develop an Indigenous-informed perspective on the nature and meaning of 'disability' and 'offending' and the identification, assessment, diagnosis and treatment of mental health disorders and cognitive disability amongst Indigenous people in Australian criminal justice systems.

Critical Indigenous theorists such as Rigney (1999), Tuhiwai Smith (2012), Sherwood (2010) and Moreton-Robinson (2014) have detailed the great harm that has been caused as a result of research that is done 'on' or 'to' or 'for' Indigenous communities rather than 'with' Indigenous people and 'with' Indigenous communities. Indigenous academics have led the critique of colonising methodologies and practices in research, challenging academics to produce research that is 'more respectful, ethical, sympathetic and useful' (Tuhiwai Smith 2012) in relation to Indigenous peoples. Privileging the worldviews, contexts and voices of Indigenous individuals, organisations and communities was a primary consideration in conducting this research, given the ongoing complexity of trauma, marginalisation and disadvantage experienced by Indigenous women and men as a result of colonisation (Baldry and Cunneen 2014; Rowe et al. 2015). Indigenous critical feminist scholarship provides a particularly prescient lens on the disproportionately high levels of violence experienced by Indigenous women and children (Davis and McGlade 2006; Payne 1992; Atkinson 1990), in particular those with mental and cognitive disability. The research methodology employed here set out to be decolonising, empowering for the Aboriginal women, families and communities who participated, and Indigenist, embodied with cultural and professional integrity (McEntyre, forthcoming; Baldry et al. 2015).

Since the 1980s, an 'intersectionality' analysis emerging from critical race and feminist scholarship has been influential, in particular, Kimberlé Crenshaw's framing of the term which has been interpreted, applied and expanded across disciplines and often employed primarily as a critique of identity-based essentialism (Crenshaw 1989, 1991 cited in Ribet 2011). Critical race theorists have challenged notions of biological inferiority underpinning social and legal discrimination against people of colour, and identified the structural and more subtle forms of racism that maintain the subordination of non-white persons (Delgado 1995). Critical feminist theorists who highlighted the gendered nature of politics and policy-making and the particular human rights issues facing women have been criticised for not sufficiently understanding or incorporating the experience of non-white women, and Indigenous women in particular (Moreton-Robinson 2000). In Crenshaw's words, 'black women are marginalized in feminist politics as a consequence of race, and they are marginalized in antiracist politics as a consequence of gender' (Crenshaw 1991, p. 1243); when feminism does not explicitly oppose racism, and antiracism does not explicitly oppose patriarchy, 'race and gender politics often end up being antagonistic to each other and both interests lose' (Crenshaw 1991, p. 1243). In particular, Crenshaw's critical analysis contends that the consequence of intersectional vulnerability results in the specific persecution of identity groups who are experiencing compounded and intersectional subordination (Crenshaw 1989, 1991 cited in Ribet 2011).

Embedded in our research is a social conceptualisation of disability. Here, the distinction is drawn between 'impairment' as a condition of the individual body or mind (such as experiencing psychosis, intellectual disability or brain injury) and 'disability' as the social experience flowing from the presence of impairment, including the range of barriers to full participation that exist in a society (Oliver and Barnes 1998; Baldry 2014). Critical disability studies has built on the social approach to understanding disability by bringing a closer examination of the dynamic interaction of social, political, cultural and economic factors to the analysis, and by exploring the ways that they define disability and shape personal and collective responses to difference. Critical disability studies also, most importantly, problematises the relegation of impairment to the domain of the medical, rehabilitative, private and personal and questions its dislocation from the social (Dowse et al. 2009, p. 38). Similarly, the critical criminological approach locates and understands the reasons for crime within wider structural and institutional contexts, with crime and social responses to it seen as deeply political and cultural matters. These contexts may be conceived of in various ways, including socioeconomic, class-based, cultural, racialised and gendered forms (Baldry 2014).

These theoretical and standpoint positions necessitate a more nuanced approach than any one of them alone provides. By merging their insights, we arrived at a hybrid critical theoretical position of cumulative and compounding disability and disadvantage (Baldry and Dowse 2013). Intersectionality by itself does not explain the effects we see in our data of the negative synergistic effects of multiple and often coinciding events and factors that create more than the sum of these parts (Baldry 2017). This is not just intersection but coalescing accumulations that compound to create vicious cycles of complex support needs. The term 'needs' (a perfectly respectable term to denote aspects or resources that are lacking and needed by a person or a community to improve their lives) has unfortunately been hijacked by the language and practice of criminal justice risk management (Cunneen et al. 2013). 'Risk-needs' in criminal justice contexts, for women, as Hannah-Moffat (2015) argues, often conflates risks with needs, because holistic structural and contextual circumstances are not taken into account. This can disadvantage women by characterising them as high risk, and as individually to blame for their 'needs'. We reclaim the term 'need' as it is the appropriate word to denote something essential (for example, people need clean water), in this case, the need for support. 'Complex support needs' in our studies is not related to criminogenic risks-needs and is structurally and contextually framed. These complex support needs (multiple compounded disabilities and disadvantages) are created by government agencies and other organisations not providing early appropriate disability and social support (as it is for more advantaged families and communities), disadvantaging the person and family. Such support would afford a socially disadvantaged child or adult and their family and community appropriate access to social resources via more equitable structural arrangements.

We next report the quantitative findings of the MHDCD Dataset that reveal the significantly earlier and more frequent levels of contact with criminal justice agencies and the more complex support needs experienced by Indigenous women compared with non-Indigenous women in the MHDCD cohort.

Quantitative Findings

This section reports on quantitative findings of the MHDCD Dataset which provided unique and unprecedented insights into the pathways and experiences of people with mental and cognitive disability who have been incarcerated (Baldry 2009; Baldry et al. 2012, 2013, 2015). The MHDCD Dataset contains lifelong administrative information from criminal justice and human service agencies on a cohort of 2731 persons who have been in prison in the Australian state of NSW, and whose mental and cognitive disability diagnoses are known. There are 93 Aboriginal and Torres Strait Islander women in the MHDCD Dataset who make up 3% of the overall cohort, 14% of the Indigenous sub-cohort and 31% of the female sub-cohort (Baldry et al. 2015). Analysis undertaken of the MHDCD Dataset reveals the particular vulnerability and disadvantage faced by Indigenous women in the cohort.

The MHDCD cohort is a purposive rather than a representative sample, intentionally focusing on those individuals with diagnosed mental health disorder and cognitive disability diagnoses who have been in prison. The MHDCD Dataset was established using a confirmed cohort of interest compiled into a relational database using MS SQL server 2008, a relational data management and analysis program. Data were drawn from Police, Corrections, Justice Health, Courts, Juvenile Justice, Legal Aid, Disability, Housing, Health and Community Services on each individual from as far back as each agency's electronic records allow (generally from around the mid-1980s) up to the date of data extraction between 2008 and 2012. These data were linked to allow detailed description and analysis of the life pathways by which people with diagnoses of mental health disorders and cognitive disability enter, move through, exit and return to the NSW criminal justice system and an understanding of the interactions between justice and human service agencies (Baldry et al. 2013).

A range of comparative analyses on the MHDCD Dataset were conducted to investigate the differences on the basis of Indigenous status and gender within the cohort. Adjusted odds ratio tests were used to reveal the likelihood that a particular outcome will occur for any group given a particular exposure, compared to the odds of the outcome occurring in the absence of that exposure. T-tests are used to compare the differences in the averages of events or occurrences in each group. For further details, see Baldry et al. (2015).

Presented below are key selected results that highlight significant findings in relation to the Indigenous and non-Indigenous women in the MHDCD Dataset. The averages in the findings below are skewed upwards by members of the cohort who did not have contact with the criminal justice system until adulthood some in mid-life, usually in connection with the onset of acute mental health issues.

> **Out of home care**
>
> Indigenous females are 3.7 times more likely than their non-Indigenous peers to have been in out of home care as a child (such as foster care, kinship care or a group home).

> **Contact with Police**
>
> Indigenous women have:
> - a significantly lower age of first police contact than non-Indigenous women: 16.4 vs. 20.5 years
> - a significantly higher number of police contacts per year than non-Indigenous women: 6.2 vs. 4.7
> - a significantly higher number of police contacts as a victim over their lifetimes than non-Indigenous women: 23 vs. 16.1
> - a significantly lower age of first police custody than non-Indigenous women: 23.8 vs. 28.3 years

Convictions

Indigenous women have:
- a significantly lower age of first conviction than their non-Indigenous counterparts: 18.4 vs. 22.4 years
- a significantly higher number of convictions than their non-Indigenous counterparts: 23 vs. 15.2
- a significantly higher rate of convictions per year than their non-Indigenous counterparts: 3.2 vs. 1.7

Juvenile Justice

Indigenous women are:
- 2.9 times more likely to be clients of juvenile justice compared to their non-Indigenous counterparts
- 3.2 times more likely to be in juvenile justice custody compared to their non-Indigenous counterparts

Adult Corrections

Indigenous women have:
- a significantly higher number of adult corrections custody counts than their non-Indigenous counterparts: 10.2 vs. 6.4
- a significantly higher rate of adult corrections custody per year than their non-Indigenous counterparts: 1.7 vs. 1.3

Remand

Indigenous women have significantly more remand episodes compared to their non-Indigenous counterparts: 8.5 vs. 5.4

Homelessness

Indigenous women are 2.2 times more likely to have been homeless at some point in life compared to their non-Indigenous counterparts.

These findings demonstrate the significantly earlier contact Indigenous women have with all aspects of the criminal justice system compared with non-Indigenous women, and highlight the multiple negative and disadvantageous events and factors that enmesh Indigenous women with mental and cognitive disabilities in criminal justice management. The following section draws on the qualitative aspects of the study to provide a depth of understanding to the quantitative findings.

Qualitative Findings

This qualitative research was premised on the principles of respecting Indigenous knowledge systems and processes; recognising the diversity and uniqueness of people as individuals; preserving the intellectual and cultural physical and knowledge property rights of Indigenous peoples and communities; and involving Indigenous researchers, individuals, organisations and communities in research as primary collaborators (Baldry et al. 2015). The approach undertaken involved five phases: engaging with and consulting key stakeholders in this Indigenous-informed research process; establishing Indigenous community research partnerships; data collection in communities; analysis, verification and validation of findings with communities; and development of education and advocacy resources for and reporting back to communities. The lived experiences of Indigenous women were the explicit focus of this strand of the IAMHDCD Project, and Aboriginal women's voices and knowledge were privileged (McEntyre, forthcoming).

The second author of this chapter, Aboriginal woman Elizabeth McEntyre, a mental health social worker and Ph.D. researcher who has worked for many years with Aboriginal women in custody, led the qualitative interviewing. The incarcerated Aboriginal women with disability, who willingly participated in the study, were imprisoned in the Silverwater Women's Correctional Centre in metropolitan Sydney, NSW and in the Alice Springs Correctional Centre in the Northern Territory. Most of the women in NSW prisons were segregated in the Mental Health Screening Unit (MHSU), Mental Health Step-Down Unit and the Mum Shirl Unit for those with severe personality disorders. Those who were interviewed were recruited by snowball sampling with Elders and community members telling the women about the study. The approach used to enable the 21 Aboriginal women participants to share their rich information was responsive to their needs and wishes. The researcher engaged various interviewing methods to gain a clear perspective of the women's lives as they saw them. Her level of engagement with the women, interviewing style, reactions to responses, use of appropriate humour and support and suggestions, when asked for them, were grounded in the researcher's experiences in the short time that she had spent with each woman, whether she was a prisoner, a parolee, on bail awaiting a court hearing, or a mother living in the community, all the while ensuring that she was being culturally and gender responsive (McEntyre, forthcoming).

More than 80% (17) of the Aboriginal women interviewed had served prison sentences during their lives; the four women who had not done prison time had been diverted into alcohol treatment, given a suspended sentence or were on bail awaiting court hearings.

The following section sets out two key themes emerging from the qualitative interviews with Aboriginal women with mental and cognitive disability regarding their perspectives and pathways into the criminal justice system. These two themes—structural violence and complex trauma, and prisons as default institutions for Indigenous women with disability—capture the key and underlying structural and contextual frameworks the women experienced and that, along with associated factors like colonial patriarchy and institutional racism, drove their criminal justice involvement.

Structural Violence and Complex Trauma

Sexual and physical violence and multiple traumatic events emerged as common and pervasive experiences for Aboriginal women with mental and cognitive disability in custody. Institutional racism and sexism were reported as factors contributing to Aboriginal women's over-representation in prison, with disability compounding this, although it was less recognised by the women themselves. Aboriginal girls with mental and cognitive disability were described as at particular risk of violence and victimisation from a young age. Community services were perceived as only becoming engaged in the lives of many Aboriginal girls and young women in the context of removal from family, not in terms of preventative or proactive support earlier in their lives. For these women, authority and agency, over their lives from the time they were young girls until adulthood, were described as dominated by the might and strength of members of their families, intimate partners, human services staff including those in mental health and disability and criminal justice agencies.

One Aboriginal women interviewed described how the 'revolving doors of prison life' began for her:

> My first partner drank heavily and would beat me senseless in front of my two beautiful boys. In [year] I had my first emotional breakdown and didn't want to live anymore. I was admitted to hospital and stayed there for two weeks. During my time at the hospital my partner went to court and gained custody of the two boys. He told me this after I was released and my world fell apart...my heart was broken but I had to leave the domestic violence relationship and my two beautiful boys before my partner killed me or I committed suicide... I turned to drugs and alcohol to dull the pain and went totally off the rails...

The majority of the women interviewed had serious unmet mental health support needs. One woman who was in the MHSU explained how she had been 'hearing voices in her head'. Another woman in the MHSU recounted how she had to deal with her post-traumatic stress disorder and complex trauma in virtual isolation. Three Aboriginal women stated that they had not received adequate treatment and care from mental health professionals and services when on the outside.

One woman in her early forties, a mother and grandmother, had lived with an acquired brain injury since she was 16 years old, but it had only been diagnosed whilst in custody after her first conviction around the age of 30. At the time of the interview, she had been on remand for more than 12 months in the MHSU with no instruction given by mental health professionals to detain her in this prison for medical reasons. She did not know why she was still in custody. A treating psychiatrist had wanted her to be transferred to the specialist forensic hospital whilst the NSW Mental Health Review Tribunal had suggested that she be detained at either there or another specialist mental health hospital in Sydney or remain a prisoner at the women's correctional facility. As a result, she was confused and concerned that no one knew what to do with her and there was no plan for her care.

This woman was being looked after by another Aboriginal woman in custody, also a mother and grandmother, aged in her early fifties who was doing a second prison term for 'acting out anger'. This woman explained that she had been diagnosed with post-traumatic stress disorder (PTSD), clinical depression and anxiety. The complex trauma experienced from her violent and abusive relationships with various men had added to her mental health issues. From the age of 17 years, she had been beaten 'senselessly', lost her children from her care to two violent partners, and self-medicated with alcohol and other drugs to 'dull the pain'. While in prison, however, she had spent no more than a few minutes in a therapy session with a correctional psychologist who just 'didn't get it'. She elaborated how the 'harsh reality of prison life' had made things harder for her while inside. This included being locked in the cells for hours by 'turn-keys' who did nothing more than open and close gates and doors and who would just 'rev you up to go off more'.

> I became angry with the world and wanted to die to end my misery once and for all...then the revolving doors of prison life began in 2012 until 2014...the justice system is by the books, they read the black and white print of law books and there are no shades of grey... I know I broke the law, but I was broken also... I believe I have lashed out in sheer frustration. Being misunderstood as aggressive and angry when I am sad and lonely...with being incarcerated under the Mental Health hold, you can be locked in the cell until the corrective service officers believe you are fit to be let out of the cell... Just another punishment making the time in prison more fearful...we are punished by our partner, police, the courts and then the corrective service officers – a quadruple dose of punishment.

This quote exemplifies how prison compounds the experience of violence and trauma for Aboriginal women with mental health issues. Another interviewee articulated how the way women with mental and cognitive disability cycling in and out of the prison system are perceived and treated by correctional officers contributes to this:

> Oh, they're [the women] just pieces of human garbage. You can see the look on their [the officers] faces sometimes, the look of superiority. You can't even – most of them are just – most of them are just so caught up in the system themselves, so much a part of the system that they don't even know what they're doing.

One woman with a cognitive disability in the mental health screening unit had been in custody more than ten times. A lack of appropriate and targeted support in prison for Aboriginal women with multiple and complex support needs was identified by many of the interviewees, particularly for the vast majority who are incarcerated for short sentences or on remand:

> There aren't enough people – qualified people – to look after people inside [prison], particularly the women. They get neglected, they get hardly anything – don't get rehab programs because they are in for very short periods of time. So it's a revolving door for the women.

The women's narratives draw out the negative, violent and harmful traumatic experiences Aboriginal women with mental and cognitive disability have had in their lives and how criminal justice agencies add to those experiences. They highlight that prison is not an appropriate place for women with disability and reveal how they experience the revolving door of criminal justice involvement with no relevant support or respect.

Prisons as Default Management Institutions for Aboriginal Women with Mental and Cognitive Disability

For the majority of Aboriginal women with mental and cognitive disability, coming from families and communities with few resources and intergenerational challenges around trauma, disability and incarceration, entry into the criminal justice system has become a common trajectory. Incarceration was reported to be the default for

Aboriginal women with multiple and complex support needs who are perceived to be 'unhelpable', as one woman described it. One participant in her early forties stated: 'prison is now my home'. The majority of women interviewed were not able to access the right kind of assistance needed to prevent their entry and re-entry to prison. The reasons for this inaccessibility were varied but linked. Women primarily had no access to culturally sound and holistic support services to deal with their determined needs due to a lack of support and care coordination between services on the outside. This segmentation of women's lives—instead of centring on the whole woman and providing integrated assistance—led to women being told to 'fit in' to whatever services or support were available. As a consequence, some women were overwhelmed and exposed to further risk of damage and incarceration.

> There is nothing [service] on the outside. I was told what is available and to fit in. I've done it all but it gets me nowhere. It's overwhelming [so I] crash and burn.

One Aboriginal woman who had been diagnosed with borderline personality disorder (which we note has been critiqued as pathologising, individualising and blaming of the ways some women respond to gendered violence, especially to child sexual abuse [Shaw and Proctor 2005]) prior to prison had on two occasions accessed community mental health services but found the psychologists she had seen 'didn't really do anything'. She felt that if she had received appropriate support services to help her deal with her mental illness, this support most likely would have prevented her from turning to drugs as a way to self-medicate and control her mind. During her childhood, she had been sexually abused and had received no therapeutic support to alleviate the trauma she had carried over decades. Moreover, she had been repeatedly 'bashed' over the course of 14 years by her male partner with her sight and hearing impaired and under these circumstances likely acquired a brain injury.

Another Aboriginal woman who had accessed metropolitan community mental health services for a 'shot and a yarn' was not even sure who she had spoken with at the community centre or who had given her the injectable medication. Another woman explained how she did not get the help she needed from community mental health professionals despite being acutely unwell:

> I ended up in [a mental health acute unit in a regional hospital]... I didn't remember a thing. I was psychotic. I'd been trying to get help in the community for four months through a clinic in [a regional centre of NSW], a mental health clinic, and they kept changing my medication every couple of days. That wasn't helping... So mum pleaded with the court for three hours to put me in [the mental health acute unit]. So they did and then that's when they diagnosed me with my mental illnesses. Then I just went from there. I started spiralling down once I hit the system.

For one Aboriginal woman with mental health issues, living in a NSW remote town on bail and awaiting a second court hearing, the stress of having contact with police, attending court and a possible prison sentence had compounded her mental ill-health. She had received no treatment from the local community mental health service that was located some distance from the town. The situation was similar for a woman who was living in a regional town and waiting to attend court for a second time. Although she had anxiety, stress, panic attacks and a fear of being around strange people, she had received no mental health care from local mental health services.

Aboriginal women interviewed identified appropriate housing and safe accommodation to be one of their greatest needs. The women explained that without a stable address, they had no independence or security, could not get their children back, had limited chance of gaining employment, were unable to access early intervention services and were more likely to have contact with criminal justice agencies. This highlights the way that structural factors compound to criminalise Aboriginal women with mental and cognitive disability. The comment: 'Once I lost my home, I lost it all' from one young woman in prison in NSW, described the impact of the loss of social housing while she was imprisoned for a short period. She then found it too difficult to access even temporary accommodation after release from prison. She articulated that housing had been one of the main things she had needed to help turn her life around from amphetamine use, implying that she might otherwise not have been incarcerated eight times during the past five years and lost the care of her three young children if she had been appropriately housed and supported. A compounding factor for this woman (and a common experience for many Aboriginal women in prison) was that she had been in the care of the state from the age of ten.

The negative impact of a lack of specialist, culturally responsive, therapeutic community-based support for all Indigenous people with mental and cognitive disabilities is compounded for Indigenous women. Women highlighted distinct issues facing them such as the lack of police responsiveness to domestic violence, access to Aboriginal Legal Services, and gender-specific diversionary programmes and post-release support.

Once in custody, a number of the women interviewed had significant concerns about the treatment of those with serious mental illness, illustrating how prison has become the damaging default institution of management for many Aboriginal women. One woman reported:

> I'll start with one [woman] specifically at Mulawa [previous name of Silverwater Women's Correctional Centre] in the segro [segregation] unit. I hated that there's women that had significant mental disorders, mental illnesses that were held in the segregation unit at Mulawa, self-harm issues, schizophrenia. It was devastating because they were locked away 23 hours out of 24 hours. You could hear their pain; literally hear their pain, their screams, their wailing. They were locked in a cell and the only way that Corrective Services, that I could see, that they were managing these women, was to put a helmet on them so they couldn't smash their heads up, to have them on heaps and heaps of medication so they were docile and take their clothes off them, which was to minimise the risk. Dehumanise them.

The majority of Aboriginal women interviewees who commented on the health care they had received in prison saw it as another form of control and were critical of some medications given to them, including methadone. One woman who had been on methadone since she was 15 years old explained how methadone was 'worse than hanging out for heroin'.

This same woman commented that although she was given a 'welcome back kiss' of anti-psychotic medication on her first day of returning to prison, the health service would not do anything further to help her get off the drugs. One woman with a cognitive disability summed up her experiences of prison health care services: 'we take a pill and you get tired, we take a pill and feel a bit better'.

Another woman described the way her experience of health care in custody had been life threatening:

> When I first went to jail I was 28. It was a bit of a scary thought… I went down to Mulawa, one of the bigger jails in Sydney, straight away because of my mental illnesses. When I got there, I was thrown in what they call a safe cell and I was left alone to my own devices. I was in a white suit. If I needed to go to the toilet, I had to buzz up. They'd come give me toilet paper. They never come near you unless they fed you. I was unmedicated [sic] for four days. I was suicidal. No attendance from any psych or anything like that. Then one day, I had to do something because I knew I was slipping between the cracks again, so I threatened to kill myself. They got a psych down. They assessed me. They got me back on my medication and then I was sent to a normal wing. I think that was the scariest part because I knew I was at the point where I could have broken myself.

This woman's narrative highlights the complete inappropriateness of prison (as seen in the previous section) for women with mental disability and of the way in which prison was clearly being used as a management tool for Aboriginal women. She also explained how it was not until her third prison sentence and longest time in custody that she was given the 'right medications'. She also reflected on her experiences as evidence that medications were being used by the system so that women could be more easily 'managed'.

> They don't mind handing the pills out once you're in the system. They like to give you medication to make you easier to be managed…they'll put you on psych pills to dope you up, which I don't agree with.

This woman's account highlights the common experience that the women are not well supported by mental health services in the community so they cycle back to prison where they may or may not receive helpful mental health care and then they are released with the cycle continuing. The women reported very little information sharing between correctional and community health care providers, which was perceived as contributing to prisons as the default option for Aboriginal women with mental and cognitive disability. Close to half of the Aboriginal women interviewed were living serially in prison, which, as Baldry and Cunneen (2014) argue, is one of the means by which colonial patriarchy continues in Australia.

Discussion

These research findings illuminate the structural disadvantage and discrimination facing Indigenous women with mental and cognitive disability, and the ways that pathways to prison become entrenched by the absence of coherent frameworks for holistic supports in the community. Drawing on critical Indigenous, feminist, disability and criminology perspectives, it is apparent that Aboriginal women with mental and cognitive disability are being serially incarcerated and 'managed' in prison in the absence of specific attention to and value placed on their lives. Aboriginal women's exposure to multiple instances of victimisation, violence and trauma over their life-course, or complex trauma (Gregorowski and Seedat 2013; Stathopoulos and Quadara 2014), has left them with little sense of safety and stability. The imposition of power and control by others has stripped Aboriginal women with mental and cognitive disability in custody of their self-determination, self-respect and self-worth. It limits their agency and capacity to make decisions about their lives, to address their mothering responsibilities, to have a home and exercise choice over where to live, to find employment, and to establish security around relationships with family; it also affects their ability to access places and people who could provide appropriate support when and where needed. Their multiple and complex support needs are created by systems and structures that fail to respond to the specific and distinct needs of Aboriginal women with mental and cognitive disability, leaving prison as the default.

While those in the MHDCD cohort are significantly more disadvantaged than the general community, Indigenous women are the most disadvantaged group in the cohort in terms of their multiple and complex support needs—they are more likely to have multiple disabilities and health problems than non-Indigenous women or Indigenous and non-Indigenous men (Baldry et al. 2015). They were 3.7 times more likely to have been in out-of-home-care than non-Indigenous women. They have earlier and more regular contact with police and significantly higher numbers of police convictions. Indigenous women in the cohort were more likely than non-Indigenous women to have been in custody as children, and had significantly more remand and custody episodes as adults. Histories of violence and abuse and ongoing trauma are common experiences for Indigenous women with mental and cognitive disabilities, as demonstrated by our qualitative and quantitative data. Indigenous women were 2.2 times more likely than non-Indigenous women to be homeless at some point in their life.

The dehumanisation, restraint and violence experienced by Aboriginal women with mental and cognitive disability in custody compounds their trauma and entrenchment in the criminal justice system. Episodes of incarceration had not prevented the women from returning to prison. Their complex trauma experiences had been ignored and the implication is that for many women, the control and management exerted by prison becomes a normal way of life, similar to their traumatic lives outside prison, which does not prepare them for a better life which they can determine for themselves outside the abnormal criminal justice system.

Keeping Aboriginal Women with Mental and Cognitive Disability Out of Criminal Justice Systems

Aboriginal and Torres Strait Islander girls and women with mental and cognitive disability must be supported and empowered from early in life to develop new life pathways of their choosing. Based on the findings detailed here and related research (Baldry et al. 2015), we have distilled a number of principles that could underpin policy and practice and forge genuine preventive approaches as well as alternatives to prison. As children and young people, they should be supported by empowering, culturally framed decisions enabling options for them and their family in the community that would assist in preventing their involvement with criminal justice in the first place. This support may prevent children and young people from being subject to abuse and violence and ensure appropriate educational pathways and culturally rich safe community contexts. In the event of criminal justice involvement, self-determination is key to improving access to and exercise of human rights and to the well-being of Indigenous women with disabilities who have been subjected to structural violence, control and serial incarceration. In turn, regular professional and cultural supervision is needed for frontline workers to limit the real risk of professional burnout, secondary traumatic stress or injury from vicarious trauma. Specific violence prevention and intervention programmes, as well as crisis, pragmatic and cultural support in Indigenous communities are also crucial. Coherent frameworks for holistic supports that are built around the specific and distinct experiences and needs of Indigenous girls and women with disability are needed to ensure that prisons are not the default response to their experiences of structural violence, disadvantage and exclusion. Aboriginal community-based culture, disability- and gender-centred policy and practice, a trauma-specific approach and integrated services in the community are key components of such a framework. These are vital to preventive approaches which provide ample support and appropriate care for Aboriginal and Torres Strait Islander girls and women with mental and cognitive disabilities.

Notes

1. The term 'Indigenous' denotes Aboriginal and Torres Strait Islander persons.
2. In this chapter, we use the NSW Law Reform Commission definitions of mental and cognitive disability: 'Mental disability' refers to a temporary or continuing impairment of emotional well-being, judgement or

behaviour so as to affect functioning in daily life to a material extent and includes psychoses, anxiety and depression. 'Cognitive disability' is used to refer to a permanent impairment in comprehension, reason, adaptive functioning, learning or memory and includes intellectual disability, learning disability, borderline intellectual disability, acquired brain injury and foetal alcohol spectrum disorder (NSW Law Reform Commission 2012).

Bibliography

Aboriginal and Torres Strait Islander Social Justice Commissioner. (2002). *Social justice report 2001*. Sydney: Australian Human Rights Commission.

Aboriginal and Torres Strait Islander Social Justice Commissioner. (2004). *Social justice report 2003*. Sydney: Australian Human Rights Commission.

Aboriginal and Torres Strait Islander Social Justice Commissioner. (2008). *Social justice report 2007*. Sydney: Australian Human Rights Commission.

Australian Bureau of Statistics (ABS). (2016, December 8). *Prisoners in Australia, 2016*. Available at: http://www.abs.gov.au/ausstats/abs@.nsf/mf/4517.0. Accessed 2 Dec 2017.

Australian Institute of Health and Welfare. (2017). *Youth justice in Australia 2015–16* (Bulletin 139). Canberra: AIHW.

Atkinson, J. (1990). Violence in Aboriginal Australia: Colonisation and gender. *Aboriginal and Islander Health Worker Journal, 14*(1), 5–21.

Atkinson, J. (2002). *Trauma trails recreating song lines: The transgenerational effects of trauma in Indigenous Australia*. North Melbourne: Spinifex Press.

Baldry, E. (2009). Prisons, institutions and patriarchy. In *ANZ Critical Criminology Proceedings* (pp. 18–30). Melbourne: Monash University.

Baldry, E. (2014). Disability at the margins: The limits of the law. *Griffith Law Review, 23*(3), 370–388.

Baldry, E. (2017). People with multiple and complex support needs, disadvantage and criminal justice systems: 40 years after the Sackville report. In A. Durbach, B. Edgeworth, & V. Sentas (Eds.), *Law and poverty in Australia 40 years after the Sackville report*. Annandale: Federation Press.

Baldry, E., & Cunneen, C. (2014). Imprisoned Indigenous women and the shadow of colonial patriarchy. *Australia and New Zealand Journal of Criminology, 47*, 276–298.

Baldry, E., & Dowse, L. (2013). Compounding mental and cognitive disability and disadvantage: Police as care managers. In D. Chappell (Ed.), *Policing and the mentally ill: International perspectives* (pp. 219–234). Boca Raton: CRC Press, Taylor and Francis Group.

Baldry, E., Dowse, L., McCausland, R., & Clarence, M. (2012). *Lifecourse institutional costs of homelessness of vulnerable groups* (Report to Australian Department of Families, Housing, Community Services and Indigenous Affairs). Available at: http://www.pwd.org.au/documents/pubs/adjc/Lifecourse-Institutional-Costs-of-Homelessness.pdf. Accessed 30 Aug 2017.

Baldry, E., Dowse, L., & Xu, H. (2013). *People with mental and cognitive disabilities: Pathways into prison* (Report on Mental Health Disorders in the Criminal Justice System Background Paper).

Baldry, E., McCausland R., Dowse, L., & McEntyre, E. (2015). *A predictable and preventable path: Aboriginal people with mental and cognitive disability in the criminal justice system*. Available at: https://www.mhdcd.unsw.edu.au/sites/www.mhdcd.unsw.edu.au/files/u18/pdf/a_predictable_and_preventable_path_2nov15.pdf. Accessed 30 Aug 2017.

Baldry, E., & McEntyre, E. (2011). Prison bars are health barriers. *O&G Magazine, 13*(3), 53–54.

Bartels, L. (2012). *Sentencing of Indigenous women* (Indigenous Justice Clearinghouse, Research Brief 14). Available at: https://www.indigenousjustice.gov.au/wp-content/uploads/mp/files/publications/files/brief014.pdf. Accessed 30 Aug 2017.

Crenshaw, K. (1991). Mapping the margins: Intersectionality, identity politics, and violence against women of color. *Stanford Law Review, 43*(6), 1241–1299.

Cunneen, C., Baldry, E., Brown, D., Brown, M., Schwartz, M., & Steel, A. (2013). *Penal culture and hyperincarceration: The revival of the prison.* Aldershot: Ashgate.

Davis, M., & McGlade, H. (2006). *International human rights law and the recognition of Aboriginal customary law* (Background Paper No. 10). Perth: Law Reform Commission of Western Australia.

Delgado, R. (1995). *Critical race theory: The cutting edge*. Philadelphia: Temple University Press.

Dowse, L., Baldry, E., & Snoyman, P. (2009). Disabling criminology: Conceptualizing the intersections of critical disability studies and critical criminology for people with mental health and cognitive disabilities in the criminal justice system. *Australian Journal of Human Rights, 15*(1), 29–46.

Gregorowski, C., & Seedat, S. (2013). Addressing childhood trauma in a developmental context. *Journal of Child & Adolescent Mental Health, 25*(2), 105–118.

Hannah-Moffat, K. (2015). Needle in a haystack: Logical parameters of treatment based on actuarial risk–needs assessments. *Criminology and Public Policy, 14*(1), 113–120.

Heffernan, E., Andersen, K., Kinner, S., Aboud, A. Ober, C., & Scotney, A. (2015). *The family business: Improving the understanding and treatment of post traumatic stress disorder among incarcerated Aboriginal and Torres Strait Islander women* (Report for Beyond Blue). Available at: https://www.beyondblue.org.au/docs/default-source/research-project-files/bw0284-the-family-business-final-report.pdf?sfvrsn=6. Accessed 2 Dec 2017.

Indig, D., McEntyre, E., Page, J., & Ross, B. (2009). *2009 inmate health survey: Aboriginal health report.* Sydney: NSW Justice Health.

Lawrie, R. (2003). *Speak out, speak strong: Rising imprisonment rates of Aboriginal women.* Sydney: NSW Aboriginal Justice Advisory Council.

MacGillivray, P., & Baldry, E. (2015). *Australian Indigenous women's offending patterns* (Research Brief 19, Indigenous Justice Clearinghouse). Available at: https://www.indigenousjustice.gov.au/wp-content/uploads/mp/files/publications/files/brief019.pdf. Accessed 2 Dec 2017.

McCausland, R. (2014). *Aboriginal women's access to diversionary programs in NSW* (Report for the Women's Advisory Council of Corrective Services NSW).

McCausland, R. (2015). *Measurement, management and marginalisation: Evaluation and the diversion of Aboriginal women from prison* (Unpublished Ph.D. thesis). University of New South Wales.

McEntyre, E. (forthcoming). *But-ton Kidn Doon-ga: Black Women Know – Re-presenting the lived realities of Australian Aboriginal women with mental and cognitive disabilities in criminal justice systems* (Unpublished Ph.D. thesis). University of New South Wales.

Moreton-Robinson, A. (2000). *Talkin' up to the white woman: Indigenous women and feminism.* Brisbane: Queensland University Press.

Moreton-Robinson, A. (2014). Towards an Australian Indigenous women's standpoint theory: A methodological tool. *Australian Feminist Studies, 28*(78), 331–347.

NSW Law Reform Commission. (2012). *People with cognitive and mental health impairments in the criminal justice system* (Report 135). Available at: http://www.lawreform.lawlink.nsw.gov.au/agdbasev7wr/lrc/documents/pdf/r135.pdf. Accessed 30 Aug 2017.

Oliver, M., & Barnes, C. (1998). *Social policy and disabled people: From exclusion to inclusion.* London: Longman.

Payne, S. (1992). Aboriginal women and the law. In C. Cunneen (Ed.), *Aboriginal perspectives on criminal justice.* Sydney: Institute of Criminology.

Productivity Commission. (2016). *Overcoming Indigenous disadvantage: Key indicators 2016.* Available at: https://www.pc.gov.au/research/ongoing/overcoming-indigenous-disadvantage/2016/report-documents/oid-2016-overcoming-indigenous-disadvantage-key-indicators-2016-report.pdf. Accessed 2 Dec 2017.

Ribet, B. (2011). Emergent disability and the limits of equality: A critical reading of the UN Convention on the rights of persons with disabilities. *Yale Human Rights and Development Journal, 14*(1), 101–150.

Rigney, L. I. (1999). Internationalisation of an Indigenous anti-colonial cultural critique of research methodologies: A guide to Indigenist research methodology and its principles. *WICAZO SA Review: Journal of Native American Studies, 14*(2), 109–122.

Rowe, S., Baldry, E., & Earles, W. (2015). Decolonising social work research: Learning from critical Indigenous approaches. *Australian Social Work, 68*(3), 296–308.

Shaw, C., & Proctor, G. (2005). Women at the margins: A critique of the diagnosis of borderline personality disorder. *Feminism and Psychology, 15*(4), 483–490.

Sherwood, J. (2009). Who is not coping with colonization? Laying out the map for decolonization. *Australasian Psychiatry, 17*, 24–27.

Sherwood, J. (2010). *Do no harm: Decolonising Aboriginal health research* (Unpublished Ph.D. thesis). University of New South Wales.

Stathopoulos, M., & Quadara, A. (2014). *Women as offenders, women as victims: The role of corrections in supporting women with histories of sexual abuse* (Report for the Women's Advisory Council, NSW Corrective Services). Available at: http://www.correctiveservices.justice.nsw.gov.au/Documents/women-as-offenders-women-as-victims-the-role-of-corrections-in-supporting-women-with-histories-of-sexual-assault.pdf. Accessed 30 Aug 2017.

Tuhiwai Smith, L. (2012). *Decolonizing methodologies: Research and indigenous peoples* (2nd ed.). London and New York: Zed Books.

9

Culture, Mental Illness, and Prison: A New Zealand Perspective

James Cavney and Susan Hatters Friedman

Indigenous Peoples, Migrant Minorities, and Colonial Cultures

Broadly speaking, indigenous people are members of an ethnic group descended from the original inhabitants of a particular geographical region. They collectively identify with and retain at least some aspects of the traditions, knowledge, and values of their ancestral culture (Sanders 1999). Since the late twentieth century, the term 'indigenous peoples' has become more precisely defined within international politics and legislation (United Nations 2009). Implicit within this definition is

J. Cavney (✉)
Auckland Regional Forensic Psychiatry Services, Auckland, New Zealand
e-mail: James.Cavney@waitematadhb.govt.nz

S. H. Friedman
University of Auckland, Auckland, New Zealand

S. H. Friedman
Case Western University, Cleveland, OH, USA

© The Author(s) 2018
A. Mills and K. Kendall (eds.), *Mental Health in Prisons*, Palgrave Studies in Prisons and Penology, https://doi.org/10.1007/978-3-319-94090-8_9

recognition that indigenous peoples have, to varying degrees, been subjugated, disenfranchised, or otherwise marginalised from socio-political influence within their traditional homelands by a more dominant colonial cultural group. The impact of colonisation upon indigenous peoples is well documented throughout history and its legacy is still seen across the globe. Indigenous people around the world are disproportionately represented across many adverse socio-demographic indices compared to the dominant colonial groups that migrated to their ancestral lands.

Although this chapter is primarily concerned with indigenous peoples, it is noteworthy that non-indigenous minority migrant groups can face a similar socio-political disenfranchisement and have similarly poor social outcomes. Moreover, new migrant groups can be vulnerable to other acculturation stressors when having to adjust to a new dominant culture, particularly if they had a traumatic migration history.

Prominent in these negative statistics are the disproportionately high rates of mental illness and incarceration among these groups. Discrimination, unemployment, poverty, substance abuse, poor education, and dysfunctional family systems are common risk factors for mental illness and incarceration in both indigenous people and migrant minorities. Notwithstanding this clear correlation, the way in which cultural factors may variably influence the disproportional rates of mental illness and imprisonment between different cultural groups is incompletely understood.

International organisations such as the United Nations now hold to the premise that protecting the cultural rights of indigenous peoples may reduce such socio-economic and political disparities and improve negative social and health outcomes (United Nations 2009). However, operationalising this principle of cultural protection into tangible interventions to reduce rates of mental illness and imprisonment is more challenging. The cultural diversity of indigenous peoples and ethnic minorities can in itself be an obstacle to finding any common cross-cultural strategies to redress these disparities.

This chapter explores a number of initiatives within a New Zealand context in relation to Māori (the indigenous people of New Zealand) at the interface of mental health and criminal justice systems. In so doing, it is hoped that strategies learnt from a New Zealand experience might assist in developing culturally informed interventions and prevention strategies to assist in service planning and delivery of such services for other indigenous and minority groups.

Culture, Colonisation, and Acculturation

Developing culturally based interventions to reduce the over-representation of mental health problems and imprisonment among diverse indigenous and minority groups is complex and challenging. To begin, there is no academic consensus on how to define culture. Any number of theoretical paradigms (both within and between disciplines) have competed with one another for saliency over the past 150 years (Kuper 1999; Moore 2012). Complexities in operationalising a definition of culture in turn complicates analyses of colonisation and acculturation processes which can also adopt specific paradigmatic perspectives. In a post-modernist era, however, all perspectives are increasingly understood to enhance our understanding of culture as a complex gestalt (Kuper 1999).

Different cultural groups may thus be expected to vary considerably in relation to the structures of their respective cultures which include their customs, symbols, language, art, values, and social behaviour. These are complex adaptations of a specific group of humans to the lands they inhabit to ensure their mutual survival. Culture thus functions as a mode of production by which specific technologies enable a group of people to meet their survival needs relative to the resources and demands of diverse geographies and climates (Wolf 1982). Culture promotes group cohesion to ensure the survival of its members through the inter-generational transition of its rules and values over time in relation to common cross-cultural themes such as preserving kinship networks, distribution of resources, reproductive strategies, and conflict resolution. In combination, the structures and functions of culture represent diverse expressions of the common need for resource acquisition and a shared existential understanding of the human experience in relation to the world in which we live (Moore 2012). For the purpose of this chapter, culture may be understood as the intergenerational expression of the relationship of a people to their ancestral land in achieving shared notions of health, well-being, justice, and survival.

When the resource needs of a cultural group are in equilibrium with the availability of their lands resources, culture is likely to change slowly, if at all. However, cultures can also change in response to new environmental challenges. Depletion of resources, in-group competition for resources, or natural disaster, may at times require population migration and cultural adaptation to meet new environmental challenges.

Throughout early prehistory, geographical distance and isolation meant small populations developed cultures to satisfy their own survival needs without reference to any other group. As human societies expanded, increased contact between different cultural groups led to the transmission of ideas and cultural 'cross pollination'. Warfare and trade became two potent vehicles for more dramatic cultural shifts in response to the demands of one cultural group for the resources of another group's land and conflicts were generally won on the basis of the superiority of the martial technologies of one group relative to another (Diamond 1997).

Colonisation is the ultimate expression of that process whereby a more powerful cultural group usurps an indigenous people's autonomous control over the resources of their land, marginalises them from political influence, and imposes different values and belief systems. History is replete with stories of colonisation, often on epic scales, whereby indigenous peoples and their cultures have variably been annihilated, enslaved, or assimilated.

The disruption of an indigenous people's relationship with their ancestral land results in an erosion of structures of their culture which, in turn, compromises the function of that culture to provide for the cultural cohesion of the group that once ensured the prosperity of its people relative to their own concepts of health and well-being. This cultural disenfranchisement has been characterised as 'cultural trauma' that is then transmitted inter-generationally instead of the values and customs of the indigenous culture (Farrelly et al. 2006).

Acculturation reflects the process by which one culture adapts or adjusts to the structures of a more dominant culture. For colonised indigenous peoples, acculturation is unavoidable, as their only home is where they are. In contrast, migrant groups may 'choose' to immerse themselves within a different culture. Although the choice to migrate may be on unfavourable terms for some groups, such as refugees, for others, it may represent an opportunity for educational, social, or financial advantage. Understanding the variable cultural dynamics of acculturation for colonised indigenous peoples and migrant minorities can provide valuable insights in beginning to consider culturally informed strategies to redress the negative social outcomes often found in these groups. Indeed, Kapoor et al. (2013) argue that an awareness of and sensitivity to the impact of acculturation on these groups are essential in working with them in correctional settings.

Colonisation and Acculturation in New Zealand

As an ethnic group, Māori are a Polynesian people whose ancestors were the part of the last wave of human migration across the Pacific region. The final phase of that migration was the settlement of New Zealand some one thousand years ago. Although initially a migrant people, Māori discovered a large and fertile landmass that was unpopulated and became the indigenous people of a land they called *Aotearoa* ('land of the long white cloud'). There they flourished and successfully exploited the rich resources of the land and sea. Māori had extensive astronomical knowledge and maritime capability and mastered Neolithic technologies. They developed cohesive social systems and trade networks based on kinship and tribal affiliation and developed a complex religious and spiritual belief system (King 2003).

Māori existed in relative cultural isolation until the arrival of Europeans (*Pākehā*) in the seventeenth and eighteenth century, most notably Captain Cook in 1769. Over the next century, New Zealand was gradually established as a British colony and all its people, including the Māori, were made subject to British rule and systems of law and justice. At first, Māori tolerated the arrival of British settlers and took advantage of the trading opportunities they brought (Salmond 1991). However, disputes began to arise as settler numbers increased and the land acquisition efforts by the British colonists intensified. Although Māori initially 'sold' some tracts of land, their beliefs and attitudes towards ownership and governance were different from those of the

Pākehā settlers. Māori did not have a concept of individual land ownership although chiefs would grant permission for the land to be used for a specific time and for a particular purpose rather more like a lease. Underpinning these early disputes about land ownership was that for Māori, land was not only an economic resource, but also a source of *mana* (pride and esteem) and formed part of Māori cultural identity by providing a connection with their ancestors who settled it (Orange 1987).

The British Government at first adopted a more humanistic approach to the colonising of New Zealand in contrast to its other colonies. In 1835, it even recognised New Zealand as an independent Confederation of United (Māori) Tribes. Nevertheless, the land requirements of the British settlers continued and led them to a treaty settlement with Māori to ensure that Māori would only sell land to representatives of Queen Victoria's government. The Treaty of Waitangi was signed on 6th February 1840 and, in return, it recognised Māori ownership of their lands and forests and other cultural assets and bestowed them the same rights as other British subjects.

However, aspects of the Treaty of Waitangi were critically mistranslated from the English version to the Māori version and resulted in a profound misunderstanding that has resonated down through subsequent generations (Orange 1987). In the English version, Māori ceded sovereignty to the Crown, in exchange for the protection of Māori culture and equal standing as subjects of the Crown. Māori, in contrast, believed that they were entering into an equal partnership with the Crown united under God. They understood that they had retained absolute sovereignty and self-determination (*tino rangatiratanga*) of their land and cultural assets. However, as the reality of Pākehā governance began to exert its influence and authority upon Māori, a series of armed conflicts arose between 1845 until 1872. In these so-called New Zealand Wars, the Government introduced legislation to confiscate Māori land to sell to settlers to offset the costs of the wars and began to systematically imprison tribal leaders as punishment for their insurgency (Belich 1986). The Suppression of Rebellion Act and New Zealand Settlements Act, both passed in 1863, allowed the seizing of land from Māori tribes who had been in rebellion against the Crown

(Belgrave 2005). Its overt intent was to establish British law and order upon Māori by using areas within the confiscated land to establish permanent settlements for further colonisation (Orange 1987).

Following the outbreak of the New Zealand Wars, the New Zealand Government continued to introduce other pieces of legislation that further discriminated against Māori and dispossessed them of their lands and cultural assets. For example, the Native Schools Act was passed in 1867 and required Māori to 'donate' more of their land for the schools and to pay for the buildings and teachers' salaries. The 1880 Native School Code further standardised the process, establishing native schools, as schooling became compulsory for Māori in 1894.

From their inception, 'native schools' were intended to teach English. Although the Māori language (*te reo Māori*) was tolerated at first, Māori children were soon punished for speaking it at school. The need to learn English to function in the Pākehā world was seen as essential to what was now an overt governmental agenda of cultural assimilation. However, the vocational curriculum of these schools focused only manual labour rather than academic opportunities, commensurate with the ethnocentric notions of the British regarding the social standing of Māori as working class (Barrington 2008).

Divested of land, language, and political influence, further erosion of Māori culture and identity occurred with the passing of the Quackery Prevention Act (1906) and the Tohunga Suppression Act in 1907. Tohunga were traditional Māori 'shaman' or healers who were considered by the Pākehā to have primitive if not dangerous practices that needed to be replaced with modern medical practice (Dow 2001). Ironically, early European settlers had noted the exceptionally good health of Māori (Salmond 1991). Tohunga were indeed experts in the use of medicinal plants and herbs (*rongoa*) relative to the challenges of a pre-European burden of disease. However, tohunga were not equipped to deal with the diseases introduced by the colonists, such as alcoholism, syphilis, influenza, and tuberculosis (Dow 2001).

Tohunga were also the holders of other cultural knowledge and by banning the practices of Māori spiritual and cultural leaders in combination with the teachings of Christian missionaries, many Māori consequently renounced their cultural traditions and accepted the new religion of the Pākehā. Subsequently, many tohunga declined to pass on their oral traditions, further impoverishing the intergenerational transmission of Māori culture (Riley 1994).

Over a period of less than 50 years, the combination of war, land confiscation, disease, forced assimilation, poverty, alcoholism, and demoralisation caused a rapid decline in the Māori population. From around 86,000 in 1769, the population declined to 48,000 by 1874, and reached its nadir of 42,000 in 1896, perpetuating the view of the time that Māori were on the verge of 'extinction' (Belich 1996). However, Māori proved to be remarkably resilient and despite their cultural disenfranchisement, their population numbers slowly began to recover during the twentieth century. In New Zealand's 2013 census, 598,605 people identified with the Māori ethnic group and 668,724 people were of Māori descent (Statistics NZ 2013).

Despite the near annihilation of Māori culture and its people, Pākehā had always believed that New Zealand race relations with Māori were exemplary. In the nineteenth century, the British Empire had proclaimed its dealings with Māori as a humanist model for colonial settlement by way of negotiation with indigenous peoples rather than bloodshed (Orange 1987). Later, the colonial government perpetuated an aspirational view of racial harmony to support an agenda of cultural assimilation (Orange 1987). Although relations between Māori and Pākehā were arguably better than many other indigenous peoples, including other Pacific territories such as Tahiti, they were far from perfect (Orange 1987).

However, because Pākehā lived primarily in urban centres and Māori in rural areas, these tensions did not fully emerge until the 1960s when Māori began to migrate from rural to urban areas in large numbers and the systemic discrimination of Māori was brought into clearer focus. Overcrowded homes, poverty, and poor school performance were early symptoms of disparity, and theorists in the 1960s began to identify the cultural disenfranchisement of Māori as the cause (Farrelly et al. 2006). Indeed, many Māori had difficulty coping with urban society, away from the stabilising influence of their final bastion of cultural identity, their extended family networks (*whānau*). Some turned to alcohol or crime, and many felt culturally isolated.

Early indicators of some of these social problems had led to the introduction of other legislation such as the Habitual Drunkards Act 1906 and the Habitual Criminals and Offenders Act 1906. Notwithstanding the debate on whether such early legislation had represented any genuine concern for the health and social welfare of Māori, by the end of the 19th century, politicians were overtly seeking to suppress Māori culture, not through the direct force of the musket, but with the rule of law (Orange 1987).

Māori had no political voice to challenge these assimilation policies that represented an institutionalised racism and gave rise to a negative stereotyping of Māori throughout the twentieth century (Farrelly et al. 2006). Durie (1999) has identified the cultural disenfranchisement of Māori as the forerunner of Māori criminalisation, imprisonment, and poor mental health perpetuated by a lack of political influence over policy, or access to the legal resources required to deal with the British criminal justice system. Moreover, the psychic expression of this cultural trauma through loss of mana also resulted in a high burden of mental health problems.

Rates of Māori Mental Health and Incarceration in New Zealand

In New Zealand, approximately 50% of prisoners are of Māori ethnicity, with an additional 11% being of Pacific Island ethnicities (Department of Corrections 2017). Yet, at the same time, Māori and Pacific Islanders made up only 15 and 7% of the general New Zealand population, respectively (Statistics NZ 2013).

A recent study of mental health disorders in New Zealand prisoners (Indig et al. 2016) found that prisoners have significantly higher rates of mental illness compared to their community counterparts—in fact, prisoners were three times as likely to have a mental disorder in the past 12 months. One fifth of prisoners had a history of comorbid mental illness and substance-use disorder in the past 12 months and 87% had a lifetime diagnosis of a substance-use disorder. Compared with community samples, among prisoners, there were elevated rates of mood disorders, post-traumatic stress disorder (PTSD), psychotic symptoms, and substance-use disorders (Indig et al. 2016). Additionally one-third of inmates were identified as having a personality disorder.

In this study, Māori were found to have a higher frequency of psychotic symptoms than other groups (Indig et al. 2016). However, rather than using a clinical diagnostic instrument for psychosis, the study listed symptoms such as hearing voices and seeing visions. The study authors suggested that the rates of psychotic disorder would require validation considering that symptoms might be transient or caused by drugs. However, one must also consider cultural factors and Māori may experience hearing voices or seeing visions as a non-psychotic experience. Indeed, Farrelly et al. (2006) are critical of labelling such symptoms as psychosis and point to systemic biases within Western diagnostic classification systems in under-diagnosing trauma-related experiences in Māori.

Nevertheless, the national New Zealand mental health survey of the general population, *Te Rau Hinengaro*, also found that Māori experienced elevated levels of mental illness, and Māori were more likely to have both comorbidities and more serious disorders than other groups (Oakley Browne et al. 2006). In contrast, Pacific people have lower rates of mental illness than the general population outside correctional settings. However, Indig et al. (2016) unexpectedly found that the highest prevalence for any mental disorder in prisons was among Pacific people.

Among women referred to and evaluated by the forensic psychiatrist in New Zealand's largest women's prison, the majority (60%) were Māori, followed by 31% Pākehā (Collier and Friedman 2016). Most of the women (54%) had been victimised by family violence, and the majority (58%) had a history of previous mental health treatment. Substance-use disorders were commonly comorbid with mental illness. Of the women, 36% had a psychotic disorder, 22% a mood disorder, and 19% PTSD (Collier and Friedman 2016). In New Zealand as elsewhere, female prisoners are more likely to have a mental health burden than their male counterparts (Indig et al. 2016) with rates of PTSD being higher among female prisoners (Friedman et al. 2016).

Despite the burden of mental illness within prisons, at the time of a national study in 1999, only 37% of inmates with psychosis were being treated, compared with 46% of those with depression and 81% of those with bipolar disorder (Brinded et al. 2001). Brinded and colleagues thus suggested that, in order to treat the large numbers of inmates with mental illnesses, a significant increase in mental health services was needed. By the time of the national study in 2016 (Indig et al. 2016), 46% of prisoners diagnosed with a mental health or substance-use disorder affecting them in the past 12 months had received treatment in the past year; this was higher than general community rates of 39%.

In order to provide effective treatment to individuals, mental health teams first need to effectively identify those in need of treatment. Cavney and colleagues (2012) analysed the clinical pathways of 925 service users entering into forensic mental health services (either via the courts or prison) and found that only a minority (30%) had no prior contact with mental health services in the three years preceding their referral to forensic mental health services. Superficially, this suggested that the majority of those in need of treatment in prison are already known to mental health services whereby improved referral and screening would be a useful intervention. However, Simpson et al. (2003) also noted that treatment for mental illness, both in prison and in the community, was less common for those of Māori and Pacific Island extraction.

Both New Zealand Māori and Pacific Islander populations are relatively young compared to the rest of New Zealanders (Ministry of Health 2012), with half of Māori being under age 23. Māori have been identified as presenting late to forensic mental health services and Māori with serious mental illness are often not identified until some time after they have been convicted and sentenced. (Skipworth et al. 2011). The delay in the identification of Māori with mental health problems can be catastrophic. For example, although Māori reported fewer suicidal thoughts than non-Māori, they evidenced similar rates of suicide attempts as non-Māori (Simpson et al. 2003).

Barriers to Care

In combination, these statistics suggest that there may be barriers to identifying Māori and Pacific Islanders with serious mental illness both in the community and upon entering the prison. To the extent that cultural disenfranchisement may contribute to the higher rates of incarceration and mental illness in indigenous peoples and migrant groups, identification of culturally specific interventions or outcomes are seldom clear. It is rare, for example, to find any specific cultural domains included in contemporary criminogenic or psychiatric assessment tools beyond demographic description. Moreover, many evaluations and screening tools are validated on different populations from the indigenous people or minority culture.

The fact that mental illness may be considered as an ethnocentric social construction (Walker 2006) that presumes the origins of an individual's experience of symptoms to lie in Western medical diagnostic nomenclatures is also relevant in misdiagnosing or 'missing' a diagnosis despite the best efforts of screening tools. Some symptoms that Western medicine considers as signs of mental illness may be attributed to spiritual causes by those indigenous people experiencing them. For example, *matakite* (clairvoyant sight) is a commonly accepted cultural reality for many Māori. Apparent perceptual disturbances can also be considered as culturally meaningful and it is not uncommon for Māori to report being visited by ancestral spirits, including when in confined custody.

Farrelly et al. (2006) also noted that the Māori experience of intergenerational trauma can contribute to three clinical presentations: *mate Māori* (sickness) as a result of *makutu* (a curse) placed by an outsider following a breach of *tapu* (a sacred rule or prohibition); *whakama* (profound shame); and *whakamomori* (variably described as profound grief or inbuilt tribal suffering associated with suicidal behaviour). These experiences they suggest may be more amendable to treatment from a tohunga than a psychiatrist.

Mistrust in communicating these spiritual experiences to Western health practitioners for fear of being labelled as psychotic is anecdotally considered to be a significant barrier to Māori engaging with non-Māori mental health professionals. Mental health professionals, and forensic psychiatrists in particular, who work with criminalised individuals from cultural minorities are very often of the majority 'dominant' culture (Friedman 2017). This is also true in New Zealand, despite a push to increase representation of Māori in medical schools and other registered health professions. Understanding the different cultural identities of incarcerated mental health patients is thus critical for the mental health professional working in the prison (Kapoor et al. 2013) and in relation to developing screening tools, engagement, diagnosis, treatment, and referral.

More systemic barriers to mental health care within correctional facilities also exist within the competing paradigms of promoting health and recovery versus crime and punishment. Moreover, attitudes and values of being an inmate ('prisonisation') in New Zealand, like the US (Winfree et al. 2002), exposes inmates to a prison culture which has been 'widely portrayed as a struggle between "captor and caged" (Branham 2011)—violent, predatory, and corrosive to mental health' (Kapoor et al. 2013, p. 273, citation in original).

Mental Health Services in New Zealand Prisons: A Cultural Renaissance

The socio-political response to the disproportionate rates of mental illness and incarceration among Māori has slowly gathered momentum since the 1950s as Māori culture began to undergo a renaissance and regain political capital. The Māori Women's Welfare League and the New Zealand Māori Council emerged to help urban Māori and provide a unified political voice, later to become the Māori protest movement. This facilitated, among many things, a revival of te reo Māori through the establishment of Kohanga Reo, schools dedicated to learning in Māori. It also empowered Māori to reassert their cultural rites through a greater recognition of the Treaty of Waitangi in the later part of the twentieth century (Orange 1987).

From the late 1960s, Māori began drawing attention to breaches of the Treaty of Waitangi, and by the 1970s, the Treaty gained prominence amid greater awareness of Māori issues and grievances. In 1975, the Waitangi Tribunal was established as a permanent commission of inquiry tasked with researching breaches of the Treaty by the Crown and suggesting means of redress. Whereas claims were at first in relation to land, this broadened to include the concepts of *taonga* (cultural treasures), and matters of health and education thus came under the Tribunal's jurisdiction (King 2003).

The passing of the Treaty of Waitangi Amendment Act in 1985 finally gave Māori a legislative right to revisit many of the hitherto neglected grievances of the past and provided a more contemporaneous interpretation of the treaty principles (Orange 1987). The so-called three 'P's' were mandated in 1989 for all New Zealand government departments, particularly the health sector. *Partnership* reflects a commitment to collaborative processes between Māori and Pākehā to achieve parity in health outcomes. *Participation* represents the enablement of Māori to participate across the health sector to reduce inequalities. *Protection* recognises the duty of Crown services to respect and preserve Māori cultural beliefs, values, and practice (Crocker 1989).

The (so-called) Mason Report (1988) reviewed the poor outcomes of Māori and Pacific Island mental health services both in the community and in prison. It recommended that when developing mental health services, particularly forensic mental health services, multi-disciplinary teams should include members who had skills and understanding of Māori culture. The New Zealand prison population has continued to rise since then, and Māori and Pacific Islanders have remained disproportionately represented. Fifteen years later, Simpson and colleagues (2003) again called for increased responsiveness of forensic mental health services to the needs of Māori and Pacific Islander peoples.

The New Zealand Ministry of Health (2012) reprioritised the development of *kaupapa Māori* services incorporating the knowledge, skills, attitudes, and values of Māori society. Clearly then, there is a desire to redress disparity for Māori in service provision, although it is equally clear that there remain barriers to achieving better outcomes. The high prevalence of Māori with serious mental illness in the prison population remains a challenge.

'Strategies for Freedom'

Durie (1999) characterised the intergenerational perpetuation of crime and mental illness as Māori being 'trapped' in these lifestyles because of the complex interaction with socio-economic circumstances and a confused or partially developed cultural identity. Farrelly et al. (2006) have referred to the same process as the intergenerational transmission of cultural trauma.

Confusion in Māori cultural identity associated with the breakdown of traditional NZ *whānau* (extended family) systems can mean that Māori may gravitate to criminal gangs who can offer a surrogate 'family' for young men and women (Gilbert 2013). In New Zealand, there are a high number of criminal gangs, many of which were founded in the late 1960s and early 1970s and some (such as Black Power, the Mongrel Mob, and King Cobras) have a predominant membership of Māori and Pacific Islanders.

Within these gangs, facial and body tattoos of gang symbols are commonly used to demarcate membership and may be considered as cultural corruptions of the traditional *moko* (tattoos) prominent in Māori and Pacific cultural traditions. Similarly, imprisonment itself has arguably become a further cultural corruption of means for some Māori, such as prospecting novice gang members, to gain respect (*mana*) from their peers on the basis of their criminal prowess. As Durie (1999) astutely observed, where disempowerment is felt most strongly, disrespect for the law brings a compensatory sense of power.

In moving towards solutions, Durie (1985) developed the *whare tapa wha* (the four walls of the house) as a metaphorical model for conceptualising Māori health and well-being. It considers physical health (*te taha tinana*), mental health (*te taha hinengaro*), spiritual health (*te taha wairua*), and family health (*te taha whanau*) to be cornerstones. This culturally informed model provides a powerful starting point in planning for strategies to redress the disparities in mental health and incarceration between Māori and non-Māori people. Indeed, a number of culturally informed initiatives have begun to be trialled within New Zealand across the spectrum of forensic mental health care.

A Culturally Informed Prison Model of Care

In New Zealand, there are currently six Regional Forensic Psychiatry Services. One of the roles of these services is to provide mental health services to remand and sentenced prisoners. The current Prison Model of Care in New Zealand entails screening for mental illness by prison healthcare staff who then refer on to a forensic prison in-reach mental health team. This model has been expanded to include referrals to forensic prison teams from any source (e.g. family, friends, prison staff, or court liaison staff), reducing the over-reliance on a single screening tool. This simple step in itself saw increases in rates of referral (Pillai et al. 2016).

The multi-disciplinary composition of a Forensic Prison Team (FPT) includes forensic psychiatrists, psychologists, nurses, social workers, and importantly, cultural advisers who then undertake a staged process of assessment following an initial referral. The role of the cultural advisor working with a triage nurse can be critical at the initial assessment juncture. In addition to having awareness of the diagnostic interface of spiritual experiences versus mental illness, the ability of a cultural advisor, and thus the FPT, to meaningfully engage with a Māori person, is substantially enhanced.

Upon the introduction of one Māori person to another, it is typical to attempt (usually successfully) to establish a common relationship on the basis of their tribal ancestry and family relationships through process known as *whanaungatanga*. Common opening questions may include 'where are you from?' and subsequently 'are you related to so and so?'. This simple step will often break down barriers and instil a degree of trust and engagement which may be beyond the ability of a non-Māori mental health worker. Cultural advisers also help in understanding the patient's mental health condition, in relation to it being an illness or *mate Māori*. Such a cultural and clinical perspective can reduce the chance of misdiagnosis or missing a diagnosis.

After initial engagement with the FPT, if evidence of mental illness is identified, inmates are assessed by a psychiatrist, and a determination is made about whether they require further psychiatric evaluation or treatment. If a prisoner requires further care upon release from custody, referral is proactively made to community mental health teams. Other social agencies are also engaged prior to release as needed, for example, for accommodation or welfare benefits. The cultural adviser can have an added role at this point in assisting the person to re-engage with whānau (if required) or otherwise act as a conduit for whānau to be involved in care planning. Use of this culturally informed assertive prison in-reach mental health model was found to be superior to 'treatment as usual' and promoted engagement with mental health services in the community after prison release (McKenna et al. 2015).

Kaupapa Māori and Pasifika Stream: Auckland Regional Forensic Psychiatric Services

A portion of those seen by the FPT may require admission to a forensic psychiatric hospital due to a perceived risk to either themselves or others stemming from mental illness. Under New Zealand Law, psychiatric treatment cannot be mandated for inmates while in prison. Therefore, if an inmate is deemed to require compulsory treatment, they are transferred to forensic hospital. Additionally, those found to be unfit to stand trial or legally insane at the time of serious offending may be committed to a forensic hospital if their risk to others is deemed serious and where long-term treatment can be mandated.

Evidence suggests that how dangerous patients are perceived to be, the provision of access to mental health services, and even the psychiatric diagnoses made—can be biased by 'race' or culture (Simpson and Friedman 2016). As noted, the urbanisation of Māori resulted in structural stigmatisation of Māori. Whether or not this contributes to the perception of the risk that Māori pose when unwell is not clear, but in 2015, Māori were 3.6 times more likely to be subject to a community treatment order than non-Māori and 3.3 times more likely to be subject to an inpatient treatment order (Ministry of Health 2016).

Auckland Regional Forensic Psychiatric Services (the Mason Clinic) is the largest provider of forensic mental health services in New Zealand. It delivers inpatient and outpatient care to a catchment region of approximately 1.5 million people. The service has approximately 110 inpatients and 50 outpatients at any given time. Of those, approximately half of service users are Māori and 20–25% are Pacific islanders. Since its establishment in 1992, the Mason Clinic has been committed to providing both Māori and Pacific cultural support. However, over the past decade, a specialised Kaupapa Māori and Pacifica stream has developed where service users can choose to participate in a culturally based therapeutic milieu. In addition to more contemporaneous rehabilitative practice, programme delivery is based on Durie's *whare tapa wha* model. The key point of difference from general rehabilitation is a focus on *wairuatanga* (spiritual health). Included in this is an emphasis on *karakia* (Māori prayer), *kapahaka* (traditional song and dance), and communal living, for example, where staff share meals with service users (Sweetman 2016).

More recent innovations have included starting to adapt an international forensic risk assessment tool, the Dundrum (Kennedy et al. 2010), to include cultural and spiritual components of significance to Māori recovery (McKenna et al. 2017). Notwithstanding anecdotal evidence of the benefits of these innovations, like many other culturally based interventions, quantifying tangible results have yet to be developed although preliminary papers in relation to that project are anticipated as being published soon.

Māori Focused Units Within Prisons and Rangitahi Youth Courts

Preliminary steps to quantify the value of culturally based interventions are also emerging from prison initiatives where a number of prisons have trialled interventions based on Māori cultural practices, including Māori Focus Units (MFUs) and Māori Therapeutic Programmes. The MFUs offer *tikanga*-based (customary Māori systems of values and practices) courses and activities. After transferring from mainstream prison units where prison culture has been characterised as often sub-therapeutic (Kapoor et al. 2013), MFUs provide a more culturally appropriate setting facilitating the involvement of local *iwi* (extended tribal kinship units) and decision-making forums which involve both prisoners and staff (Department of Corrections 2009). Enhanced cultural identity and knowledge among participants and change in attitudes about criminal lifestyles have been found among participating inmates, as have modest changes in reoffending rates (Department of Corrections 2009).

Even more promising, however, has been the adoption of a different crime and punishment paradigm for Māori and Pacific Island youth offenders. For example, Rangatahi and Pasifika Courts are designed to involve young Māori and Pacific Island offenders, their families, and their communities in youth justice processes. These courts work within the same legal structures as New Zealand Youth Courts and have the same laws and consequences. In contrast, however, they are not held in a courtroom, but Rangatahi courts are instead held on marae (traditional Māori meeting houses), and Pasifika courts in Pasifika churches or community centres. They both follow their respective cultural processes. Like MFUs it is hoped that by instilling self-esteem and pride through engagement and immersion in aspects of the Māori and Pasifika cultures, a youth offender may be diverted out of the criminal justice system with a long-term reduction in rates of recidivism. Again, outcomes are at present limited to qualitative data indicating a high level of endorsement of the processes (Ministry of Justice 2012) although quantitative data, for example about actual reductions in recidivism, have yet to be developed.

Conclusions and Recommendations

Kapoor and colleagues (2013) have discussed the adaptation of the cultural formulation, a diagnostic tool from the DSM-IV designed to elicit culturally relevant clinical information, for people with mental health problems within the correctional setting. This includes understanding the explanations for mental illness within the inmates' culture of origin and cultural elements of the doctor–patient relationship. It also incorporates explanations for incarceration according to the inmate's culture of origin, consideration of the prison sub-culture, and consideration of how culturally appropriate treatment can be best discussed with corrections staff, who must retain their focus on security and safety (Kapoor et al. 2013). Culture describes rituals, traditions, behaviours, attributes, and meanings of a group of people (Simpson and Friedman 2016). All of us are cultural beings, with our own beliefs and attitudes related to culture. Treatment teams must keep in mind that they too are products of their own—different—culture. Teams must, in addition to possessing a level of knowledge about other groups, use their skills in culturally appropriate ways, and be self-aware, including about their own limitations (Friedman 2017). They must seek to understand the colonial history of the indigenous person before them, their behaviour, motivations, and mental illness on a backdrop of their cultural identity. Treatment teams need to guard against countertransference feelings towards those of other cultures and personal beliefs that they may not understand in relation to the patient's cultural issues and needs (Friedman 2017).

Nevertheless, Durie (1999) has noted that, 'by itself [cultural] identity is not an insurance against offending, nor does it offer a passport to good health'. However, cultural identity is one important factor in mental health recovery. In turn, the process of recovering from a mental illness may also help contribute to one's cultural identity (Pere 2006). New Zealand has pioneered a number of cultural-based intervention strategies in forensic mental health and correctional settings as a result of increased legislative partnerships between Māori and Pākehā to ensure the participation of Māori in service delivery at all levels to protect their cultural identity. This has been a slow but significant intergenerational reclamation of socio-political self-determination over the past century. The fact that quantitative data clearly demonstrating improved outcomes have yet to eventuate should not be a deterrent to continuing this commitment but rather understood as part of a process of research, service development, and evaluation. It is hoped that the emerging qualitative data indicating the enthusiasm and support for these programmes will continue to ensure political commitment to establishing culturally based interventions in New Zealand and inspire other indigenous people and cultural minorities across the globe.

Acknowledgements The authors would like to thank Mr. Tipene Paul (cultural advisor, Mason Clinic Forensic Prison Team) and the Taumata of Mason Clinic for endorsing the authors to write this chapter and providing cultural oversight and support.

Bibliography

Barrington, J. (2008). *Separate but equal? Māori schools and the Crown, 1867–1969*. Wellington: Victoria University Press.

Belgrave, M. (2005). *Historical frictions: Māori claims and reinvented histories.* Auckland: Auckland University Press.

Belich, J. (1986). *The New Zealand wars*. Auckland: Penguin Press.

Belich, J. (1996). *Making peoples*. Auckland: Penguin Press.

Brinded, P. M., Simpson, A. I. F., Laidlaw, T. M., Fairley, N., & Malcom, F. (2001). Prevalence of psychiatric disorders in New Zealand prisons: A national study. *Australian and New Zealand Journal of Psychiatry, 35,* 166–173.

Cavney, J., Skipworth, J., Madell, D., & McKenna, B. (2012). Patterns of mental health service contact before and after forensic mental health contract in New Zealand. *Australasian Psychiatry, 20*(3), 225–227.

Collier, S., & Friedman, S. H. (2016). Mental illness among women referred for psychiatric services in a New Zealand women's prison. *Behavioral Sciences & the Law, 34,* 539–550.

Crocker, T. (1989). 'Introduction' in principles for Crown action on the Treaty of Waitangi. Wellington: Treaty of Waitangi Research Unit, Victoria University.

Department of Corrections. (2009). *Māori focus units and Māori therapeutic programmes: Evaluation report.* Department of Corrections, Wellington. Available at: http://www.corrections.govt.nz/__data/assets/pdf_file/0008/854675/MFU_MTP_evaluation_final_report.pdf. Accessed 30 Nov 2017.

Department of Corrections. (2017). *Prison facts and statistics—September 2017.* Available at: http://www.corrections.govt.nz/resources/research_and_statistics/quarterly_prison_statistics/prison_stats_september_2017.html. Accessed 30 Nov 2017.

Diamond, J. (1997). *Guns, germs, and steel: The fates of human societies.* New York: W.W. Norton.

Dow, D. A. (2001). "Pruned of its dangers": The Tohunga Suppression Act 1907. *Health and History, 3*(1), 41–64.

Durie, M. H. (1985). Māori perspective of health. *Social Science and Medicine, 20*(5), 483–486.

Durie, M. H. (1999). *Imprisonment, trapped lifestyles, and strategies for freedom.* Paper presented at the indigenous people and Justice conference, Wellington, New Zealand.

Farrelly, S., Rudegeair, T., & Rickard, S. (2006). Trauma and dissociation in Aotearoa (New Zealand): The psyche of a society. *Journal of Trauma Practice, 4*, 203–220.

Friedman, S. H. (2017). Culture, bias, and understanding: We can do better. *Journal of the American Academy of Psychiatry and the Law, 45*(2), 136–139.

Friedman, S. H., Collier, S., & Hall, R. (2016). Post-traumatic stress disorder among women in prison. In C. Martin, V. R. Preedy, & V. B. Patel (Eds.), *The comprehensive guide to post-traumatic stress disorders* (pp. 1497–1512). Switzerland: Springer International Publishing.

Gilbert, J. (2013). *Patched: The history of gangs in New Zealand.* Auckland: University of Auckland Press.

Hayward, J. (2004). Flowing from the Treaty's words: The principles of the Treaty of Waitangi. In J. Hayward & N. Wheen (Eds.), *The Waitangi Tribunal: Te Roopu Whakamana i te Tiriti o Waitangi* (pp. 29–40). Wellington: Bridget Williams Books.

Indig, D., Gear, C., & Wilhelm, K. (2016). *Comorbid substance use disorders and mental health disorders among New Zealand prisoners.* Wellington: New Zealand Department of Corrections.

Kapoor, R., Dike, C., Burns, C., Carvahlo, V., & Griffith, E. E. H. (2013). Cultural competence in correctional mental health. *International Journal of Law and Psychiatry, 36*, 273–280.

Kennedy, H. G., O'Neill, C., Flynn, G., & Gill, P. (2010). *The Dundrum toolkit. Dangerousness, understanding, recovery and urgency manual (The Dundrum Quartet). Four structured professional judgment instruments for admission triage, urgency, treatment completion and recovery assessments.* Dublin: Trinity College Dublin.

King, M. (2003). *The Penguin history of New Zealand.* Auckland: Penguin Books.

Kuper, A. (1999). *Culture: The anthropologists' account.* Cambridge, MA: First Harvard University Press.

Mason, K., Bennett, H., & Ryan, E. (1988). *Report of the committee of inquiry into procedures used in psychiatric hospitals in relation to admission discharge or* release on leave of certain classes of patient ('The Mason Report'). Wellington: Department of Health.

McKenna, B., Skipworth, J., Tapsell, R., Madell, D., Pillai, K., Simpson, A., et al. (2015). A prison mental health in-reach model informed by assertive community treatment principles: Evaluation of its impact on planning during the pre-release period, community mental health service engagement and reoffending. *Criminal Behaviour and Mental Health, 25*(5), 429–439.

McKenna, B., Wiki, N., Cavney, J., Field, T., Cooper, E., & Wharewera, J. (2017). *The face validity of the DUNDRUM-3 and DUNDRUM-4 structured clinical judgment instruments: A Māori participatory action research perspective.* Paper presented at the International Association of Forensic Mental Health, Split, Croatia.

Ministry of Health. (2012). *Rising to the challenge: The mental health and addiction service development plan 2012–2017.* Wellington: Ministry of Health.

Ministry of Health. (2016). *Office of the Director of Mental Health annual report 2015.* Wellington: Ministry of Health.

Ministry of Justice. (2012). *Rangatahi Court: Evaluation of the early outcomes of Te Kooti Rangatahi.* Wellington: Kaipuke Limited.

Moore, J. D. (2012). *Visions of culture: An introduction to anthropological theories and theorists* (4th ed.). Lanham, MD: AltaMira Press.

Oakley Browne, M. A., Wells, J. E., & Scott, K. M. (2006). *Te Rau Hinengaro: The New Zealand mental health survey.* Wellington: Ministry of Health.

Orange, C. (1987). *The Treaty of Waitangi.* Wellington: Allen and Unwin.

Pere, L. M. (2006). *Oho Mauri: Cultural identity, wellbeing and Tangata Whai Ora/Motohake.* Unpublished Ph.D. dissertation, Massey University, New Zealand.

Pillai, K., Rouse, P., McKenna, B., Skipworth, J., Cavney, J., Tapsell, R., & Madell, D. (2016). From positive screen to engagement in treatment: A preliminary study of the impact of a new model of care for prisoners with serious mental illness. *BMC Psychiatry, 16*(9), https://doi.org/10.1186/s12888-016-0711-2.

Riley, M. (1994). *Māori healing and herbal.* Paraparaumu: Viking Sevenseas N.Z.

Sanders, D. (1999). Indigenous peoples: Issues of definition. *International Journal of Cultural Property, 8,* 4–13.

Salmond, A. (1991). *Two worlds: First meetings between Māori and Europeans 1642–1772.* Auckland: Viking.

Simpson, A. I. F., Brinded, P. M., Fairley, N., Laidlaw, T. M., & Malcom, F. (2003). Does ethnicity affect need for mental health service among New Zealand prisoners? *Australian and New Zealand Journal of Psychiatry, 37,* 728–734.

Simpson, A. I. F., & Friedman, S. H. (2016). Culture and forensic psychiatry. In R. Rosner & C. Scott (Eds.), *Principles and practice of forensic psychiatry* (pp. 785–792). Boca Raton, FL: CRC Press.

Skipworth, J., Cavney, J., Madell, D., McKenna, B., Nicholson, I., & Southen, C. (2011). *Auckland Regional Forensic Psychiatry Services clinical pathways project report*. Auckland: Northern District Health Board Support Agency Ltd.

Statistics NZ. (2013). *2013 census quick stats about culture and identity*. Wellington: Statistics NZ.

Stevenson, B. (2001). *The relationship between Māori cultural identity and health*. Unpublished Masters thesis, Massey University, New Zealand.

Sweetman, L. (2016). *Ngā Waiata O Tāne Whakapiripiri (The music of Tāne Whakapiripiri): Cultural expression, transformation, and healing in a Māori forensic psychiatric unit*. Unpublished Ph.D. dissertation, New York University, New York.

United Nations. (2009). *State of the world's Indigenous peoples*. New York: United Nations Secretariat of Permanent Forum on Indigenous Issues.

Walker, M. T. (2006). The social construction of mental illness and its implications for the recovery model. *International Journal of Psychosocial Rehabilitation, 10*(1), 71–87.

Winfree, L. T., Newbold, G., & Tubb, S. H. (2002). Prisoner perspectives on inmate culture in New Mexico and New Zealand: A descriptive study. *The Prison Journal, 82,* 213–233.

Wolf, E. (1982). *Europe and the people without history*. Oakland: University of California Press.

10

'Malignant Reality': Mental Ill-Health and Self-Inflicted Deaths in Prisons in England and Wales

Joe Sim

Introduction

A number of critical issues regarding prisoners with mental ill-health have been raised by academics and activists researching and working in this area. These include: the prevalence of ill-health amongst this population; their lack of access to treatment; the difficulties in transferring them to community programmes; the poor standard of prison care compared with the care delivered by outside agencies; and the lack of radical alternatives to the often-lamentable policies currently being pursued by the state (Mills and Kendall 2016). Building on this literature, this chapter has a more specific focus. It is concerned with the deaths in custody of these prisoners and addresses three areas in particular.

'Malignant Reality', in the title, is a phrase used by Thompson (2011, p. 145).

J. Sim (✉)
Liverpool John Moores University, Liverpool, UK
e-mail: J.Sim@ljmu.ac.uk

© The Author(s) 2018
A. Mills and K. Kendall (eds.), *Mental Health in Prisons*, Palgrave Studies in Prisons and Penology, https://doi.org/10.1007/978-3-319-94090-8_10

235

First, it considers the abject failure on the state's part to follow its own guidelines and policies for the care and protection of the deceased. In failing to deliver a coherent and humane strategy, state policies have reinforced the emotional scarring of this population, reproducing a subaltern, dispossessed group who are physically corralled, emotionally shredded and psychologically mortified in often-excruciating conditions, with the devastating impact that inevitably follows in terms of self-harm and self-inflicted death. Second, the chapter develops a critical, theoretical framework for analysing these deaths which challenges both liberal academic and state-defined discourses which have dominated the debate in this area and created, in Gramscian terms, a common-sense, reductive understanding of a complex social phenomenon. Finally, it outlines a number of radical, policy alternatives which transgress those currently being pursued by the state, which have failed to alleviate the distress of, and offer protection to, the confined and their families. As examples of 'abolitionist praxis' (Brown and Schept 2016, p. 451), these alternatives are designed to humanise prisoners with mental ill-health, drastically reduce the number of deaths inside and prevent families from experiencing the anguish they feel when a relative takes his or her own life.

State Incompetence and Systemic Neglect

In 2016, there were 120 self-inflicted deaths in prisons in England and Wales, almost double the number from four years previously and 'higher than any previous year on record' (National Audit Office [NAO] 2017, p. 5).[1] According to the Prisons and Probation Ombudsman, '70% of those who had taken their own lives between 2012 and 2014 had been identified as having mental health needs' (cited in ibid., p. 15). In December of the same year, the Joint Committee on Human Rights (JCHR) launched an inquiry into the deaths in detention of adults with mental health conditions (JCHR 2016). Eight specific issues were identified: the appropriateness of prison for those with mental health issues; the identification and assessment of risk; the safety of the prison environment; access to specialist mental health services and other treatments/interventions; maintaining family relationships; providing purposeful activity; the question of segregation/solitary confinement and the appropriate use of restraint; and, finally, learning lessons for the future. The Committee was particularly concerned about the state's neglect in implementing the recommendations it had made previously (JCHR 2016).

The inquiry followed an earlier report by the Equality and Human Rights Commission which noted that there were 1998 deaths in police, prison and psychiatric detention between 2010 and 2013. Just over 1200 of these deaths involved detainees with mental ill-health who were in, or following, police custody or who were in-patients detained under the Mental Health Act. A further 367 adults died from 'non-natural causes' in police and psychiatric detention while many of the 295 individuals who died from 'non-natural causes' in prison had mental health issues (Equality and Human Rights Commission 2015, p. 3). The Commission was unable to be more numerically precise as, scandalously, those responsible for managing the prison system did not record the number of prisoners with mental ill-health; the most recent data available derived from 1997, nearly two decades earlier (ibid., p. 5). For the Commission:

> ...the debate about how people are detained needs to go beyond the minimum standards that keep people alive. Those responsible for detention must ensure that people are not punished for behaviours that are viewed as disruptive but in fact are symptomatic of illness... It is impossible to talk about the high levels of people with mental health problems without questioning whether imprisonment is the appropriate place. (ibid., p. 7)

The report catalogued systemic failures, institutionalised negligence and sheer incompetence on the part of the state including: the failure to use the Assessment Care in Custody and Teamwork (ACCT) procedures to assess prisoners at risk; the failure to transfer essential information about individual prisoners even between prison wings; the failure of staff to understand data protection legislation; and the failure to acknowledge, pass on or act upon information from prisoners' families, thereby possibly increasing the level of risk their relatives faced. Additionally, the processes for identifying and managing risk were poor; medical records were unavailable or were difficult to access; there was a lack of awareness regarding changes in prisoners' circumstances around bereavement 'trigger dates' and with respect to individual histories of self-harm (ibid., pp. 38–40). Finally:

> In the course of our Inquiry we have come across cases from PPO [Prison and Probation Ombudsman] investigation reports where deaths have resulted from the failure to identify a prisoner's mental health condition and where concerns were identified but not shared with colleagues. *These deaths could have been prevented if prisons got the basics right.* (ibid., pp. 7–8, emphasis added)

The PPO supported the Commission's dispiriting conclusions. The Ombudsman investigated 557 deaths that had occurred between 2012 and 2014 and, once again, highlighted a catalogue of poor practices, errors and lack of compliance:

> While there were many examples of very good practice, there were also many cases where practice could and should have been better. Issues ranged from poor monitoring of compliance with medication and lack of encouragement to take prescribed drugs to inappropriate care plans which were not reviewed and updated, and did not include meaningful actions. Unfortunately, there have also been investigations where the provision of mental health care was simply inadequate...*it is not surprising that this review identifies significant room for improvement in the provision of mental health care.* (PPO 2016, p. 3, emphasis added)

In 2017, the NAO identified a range of other issues: the lack of clarity regarding how the objectives around mental health care in prison were to be achieved; the poor nature of healthcare data which made it difficult to ensure that services were planned and outcomes monitored; the impact of austerity cuts on the prison service; the lack of access to GP records; the difficulty in transferring prisoners to secure hospitals; and the lack of continuity in mental health care when prisoners were released (NAO 2017, pp. 7–10). Furthermore:

NHS England...does not know how much it spends on mental healthcare in prisons which means it cannot know whether it is providing value for money... The payment system for health services in prison is less mature than for acute physical health services in hospitals and does not enable the provider to change provision to meet need... There are also no mechanisms built into contracts that create an incentive to provide a better standard of care. (ibid., pp. 26 and 28)

Additionally, training for prison officers in mental healthcare provision was 'inadequate'. There were no refresher courses in 40% of the prisons in the NAO's study while officials failed to provide direction on how often training should take place (ibid., p. 36). The report noted that the Ministry of Justice had developed a four-hour training programme for staff who were also guided in 'how to approach a conversation with a vulnerable person' and 'when and how to refer prisoners to other services' (ibid., p. 37). All new staff were to undergo this training from May 2017 and there were plans to 'deliver training to existing staff who have not received other relevant training. *Not all training for existing staff will include all modules*' (ibid., emphasis added). Finally, although prison staff screened every prisoner coming into prison, scandalously:

> ...records do not give a complete picture. Staff did not enter data on the 'risk of suicide' in 68% of screening records, or on the 'risk of self-harm' in 59% of records. (ibid., p. 31)

The Reality of Self-Inflicted Death

The stark evidence presented in coroners courts between 2015 and 2017 illustrated the brutal dehumanisation experienced by prisoners with mental ill-health in the last hours of their lives. In Carl Foot's case, the inquest jury heard that he died four days after he was found hanging from a noose constructed from his bedsheet. His emergency cell bell had been left ringing for 27 minutes. A number of issues were highlighted at his inquest including: 'the failure to realise Carl was at risk, check his records or answer his bell within five minutes...along with a lack of managerial control over emergency bell services' (*Private Eye* 2015, p. 38).

In the case of Neal Price, although Salford prison had been made aware of his mental health condition, the institution had failed to put him on suicide alert despite Neil, himself, indicating to mental health assessors that:

> he had suicidal thoughts, felt depressed, and was concerned that he might lose his home…he told a nurse he felt his medication was not reducing his 'violent thoughts'. The nurse emailed the mental health team, but no one acted on it. In the early hours of 4 March, Neal was found dead, the 15th anniversary of his mother's suicide. (ibid.)

In April 2017, a coroner heard evidence concerning Chris Beardshaw, a remand prisoner who had killed himself in the segregation unit of the prison. He had 40 cuts to his arms. The inquest jury noted that:

> …poor training and a lack of communication meant inadequate care plans were drawn up…after he started self-harming. While a report registering concerns about his mental health had been opened, he was not relocated to a safe cell, nor checked five times an hour as he should have been. (*Private Eye*, May 2017, p. 36)

Matthew Stubbs had also tried to kill himself. He had been moved between different institutions before being isolated in the segregation unit in Leeds. Matthew received 'no medication for 24 hours'. He self-harmed but remained in segregation and was found hanging in his cell. Matthew's care was criticised by an independent consultant for 'the lack of urgent assessment of his deteriorating mental condition' (*Private Eye* 2015, p. 38). By April 2017, there had been a further 10 self-inflicted deaths in the prison making it second only to Woodhill, as the institution with the highest death rate in England and Wales (*Private Eye* 2017, p. 36).

The impact of the brutal cuts pursued by the state in the name of austerity was seen in individual cases. According to the charity INQUEST, in the case of Dean Saunders, who was found dead in Chelmsford prison in January 2016, the inquest jury found that:

Dean and his family were 'let down by serious failings in both mental health care and the prison system' and said that Care UK, the private company that runs healthcare at the prison, 'treated financial consideration as a significant reason to reduce the level of observations' of Dean, despite repeated warnings of his state of mind. They concluded that Dean killed himself while the balance of his mind was disturbed and that the cause of death was 'contributed to by neglect'. (INQUEST 2017a, p. 1)

Deborah Coles, INQUEST's Director, noted that Dean:

...a young father in serious mental health crisis, should never have been in prison in the first place. His death was entirely preventable. The responsibility for his death lies with a system that criminalises people for being mentally ill. As a society, we should not accept that deaths such as Dean's are inevitable: they are not. Time and again, we hear the empty words "Lessons will be learned". Without action and accountability, nothing will change. Until this government properly invests in mental health provision, and stops the use of prison for people in mental health crisis, these tragic and needless deaths will continue. (ibid.)

For Dean's father, there was '[a] toxic mix of understaffing, inadequate training, inadequate information, complacency, lack of passing information between all of them [the agencies involved]' (cited in Gentleman 2017, p. 11).

INQUEST has also documented the relationship between mental ill-health, self-harm and self-inflicted deaths in relation to women in prison highlighting 'sadly familiar patterns' of systemic, institutional neglect underpinning these deaths including: a history of disadvantage and complex needs; the inappropriate use of detention; isolation from family contacts; poor medical care including lack of access to therapy in prison; and unsafe environments. The lamentable, but avoidable, failure in communication within, and between prisons, was also apparent in the case of Melanie Beswick who was initially sentenced for fraud, which was her first offence. She was then sentenced to a further 12 months for defaulting on repaying the initial fraud. The inquest jury found that the lack of communication within the prison and between the outside hospital and the prison played a part in Melanie's death (INQUEST 2013, pp. 10–14).

Sarah Reed, a '32 year old black woman with mental ill- health' was the last woman to die in Holloway before the prison was closed. According to INQUEST, she 'died as a result of institutional racism, neglect and indifference'. Sarah had been assaulted by a police officer in 2012 and had been remanded to Holloway so that two psychiatric assessments could be conducted regarding her fitness to plead. The inquest jury concluded that 'unacceptable delays in psychiatric assessment and failures in care contributed to her death' (INQUEST 2017b, p. 1). In the light of her case, Deborah Coles, commented that:

> Serious mental health problems are endemic in women's prisons, with deaths last year [2016] at an all-time high. They continue because of the failure of the governments to act. The legacy of her death and the inhumane and degrading treatment she was subjected to must result in an end to the use of prison for women. The state's responsibility for these deaths goes beyond the prison walls and extends to the failure to implement the Corston review, tackle sentencing policy and invest in alternatives to custody and specialist mental health services for women. (ibid., pp. 1–2)

Thus, even on its own terms, the state's ability, or indeed desire, to fulfil its duty of care for those with mental health needs was failing, often catastrophically. These cases also demonstrated the desperate lack of accountability of those state servants responsible for protecting them. Time and again, as INQUEST has consistently noted, recommendations from juries, coroners, official reports and inquiries were simply ignored leaving some of the most vulnerable individuals in prison at the mercy of a culture where humanity, understanding and social justice were regarded as antithetical to the system's punitive ethos and where the whims of tickbox managerialism and short-term expediency were the norm.

Thinking Critically About Mental Ill-Health and Self-Inflicted Deaths in Prison[2]

In 2015, according to the NAO, there were:

...ten times more self-inflicted deaths per 1000 people in custody than there were suicides per 1000 people in the community. Men in prison were six times more likely to take their own life than men in the community, and women in prison were 24 times more likely to take their own life than women in the community. (NAO 2017, p. 15)

It would be easy to conclude from these stark data that self-inflicted deaths are not entirely unexpected given the alleged 'pathologies' of the prison population. In terms of theory, policy and practice, prison deaths in general, and those involving individuals with mental ill-health in particular, have been explained, and responded to, through a positivist lens which, at different historical moments, has emphasised, singularly, or in combination, discourses of pathology, risk and vulnerability. Consequently, this has allowed the state, supported by accredited psychiatric and criminological experts, a compliant and incorporated penal reform lobby and a sensationalist, monstering mass and (anti) social media, to socially construct the deceased as 'a pathological dysfunction in relation to the normal' (Foucault 2003a, p. 163). The facile, social construction of these prisoners as abnormal, in turn, has legitimated policy interventions which, theoretically, are supposed to lessen risk, reduce vulnerability and prevent future deaths. However, there are a number of problems with conceptualising the lives and deaths of prisoners through this simplistic and reductive discourse.

First, according to Diana Medlicott, not only are prisoners institutionally and systemically dehumanised but socially constructing some prisoners as being at risk of self-inflicted death allows the state to categorise 'the rest as invulnerable'. Crucially, she maintains that this binary divide is problematic and that it is the 'very special place characteristics of the prison [that] render *all* male prisoners socially vulnerable' (Medlicott 2001, p. 58, emphasis added). For Sim and Tombs (2014), if the prison environment is experienced:

as a punitive attack on [prisoners'] sense of self due to the nature of the prison's culture, then self-harming or death are, from their perspective, often the only options available to them. Therefore, rather than endlessly constructing, and concentrating on, categories of risk and vulnerability we would suggest an alternative perspective built on recognising the often harmful events experienced by prisoners, and the meanings they, and their families, attribute to these experiences. (p. 2)

Second, the focus on risk and vulnerability is legitimated by experts, operating as self-proclaimed, and self-serving, 'judges of normality' (Foucault 1979, p. 304). However, their capacity for predicting human behaviour is at best variable and, at worst, simply wrong. Despite the many theoretical and methodological weaknesses in expert knowledge around risk, specific groups and individuals within prisons continue to be socially constructed as susceptible to engaging in self-harm and acts which are likely to induce self-inflicted death. This focus on the pathological vulnerabilities of the few individualises the problem and distracts attention away from the destructive, structural operationalisation of power inside. For Cutcliffe and Riahi (2014, p. 238), not only is the 'diagnosis of so-called mental illness...more an art than a science' but the link between mental health and suicide is more problematic than first appears. Their evidence:

...casts doubt on, if not actually refutes, that suicide is a mental health disorder or rarely occurs without the presence and influence of a so-called mental illness. While it is abundantly clear that there is a relationship between suicide and mental health problems, it is also abundantly clear that it is epistemologically premature to convert suicide into depression. (ibid., p. 245)

Mobilising the discourse of vulnerability also misses another key point, namely that this classification:

sometimes operates to strip power away from populations that are already marginalised... Although they help some individuals to avoid blame for their difficulties, vulnerability discourses emphasise personal reasons for difficulties experienced by individuals, *diverting attention from structural issues*. (Brown 2016, pp. 45 and 51, emphasis added)

Third, the prison has *never* been a site for rehabilitation and reform. It is a state institution, which prisoners directly experience as meaningless, tormenting, terrorising, traumatising, humiliating and degrading. Within this punitive site:

> All prisoners can feel bereft and terrified through living in often-abject penal regimes that are built on the delivery of punishment and pain. Feeling bereft can generate a deep sense of loss, a lack of self-worth and self-esteem, underpinned by feelings of alienation, humiliation and uncertainty… These places traumatise the already-traumatised. Contrary to the state's official discourse, they make *all* prisoners vulnerable not just those who are defined as at risk… (Carlton and Sim 2018, p. 61, emphasis in the original)

Places of the 'Loneliest Loneliness'[3]: Death and Solitary Confinement

The specific issue of solitary confinement, mental ill-health, self-harm and self-inflicted death has also been highlighted by academics and activists who, again, have pointed to the state's failure to live up to its own rhetoric in terms of providing a duty of care to prisoners in segregation. In 2013–2014, 'there were eight self-inflicted deaths in segregated conditions' the highest number since 2005 (Prisons and Probation Ombudsman, cited in Shalev and Edgar 2016, p. 97). The institutional environment in segregation places often intolerable psychic pressures on the detained, through denying them the essence of their humanity: human contact, interpersonal support and social interaction. Scandalously, the Chief Inspector of Prisons found that, although not all cases were related to prisoners with mental ill-health, those 'who had been identified as at risk were being held in segregation without adequate justification in half of the prisons he reported on…' (NAO 2017, p. 41).

In their study of prisoners in segregation with mental ill-health, Shalev and Edgar (2016) identified a catalogue of failures in this area: health workers misunderstanding their role in the process of segregating prisoners; nursing staff deferring to custody staff in risk assessment procedures; little managerial consideration about the risk of prisoners harming themselves if they were segregated, particularly those already identified as being at risk;

the wide variation in the level of detailed documentation in ACCT forms; forms being filled in retrospectively; cursory examinations by mental health professionals; the lack of privacy which undermined medical confidentiality; and poor record keeping (ibid., pp. 96–102). They noted that:

> The three key components inherent in segregated confinement - social isolation, reduced sensory input (and enforced idleness), and increased control of prisoners even more than is usual in the prison setting, combine together to make for a toxic environment... This environment is known to have negative effects on health and wellbeing. (ibid., p. 91)

Segregated prisoners provided powerful, poignant testimonies about their experiences:

> All my mental health problems start kicking in—been really depressed listening to all the voices a lot more, just stuck in my thoughts.
>
> [Segregation] just made me worse and made me mentally even more ill.
>
> Ten suicide attempts so far, and my mental health is deteriorating, but I am doing better than a lot of the others.
>
> Before CSC, [Close Supervision Centre] I was on no medications. Now I am on anti-depressants, anti-psychotics, and valium. That is just the pressure of being here. Most CSC prisoners end up in hospitals.
>
> I'm in solitary confinement, and I know I'm deteriorating especially when I feel aggrieved by the injustice. Everything exacerbates my situation. My mental health will deteriorate, I have no doubt. I am pro-active. I read Sharon's books [about it]. I'm aware of how it's getting to me. This is just existence, with no quality of life. (ibid., pp. 94–95)

For some, self-harm and segregation were linked:

> The only time I hurt myself is when I'm down here (segregated).
>
> How ridiculous is this: you feel you are nobody's business. This is why people take overdose, die in seg.
>
> Question: How do you fill your time in segregation?

Answer: Feeling suicidal, neglected, victimised, locked up 23 hours, on my bed covering my head. I was cold, depressed, and suicidal. Cry myself to sleep not mentally able to do anything. Die, I wanted to die. (ibid., p. 99)

Shalev and Edgar (2016) proposed a number of reforms including: developing multi-disciplinary management strategies with a focus on mental health needs; avoiding using segregation for those awaiting transfer to NHS hospitals or on open ACCTs or receiving antipsychotic medication; improving communication between different groups within the prison system, i.e. mental health professionals and officers working in segregation; strict practices around medical records especially relating to the relationship between segregation and the risk of deterioration; ensuring medical confidentiality; training segregation officers in understanding different aspects of mental ill-health; training managers about the impact of segregation and the need for prisoner-focussed interventions (ibid., pp. 107–108).

The report by the NAO, discussed above, also pointed to the failure of the state's policies around solitary confinement. In 2016–2017, the 14-day period allowed under the Mental Health Act for transferring prisoners from prison to secure hospitals was only achieved in around one-third of cases while the waiting time for 7% of prisoners was over 140 days. Neither prison health care, nor the secure hospital system, had 'overall responsibility' for ensuring that the recommended time period of 14 days was met (NAO 2017, p. 43).

More generally, the NAO revealed that NHS England and the National Offender Management Service (NOMS),[4] the agency responsible for the management of the prison system, did not 'routinely track' how many prisoners were awaiting transfer to a secure hospital but did find that 'prisoners had waited an average of 47 days for their first assessment, a further 36 days for their second assessment and a further 13 days for the Secretary of State to sign a warrant for them to move to a secure hospital' (ibid., p. 44). There was also disruption to prisoners' care when they were transferred between prisons, their medical history was not always reviewed by healthcare staff, data were 'not always complete…and some prisoners told us that they did not get the same medication after transfer' (ibid.). Finally, there were issues around continuity of care as there was 'currently no routine follow-up to assess whether people who have received mental healthcare in prison continue to receive care on release' (ibid., p. 45).

Therefore, following the accounts above, and the systemic failings in the state's policies, rather than focussing on the peculiarities, dangers, failings or risks that individuals who are in segregation *might* pose to the social order of the prison, what is required is a psycho-social analysis of the harms generated by this gruelling environment. *This involves understanding what solitary confinement means and does to individuals and the destruction of their sense of selfhood.* As Stauffer has noted:

> Selves are formed intersubjectively, in the presence of others, for better and worse and regardless of whether any of us would have willed it to be this way. Acknowledging that brings us closer to understanding how selves and worlds can be destroyed by human violence, and why human beings can be wounded – not only physically – in such deep and lasting ways. *Being abandoned by those who have the power to help produces a loneliness more profound than simple isolation.* (Stauffer 2015, p. 5, emphasis added)[5]

Challenging State 'Truth': Death and Mental Ill-Health as 'Criminology from Below'[6]

In challenging, and seeking to radically transform, the current demoralising and destructive system, it is important to recognise that knowledge about prison deaths has *not* materialised as a result of state benevolence or a desire to make visible the distress and harm that prisoners experience. Nor has this knowledge appeared as a result of political concern. For politicians, as Deborah Coles has noted, 'dead prisoners do not win votes' (cited in Gentleman 2017, p. 9).

What *is* known about these deaths has been generated through radical praxis involving a combination of 'the tools of scholarship' (Foucault 2003b, p. 7) and the interventionist activism of families and grassroots organisations like INQUEST who have refused to be incorporated onto the terrain of the state and be 'defined-in' by its language, institutions and policies (Mathiesen 1980). The slogan, *Truth, Justice and Accountability*, is central to INQUEST's research and casework. This has allowed the charity to contest both the hypocritical expediency of the state's response to deaths in custody and challenge the interventions of liberal pressure groups whose often-futile, reform agenda has done little since the emergence of the prison to curtail the institution's deadly capacity for inflicting pain and punishment on the confined. This is not to decry the principled efforts of *some* in the prison reform lobby. However, taken as a whole, the lobby's incorporation into the state's policy formation network, *has* seen reformers defined into, and onto, the state's terrain (Ryan 1978; Sim 2018).

INQUEST's interventions have been built on utilising the harrowing accounts of prisoners, and their families, whose negative labelling and callous stereotyping have intensified the 'primal wound[s]'[7] of anguish and soul-crunching desolation they experience over the deaths of their relatives (INQUEST 2007a). As examples of the 'insurrection in subjugated knowledges' (Foucault 2003b, p. 7), these accounts have been crucial in challenging the state's definition of 'truth' concerning deaths in prison. They have also been central in shifting the focus towards understanding the experiences of prisoners as a form of social harm where the delivery of pain and punishment subverts and dominates the discursive window-dressing of rehabilitation and reform (Sim 2009; Scott 2016). These interventions have also contested the state's belligerent commitment to a highly contentious, unproven, manifestly misplaced, positivist discourse around self-inflicted deaths. In this discourse, the fault lies with the individual rather than with the structural processes of unfettered, discretionary power operating within bleak regimes, an authoritarian and heavily masculinised prison officer culture, systemic neglect and the threat and use of violence (Sim 2009).

Ideologically, because of this critical research, casework and activism, the state has not achieved hegemonic domination in terms of its definition of, and explanation for, the reality of deaths inside, nor for the policies it wishes to pursue. Its 'truth' has been seriously challenged, a challenge which has also dragged liberal reform groups onto a more critical and radical terrain without totally uncoupling them from its nefarious, incorporating power networks and processes (Sim 2018).

Within any social system and state institution '[t]here are always cracks and contradictions - and therefore opportunities' (Hall et al., cited in ibid., p. 182). It is these 'cracks and contradictions' which have been explored and exploited by critical researchers and activists who have, in Gramscian terms, turned 'common sense' into 'good sense' with respect to self-inflicted deaths in prison. The question, then, is, how can this work be developed, strategically and politically, with particular reference to the self-inflicted deaths of prisoners with mental ill-health? It is to this issue that the chapter now turns.

Developing Radical Alternatives and Structures of Democratic Accountability

Liberal reforms have dominated the debate around self-inflicted deaths in this area and have included: attempting to reduce the high number of prisoners with mental health issues in prison; improving mental health services for them; and diverting them from custody into the community. However, these reforms have 'simply tinker[ed] at the edges without getting to the root of the problem' (Mills and Kendall 2016, p. 198). Mills and Kendall rightly call for radical changes involving 'alternatives to confinement which embody values of justice, humility and compassion'. Following Ballatt and Campling, they argue for adopting the practice of 'intelligent kindness [which] suggests that we address social problems through practices that recognise our interdependence and bond us rather than by those that divide us and exclude the poor and most vulnerable' (ibid., p. 199). Similarly, Medlicott has argued for building a prison environment which recognises that '[all] prisoners require attention which is other than punitive, care that recognises their social rather than strictly medical needs, and opportunities to talk unguardedly and empathetically' (Medlicott 2001, p. 220).

This progressive transformation in the philosophical basis of the prison needs to be underpinned by radical shifts in penal practices inside, and criminal justice and social policies outside the walls. For example, fundamentally changing the sentencing culture in England

and Wales, running parallel with a moratorium on prison building, as well as shutting prisons down, would begin to seriously dent the country's reputation as the punishment capital of Europe. The statistics are damning. There were over 202,000 'arrivals' in prisons in England and Wales in 2016.[8] Over 86,000 were new prisoners, nearly 21,000 were recalls and over 95,000 were transfers between prisons. Over half—52%—of receptions were remand prisoners, while 58% of the sentenced population were serving sentences of less than 12 months. The entire population of an average, local prison was being replaced every three months (NAO 2017, pp. 4, 30, 31, and 38).

Prior to entering the social oblivion of the penal revolving door, many of these men and women were unemployed, poorly educated, homeless, had drug and alcohol problems, been sexually and physically abused and had mental health issues. These background data provide a stark and compelling illustration of the expurgatory role that the prison plays in the social cleansing of those on the economic and political margins of the wider society (Mathiesen 1974). They are 'social junk' (Spitzer 1975, p. 645). However, prisoners who have mental health issues are not *just* 'social junk'. Because of their ascribed, psychological status, they are *doubly* demonised: unloved, undesired, unappreciated and, above all, unwanted, a dispossessed, residual class for whom the society, in its most capricious, pitiless and virulent neoliberal form, has no need. They have been psychologically dismembered by wider economic, political and ideological processes, and by prisons themselves, operating as 'regions of sorrow' (Milton, cited in Solomon et al. 2015, p. 200) in, and on, their lives.

Internally, the redirection of the prison budget towards mental health services, the development of well-funded, non-privatised, radical alternatives to custody and training staff in the application of psychotherapeutic techniques and small group therapy, utilised in institutions like Grendon Underwood (Stevens 2013), would ensure that prisoners with mental ill-health would not suffer the often-ignominious treatment that they currently experience, and the intensification in their unresolved pain which the prison engenders. Focussing on the *pathology of the prison rather than on the pathology of the individual* would be a small, but important first step, in generating this fundamental change.

INQUEST has called for radical changes arising from its casework which has pointed to mental health care being 'a recurring feature of deaths in custody. Many inquests have revealed frequent shortcomings in the ability of the police and prisons to offer appropriate care to these individuals' (http://www.inquest.org.uk/issues/mental-health-deaths). The charity has demanded that robust structures of democratic accountability should be embedded within prisons including implementing recommendations from official bodies designed to prevent further deaths. As noted above, it has consistently pointed to the state's systematic failure to implement recommendations made by the Prisons and Probation Ombudsman, HM Chief Inspector of Prisons, coroners and, from outside the state, by INQUEST itself. These recommendations have been blatantly and routinely disregarded by those responsible for managing and operating prisons on a daily basis.

INQUEST, and others, have maintained that the Corporate Manslaughter and Corporate Homicide Act (CMCH) 2007 could be utilised when there is evidence of systemic failings in the system and gross negligence by prison staff (INQUEST 2007b). As Steve Tombs has pointed out:

> Many deaths in prison are the result of gross breaches in the duty of care through attitudes, policies and practices woven into the fabric of the prison service. The time is overdue for the CMCH Act to be tested there…a successful prosecution under the Act would provide a powerful, symbolic message that the routine, systematic deaths of those to whom the state and the prison service has a duty of care cannot continue without legal accountability. (Tombs 2016, p. 4)

Finally, a radical reconceptualisation of prison deaths would mean moving beyond the reductive, legalistic discourse of intent and towards critically considering the systemic negligence, incompetence, indifference and moral corruption of state servants which underpins the attitudes and behaviour of many of them (Carlton and Sim 2018). In other words, it would involve thinking about state servants as *active*, social agents in the deaths of the deceased:

The fact many deaths in prisons occur as a result of the failure to learn lessons from previous deaths or from the inept, incompetent and indifferent behaviour of state servants, either individually or collectively, has been well documented by INQUEST, the Chief Inspector of Prisons, the Prisons and Probation Ombudsman and different coroners. Given this...it is not necessary for intent to be present in the conventional, legalistic sense, for deaths in prison to be conceptualised as a form of violence. Indifference and neglect can and do kill and, further, generate a sense of bereavement and deeply-felt loss which can be as wounding for the families of the deceased as the intentional killing of their relative. (Carlton and Sim 2018, pp. 58–59)

Conclusion

Michel Foucault has noted that:

The whole penal system is essentially pointed toward and governed by death. A verdict of conviction does not lead, as people think, to a sentence of prison or death; if it prescribes prison, this is always with a possible added bonus: death... Prison is not the alternative to death: it carries death along with it... Prison is a death machine. (Foucault 2002, p. 419)

Throughout 2017, (when this chapter was written), Foucault's point was consistently and harrowingly highlighted as prisoners continued to live and die in penal and mental health institutions with no transparent systems of accountability with respect to attributing responsibility, determining blame, prosecuting offenders and seeing justice done for the dead and their families (INQUEST 2012, 2015). David Scott has developed this argument further by pointing out that prisons do not just induce physical death but also they are structured:

...to exhaust meaningful space and relationships, becoming a tomb for the living and a graveyard for those unable to cope with prison time... Systematically undermining forms of mutual aid, respect and recognition on the inside, the prison breaks connections with people on the outside and the ability of prisoners to build new relationships when released... It is the negation of the fulfilled life. [It] is a place which generates corporeal, civil and social death... (Scott 2016, p. 52)

This abject situation extends to other 'sites of state confinement' involving the deaths of individuals with mental ill-health (Carlton and Sim 2018). Between April 2011 and March 2015, the Southern Health NHS Foundation failed to investigate the deaths of over 1400 patients. And while the Trust examined the deaths of 30% of those with mental ill-health—which itself is scandalously low—this figure declined to 1% for those with learning disabilities and 0.3% for those over 65 (*The Guardian*, 10 December 2015, p. 4). Thus, the hierarchy of powerlessness is itself hierarchically organised in terms of classifying those with mental health issues into the deserving and undeserving for the purposes of investigating the causes of these deaths and ensuring accountability for them.[9]

Marx noted that the workhouse in the nineteenth century was a place of 'punishment for misery' (Marx cited in Palmer 2013, p. 55). This phrase aptly crystallises the systemic physical violence and aching desolation intrinsic to twenty-first century, neoliberal state institutions— penal and welfare, public and private, political and civil (Sim 2014). Responding empathically, humanely and radically to this aching desolation, and alleviating the suffering of *all* prisoners, including those with mental health issues, should be a moral, as well as a political duty, for the state. However, such enlightened responses are light years away from the state's current discourses and practices where, despite some honourable exceptions, a hypocritical, punitive expediency dominates the implementation of penal policy. Until this punitive, corrosive mentality is finally removed from the prison, and from the wider political culture, then, shamefully, for many prisoners, self-harm and self-inflicted death will appear to offer rational and meaningful alternatives to their existence given what they endure on a daily basis in the pathological culture of the prison system in England and Wales in the twenty-first century.

Acknowledgements Thanks to the staff at INQUEST and to David Scott and Carly Speed for discussing this issue with me, to Maureen Kenny for her technical support and to Kathy Kendall and Alice Mills for their patience.

Notes

1. It is also worth noting that between 2000 and 2013, there were 4573 deaths in psychiatric detention in England and Wales. This figure accounted for 60% of all deaths in state custody during this time (*Independent Advisory Panel on Deaths in Custody*, cited in Speed 2017a). Additionally, between April 2014 and March 2015, there were 227 patient deaths. This compared with 198 deaths that were reported between 2013 and 2014 (*Care Quality Commission*, cited in Speed 2017b).
2. What follows in this section is derived from the analysis developed in Carlton and Sim (2018) which, itself, built on the analysis developed by Canning (2014).
3. This is a phrase used by Nietzsche, cited in Atkinson (2014, p. 11).
4. NOMS is now known as Her Majesty's Prison and Probation Service.
5. Thanks to David Scott for pointing out this reference to me.
6. This is a phrase used by Sim et al. (1987, p. 7).
7. 'Primal wound' is a phrase used by David Remnick in an article entitled 'Leonard Cohen Makes It Darker' published in the New Yorker magazine. https://www.newyorker.com/magazine/2016/10/17/leonard-cohen-makes-it-darker (accessed 28 October 2016).
8. 'Arrivals' are classified as individuals coming to prison for the first time, or who were recalled to prison or who were moving between prisons.
9. Premature death also disproportionately impacts on the poor and the powerless in England and Wales who live, or simply exist, at the razor-sharp end of the social divisions that scar the social landscape. These deaths cut across this landscape generated, as they are, by poverty and disease, air pollution which disproportionately affects minority ethnic groups, dangerous and alienating working conditions and the pitiless welfare sanctions inflicted on the poor, pejoratively labelled as 'bodies without brains' (Wilson and Anderson 2011, p. 50).

Bibliography

Atkinson, K. (2014). *Life after life*. London: Black Swan.

Brown, K. (2016). Beyond protection: "The vulnerable" in the age of austerity. In M. Harrison & T. Sanders (Eds.), *Social policies and social control: New perspectives on the 'not-so-big' society* (pp. 39–52). Bristol: Policy Press.

Brown, M., & Schept, J. (2016). New abolition, criminology and a critical carceral studies. *Punishment and Society, 19*(4), 440–462.

Canning, V. (2014). Introduction. In V. Canning (Ed.), *Sites of confinement* (pp. 1–5). Weston-Super-Mare: European Group for the Study of Deviance and Social Control.

Carlton, B., & Sim, J. (2018). Deaths in sites of state confinement: A continuum of routine violence and terror. In S. Read, S. Santazoglou, & A. Wright (Eds.), *Loss, bereavement and the criminal justice system: Issues, possibilities and compassionate potential* (pp. 54–63). London: Routledge.

Cutcliffe, J. R., & Riahi, S. (2014). Twenty-first-century "snake oil" salesmanship: Contemporary care of the suicidal person in formal mental health care. In D. Holms, J. D. Jacob, & A. Perron (Eds.), *Power and the psychiatric apparatus* (pp. 235–250). Farnham: Ashgate.

Equality and Human Rights Commission. (2015). *Preventing deaths in detention of adults with mental health conditions*. London: Equality and Human Rights Commission.

Foucault, M. (1979). *Discipline and punish: The birth of the prison*. Harmondsworth: Peregrine.

Foucault, M. (2002). Pompidou's two deaths. In J. Faubion (Ed.), *Michel Foucault: Essential works of Foucault 1954–1984* (pp. 418–422). London: Penguin.

Foucault, M. (2003a). *Abnormal: Lectures at the College de France 1974–1975*. London: Verso.

Foucault, M. (2003b). *Society must be defended*. London: Penguin.

Gentleman, A. (2017, January 25). We were told: He is safe, he is secure, don't worry. *The Guardian*, pp. 9–11.

The Guardian (2015, December 10), p. 4. Available at: http://www.inquest.org.uk/issues/mental-health-deaths. Accessed 24 Aug 2017.

INQUEST. (2007a). *Unlocking the truth—Families' experience of the investigation of deaths in custody*. London: INQUEST.

INQUEST. (2007b). *Briefing on the Corporate Manslaughter and Homicide Bill 2006–07*. London: INQUEST.

INQUEST. (2012). *Learning from death in custody inquests: A new framework for action and accountability*. London: INQUEST.

INQUEST. (2013). *Preventing the deaths of women in prison: The need for an alternative approach.* London: INQUEST.

INQUEST. (2015). *Deaths in mental health detention: An investigation framework fit for purpose?* London: INQUEST.

INQUEST. (2017a). *Jury concludes neglect contributed to death of Dean Saunders at HMP Chelmsford.* London: INQUEST. Available at: http://www.inquest.org.uk/media/pr/jury-concludes-neglect-contributed-to-death-of-dean-saunders-at-hmp-chelmsf. Accessed 7 Sept 2017.

INQUEST. (2017b, June/July). *Newsletter.* London: INQUEST.

Joint Committee on Human Rights (JCHR). (2016, December 15). *Press Notice No 20.* Session 2016–17. London: Houses of Parliament.

Mathiesen, T. (1974). *The politics of abolition.* London: Martin Robertson.

Mathiesen, T. (1980). *Law, society and political action.* London: Academic Press.

Medlicott, D. (2001). *Surviving the prison place.* Aldershot: Ashgate.

Mills, A., & Kendall, K. (2016). Mental health in prisons. In Y. Jewkes, J. Bennett, & B. Crewe (Eds.), *Handbook on prisons* (pp. 187–204). London: Routledge.

National Audit Office (NAO). (2017). *Mental health in prisons.* HC 42 Session 2017–18. London: National Audit Office.

Palmer, B. (2013). Reconsiderations of class: Precariousness as proletarianization. In L. Panitch, G. Albo, & V. Chibber (Eds.), *The socialist register 2014* (pp. 40–62). London: The Merlin Press.

Prisons and Probation Ombudsman (PPO). (2016). *Learning from PPO investigations prisoner mental health.* London: Prisons and Probation Ombudsman.

Private Eye. (2015, November 13–26). No. 1405.

Private Eye. (2017, April 21–May 4). No. 1442.

Ryan, M. (1978). *The acceptable pressure group.* London: Saxon House.

Scott, D. (2016). Regarding rights for the Other: Abolitionism and human rights from below. In L. Weber, E. Fishwick, & M. Marmo (Eds.), *The Routledge international handbook of criminology and human rights* (pp. 50–60). London: Routledge.

Shalev, S., & Edgar, K. (2016). *Deep custody: Segregation units and close supervision centres in England and Wales.* London: Prison Reform Trust.

Sim, J. (2009). *Punishment and prisons.* London: Sage.

Sim, J. (2014, May) "Welcome to the machine": Poverty and punishment in austere times. *Prison Service Journal, 213,* 17–23.

Sim, J. (2018). We are all (neo) liberals now: Reform and the prison crisis in England and Wales. *Justice, Power and Resistance, 2*(1), 165–188.

Sim, J., & Tombs, S. (2014). *Submission to The Harris Review. Independent review into self-inflicted deaths in NOMS custody of 18–24 year olds.* Available at: http://iapdeathsincustody.independent.gov.uk/wp-content/uploads/2015/08/Submission-to-Harris-Review-from-Professor-Sim-and-Professor-Tombs.pdf. Accessed 24 Aug 2017.

Sim, J., Scraton, P., & Gordon, P. (1987). Introduction: Crime, the state and critical analysis. In P. Scraton (Ed.), *Law, order and the authoritarian state* (pp. 1–70). Milton Keynes: Open University Press.

Solomon, S., Greenberg, J., & Pyszczynski, T. (2015). *The worm at the core: On the role of death in life.* London: Random House.

Speed, C. (2017a). Deaths in psychiatric detention. In S. Morley, J. Turner, K. Corteen, & P. Taylor (Eds.), *Companion of state power, liberties and rights* (pp. 57–59). Bristol: Policy Press.

Speed, C. (2017b). As little regard in life as in death: A critical analysis of subjugation and accountability following deaths in psychiatric detention. *Illness, Crisis and Loss, 25*(1), 27–42.

Spitzer, S. (1975). Toward a Marxian theory of deviance. *Social Problems, 22,* 638–651.

Stauffer, J. (2015). *Ethical loneliness: The injustice of not being heard.* New York: Columbia University Press.

Stevens, A. (2013). *Offender rehabilitation and therapeutic communities: Enabling change the TC way.* London: Routledge.

Thompson, H. (2011). *The Gonzo papers anthology.* Basingstoke: Pan/Macmillan.

Tombs, S. (2016). Prison deaths: A case of corporate manslaughter? Available at: https://theconversation.com/prison-deaths-a-case-of-corporate-manslaughter-69729. Accessed 30 Oct 2017.

Wilson, D., & Anderson, M. (2011). Understanding Obama's discourse on urban poverty. In A. Bourke, T. Dafnos, & M. Kip (Eds.), *Lumpencity* (pp. 43–74). Ottawa: Red Quill Books.

11

Institutional Captives: US Women Trapped in the Medical/Correctional/Welfare Circuit

Maureen Norton-Hawk and Susan Sered

You could hear Katie coming before she ever arrived at our office door. She was always talking rapidly, at least one or two octaves above normal. Plopping down on the office chair she would reach into the rolling suitcase that was her constant companion and pull out a package of orange frosted Hostess Cupcakes. With a grin, she would hand the confectionary to us as she knew that we had a soft spot for them. We never asked how she, as a poor, often homeless, woman, could and would give so generously. But that was Katie.

Given her history of abuse, mental illness, homelessness and addiction, one might expect an angry, bitter, vengeful woman, beaten up by life one time too many. Instead of anger, she was an unusually smiling and trusting person who, because of these traits, often found herself exploited or abused. Each time she was victimised, she would pick herself up and start again.

M. Norton-Hawk (✉) · S. Sered
Suffolk University, Boston, MA, USA
e-mail: mnhawk@suffolk.edu

S. Sered
e-mail: ssered@suffolk.edu

A. Mills and K. Kendall (eds.), *Mental Health in Prisons*, Palgrave Studies in Prisons and Penology, https://doi.org/10.1007/978-3-319-94090-8_11

Six years after we first met her, she was brutally murdered, her body dumped by the roadside. She did not deserve to die this way. More importantly, she did not deserve to live the way that she had to live. In addition to fighting her own personal struggles, she was faced with well-intentioned agencies that always fell short of what she needed. Again and again, she would start down the long road to recovery and then fail when programs ended, support was withdrawn, or when she did not live up to the myriad requirements and regulations of the institutional circuit. Again and again, she would start from scratch with a whole new set of intake procedures, new therapists, new counsellors, new doctors, new advocates, and new parole and probation officers, each with their own set of rules, prescriptions, carrots and sticks. Even her death did not lead to institutional resolution: her murder has never been solved.

Introduction

Of the 1.6 million incarcerated Americans in 2015, 111,000 (7%) are women (Carson 2016). Females incarcerated in Massachusetts—the state where we followed a cohort of women post-incarceration for five years—account for a similar 7% (720) of total inmates (Cannata and Papagiorgakis 2017). While still representing only a small percentage of the larger prison population, from 1980 to 2015, the number of women imprisoned nationally has experienced a 744% increase from the 13,206 women incarcerated in 1980 (Kalish 1981). Massachusetts outpaced national statistics with a 1025% increase over these thirty-five years (Cannata and Papagiorgakis 2017; Minor-Harper 1982).

The majority of prisoners are eventually released (Hughes and Wilson 2002). Of the 2328 individuals freed from Massachusetts' prisons into the community in 2016, 523 were female (Cannata and Papagiorgakis 2017). Successful re-integration of released prisoners is the formal mission of the Massachusetts Department of Corrections (2011, p. 5): 'Our mission is to promote public safety by managing offenders while providing care and appropriate programming in preparation for successful re-entry into the community'.

Successful re-entry typically is determined by the rate of recidivism. One year after release, 17% of women incarcerated in Massachusetts are rearrested (Papagiorgakis 2016a); after 3 years, the percentage more than doubles to 35% (Papagiorgakis 2016b). Numerous studies have been conducted to determine what individual traits are associated with female re-incarceration so that programs could be developed to help these women avoid criminal activity. Variables that impact on recidivism are age, criminal history, lacking a pro-social network, failing to obtain employment, limited education, having an extensive criminal history and substance abuse (Sweeten et al. 2013; Huebner and Berg 2011; Bender et al. 2010; Deschenes et al. 2007; Stuart and Brice-Baker 2004; Kruttschnitt and Gartner 2003; Laub and Sampson 2001).

But simply staying out of prison is an inadequate measure of success. For that reason, we launched a five-year study in which we followed the experiences of a cohort of women after their release from the Massachusetts' women's state prison. Over the course of the five years, we saw that not all of the women were re-incarcerated, but virtually none of the women moved into a safe and stable lifestyle with independent secure housing and employment. We began to understand that their failure transcended their individual shortcomings. It involved societal constraints reinforced by a variety of often well-intended social service and healthcare institutions.

Programs have been developed to address individual challenges, but, on the whole, success in programs is measured in terms of completion rate and rarely in terms of the ongoing impact of the program. Indeed, all of the women in our study entered and often completed multiple programs over the course of the five years.

Research

Prior to 2008, we conducted extensive research on the challenges that confront post-incarcerated women. This preliminary research included exhaustive literature reviews as well as interviewing the personnel of numerous agencies that provide services to women after they are released from prison. With this information, we created an initial intake survey that covered housing, money and jobs, education and programs, romantic relationships, family, children, health, drug use, contact with the correctional system, recreational activities, frightening and unpleasant events, and plans for the future. These data provided quantitative, baseline information as well as permitting confirmation that the samples from the two facilities were not significantly different.

After receiving approval from Suffolk University's Institutional Review Board as well as the directors of the two facilities, we recruited participants in the spring of 2008. For three months, we frequented the women's centre of a Boston multi-service facility serving poor and homeless adults and a nearby halfway house for women on parole. The intended sample size was 50. From March to June, the researchers attended weekly gatherings at the two facilities to explain the research and recruited 47 volunteers. If a woman was willing to participate, arrangements were made to conduct an initial comprehensive intake questionnaire. At this first interview, the women signed consent forms following a description of potential risks and benefits of the study. Each woman was assigned a code to protect her anonymity.

The volunteers agreed to meet monthly, at which time they would be rewarded with a monthly pass to the city's mass transit system. Every three months, the women met for a longer in-depth interview. While the initial intake provided the researchers with a considerable amount of quantitative data, the monthly interviews were more qualitative. At the quarterly meetings, the researchers used primarily open-ended questions to provide detailed information about the lives of these women post-incarceration. Extensive written notes were taken during the interviews and then coded. We also regularly spent time at the various facilities that the women frequented. As the women came to know us, we accompanied them to numerous court hearings, medical appointments, parties, shopping trips, christenings, and program graduations. Notes on these gatherings were also collected. As the qualitative data accumulated, patterns emerged that helped to identify, define, and clarify the concepts that are the basis of our research. Because most of the women did not have permanent addresses or a regular telephone service, keeping in touch was an enormous challenge. However, thirty-two women remained in touch with us throughout the five-year study period and beyond.

Their stories emerged bit by bit over time. Often, we did not hear the real story until several years into the study. And still today, we hear different versions and we witness diverse interactions with their friends and family. While five years is an arbitrary timeframe, it allowed us to develop quite significant relationships with at least some of the women and to have opportunities to be with them as their lives have changed. In several instances, the rapport with us became one of the longest lasting and most stable relationships the subjects had ever experienced. Several women have told us that they have stuck with us because they are determined to finish one thing in their lives. A few make a point of telling us about insights for us to pass along to policy-makers.

Participants

At the time we began the study, 34% of the women were aged 41 or older; 43% were aged 31–40; 23% were aged 20–30. This demographic—slightly older than the typical incarcerated female population in Massachusetts and quite a bit older than comparable populations in other states—has allowed us to get a sense of women's experiences beyond the life stage at which they are most likely to be incarcerated. Very similar to the larger female incarcerated population, the majority of the women were single, and had never married (57%). However, most of the women were engaged in numerous, often unstable relationships over the study period.

The women have multiple inter-related problems of physical and mental illness, poverty, low level of education, disabilities of various sorts (developmental, hearing, physical and mental), troubled families, little or no work histories and more. Over 40% had less than a high school education. This may explain, in part, the reason that only a third were regularly employed prior to their involvement in the study. Social Security Disability Insurance (SSDI), food stamps, food banks, and financial help from family or friends helped to offset the lack of a stable income. Most of the women we came to know did not complete high school and quite a few struggle with basic literacy. When they do find employment, they often are confronted with sexual harassment from bosses or clients, and they typically are the first to be fired. The salaries they receive are not sufficient to cover rent and food, thus they continue to rely on a variety of agencies for housing subsidies, food stamps, and emergency assistance. In short, even when one problem is effectively addressed, another problem is likely to offset any gains made by the woman.

The racial make-up of the study participants is nearly identical to that of the overall population of incarcerated women in Massachusetts (72% White, 19% Black, 11% Asian/Hispanic). This racial make-up is not typical for most of the United States. In general, the black women were somewhat more likely to have good relationships with their natal families, were somewhat less willing to go to halfway houses, more likely to finish out a prison term than choosing early release into community supervision, and were somewhat more likely to struggle with literacy and the ability to fill out forms. White women were somewhat more likely to have been sexually abused, rejected by their natal families, have had some post-secondary school education and were more interested in various rehabilitation and sobriety programs.

By far, the most likely reason for incarceration was for a drug offense (37%), usually possession, followed by property offenses (17%). Drug use by marginally employed women necessitates involvement in property crimes like shoplifting, bad checks, and robbery. Only 13% of the participants in the study were convicted of a violent offense, far lower than the 34% of women in custody of Massachusetts Department of Corrections. This may be because drug offenders cycle in and out of prison more frequently than those convicted of violent crimes.

Post-incarceration, women are confronted with a myriad of problems that somehow must be resolved. Lack of education creates hurdles to employment. Thirty-one per cent of the women committed to the Massachusetts state prison in 2016 had less than a 9th grade reading level and less than a 6th grade math level, leaving no realistic employment choices beyond low wage work. Employment and social engagement become particularly challenging when you suffer from a mental illness. In 2016, 74% of women incarcerated in Massachusetts had open mental health cases, 15% were diagnosed with a serious mental illness (SMI), and 61% were on psychotropic medication

(Cannata and Papagiorgakis 2017). Additionally, upon release, many women return to the same disadvantaged neighbourhood, making personal and financial stability unlikely. After the city of Boston, which accounts for the largest percentage of women released to that community, women were most likely to return to Lynn, Lowell, Lawrence and Brockton (Papagiorgakis 2017). These four cities have median incomes far below the state average (Massachusetts Median Household Income City Rank 2012–2014).

Captives of the Institutional Circuit

Institutional Circuit

The term 'institutional circuit' was coined by Hopper et al. (1997) to describe the loop of agencies, programs and facilities providing services to people who are homeless and mentally ill. Despite ostensibly different mandates (punishment, protection and helping), the various institutions of the penal-welfare-healthcare system constitute one interlocking meta-system ('the system') in the experiences of the American caste of the ill and infirm, abused and afflicted. This circuit has many of the attributes of what sociologists call 'total institutions' (Goffman 1961); that it is composed of all-encompassing hierarchical facilities in which similarly situated people are cut off from the wider community and culture, obligated to follow detailed rules and regulations, dispossessed of their 'outside' identities and statuses, and drilled in institutional values and norms. The 'total-ness' of these institutions serves, over time, to persuade inmates that the institutions' ways are the only ways. Unlike conventional total institutions such as prisons, boarding schools and army camps, the institutional circuit does not confine its captives within a single building (although there are certain neighbourhoods in which free clinics, food banks, methadone clinics, homeless shelters and other services are concentrated, thus containing the marginalised populations who frequent these services). Rather, the power of the institutional circuit is diffuse, hard to identify. Following Foucault, we see this type of power as particularly difficult to resist or escape. It is everywhere, rather than confined to particular buildings. It is hard to identify in that it is composed of both punishing and 'helping' institutions.

Dewey and St. Germain (2016) in their research on street prostitution use the phrase 'the criminal justice and social services alliance' to discuss the power of these integrated, bureaucratic, ideological institutions. This alliance promotes a belief that the women's history of victimisation is the cause of their illegal and immoral behaviour, that combinations of punishment and treatment are the answer and that women must affirm a readiness for change. These interlocking institutions are often well-intentioned, always underfunded and typically ineffective, bureaucratic agencies. On the surface, the mission of the circuit is to provide services to poor, mentally ill, homeless, marginalised, 'deviant' populations. In reality, the cumulative power of this circuit isolates these populations in economically segregated areas, constraining the choices of those unlucky enough to have to cycle through the institutional circuit.

Institutional Captivity

We introduce the term 'institutional captivity' to describe the experiences of women trapped in an institutional circuit made up of battered women's shelters, homeless shelters, prisons, jails, probation, parole, rehabilitation facilities, detoxification facilities, clinics, respite care, hospitals, welfare offices, food stamp and WIC (Women, Infants and Children) offices, psychiatric units, child welfare offices, family court, drug courts, public housing, sober houses, recovery meetings and parenting classes.

The women 'institutional captives' were born or drawn into the system of corrections, social services and public health care. Many of these women have known only this system. Their parents before them moved between corrections (either their own incarceration or that of a family member), social services (public assistance for housing, food, foster care) and the public healthcare providers. Many of the women come from homes that were already part of the institutions (i.e. welfare, subsidised housing and foster care) so they grew up learning how to be a good 'institutional captive'.

Other women were drawn in through the correctional system as teen-agers when they ran away from abusive homes, or as young adults when they were first picked up on minor charges. In prison, they learned the tactics that allowed them to survive. Charlotte grew up in a typical, middle-class family. She was involved in school activities and sports. She loved to go skiing in the winter, heading for the mountains any chance she got. Charlotte also drank heavily. After she was arrested and con-victed of a DUI (driving under the influence), she had her first intro-duction to the prison system. Charlotte did not see herself as having any similarity to most of the women she met. However, 'you have to play the game when you are in there'. She explains that you need to find a group that accepts you, women who you can trust, and you have to learn the informal rules. She said these norms, which allow you to sur-vive in prison, do not translate well to mainstream society. Even though Charlotte identified herself as 'not like those other women' she, like the others, was caught up in the institutional circuit on her release.

These often-marginalised women are increasingly dependent on well-intentioned institutions that require adherence to complex, often arbitrary and counterproductive rules. The women are taught to be dependent on these services, thus taking away any sense of independ-ence. Even when they qualify for assistance, it turns out that Social Security Insurance (SSI) and Temporary Assistance to Needy Family (welfare) remittances are not sufficient to live on. As a result, recipi-ents also are drawn into homeless shelters or other housing programs. Homeless shelters, while better than the street in most instances, are structured around rules that seem designed for people to break them. For a mother, residence in a homeless shelter is a sure-fire way to draw in child welfare services. Child welfare services often require drug testing which in turn easily leads them into the correctional system when they relapse. Probation and parole often require constant urine tests which make it impossible to hold down a job. And children like Nancy's son, who were drawn into child welfare services, are more likely than other children to end up in juvenile detention facilities, jails and prisons—all but guaranteeing that they will remain stuck in the same institutional circuit that failed them from the start.

Once released, the system still controls these women, both through the overt restraints of parole or probation and through subtler social forces that limit their ability to successfully navigate mainstream society. As Isabella explained, 'It's a system that is designed for us to fail'. For example, people eagerly agree to long probations because they want to minimise jail time. But the probation conditions make it impossible for them to hold down jobs after they are released. They must come in for frequent urine tests and meetings with the parole office and they are required to attend numerous (sometimes daily) AA or NA meetings. 'Employers are not interested in keeping employees who constantly are leaving work for these things'. Isabella articulated, 'I hit the junkie ceiling – like the glass ceiling for women. I can't go further because of my record and probation conditions. I don't earn enough money for a decent life so I go back to using'.

At this point, nearly all of the study women have qualified for SSDI on the basis of mental illness. While their monthly SSDI payments allow them to scrape by, they also keep them locked in the circuit. On the one hand, they cannot risk losing Disability by taking a job. On the other hand, the disability payments are so small (a little over $700/ month) that they continue to use other social services as well as engage in petty crime such as shoplifting or low-level drug dealing that eventually sends them back to prison.

Constrained Choices

Over the past five years, we have seen the same study participants sober and on drug runs; homeless and housed; employed and unemployed; in a supportive relationship and abused by a boyfriend; enthusiastically attending church and absolutely disinterested in religion; involved on a daily basis with their child and out of the children's lives; sick and healthy, happy and despondent. Sometimes when we talked to them, they would tell us how well things are going; perhaps they finally got housing, a kind boyfriend, sobriety, charges dropped, health care, surgery, better medication, food stamps, visits with children, a part-time job, a wonderful new caseworker, or reconciliation with estranged family members. But as we have learnt over the years, how well things are going one month or one year are unlikely to predict how things will go later down the line.

Social position and policies determine what options are available when making decisions that impact one's lifestyle. One often hears, 'well it is the women's choice' to use drugs, be a single mom, be on welfare, be involved with a violent partner or commit a crime. While women do have choices, these choices are constrained by their gender, social class, economic status, and race. Most of the women post-incarceration return to the same poor, marginalised, urban neighbourhood from which they came. These locations provide easier access to agencies like probation offices, courts, medical and mental health care for the poor, homeless shelters, drug treatment facilities, meals, food stamps, job training, and family members.

These neighbourhoods have few opportunities for the women to escape the institutional circuit, the poverty and lack of opportunity that is endemic in these areas. While providing few avenues to improve their situation, the neighbourhoods provide easy access to illegal behaviour which the women often return to in desperation. These illegal activities may look promising to women who have few other options but they further draw them deeper into the circuit. The longer one remains in the circuit, whether they are born into it or drawn into it, the more reified the norms that support illegal behaviour become. Women who are poor and unemployable due to a criminal record, lack of job experience or ongoing health or mental health issues may resort to legally tapping public financial assistance, but this assistance locks them into the circuit. SSDI is available (though typically requires repeated applications and medical assessments) for women who are diagnosed with a mental illness. However, they cannot ever become 'well' because they would lose their only source of income.

Katie: Stuck in the Institutional Circuit

This mostly toothless, somewhat inarticulate, warm, sensitive and giving (she brought us presents like candy which we are pretty sure she 'lifted') 49-year-old white woman is a good example of 'convicted at birth'.

Katie was born in Ohio in a family with four siblings, three brothers and one sister, and none who would be considered a success. Their problems range from alcoholism to mental illness to criminality. Her father physically abused the mother and all the children. One day Katie fell while playing during recess. She had to go to the Emergency Room. Her father was so angry at the expense of the hospital visit that he beat her until she lost consciousness.

Her father was also sexually abusive. Katie felt a bit lucky because her father seemed to be more attracted to her younger sister. That sister now has a major depressive disorder and has attempted suicide multiple times. The mother was too afraid (according to Katie) to confront the father. In many ways, she was complicit, even if the complicity was based on fear. 'My mother would send one of the girls into the bathroom with toilet paper for my father. We all knew what was going on'.

The familial dysfunction may explain why the family was so mobile, moving at least two times a year. 'We moved around a lot. I use to go to school with bruises and black and blue marks. No one ever asked me about it. I guess because we never stayed in the same place long enough'. In California, Katie entered the military as a way to avoid the abuse at home. Like many abused children, Katie found herself involved with abusive men in adulthood. Sam, the father of two of her five children, was very abusive. On Sam's release from prison, Katie was so afraid that he would come looking for her that she lived under a highway overpass for weeks in order to avoid him.

Navigation of large bureaucracies has frustrated most Americans at one time or another. Women who are poor, under-educated, suffering from mental illness, drug-addicted and homeless find these agencies particularly challenging. For example, at various times, Katie received services for her drug addiction through the Bureau of Substance Abuse Services which was one sub-agency of the Department of Public Health, a division of the Office of Health Services under the administration of the Executive Office of Health and Human Services. Each level of each agency has its own rules, regulations, administration and culture. For women with multiple issues, the complexity of these bureaucracies poses enormous challenges. The women must remember the regulations that apply to each agency, expect sudden rule and personnel changes, keep appointments, and retain important documents like birth certificates, health information, identification, and any other pertinent information that will ensure eligibility. As one woman stated, 'obtaining services becomes a full-time job'.

Katie was provided services by numerous bureaucratic agencies (highlighted agencies in Fig. 11.1, Organisational Chart Massachusetts Executive Offices). She was a frequent client of The Veterans Administration (VA), whose mission was to provide shelter, counselling and job training. She had multiple stays at The Kingston House, which was under contract with the Department of Corrections. The Kingston House's formal mission is to support people who have a history of substance abuse, incarceration and homelessness. This support takes the form of highly structured and supervised residential programs. St. Francis House provided medical and psychological care. The Boston Housing Authority (BHA), a division of the Department of Housing and Community Development, at various points in her adult life, provided subsidised housing. Katie received a monthly SSDI check from the federal program that provides assistance to people with mental and physical disabilities. She served multiple, often short-term, incarcerations at the county and state prison for women, an institution that, in part, states their mission is rehabilitation. Before losing her children,

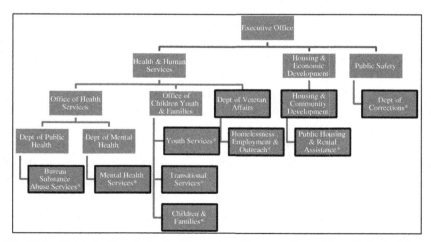

Fig. 11.1 Organisational chart—Massachusetts executive offices (Adapted from state government organizational chart—Commonwealth of Massachusetts, 1 January 2008)

she was immersed in the various departments of the Office of Children, Youth and Families.

While Katie received services from countless social agencies, whose formal mission indicated a desire to provide assistance and/or rehabilitation, these services, while sometimes providing temporary relief, were ineffective and often counterproductive.

Housing

When we first met Katie, she was in the process of moving from the Kingston House to the Veterans Homeless shelter. After a month, she relapsed so was sent back to detox then again back to the VA. She stayed a month and went out and used again. She was sent back to detox and returned to the VA shelter. 'It is not bad there. You can't be in your room from seven to three so I just go to the common and take a nap'. After leaving the VA shelter, Katie found herself homeless and eventually residing at the Woods Mullen Shelter. She kept her things at Pine Street Inn because too much gets stolen at Woods Mullen. Katie also sometimes stayed on the Cape with Sam's (abusive boyfriend) mom so that she could be close to her oldest son who lives in Hyannis. She was looking for other housing as Sam's release from prison was imminent.

Two years after we first met, Katie moved back to the VA shelter in Boston. Things did not go well at the VA. One problem was that some women refused to follow any type of proper hygiene. Katie talked about one woman in particular 'who was dirty and who stunk up the place'. She said she used to spray with Lysol when she was there. Since leaving the Kingston House, Katie had lived in six different places: the VA, homeless shelters (three), Sam's mom's and back to the VA.

At two and a half years, Katie finally had subsidised housing and moved to Malden in a rent-subsidised apartment. She was paying about $250 a month. Katie became afraid to stay there after a woman was stabbed in the apartment building. She said it was awful, with blood splatted everywhere. Katie said the police descended on the apartment complex, interrogating her about what she knew. To deal with the distressing situation, Katie returned to drug use. She had no problem getting the drugs because the subsidised apartment complex was a haven for drug traffickers.

Criminal Justice System

Katie was still on probation at this time. Her probation officer ordered an unscheduled drug test. Katie's test was positive, which violated her probation. She was sent back to South Bay House of Corrections for 30 days. Because she violated her probation, she lost her eligibility for housing subsidies. After spending two years to become eligible for housing vouchers, she had to start at square one again. Because she lost the housing, she no longer had an address so her SSDI checks were cancelled. She had to re-apply for SSDI benefits.

Employment

At the VA, Katie was assigned a job counsellor. She was sent to Workplace, a local non-profit agency, to learn skills that would make her employable. The counsellor thought telemarketing was a good fit. She had an interview with a telemarketing company but did not get the job. Part of the reason is that she had no upper teeth so she could not speak clearly. She had been provided with an inexpensive set of upper dentures. These did not fit well so she often did not wear them as the dentures often hurt, fell out, distorted her face and speech. So, rather than fix the problem, pay for a good pair of dentures, the VA had Katie take courses on money management and computers. Not surprisingly, these courses did not lead to employment for Katie.

Mental Health Care

In the early 1990s, Katie started seeing a therapist. She was diagnosed as having anxiety attacks, Post Traumatic Stress Disorder (PTSD), depression, and drug addiction. Katie always saw her illegal drug use as 'self medication – the drugs work'. In 1995, she was diagnosed as manic-depressive after a suicide attempt. Katie complained about the number of different therapists that she had seen over the years. She thinks the reason that most therapists rarely stayed at the agencies for any length of time was because the pay was so low:

> So when my therapist at the VA left, my Probation Officer insisted that I needed to find another one. It is really a pain starting all over again with a new therapist. You tell the same story over and over again to different people. Then they leave and you start over again. Nothing seems to change. You just get real good at telling your story.

Melanie: Drugs, Gender and the Institutional Circuit

We have often wondered if being 'crazy'—being a poster child for PTSD—was an identity Melanie earned on the institutional circuit. It is not that she did not experience a dysfunctional and abusive childhood, but it was on the circuit that she learned to rationalise using drugs because of her history of victimisation. She seemed to embrace the victim role, telling and retelling with gusto all of her bad experiences. We often had the feeling that her recitals were rehearsed. And indeed, she had told them a myriad of times to caseworkers, correctional officers and therapists.

A slender white woman in her mid-thirties, life was relatively normal until the death of her mother. She had many close friends, was active in sports and did well in school. After the death of her mother, Melanie's father started using valium, graduated to heroin and eventually was arrested for drug trafficking. As news of her father's arrest became public, Melanie's friends drifted away. Melanie was taken in by the grandparents but they could not deal with her so she was bounced around among various family members and finally put under the care of an uncle who repeatedly sexually assaulted her. When she tried to alert other family members regarding the abuse, she was met by disbelief and anger. How could she say such a thing about her uncle?

Melanie began running away at age fourteen. As a teenager she started trying different drugs, first marijuana and then graduating to heroin, which she used together with her father after his release from prison. By the time she aged out of child welfare services, she was a homeless and steady drug user. In fairly short order, she had a pimp 'to take care of me' by providing shelter and drugs. 'I even taught him how to use Craig's List which brought in more customers'.

Criminal Justice System

Before long, she ended up in prison. While there she was given a number of different psychiatric medications, but each had side effects so the doctors 'would try something different'. Melanie calls this her 'guinea pig time.' Over the years, both in and out of prison, she has been prescribed Clonidine, Remaron, Topimax, Clonopine, Celexa, Welbutrin and Amitriptyline. She thinks there were others but cannot remember the names.

Housing

After serving several months in prison, she was sent to a halfway house. When she finished her time at that facility, with few other options, she moved in with her aunt and uncle, the uncle who had been sexually abusive when she was a child. Her psychiatrist recommended that she leave. While the psychiatrist could make recommendations to protect Melanie, he did not have any resources to help her arrange other housing. Left with few options she moved in with a woman who was addicted to crack cocaine. Melanie recalls the night that her roommate, who was high on crack, assaulted her. She ended up in the emergency room as she has done dozens of times before.

Employment

With the help of a job training program, Melanie landed a temporary job as a telemarketer. As we have learned, this is the typical routine: women attend job training programs that teach them how to be a 'good' employee (that is, how to set an alarm clock, how to write a resume, what to wear for a job interview), but these programs rarely, if ever, lead to permanent jobs. More often, after a few months of work for a stipend, the grant-funded program ends. Melanie continued applying for jobs but because of her Criminal Offender Record Information (CORI), she remained unemployable. In particular, she was interested in working with the elderly but due to her criminal history was ineligible for employment at these facilities. She told us:

> When money is tight and I can't find a job I think about going back to it [prostitution]. The thought rolls around in my head and says you could do it once. I know that if I did it once I would do it again and then I would be using again. Drugs and prostitution go together.

Mental Health Care

A few years ago, Melanie decided to try to get into Massachusetts Rehabilitation Commission (MRC) to access job training and job placements for people with disabilities. She was told that she did not qualify as disabled because she 'only' had PTSD and anxiety disorder. To be eligible she had to have PTSD and anxiety disorder and one other mental disorder. She went back to the therapist who sent her back to the psychiatrist. The psychiatrist said, according to Melanie, 'I will write anything... tell me what you need to qualify'. She told him she needed a depressive disorder which he quickly added to the list of mental disorders. She then became eligible for Massachusetts Rehabilitation Services. She was hoping to be trained as a counsellor. As finding a permanent job became less likely, she applied for SSDI. After three years and three denied applications (for each application, she needed letters from psychiatrists and therapists, as well as an evaluation by a government clinician), she hired a lawyer and was approved. Her monthly check was $771 per month.

During these years of applications for jobs and disability insurance, she moved around to various residential programs, shelters, and friends' houses. Eventually, she moved back in with her father and we lost touch with her. The next we heard of her was her obituary. It was reported that when her body was found, she still had a needle protruding from her arm, suggesting that she died from a drug overdose.

Gender, Mental Health and Ideology in the Institutional Circuit

Nearly all of the women we have come to know have spent far more time dealing with medical institutions than with correctional ones. We have come to understand that medicalisation and criminalisation are two sides of the same coin. The women of this project are treated by doctors and psychiatrists for the very same conditions (pain and fear), and with the same or similar psychotropic and pain medications for which they are sent to prison. There is not much of a boundary between punishing and helping institutions when women attend the same Twelve Step type programs and classes in both sets of institutions, see the same brands of therapists and psychiatrists in both sets of institutions and are tested for 'dirty urines' in both sets of institutions.

Medicalisation—the social propensity to characterise problems or conditions in medical terms and adopt a medical approach to address those problems—is a greedy social force. In contemporary Western cultures, we have come to define more and more phenomena, sensations and experiences as pathological: menstruation and menopause, pregnancy and lactation, being too thin or too fat, homoerotic feelings, fear or shyness, consuming alcohol or junk food, homelessness, expressing too much anger or too little, rejecting normative gender roles and expectations, suffering and rebelliousness have all become targets of pharmaceutical interventions (Conrad 1992).

Medicalisation is a powerful form of social control. In medicalised cultures, doctors boast an expert scientific status and an aura of objectivity that few other professions can claim. Physicians are employed to control and supervise those who are deemed to be deviant, adjudicate punishment within carceral institutions, justify insanity defences and decide who is mad and who is bad—who is helped (treated) and who is punished. With the authority to determine SSDI and SSI eligibility, physicians are gatekeepers to the range of services upon which poor and disabled Americans depend in order to survive.

Reliance upon physician-documented illness as the justification for social benefits frames structural inequalities and violence as personal pathology. On many levels, medicalisation allows us as a society NOT to talk about human rights to basic minimum standards of food, housing, health care and safety—a collective framework, but rather to talk about individual defects, flaws, imperfections and disease.

It seems to us that framing structural violence in terms of mental illness and treating it through drug use (whether legal prescriptions or illegal 'self-medication') simultaneously signifies and crafts a loss of agency. In the case of illegal substances that loss is direct—incarceration. But we also wonder whether the epidemic of drug use (legal and illegal) in America is part of a larger landscape in which those on the wrong side of racial, gender and economic stereotypes are encouraged to believe that they are the cause of their own suffering, whether through bad choices or through genetic defects.

There are important differences in the nature of men's and women's institutional captivity. Both before entering the circuit and while on the circuit, women are more likely than men to experience poverty, be heads of households, actively engage in parenting (Rabgy and Kopf 2015), and be diagnosed with mental and physical illnesses (Fig. 11.2). Criminalised women have a higher rate of welfare dependency than men or non-criminalised women (Butcher and LaLonde 2006), they suffer from numerous serious physical and mental health challenges (Cannata and Papagiorgakis 2017; Maruschak 2004) that keep them intensively involved with the healthcare system, and as mothers they are likely to be heavily involved with child service agencies. These agencies shuffle personnel and shift policies on a regular basis, and typically require women to attend therapy and parenting classes as well as show up for frequent urine tests to show that they are not using drugs. In these ways, women are scrutinised as parents.

A great deal of effort is put into explaining why their lives are so bad and teaching them to change the character traits that are said to be the source of their struggles. Examining and re-examining their propensity

> Gendered childhood abuse → diagnosis of mental and physical health problems → school failure → medication → unstable jobs → poverty → involvement with problematic men → deteriorating health → medication and self-medication → arrest and incarceration → unemployability → loss of custody of children → homelessness → vulnerability to violence and exploitation → increased use of medications → dependence upon problematic men → increased likelihood of accidents, attacks and severe health problems → death.

Fig. 11.2 Pathways in the institutional circuit

for being both victims of crime and perpetrators of crime, women learn that they are inherently flawed—an answer that is both gendered and highly consonant with the neo-liberal script.

In Massachusetts, criminalised women typically are incarcerated for shorter times than men. They do more institutional shuffle than men, which means more scrutiny and interpretation ('intake') and less stability. Women bounce among dozens of programs and facilities, each of which requires them to reveal intimate body parts to the gaze of a procession of doctors and nurses. Far more than men, women are compelled to expose intimate psychic wounds to an assortment of therapists, caseworkers, probation officers, and parole officers and submit to extensive interpretations and reinterpretations of their behaviour.

Medicalisation and criminalisation are complementary devices for operationalising and enforcing the grand narrative of personal choice, and that narrative plays out in a highly gendered manner. Despite ostensibly different mandates, both the correctional and the therapeutic stations on the institutional circuit reinforce a cultural ethos that overdetermines gender (Sered and Norton-Hawk 2011a), casts women as victims who are, in a variety of ways, responsible for their own victimisation and suffering, and locks women into needing help from the benevolent parts of the circuit in order to escape the clutches of the punishing parts. As victims, the women are dependent on the police to protect them and the state to provide basic resources. If they do not stay victims, always acknowledging how they are responsible for their victimhood, they lose these services that allow them to survive, thus they stay locked into the circuit. As Crawford (2006) has argued, this neo-liberal trope, operationalised through local and federal laws and policies, ignores structural inequalities, and absolves governments and corporate leadership from public responsibilities for the well-being of citizens.

Throughout the institutional circuit, criminalised women are drilled in quite specific interpretations of their experiences and suffering that actually serve to keep them captives of the circuit (Trammell et al. 2017). In court, therapists' offices, churches, television and Twelve Step meetings, they are taught a highly gendered version of a neo-liberal trope that casts suffering as a matter of individual choice and responsibility (Sered and Norton-Hawk 2011b). If it is your problem, you should be able to change it. The scripts taught to criminalised women focus on female psychological and emotional weaknesses; as a woman you are especially vulnerable to low self-esteem and co-dependency, which in turn leads you to make bad choices, including the 'choice' to be a victim. The way out is to own up to your flaws, keep all of your appointments with counsellors and other officials. If men on the circuit are punished for being too aggressive, women are berated for being victims, traits that are said to be the source of their struggles.

Conclusion

Throughout our research, we have been puzzled by studies indicating high levels of success for a variety of re-entry programs for women. Researchers rarely follow post-incarcerated women for sufficient time to evaluate long-term outcomes. This five-year study provides insight into the bureaucratic and social structures that limit success of even high-quality, well-resourced programs. While these agencies provide a stepping stone towards a mainstream life, they simultaneously relegate too many clients into a long-term relationship with the institutional circuit.

The women of this study typically do not suffer from a lack of access to institutional services. In that way, they likely differ from women in states that do not have the generous health and social service resources of Massachusetts. Virtually all of the women in this study have seen dozens of counsellors, therapists and psychiatrists who have prescribed a wide variety of medications and therapeutic programs. Ironically, many of the women actually have suffered from too many interventions, particularly on the part of healthcare providers.

The lack of coordination between programs results in duplication and ineffective long-term solutions to the numerous challenges faced by the women. The woman is not seen as a whole person who has psychological issues, and is poor, and is homeless, and is undereducated and is a parent. Rather, the woman is viewed as a person suffering a mental illness, or is a drug addict, or is a homeless person or the primary caregiver according to the specialisation of the analyser. With each diagnosis, the woman is referred to a different agency in the institutional circuit. One issue may get resolved temporarily but unaddressed issues will arise to sabotage other penal, welfare, or healthcare agencies' efforts. For example, almost all the women received mental health care in the form of medication. Achieving mental stability is important but, if the woman is homeless, she is unlikely to stay current with her medication or appointments. The woman relapses. Once again she faces depression,post-traumatic stress disorder, anxiety or addiction. One step forward-one step backwards. The woman never makes any significant progress.

As a first step towards improving the allocation of services, we propose a program that mirrors the America's mainstream healthcare system, where, at least in theory, each patient is assigned a primary care physician who coordinates treatment. Each post-incarcerated woman would be assigned a case manager whose job is to assess the totality of the woman's needs, then coordinate the services that are provided. The case manager would monitor all the various interventions to utilise resources in the most efficient and effective manner. Below is a suggested format for this program (Fig. 11.3).

While we suggest remedies for the bureaucratic problems that make success post-incarceration less likely, the unfortunate reality is that solutions to the broader structural gendered, racial and economic problems in communities in which poor and marginalised women live remain largely unresolved. To dismantle the institutional circuit and free the institutional captives still remains a vision for the future.

- Mentoring by case manager
- Intensive supervision if needed
- Therapeutic activities
- Meeting safety and stability needs
- Drug testing as needed
- Health and mental/health assessments
- Treatment placements
- Counselling
- Outreach services for housing, children's services, vocational training

Fig. 11.3 Primary care for post-incarcerated women

Bibliography

Bender, K., Tripodi, S., Aguilar, J., & Thompson, S. (2010). Predicting arrest in early adulthood: The relationship between internal and external sources of control. *Social Work Research, 34*(1), 58–64.

Butcher, K. R., & LaLonde, R. J. (2006). *Female offender's use of social welfare programs before and after jail and prison: Does prison cause welfare dependency?* (Working Paper No. 2006–13). Chicago: FRB.

Cannata, N., & Papagiorgakis, G. (2017). *Prison population trends 2017.* Massachusetts Department of Corrections. Available at: http://www.mass.gov/eopss/docs/doc/research-reports/pop-trends/prisonpoptrends-2016-final.pdf. Accessed 2 Dec 2017.

Carson, E. A. (2016). *Prisoners in 2015.* U.S. Department of Justice: Bureau of Justice Statistics. Available at: https://www.bjs.gov/content/pub/pdf/p15.pdf. Accessed 2 Dec 2017.

Conrad, P. (1992). Medicalization and social control. *Annual Review of Sociology, 18,* 209–232.

Crawford, R. (2006). Health as a meaningful social practice. *Health: An Interdisciplinary Journal for the Social Study of Health, Illness and Medicine, 10*(4), 401–420.

Deschenes, E. P., Owen, B., & Crow, J. (2007). *Recidivism among female prisoners: Secondary analysis of the 1994 Bureau of Justice Statistics recidivism data set.* Long Beach, CA: NCJRS.

Dewey, S., & St. Germain, T. (2016). *Women of the street: How the criminal justice-social services alliance fails women in prostitution*. New York: New York University Press.

Goffman, E. (1961). *Asylums: Essays on the social situations of mental patients and other inmates*. Garden City, NY: Anchor Books.

Hoper, K., Jost, J., Hay, T., Welber, S., & Haugland, G. (1997). Homelessness, severe mental illness and the institutional circuit. *Psychiatric Service, 48*(5), 659–665.

Huebner, B. M., & Berg, M. T. (2011). Examining the sources of variation in risk for recidivism. *Justice Quarterly, 28*(1), 146–173.

Hughes T., & Wilson, D. J. (2002). *Reentry trends in the United States*. U.S. Department of Justice: Bureau of Justice Statistics. Available at: https://www.bjs.gov/content/reentry/reentry.cfm. Accessed 2 Dec 2017.

Kalish, C. B. (1981). *Prisoners in 1980*. U.S. Department of Justice: Bureau of Justice Statistics. Available at: https://www.bjs.gov/content/pub/pdf/p80.pdf. Accessed 2 Dec 2017.

Kruttschnitt, C., & Gartner, R. (2003). Women's imprisonment. In M. Tonry (Ed.), *Crime and justice: A review of research* (Vol. 30, pp. 1–82). Chicago, IL: University of Chicago Press.

Laberge, K. (1991). Women's criminality, criminal women, criminalized women? Questions in and for a feminist perspective. *Critical Criminology, 2*(2), 37–56.

Laub, J. H., & Sampson, R. F. (2001). Understanding desistance from crime. In M. Tonry & N. Morris (Eds.), *Crime and justice* (Vol. 28, pp. 1–69). Chicago, IL: University of Chicago Press.

Maruschak, L. M. (2004). *Medical problems of prisoners*. U.S. Department of Justice. Office of Justice Programs. NCJ 221740. Available at: https://www.bjs.gov/content/pub/html/mpp/mpp.cfm. Accessed 2 Dec 2017.

Massachusetts Department of Corrections. (2011). *Annual report*. Available at: http://www.mass.gov/eopss/docs/doc/annual-report-2011-final-08-01-12.pdf. Accessed 2 Feb 2017.

Massachusetts Median Household Income City Rank. (2012–2014). Available at: http://www.usa.com/rank/massachusetts-state—median-household-income—city-rank.htm. Accessed 2 Dec 2017.

Minor-Harper, S. (1982). *Prisoners in state and federal institutions on December 31 1980*. U.S. Department of Justice: Bureau of Justice Statistics. Available at: https://www.bjs.gov/content/pub/pdf/psfi80.pdf. Accessed 2 Dec 2017.

Papagiorgakis, G. (2016a). *One year recidivism rates 2014 release cohort*. Massachusetts Department of Corrections. Available at: http://www.mass.

gov/eopss/docs/doc/research-reports/recidivism/recidivism-rates-2014-releases-1year.pdf. Accessed 27 Nov 2017.

Papagiorgakis, G. (2016b). *Three year recidivism rates 2012 release cohort.* Massachusetts Department of Corrections. Available at: http://www.mass.gov/eopss/docs/doc/research-reports/recidivism/recidivism-rates-2012-releases-3year.pdf. Accessed 2 Dec 2017.

Papagiorgakis, G. (2017). *Communities inmates released to in 2017.* Massachusetts Department of Corrections. Available at: http://www.mass.gov/eopss/docs/doc/research-reports/release-reports/communities-inmates-released-2016.pdf. Accessed 2 Dec 2017.

Rabgy, B., & Kopf, D. (2015). *Prison of poverty: Uncovering the pre-incarceration incomes of the imprisoned.* Prison Policy Initiative. Available at: https://www.prisonpolicy.org/reports/income.html. Accessed 2 Dec 2017.

Sered, S., & Norton-Hawk, M. (2011a). Gender overdetermination and resistance: The case of criminalized women. *Feminist Theory, 12*(3), 317–333.

Sered, S., & Norton-Hawk, M. (2011b). Whose higher power: Criminalized women confront the twelve steps. *Feminist Criminology, 6*(4), 308–322.

Stuart, B., & Brice-Baker, J. (2004). Correlates of higher rate of recidivism in female prisoners: An exploratory study. *Journal of Psychiatry and Law, 32*(1), 29–70.

Sweeten, G., Piquero, A., & Steinberg, L. (2013). Age and the explanation of crime, revisited. *Journal of Youth and Adolescence, 42,* 921–938.

Trammell, R., Wulf-Ludden, T., Pyfer, N., Jakobitz, E., Mullins-Orcutt, J., & Nowakowski, N. (2017). Doing gender as self-improvement. *Feminist Criminology.* https://doi.org/10.1177/1557085116687034.

12

Queer and Trans Incarceration Distress: Considerations from a Mad Queer Abolitionist Perspective

Andrea Daley and Kim Radford

Introduction

In this paper, we articulate a mad queer abolitionist perspective to expose the limitations of a lesbian, gay, bisexual, transgender, and queer (LGBTQ) rights framework, and relatedly, the Minority Stress Model (Meyer 2003) for recognising and responding to mental and emotional distress experienced by incarcerated queer and trans people. In this work, we engage with key ideas from Mad Studies[1] to reveal the ways in which a LGBTQ rights framework and the minority stress model are implicated in reformist interventions that individualise and pathologise incarcerated queer and trans distress (Rimke 2016; Menzies et al. 2013). We draw upon Queer Abolitionist[2] literature to position such interventions as particularly

A. Daley (✉)
School of Social Work, Renison University College, Waterloo, ON, Canada
e-mail: adaley@yorku.ca

K. Radford
Ottawa, Canada
e-mail: kim.radford@icloud.com

© The Author(s) 2018
A. Mills and K. Kendall (eds.), *Mental Health in Prisons*, Palgrave Studies in Prisons and Penology, https://doi.org/10.1007/978-3-319-94090-8_12

285

limited given the heteronormative and cisnormative logics of the prison system. In doing so, a mad queer abolitionist framing of incarcerated queer and trans distress is conceptualised as a critical intervention intended to interrupt pathologising accounts of 'normal' reactions by queer and trans people to structural violence that is foundational to the prison system.

Our focus upon the category, 'incarcerated queer and trans people', may initially seem unclear. Not only does it reference an incredibly diverse spectrum of people, this population is usually omitted within academic chapters on the LGBTQ rights movement and critical prison studies (Vitulli 2013). Increasingly, discussion of incarcerated queer and trans people within critical theory, and including this paper, is adopted to reference the social exclusion of *some* queer and trans people during a period of wealth and rights acquisition for lesbian, gay, and bisexual populations who are race and class privileged. This social exclusion manifests in the systemic criminalisation of *some* queer and trans people based not only upon their sexual orientation and/or gender identity, but also the specific intersection of their queer and trans identities with racism, poverty, sanism,[3] and/or disableism. This discrimination is further illustrated in the harsher sentences and more stigmatising charges they accumulate within the criminal legal system, as well as heightened experiences of violence once behind bars. Following this, our analysis is premised on a formulation of mental and emotional distress that implicates intersecting unjust social, political, and economic systems of sexuality, gender, race, class, and ability that permeate all social institutions including, and particularly, places of discipline and punishment.

Before, delving into the paper, we preface this review by locating ourselves as non-incarcerated, white cis-gendered lesbian/queer women writing from the academy. We are mindful of Stanley's cautionary comment, which calls for scholars to honour the grassroots work that underlies the expansion of critical prison studies. He states: 'if there has been a cultural shift, it is primarily because of the organising that has made, and continues to make, space for trans and queer critiques of imprisonment' (Stanley et al. 2012, p. 116). Acknowledging our academic standpoint, we position this piece as contributing to the capacity of queer abolitionist scholarship to consider incarcerated sexual and gender minority mental and emotional distress through the lens of Mad Studies.

Queer and Trans Incarceration

The central queer abolitionist claim that some queer and trans populations are over-represented in carceral spaces implies the presence of statistical figures. However, there is a paucity of empirical evidence on the incarceration rates in prisons of queer and trans people. Since 2003, the U.S. Department of Justice, Bureau of Justice Statistics (BJS) has collected information about the sexual orientation, gender identity, and experiences of sexual violence during present sentences. This information represents the first sample of jailed or imprisoned queer and trans people that can be generalised nationally. To our knowledge, it is the only comprehensive administrative data set ever produced for study. Findings from the National Inmate Survey[4] have been interpreted by Meyer et al. (2017), as demonstrating that self-identified lesbian, gay or bisexual (LGB) populations are incarcerated at three times the general population rate (1882 per 100,000 LGB people vs. 612 per 100,000 US residents). Overall, the results confirm the observations of advocates, who have long articulated that queer and trans people are more likely than the general population to be incarcerated, to serve longer sentences, and to experience administrative segregation.

Research on the likelihood of police harassment and brutality (e.g. police brutality against queer and trans persons for failing to reinforce normative sexuality and/or the gender binary) suggests that queer and trans people often suffer substantial levels of surveillance in the community (e.g. profiling), and therefore, heightened vulnerability to being criminalised and incarcerated (Grant et al. 2016). Poor and racialised queer and trans people are particularly vulnerable to criminalisation and incarceration, as they are more rigorously surveilled (BreakOut! 2014; Sylvia Rivera Law Project 2007). In terms of the latter, the contemporary phrase, 'walking while trans' (BreakOut! 2014, p. 1), reveals the injustice of trans people's everyday criminalisation. Importantly, Daniel-McCarter et al. (2016) note the colonial legacy of trans incarceration stating:

> The cause of such disproportionate numbers of trans people in detention - especially black, indigenous, and Latino/a trans people - is linked to a legacy of the criminal sexualisation of trans bodies of color. Even from the

time of "first conquest" on what is now known as North America, people who today might identify as trans women, gender expansive, or two-spirit were labeled "berdache" by Europeans, a term that derives from the French and Arabic word for "prostitute." Trans people have been profiled on this land as sexual deviants ever since. (Daniel-McCarter et al. 2016, p. 116)

The U.S. 2011 National Transgender Discrimination Survey demonstrates that about 22% of respondents indicated being harassed by the police. When disaggregated by race, large disparities are revealed: 38% of Black respondents and 36% of multiracial respondents reported police harassment compared to 18% of white respondents (Grant et al. 2016). The Trans PULSE project indicates that 24% of 433 transgender respondents in Ontario, Canada, have experienced police harassment[5] (Bauer and Scheim 2016). Of the total sample, 6% of respondents indicated a lifetime history of incarceration in their felt gender. Of this 6%, 26% were Aboriginal, while another 9% were racialised non-Aboriginal (Scheim et al. 2013).

Queer and Trans Mental Health and Minority Stress

A growing body of international research literature has identified greater prevalence of 'mental disorders' among queer and trans persons compared to non-queer and trans populations (i.e. heterosexual, cisgendered). For example, research indicates that suicide attempts, depression, anxiety, and substance abuse are all more frequently experienced among queer and trans persons (Gevonden et al. 2014; Grant 2010; Meyer et al. 2008; Balsam et al. 2005; Mays and Cochran 2001). To further nuance and articulate the complexities of distress experienced by queer and trans persons, intersectional analyses (Crenshaw 1993) are offered to reveal differences in prevalence rates across and within sexual and gender identity categories as they intersect with other aspects of identity including race, class, disability, and age (Fish 2008). For example, studies have determined differences in prevalence rates of lifetime mood disorder diagnoses between lesbian (11.4%) and bisexual (25.2%) women, and older bisexual and transgender adults have been described as having poorer mental health outcomes than older gay men and lesbians (King and Richardson 2017). Research studies note substantial risk of depression among gender minority (i.e. trans, non-binary) persons with 61.2% of male-to-female spectrum transgender persons (Rotondi et al. 2011a) and 66.4% of female-to-male-spectrum transgender persons (Rotondi et al. 2011b) reporting depression. Other research suggests that transgender women report more suicidal ideation, take more prescribed psychotropic medications, and experience more alcohol problems than transgender men (King and Richardson 2017). Attending to how intersecting effects of privilege and oppression contribute to quantitatively and qualitatively different experiences of mental and emotional distress is signalled as a critically important intervention towards resisting the homogenising of diversely located queer and trans persons (Murphy et al. 2009).

Differences in experiences of mental and emotional distress within sexual identity categories that are identified in the existing research literature account for the productive effect of intersections between sexual and gender identity and race, class, disability, and age. For example, Meyer et al. (2008) identify an elevated risk for suicidality among queer and trans persons of colour compared to white counterparts, and it is posited that queer and trans asylum seekers may experience heightened susceptibility to mental and emotional distress because of persecution suffered in their country of origin and the relative isolation they experience in a new country (Laing 2016). Existing data on the experiences of queer, trans, and Two-spirit[6] Indigenous persons suggest a greater risk for negative mental health outcomes than their non-Indigenous peers, with some studies reporting higher rates of depression, anxiety, and substance use among queer, trans, and Two-spirit Indigenous persons than non-Indigenous queer and trans persons (Laing 2016). Finally, Williams et al. (2017) found that among transgender/gender non-binary persons, lower income and intersections of race with other marginalised identities are associated with more depression.

Less information is available on the mental and emotional distress experiences of incarcerated queer and trans people; however, our brief review of the existing mental health literature suggests that many queer and trans persons will enter prison already having experiences of distress related to sexual and/or gender minority identities and intersecting oppressions. Moreover, there is strong evidence that incarcerated queer and trans persons suffer heightened risks for discrimination, harassment, harm, and/or sexual victimisation that undoubtedly result in or exacerbate existing distress. Indeed, sexual orientation has been identified by the Bureau of Justice Statistics as the single greatest determination of sexual abuse in prisons (Tiffe 2015), with other US studies indicating that within prisons for men, Black and Latina transgender women and gay men are primary targets for sexual violence by both prison staff and other incarcerated persons (Lydon et al. 2015; Hill 2014; Shay 2014).

Within women's prisons, the frequency of sexual victimisation of lesbians by other incarcerated women is similar to that of incarcerated heterosexual women (13%); however, the rate of assault by prison staff is reported as being at least double (8%) that of incarcerated heterosexual women (4%) (Hill 2014). Among bisexual women, the rate of victimisation by other incarcerated persons is 18% and staff sexual assault is similar to that of incarcerated lesbians (8%) (Hill 2014). Importantly, Shay (2014) notes that non-heterosexual incarcerated persons with 'serious psychological distress' (p. 346) report the highest incidence of sexual victimisation. Finally, queer and trans persons are more likely than non-queer and trans persons to be targeted for their consensual relationships, receiving disciplinary tickets, loss of privileges, and being placed in solitary confinement for consensual affectionate and/or sexual contact (Lydon et al. 2015).

Incarcerated trans and gender non-binary persons are particularly at risk for violence that undoubtedly causes severe mental and emotional distress. These experiences include sexual victimisation and rape, having their appearance and gender expressions monitored, having gender identities refused/denied/rejected, being denied hormones, assigned housing based upon genitalia rather than their gender identity, and being subjected to excessive strip searches, often by a staff person of the gender the individual was assigned at birth (i.e. not of the same felt and/or lived gender) (Carr et al. 2016; Lydon 2016; Hill 2014; Sylvia

Rivera Law Project 2007). It is widely acknowledged that trans people are often forced into carceral spaces based upon their birth sex assignment; however, findings from Trans PULSE suggest that over several decades, some trans people have been placed in institutions according to their felt gender. With this said, 35% of these respondents reported experiences of transphobic physical violence while incarcerated. Scheim et al. (2013) conclude that gender-appropriate facility placement does not automatically protect many transgender people.

Given the violence to which incarcerated queer and trans persons are subjected, it is very likely that the limited statistics on their mental health misrepresent their mental and emotional distress experiences. For example, a U.S. national prison survey found that more than two-thirds (67%) of 1118 LGBT respondents had a 'mental illness diagnosis' (Lydon et al. 2015, p. 48). Other research notes a high prevalence of mental health and substance-use disorders among incarcerated queer and trans persons more generally (Marksamer and Tobin 2014). Beyond this, queer and trans persons are undoubtedly represented in general statistics that note high rates of mental and emotional distress among the general incarcerated population (Kouyoumdjian et al. 2016). Fazel and Danesh (2002, p. 548), for example, found that 'typically about one in seven prisoners in western countries have psychotic illnesses or major depression', while Canadian statistics indicate that 13% of incarcerated men and 29% of incarcerated women offenders in federal custody self-identified at intake as having mental health problems (Correctional Service Canada 2009).

Queer and trans mental and emotional distress is most commonly understood and responded to as an outcome of stigma, prejudice, and discrimination as it is framed through the minority stress model (Meyer 2003). The model acknowledges that sources of stigma, prejudice, and discrimination can include overt discriminatory events as well as micro-aggressions that occur in the everyday lives of queer and trans persons including brief frequent assaults which can be social or environmental, verbal or nonverbal, as well as intentional or unintentional (Sue et al. 2007). Unrelenting and converging structural inequalities such sexism, homophobia/heterosexism, cissexism, racism, classism, ageism, sanism, and disablism constitute stressful social environments for queer and trans persons, resulting in deleterious impacts on their mental health (Carr et al. 2016; Montesanti and Thurston 2015). For example, Williams et al. (2017) research on depression and unmet need for mental health care among women and trans/non-binary persons reveals that discrimination was the strongest predictor of depression, and that race, gender, class, and sexuality all corresponded to significant differences in exposure to discrimination and experiences of depression. As a second example, mental and emotional distress among Two-spirit and Indigenous queer and trans persons is recognised as an outcome of colonialism (e.g. being subjected to the violence of the residential school system) and racism as they intersect with sexual and gender minority identities to produce high levels of poverty and homelessness for these communities (Laing 2016).

In similar ways, the minority stress model may be used to conceptualise mental and emotional distress experienced by incarcerated queer and trans persons in relation to intersecting systems of power—sexism, racism, heterosexism, cissexism, and colonialism, among other systems—within the prison context. In this regard, the *Handbook on Prisoners with Special Needs* (Atabay 2009, p. 104) notes with respect to the experiences of incarcerated queer and trans persons in various countries, 'the prejudices with which society responds to LGBT persons in the community and the myths that surround these populations are intensified in the criminal justice system'. As such, similar relationships between queer and trans mental and emotional distress and structural inequalities are imagined as persisting throughout the incarceration period.

In response, interventions for queer and trans people in both community and incarceration settings seek to redress stigma, prejudice, and discrimination and institutionalised barriers to safety and support by facilitating queer and trans access to mental health services and adequate medication as well as LGBTQ (culturally) competent mental health services including individual and group talk therapy (Lydon et al. 2015). Specific to incarceration settings is an attempt to interrupt the impact of structural inequalities on queer and trans mental health by identifying these populations as 'vulnerable' (Carr et al. 2016), often resulting in their placement in administrative or protective segregation and/or gay or trans specific ranges or common areas (Hill 2014; Shay 2014).

A Mad Queer Abolitionist Framework

As established above, the minority stress model draws important connections between queer and trans distress and structural inequalities such as heterosexism, cissexism, racism, classism, sanism, and disablism. As such, it is lauded as a progressive response to historical and contemporary discourses that frame sexual and gender minority identities and expressions as pathologies and/or the cause of queer and trans mental and emotional distress (Simeonov et al. 2015). Additionally, it has contributed to rebutting mental health practices and interventions that are harmful to queer and trans persons (e.g. 'reparative therapies') because they attribute poor mental health to having a sexual and/or gender minority identity (Williams et al. 2017). However, we critique the minority stress model through a mad queer abolitionist framework in order to articulate its convergence with individualising, normalising, and pathologising discourses of a LGBTQ rights politic, and the regulatory and disciplinary aims of the prison system. Our critique raises critical questions about the ability of this conceptualisation of queer and trans mental health to effectively reveal and respond to structural violence within the prison system.

An articulation of queer and trans mental and emotional distress through the minority stress model takes on the primary goal of queer and trans recognition and inclusion, as it is informed by the contemporary LGBT rights framework (Stanley et al. 2012). As a reformist framework, LGBT rights politics has resulted in some benefits for some queer and trans people. However, it is critiqued by radical factions of queer and trans movements for its prioritising of homonormative goals, representing the interests and desires of dominant class (middle-class) and racial (white) groups (e.g. same-sex marriage) to the neglect of a social action agenda that addresses injustices experienced by poor and racialised queer and trans persons including criminalisation and incarceration (Stanley et al. 2012). This is evident, for example, in the departure from the pre-Stonewall era commitment to a prison justice analysis in queer and trans communities (Daniel-McCarter et al. 2016; Stanley et al. 2012). Tiffe (2015, p. 8) infers the historical imperative of a prison justice analysis within the gay and lesbian liberation movement noting that, '[A]longside an extensive history of police brutality against queer bodies is a history of queer resistance against it'. Lewis (2016, p. 87) argues that the departure of the LGBT rights movement from a prison justice analysis is inextricably connected to the declassification of 'homosexuality' as a mental disorder, underscoring that declassification activism signalled a critical moment in the gay and lesbian liberation movement as reformist and radical factions within the movement were reified. Radicals maintained a stance of 'wariness' towards psychiatry during and after the declassification campaign, embracing dissent, difference, and madness, while claiming 'insanity as a privileged political position' (Lewis 2016, p. 87). Conversely, reformers encouraged an alliance, of sorts, with psychiatry by promoting a strategy of declassification that aligned 'homosexuality with health, happiness, and functionality' (Lewis 2016, p. 92). Central to the reform strategy were appeals to the scientific method in psychiatry to distance 'homosexuality' from 'criminality, pathologized affect, and mental disability' (Lewis 2016, p. 92). In this regard, Lewis (2016) asserts:

> For DSM [Diagnostic and Statistical Manual of Mental Disorders] reformers, establishing homosexuality's essentially "healthy" character required its discursive disarticulation from putatively "unhealthy" conditions like gender nonconformity, criminality, negative affects, and mental illness—all of which were, in these efforts, subsequently reproduced and naturalized as pathological. (p. 86)

Citing Regina Kunzel (forthcoming), Lewis further articulates the reliance of DSM reformers on normalising discourses and empirical evidence of 'homosexuality's "representative" characteristics' (Kunzel, cited in Lewis 2016, p. 90), thus implicating declassification efforts in 'a larger institutional push to refine psychiatry as a scientific discourse, contributing to the more elaborate psychiatrisation of human behavior inaugurated by the DSM-III' (Lewis 2016, p. 97). Conceivably then, the minority stress model is an outgrowth of the declassification campaign as it inspires the individualising and normalising psychiatric discourses or rather psychocentric[7] (Rimke 2016) ways of 'thinking, behaving, relating, and being' (Menzies et al. 2013, p. 13), which serve to obscure structural violence and injustice (Menzies et al. 2013). That is, while the minority stress model allows for the possibility of de-pathologising sexual minority identities, it continues to rely on 'the psychiatric discourse of normality/abnormality', and a normalised idea of 'mental health' that not only sets the parameters of 'what the problem is', but also 'the limits of the discussion' (Overboe 2007, p. 28). So, while it may shift the focus away from the pathologising of queer and trans identities, the minority stress model operates as a psychocentric discourse (Rimke 2016) within a deficit paradigm to individualise and pathologise the reactions of queer and trans persons to structural violence. Thus, the 'problem' becomes the reactions of queer and trans persons to structural inequalities, and the limits of the discussion are manifest in interventions aimed at ameliorating 'pathological' reactions. In other words, the model invokes structural violence as a cause of queer and trans mental and emotional distress; yet, it remains firmly committed to the notion of individual pathology, and thus, continues the well-established pattern of psychiatrising queer and trans people.

Drawing upon queer abolitionist literature, we are able to locate our critique of the minority stress model in relation to abolitionist critiques of the prison system as a colonial tool of class and racial control, with the purpose of regulating and disciplining people who threatened systems of economic and racial power and privilege (Lydon 2016; Stanley et al. 2012). Lydon (2016) succinctly details this purpose in reference to the US prison system:

> ...[the US prison system] has been built up with the purpose of, among other things, maintaining systems of "anti-Blackness" (Alexander 2012), regulating and disciplining non-normative gender/sexuality (Mogul, Ritchie, and Whitlock 2012), controlling im/migration (Walia 2013), suppressing resistance (Churchill 2001), and establishing a capitalist response to surplus labor (Gilmore 2007). (p. 62, citations in original)

Working from the intersection of critical race analysis, queer theory, and transgender studies, queer abolitionists challenge the prison industrial complex (PIC) generally, and the criminalisation and imprisonment of queer and trans people specifically (Daniel-McCarter et al. 2016; Stanley et al. 2012). Queer abolition interrogates the intended purpose of the prison system to produce appropriately sexualised and gendered bodies, troubling oppressive systems of domination enforced by the prison system such as heteronormative patriarchy and its intersection with white supremacy and institutionalised racism, as they are implicated in regulating and disciplining queer and trans persons, particularly racialised and poor queer and trans persons (Vitulli 2013; Tiffe 2015; Mogul et al. 2011). In this regard, Girshick (2011, p. 191) describes prisons as mirroring 'a hyper expression of traditional gender roles'.

From this perspective, the minority stress model of queer and trans distress and associated interventions constitute reformist strategies by serving to improve conditions for incarcerated queer and trans persons while converging with the disciplinary aims of the prison system. These reformist strategies reinforce 'the status quo by validating the system through the process of improving it' (Faith cited in Lawston and Meiners 2014, p. 5). Individualised interventions that aim to 'fix' (i.e. normalise) individuals within dangerous spaces may serve an intended purpose of safety; however, they construct queer and trans 'vulnerability' as individual accounts of violence perpetrated by incarcerated peers rather than as an outcome of structural violence that is inherent to the prison system. In short, these interventions are unable to robustly identify and interrupt 'gender normativity and anti-trans and anti-queer violence' as 'central logics of the [US] prison system' (Vitulli 2013, p. 116). To this point, Lawston and Meiners (2014, pp. 8–9) note, reformist strategies 'rarely have the capacity to frame [their] work within the carceral state with an analysis of institutional racism, heterosexism, and classism'. On the contrary, Hanssens et al. (2014) argue that reformist strategies may actually contribute to further distress for queer and trans persons:

> For many LGBT and gender non-conforming persons, protective custody remains the default placement for periods of days, months, years, and in some cases, decades. In addition to the conditions themselves amounting to torture, solitary confinement usually restricts a person's access to education, work, and program opportunities. These opportunities are not only essential for maintaining a person's mental health, but are usually

necessary for achieving good time credit and being paroled. This means that LGBT persons, who are likely to serve much of their sentence in isolation, are also more likely to serve the maximum time (or longer) of non-life sentences. (p. 21)

Intertwining a mad critique of the minority stress model with queer abolitionist critiques of the heteronormative and cisnormative imperative of the prison system troubles and complicates the notion that societal prejudices against queer and trans people are simply 'intensified' in the prison system as cited above from the *Handbook on Prisoners with Special Needs* (Atabay 2009). Indeed, a mad queer abolitionist framework shifts the parameters of 'what the problem is' and the 'limitations of the discussion' (Overboe 2007, p. 28), reframing pathological accounts of incarcerated queer and trans distress as 'normal' reactions to structural violence—homophobia and transphobia, and racism, sexism, and classism—that are *foundational* to the prison system, and thus, resists psychiatrising queer and trans people.

A Mad Queer Abolition Strategy

How might we imagine a mad queer abolition strategy? We contend that a mad queer abolition strategy necessarily rests upon revealing points of intersection between queer, abolition, and mad activist scholarship, and that revealing such points of intersection is useful to imagining coalition building across queer, abolition, and mad movements. As a starting point for and invitation to ongoing critical dialogue and exchange, we offer the following ideas.

In recent years, some factions of LGBTQ communities have witnessed a resurgence of their radical gay liberationist roots in response to the homonormativity of contemporary LGBT rights politics, and relatedly, neoliberal corporatisation within mainstream LGBTQ communities (e.g. corporatised Pride Parades). As 'collectivist, grassroots, and movement-based, with applied goals of effecting change through activism' (Mulé 2015, p. 19) queer liberation diverges from an assimilationist, mainstream LGBT rights politics by seeking 'civil rights as a means to an end, but not an end in and of themselves' (Mulé 2015, p. 19). Queer liberationists 're-emphasize the political origins of gay liberation as being founded in disruption and riot' (Rajala 2017, para. 3), while recognising the 'collective liberation of *all* struggles as being inextricably linked by systemic marginalization' (Rajala 2017, para. 5). Queer liberation challenges the heteronormative, cisnormative, racist, and classist social order:

> Being queer is being anti-racist, being queer is being anti-classist. Acknowledging the struggles of people who aren't white, who aren't cis, who aren't economically privileged, who don't have access to the victories that have already been won isn't being divisive, it's being inclusive. And that's what equality means. (Phoenix 2012, para. 7)

Contemporary examples of queer liberationist activism within LGBTQ communities might include successful challenges by Black Lives Matter in Toronto, Canada and Vancouver, Canada to the presence of uniformed police in annual Pride Parades. Undergirding these challenges is recognition of disproportionate state violence and anti-Black racism against Black queer people, and subsequently, their disproportionate criminalisation and incarceration. In some cities across the globe, anti-capitalist queer liberationist networks are organising alternative Pride events, for example, in the U.K., The London Queer Social Centre (2014) posted a call for an alternative Pride urging that queer folks:

> Come plot and plan with us and help us take pride back to its militant, intersectional roots but with fresh ideas as well. There are enough people out there who still don't want to get married, be well-behaved, fight colonial wars or march shoulder to shoulder with the police. (para. 3)

These examples of activism and disruption suggest the 'collective liberation' potential of the queer liberation movement to (re)mobilise a prison justice analysis. In fact, grassroots groups across North America are responding to Richie's provocative question, 'what would it be like to 'queer' anti-prison work?' (2005, p. 80) by 'living' queer abolition.

This question not only illustrates the importance of theory as a facilitator of social justice, but theory is simultaneously positioned as work to be lived in practice. Furthering this point, Richie proposed that integrating a queer analysis into abolition results in 'more radical anti-prison praxis' (p. 76). This ranges across the spectrum of macro to micro action. Systemic advocacy has been enacted by queer and trans grassroots organisation to voice the deleterious impact of police surveillance upon incarcerated racialised queer and trans people (e.g. Silvia Rivera Law Project; Movement Advancement Project), and grassroots initiatives have served to facilitate 'inside'/'outside' connections such as the Prisoner Correspondence Project[8] (Canada), Bent Bars Project[9] (UK), and Black and Pink[10] (U.S.), as well as community-based organisations such as BreakOUT![11] and Hearts on a Wire.[12]

While the examples above suggest an intersection between the queer liberation movement and the abolition movement, it is less evident how either movement takes up advocacy and activism in response to the criminalisation and incarceration of queer madness. In fact, increasingly, within the field of Mad Studies attention is being directed to critiques of mass incarceration and the prison industrial complex (PIC) for their failure to consider disability. For example, Remblis (2014) asserts that such critiques implicate the surveillance and criminalisation of racialised and poor people:

> We cannot begin to grasp the complex and powerful role that mass incarceration has taken on in the era of neoliberalism without making serious consideration of the extent to which our modern lives have become embedded within and dependent on a medicalized, psychiatrized, and ultimately punitive, discourse of madness. (p. 140)

Remblis's analysis (2014) reveals connections between the deinstitutionalisation of psychiatric hospitals in the 1960s and 1970s, the criminalisation of madness, and incarceration of mad people and the deep connection between the criminal justice system and 'modern medical, health care and social welfare policies and practices' (p. 155). His analysis foregrounds the concept of transinstitutionalisation as a significant consideration for abolitionist critiques of mass incarceration and the PIC. Similarly, Ben-Moshe (2011) brings forth a consideration of disability in abolitionist critiques of incarceration and the PIC, centring the concept of trans-incarceration in her analysis of the intersection between incarceration and disability. Trans-incarceration or rather the 'move from one carceral edifice such as a psychiatric hospital to another such as a jail' (p. 385) advances an understanding of incarceration as a continuum, and as with Remblis's analysis, queries the role of medico-judicial discourse in the criminalisation and incarceration of madness (i.e. mad bodies). We underscore the significance of this scholarship for organising towards a mad queer abolition strategy that vigorously interrogates and challenges the individualising, normalising, and pathologising discourses of a LGBTQ rights politic as it converges with the regulatory and disciplinary aims of the prison and related systems (i.e. psychiatric) vis-à-vis reformist interventions that rely upon the minority stress model to explain incarceration distress. Beyond this, the mad analyses put forth by Remblis (2014) and Ben-Moshe (2011) raise questions about where the points of connection/collaboration/coalition might be between queer abolitionist activism and mad activism.

Conclusion

It is well articulated that the topic of queer and trans incarceration exposes the limitations of critical accounts of a LGBT rights framework, the minority stress model, and the prison system. Our analysis centres a critique of individualised and pathologised accounts of incarcerated queer and trans distress produced through the minority stress model, and associated interventions. As an intended response to this critique, we posit a mad queer abolitionist framework. We argue that a mad queer abolitionist framework holds significant relevance for reframing mental and emotional distress away from individualised and pathologised accounts to consider such distress as an expected and 'normal' reaction by incarcerated queer and trans people who are subjected to the unrelenting structural—gendered—violence of the prison system. Our analysis suggests that a mad queer abolitionist framework demands that interventions unsettle heteronormativity and cisnormativity, and their intersections with white supremacy and institutionalised racism within the prison system to reveal queer and trans *incarceration distress*. As such, a mad queer abolitionist framework serves as a critically important intervention, challenging the idea that structural violence (homophobic and transphobic violence) inherent in the prison system can simply be severed from the mental and emotional distress experiences of queer and trans people vis-à-vis the implementation of reformist interventions such as queer and trans culturally competent services and administrative segregation. We conclude our analysis with an invitation to explore ideas related to a mad queer abolition strategy that is built upon the intertwined spaces of queer, abolition, and mad activist scholarship and activism.

Notes

1. Mad Studies is defined by Menzies et al. (2013, p. 13) as 'a project of inquiry, knowledge production, and political action devoted to the critique and transcendence of psy centred ways of thinking, behaving, relating, and being that validates and celebrates survivor experiences and cultures'.

2. Over the past decade, grassroots advocacy groups and critical queer and trans scholars have co-created a movement focused on the over representation of queer and trans people in the prison system and the prison industrial complex.

3. Meerai et al. (2016, p. 18) describe sanism as 'an oppression', stating that 'it makes normal the practice of discrimination, rejection, silencing, exclusion, low expectations, incarceration, and other forms of violence against people who are othered through mental 'illness' diagnosis, history, or even suspicion'.

4. The National Inmate Survey referenced here was administered throughout 2011 and 2012, and is a recent Bureau of Justice Statistics probability sample of over 100,000 inmates across US prisons and jails.

5. While the authors caution that these statistics are not representative of the incarcerated transgender Canadian population, we suggest the Trans PULSE data set nevertheless represents the best Canadian information upon this topic.

6. The term 'Two-spirit' has various meanings within Indigenous communities; it is used to refer to a person who possesses both masculine and feminine spirits, but also 'to distinguish the wide variety of Indigenous concepts of gender and sexual diversity as separate from the European gender binary, which was violently imposed on Indigenous communities through Christianisation and the residential school system' (Laing 2016, p. 1). Please see Laing (2016) for more information.

7. The concept of psychocentrism, developed by Heidi Rimke (2016), refers to the 'dominant Western view that pathologies are intrinsic to the person, promoting an individualistic perspective at the expense of social, political, economic, historical and cultural forces that shape human experience' (Croft et al. 2016, p. 2). Intertwined with the values of neoliberalism, psychocentrism is conceptualised as a governing neoliberal rationality (Dej 2016).

8. The Prisoner Correspondence Project is a solidarity project for gay, lesbian, transsexual, transgender, gender-variant, two-spirit, intersex, bisexual and queer prisoners in Canada and the United States, linking them with people who are a part of these same communities outside of prison (https://prisonercorrespondenceproject.com/).

9. The Bent Bars Project is a letter-writing project for lesbian, gay, bisexual, transgender, transsexual, gender-variant, intersex, and queer prisoners in Britain. The project was founded in 2009, responding to a clear need to develop stronger connections and build solidarity between LGBTQ communities inside and outside prison walls (http://www.bentbarsproject.org/about).

10. Black & Pink is an open family of LGBTQ prisoners and 'free world' allies. Its work towards the abolition of the prison industrial complex is rooted in the experience of currently and formerly incarcerated people (http://www.blackandpink.org/).

11. BreakOUT! seeks to end the criminalisation of lesbian, gay, bisexual, transgender, and questioning (LGBTQ) youth to build a safer and more just New Orleans (http://www.youthbreakout.org/who-we-are/).

12. Hearts on a Wire includes trans and gender variant people building a movement for gender self-determination, racial and economic justice, and an end to policing and imprisoning our communities (https://www.scribd.com/user/78046739/Hearts-on-a-Wire).

Bibliography

Atabay, T. (2009). *Handbook on prisoners with special needs*. New York: United Nations Office on Drugs and Crime. Available at: https://www.unodc.org/pdf/criminal_justice/Handbook_on_Prisoners_with_Special_Needs.pdf. Accessed 15 July 2017.

Balsam, K. F., Beauchaine, T. P., Mickey, R. M., & Rothblum, E. D. (2005). Mental health of lesbian, gay, and bisexual adults and their heterosexual siblings: Effects of gender, sexual orientation, and family. *Journal of Abnormal Psychology, 114*(3), 471–476.

Bauer, G., & Scheim, A. (2016). *Transgender people in Ontario, Canada: Statistics from the Trans PULSE project to inform human rights policy*. London, Ontario: University of Western Ontario. Available at: http://transpulseproject.ca/wp-content/uploads/2015/06/Trans-PULSE-Statistics-Relevant-for-Human-Rights-Policy-June-2015.pdf. Accessed 6 May 2017.

Ben-Moshe, L. (2011). Disabling incarceration: Connecting disability to divergent confinements in the USA. *Critical Sociology, 39*(3), 385–403.

BreakOut! (2014). *We deserve better: A report on policing in New Orleans by and for queer and trans youth of colour*. Available at: http://www.equityprojects.org/wp-content/uploads/2014/12/WE-DESERVE-BETTER-REPORT.pdf. Accessed 18 Mar 2017.

Carr, N., McAlister, S., & Serisier, T. (2016). *Out on the inside: The rights, experiences and needs of LGBT persons in prison*. Dublin: Irish Penal Reform Trust. Available at: http://www.iprt.ie/files/IPRT_Out_on_the_Inside_2016_EMBARGO_TO_1030_Feb_02_2016.pdf. Accessed 12 Aug 2017.

Correctional Service Canada. (2009). *The changing federal offender population: Highlights*. Ottawa: Author. Available at: http://www.cscscc.gc.ca/text/rsrch/special_reports/sr2009/sr-2009-eng.shtml. Accessed 12 July 2017.

Crenshaw, K. (1993). Mapping the margins: Intersectionality, identity politics, and violence against women of color. *Stanford Law Review, 43*, 1241–1299.

Croft, L., Gray, M., & Rimke, H. (2016). Mental health and distress as a social justice issue: Guest editors' preface and acknowledgments. *Studies in Social Justice, 10*(1), 1–3.

Daniel-McCarter, O., Meiners, E. R., & Noll, R. (2016). Beyond queer disavowal to building abolition. *PhiloSOPHIA, 6*(1), 109–123.

Dej, E. (2016). Psychocentrism and homelessness: The pathological/responsibilization paradox. *Studies in Social Justice, 10*(1), 117–135.

Faith, K. (2000). Reflections on inside/out organizing. *Social Justice, 27*(3), 158–167.

Fazel, S., & Danesh, J. (2002). Serious mental disorder in 23,000 prisoners: A systematic review of 62 surveys. *The Lancet, 359*(9306), 545–550.

Fish, J. (2008). Navigating queer street: Researching the intersections of lesbian, gay, bisexual and trans (LGBT) identities in health research. *Sociological Research Online, 13*(1), 1–12. https://doi.org/10.5153/sro.1652. Available at: http://www.socresonline.org.uk/13/1/12.html. Accessed 12 May 2017.

Gevonden, M. J., Selten, J. P., Myin-Germeys, I., de Graaf, R., ten Have, M., van Dorsselaer, S., et al. (2014). Sexual minority status and psychotic symptoms: Findings from the Netherlands mental health survey and incidence studies (NEMESIS). *Psychological Medicine, 44*(2), 421–433.

Girshick, L. (2011). Out of compliance: Masculine-identified people in women's prisons. In E. Stanley & N. Smith (Eds.), *Captive genders: Trans embodiment and the prison industrial complex* (pp. 189–208). Oakland: AK Press.

Grant, J. M. (2010). *Outing age: Public policy issues affecting lesbian, gay, bisexual and transgender elders.* Washington, DC: National Gay and Lesbian Policy Task Force Institute. Available at: http://www.thetaskforce.org/static_html/downloads/reports/reports/outingage_final.pdf. Accessed 15 May 2017.

Grant, J. M., Mottet, L. A., Tanis, J., Harrison, J., Herman, J. L., & Keisling, M. (2016). *Injustice at every turn: A report of the national transgender discrimination survey.* Washington, DC: National Centre for Transgender Equality and National Gay and Lesbian Task Force.

Hanssens, C., Moodie-Mills, A. C., Ritchie, A. J., Spade, D., & Vaid, U. (2014). *A roadmap for change: Federal policy recommendations for addressing the criminalization of LGBT people and people living with HIV.* New York: Center for Gender & Sexuality Law at Columbia Law School.

Hill, T. (2014). Sexual abuse in California prisons: How the California rape shield fails the most vulnerable populations. *UCLA Women's Law Journal, 21*(2), 89–141.

James, D. J., & Glaze, L. E. (2006). *Mental health problems of prison and jail inmates.* Washington, DC: U.S. Department of Justice, Office of Justice Programs, Bureau of Justice Statistics.

King, S. D., & Richardson, V. E. (2017). Mental health for older adults. *Annual Review of Gerontology & Geriatrics, 37,* 59–77.

Kouyoumdjian, F., Schuler, A., Matheson, F. I., & Hwang, S. W. (2016). Health status of prisoners in Canada narrative review. *Canadian Family Physician, 62*(3), 215–222.

Laing, M. (2016). *Two-spirit and LGBTQ Indigenous health: Evidence brief.* Toronto: Rainbow Health Ontario. Available at: https://www.rainbowhealthontario.ca/wp-content/uploads/2016/07/2SLGBTQINDIGE-NOUSHEALTHFactHeet.pdf. Accessed 14 July 2017.

Lawston, M. J., & Meiners, E. R. (2014). Ending our expertise: Feminism, scholarship, and prison abolition. *Feminist Formations, 26*(2), 1–25.

Lewis, A. J. (2016). "We are certain of our own insanity": Antipsychiatry and the gay liberation movement 1968–1980. *Journal of History of Sexuality, 25*(1), 83–113.

London Queer Social Centre. (2014). *An alternative pride.* Available at: https://houseofbrag.wordpress.com/2014/04/09/an-alternative-pride/. Accessed 12 Dec 2017.

Lydon, J. M. (2016). Once there was no prison rape: Ending sexual violence as a strategy for prison abolition. *PhiloSOPHIA, 6*(1), 61–71.

Lydon, J., Carrington, K., Low, H., Miller, R., & Yazdy, M. (2015). *Coming out of concrete closets: A report on Black & Pink's national LGBTQ prison survey.* Black & Pink. Available at: http://www.blackandpink.org/. Accessed 7 May 2017.

Marksamer, J., & Tobin, H. J. (2014). *Standing with LGBT prisoners: An advocate's guide to ending abuse and combatting injustice.* Available at: http://transequality.org/PDFs/JailPrisons_Resource_FINAL.pdf. Accessed 4 June 2017.

Mays, V. M., & Cochran, S. D. (2001). Mental health correlates of perceived discrimination among lesbian, gay, and bisexual adults in the United States. *American Journal of Public Health, 91*(1), 1869–1876.

Meerai, S., Abdillahi, I., & Poole, J. (2016). An introduction to anti-black sanism. *Intersectionality: A Journal of Social Work Analysis Research, Polity, and Practice, 5*(3), 18–35.

Menzies, R., LeFrançois, B. A., & Reaume, G. (2013). Introducing mad studies. In B. A. LeFrançois, R. Menzies, & G. Reaume (Eds.), *Mad matters* (pp. 1–18). Toronto: Canadian Scholars' Press Inc.

Meyer, I. H. (2003). Prejudice, social stress, and mental health in lesbian, gay, and bisexual populations: Conceptual issues and research evidence. *Psychological Bulletin, 129*(5), 674–697.

Meyer, I. H., Dietrich, J., & Schwartz, S. (2008). Lifetime prevalence of mental disorders and suicide attempts in diverse lesbian, gay, and bisexual populations. *American Journal of Public Health, 98*(6), 1004–1006.

Meyer, I. H., Flores, A. R., Stemple, L., Romero, A. P., Wilson, B. D., & Herman, J. L. (2017). Incarceration rates and traits of sexual minorities in the United States: National Inmate Survey 2011–2012. *American Journal of Public Health, 107*(2), 267–273.

Mogul, J. L., Ritchie, A. J., & Whitlock, K. (2011). *Queer(in)justice: The criminalization of LGBT people in the United States.* Boston: Beacon Press.

Montesanti, S. R., & Thurston, W. E. (2015). Mapping the role of structural and interpersonal violence in the lives of women: Implications for public health interventions and policy. *BioMed Central Women's Health, 15*(100). https://doi.org/10.1186/s12905-015-0256-4.

Mulé, N. J. (2015). The politicized queer, the informed social worker: Dis/re-ordering the social order. In B. O'Neill, T. A. Swan, & N. J. Mulé (Eds.), *LGBTQ people and social work: Intersectional perspectives* (pp. 17–36). Toronto: Canadian Scholars Press.

Murphy, Y., Hunt, V., Zajicek, A. M., Norris, A. N., & Hamilton, L. (2009). *Incorporating intersectionality in social work practice, research, policy, and education.* Washington, DC: NASW Press.

Overboe, J. (2007). Vitalism: Subjectivity exceeding racism, sexism, and (psychiatric) ableism. *Wagadu, 4*(Summer), 23–34.

Phoenix. (2012). *Gay rights are not queer liberation.* Available at: https://www.autostraddle.com/gay-rights-are-not-queer-liberation-the-nation-interviews-amber-hollibaugh-140431/. Accessed 25 Nov 2017.

Rajala, K. (2017). *Against Canada, towards queer liberation.* Available at: http://themainlander.com/2017/06/24/against-canada-towards-queer-liberation/. Accessed 26 Nov 2017.

Remblis, M. (2014). The new asylums: Madness and mass incarceration in the neoliberal era. In L. Ben-Moshe, C. Chapman, & A. Carey (Eds.), *Disability incarcerated* (pp. 139–159). New York: Palgrave.

Richie, B. (2005). Queering antiprison work: African American lesbians in the juvenile justice system. In J. Sudbury (Ed.), *Global lockdown: Race, gender, and the prison-industrial complex* (pp. 73–85). New York: Routledge.

Rimke, H. (2016). Introduction—Mental and emotional distress as a social justice issue: Beyond psychocentrism. *Studies in Social Justice, 10*(1), 4–17.

Rotondi, N. K., Bauer, G. R., Scanlan, K., Matthias, K., Travers, R., & Travers, A. (2011a). Prevalence of and risk and protective factors for depression in female-to-male transgender Ontarians: Results from the Trans PULSE Project. *Canadian Journal of Community Mental Health, 30*(2), 135–155.

Rotondi, N. K., Bauer, G. R., Travers, R., Travers, A., Scanlan, K., & Matthias, K. (2011b). Depression in male-to female transgender Ontarians: Results from the Trans PULSE Project. *Canadian Journal of Community Mental Health, 30*(2), 113–133.

Scheim, A., Cherian, M., Bauer, G., & Zong, X. (2013). *Joint effort: Prison experiences of trans PULSE participants and recommendations for change.* Ontario, Canada: Trans PULSE E-Bulletin.

Simeonov, D., Steele, L. S., Anderson, S., & Ross, L. E. (2015). Perceived satisfaction with mental health services in the lesbian, gay, bisexual, transgender and transsexual communities in Ontario, Canada: An internet-based survey. *Canadian Journal of Community Mental Health, 34*(1), 31–44.

Shay, G. (2014). PREA's elusive promise: Can DOJ regulations protect LGBT incarcerated persons? *Loyola Journal of Public Interest Law, 15*, 343–356.

Stanley, E. A., Spade, D., & (In)Justice, Q. (2012). Queer prison abolition, now? *American Quarterly, 64*(1), 115–172.

Sue, D. W., Capodilupo, C. M., Torino, G. C., Bucceri, J. M., Holder, A. M. B., Nadal, K. L., et al. (2007). Racial microaggressions in everyday life—Implications for clinical practice. *American Psychologist, 62*(4), 271–286.

Sylvia Rivera Law Project. (2007). *'It's war in here': A report on the treatment of transgender and intersex people in New York State men's prisons.* New York: The Sylvia Rivera Law Project.

Tiffe, R. (2015). Interrogating industries of violence: Queering the labor movement to challenge police brutality and the prison industrial complex. *QED: A Journal in GLBTQ Worldmaking, 2*(1), 1–21.

Tjepkema, M. (2008). Health care use among gay, lesbian and bisexual Canadians. *Health Reports, 19*(1), 53–64.

Vitulli, E. W. (2013). Queering the carceral: Intersecting queer/trans studies and critical prison studies. *GLQ: A Journal of Gay and Lesbian Studies, 19*(1), 111–123.

Williams, C., Curling, D., Steele, L. S., Gibson, M., Daley, A., Green, D. C., et al. (2017). Depression and discrimination in the lives of women, transgender and gender liminal persons in Ontario, Canada: Applying an intersectional lens to the question of why some persons are more likely to be depressed. *Health and Social Care in the Community, 25*(3), 1139–1150. https://doi.org/10.1111/hsc.12414.

Part IV

Alternative Penal Practices and Communities

13

A Sense of Belonging: The Walls to Bridges Educational Program as a Healing Space

Shoshana Pollack and Denise Edwards

Introduction

In *A Hidden Wholeness* Parker Palmer speaks of the healing power of 'circles of trust' in which communication is about reflection, collaboration and listening, rather than explaining, advising or helping (Palmer 2014). This basic premise underpins the Walls to Bridges (W2B) program, a university-based educational program in which incarcerated and non-incarcerated students study together for semester-long courses in a correctional setting. Courses are for-credit and are offered in a variety of disciplines such as Social Work, Criminology, English Literature, Sociology, Urban Studies, Philosophy and Gender Studies. W2B is an experiential learning model designed to create spaces of analysis, reflection and action within university classes held in prisons. While not a

S. Pollack (✉)
Wilfrid Laurier University, Waterloo, ON, Canada
e-mail: spollack@wlu.ca

D. Edwards
Walls to Bridges Community Collective, Toronto, ON, Canada

© The Author(s) 2018
A. Mills and K. Kendall (eds.), *Mental Health in Prisons*, Palgrave Studies in Prisons and Penology, https://doi.org/10.1007/978-3-319-94090-8_13

'therapeutic' service, both incarcerated and university-based students report that participation in this program cultivates a sense of personal 'voice' and agency and creates a community of learners that feels personally healing and socially transformative (Pollack 2016).

This chapter is a collaboration between Denise, a formerly incarcerated alumnus of W2B classes and Shoshana, an instructor of W2B classes and the director of the National W2B program in Canada. In this chapter, we explore several aspects of the W2B program that students experience as healing and transformative (Pollack 2016): these include W2B's commitment to destabilising power in the classroom, avoiding stigmatising labels and categories, and developing a classroom space in which 'difference' is valued. In keeping with W2B principles that honour lived experiences as sources of knowledge, we have written this chapter using first-person narration to explore the transformative impact of W2B classes. Shoshana begins the chapter by outlining the central components of the W2B program pedagogy and how it differs from both conventional university education and correctional programs. This is followed by Denise's account of the ways in which race, class and gender dynamics shaped her experiences of (un)belonging in Canada (which were then reproduced while incarcerated) and her contrasting experiences of being a W2B student. In this chapter, we discuss how lived experience, non-stigmatising discourses and practices, and mutually reciprocal relationships are crucial for cultivating mental health for incarcerated people.

The Walls to Bridges Program: Creating a Learning Community Within a Prison Classroom

Based on the U.S. Inside-Out Prison Exchange Program, the Canadian W2B program shares many of its practices and premises.[1] I (Shoshana) took the seven day Inside-Out instructor training in the United States in 2011. Although we have made changes to suit the Canadian cultural and correctional context, pedagogically we use a similar teaching model as described by Lori Pompa (2013), founder of the Inside-Out

Prison Exchange Program. Inside-Out and Walls to Bridges classes are not about students from the 'outside' helping, researching, or mentoring incarcerated students; but rather all students study academic material together within the context of a classroom in a prison or jail. Further, the instructor of a W2B class is considered a facilitator of the learning process—she or he does not lecture but through a variety of teaching techniques holds the space in which students can explore complex and challenging ideas from a variety of perspectives, lived experiences, and contexts.

For many instructors, this can be daunting as we have been trained to consider ourselves experts and to think of education as only effective if delivered through the 'banking model' (Freire 1970) in which we 'deposit' our knowledge into the minds of students. Both Inside-Out and W2B consider the instructor a facilitator and develop teaching tools that help to destabilise power relations between professor and student and between students themselves. The Canadian W2B program has been influenced by Indigenous Elders and Indigenous scholars such Dr. Pricilla Settee, Larry Morrison, Gayle Cyr and Dr. Kathy Absolon, all of whom participated in circles with us, and provided teachings on Indigenous holistic ways of knowing. The use of learning circles, in which participants take turns speaking while others reflectively listen, is integral to Indigenous ways of learning and healing (Hart 2002).

Participants are encouraged to listen openly and reflectively to the perspectives of others and to their own inner dialogue. In W2B classes, this fosters a classroom climate that values different perspectives and supports an understanding of self as situated within the contexts of gender, race, class, culture, sexual orientation and other forms of othering. Such an approach is particularly well suited for working with students who may be living in very different contexts, such as those who are incarcerated and those who are not. Incarcerated students enter into W2B classes feeling concerned that the university or 'outside' students will look down on them, judge them as stupid or as ill-equipped for university level studies (Pollack 2016). A pedagogy that explicitly values all sorts of knowledge, including lived experience and emotions, creates an inclusive learning environment.

We have also been influenced by Parker Palmer, a U.S. Quaker and educator. In *A Hidden Wholeness: The Journey Toward An Undivided Life*, Palmer (2014) outlines principles and guidelines for creating a community that fosters a space in which authenticity is encouraged and valued; in which a 'whole self' is permitted to emerge. In W2B, we do this by explicitly valuing emotions, spirit, body, and mind as legitimate forms of knowledge and by creating in-class activities that foster reflective listening, rather than debating or competing for the 'right' answer. Instead, as Palmer (2014) writes:

> We speak from our own center to the center of the circle— to the receptive heart of the communal space— where what we say will be held attentively and respectfully. This way of speaking differs markedly from everyday conversations in which we speak from our own intellect or ego directly to the intellect or ego of someone on whom we hope to have an impact. (p. 118)

Not only is this a countercultural approach to conventional university teaching but it also deviates from most correctional programming. Correctional programming is typically cognitive-behavioural, explicitly designed to change thinking patterns and behaviours considered to be criminogenic. The facilitator is considered the expert on the material and the very purpose of such program is to impact/change participants' selves (Kendall and Pollack 2003). If participants fail to adopt the discursive framing of crime and criminality promoted in these programs, they are considered to be 'engaging in "techniques of neutralisation" which Sykes and Matza (1957) describe as the discursive methods through which individuals justify their delinquent or illegal actions' (Fayter 2016, p. 60).

People experiencing incarceration are rarely considered 'knowers' or as having much to contribute to understandings of mental health, crime, addiction and other social issues. In contrast, all students and instructors in W2B classes are considered both teachers and learners who have intellectual, experiential, academic and emotional knowledge important for the exploration of course content. As it is a university-class, not a correctional program, there is no focus on criminogenic factors, changing behaviour, or labelling. In fact, our classes adopt Palmer's suggestion that there be 'no fixing, no advising, no setting each other straight' (2014, p. 115) so that we can foster an environment in which students collaboratively explore the course materials from their own unique perspectives and contexts, without fear of being admonished or diminished.

Narratives About Criminalised Women and Mental Health

I worked as a psychotherapist in a women's prison before I became an academic. I worked with a group of feminist psychologists and social workers to provide trauma counselling, group work, and advocacy for the women inside. These early experiences form the foundation of my commitment to shared work with criminalised women, challenging professional (correctional, psychiatric, psychological) discourses that decontextualise lived experience from social structures; and promoting continual reflexivity in practice and research. The W2B program contributes to destabilising public, legal, correctional and academic discourses that pathologies women's mental health by individualising behaviours without placing them within the context of lived experience of poverty, gendered violence, racism and colonialism. In W2B classes, we do this in part, by valuing incarcerated students' own analyses of what they have experienced within the criminal justice system and in their lives more generally. Although no student (incarcerated or otherwise) is expected to share any particular aspect of their lives, the circle process and small group activities allow opportunities to use course material to reflect on lived experience; therefore, personal stories are sometimes shared in the interest of developing a more robust understanding of course content and academic scholarship.

Over the past 27 years, I have been to countless conferences, have read hundreds of articles on 'female offenders', and have seen endless and repetitive statistics on the mental health, substance use, mothering, and behavioural problems of criminalised women. Yet, only on the rare occasion are the subjects of all this analysis and intervention given an opportunity to represent themselves and their own perspectives on crime and punishment. Of course, there are occasional opportunities for incarcerated people to share their stories at some criminological and/or correctional conferences and workshops. Nonetheless, how these stories are shared and structured is typically shaped by the agenda of those who are putting on the event, and thus they often take the predictable shape of a reformation narrative, identifying low self-esteem, faulty thinking, and poor choices as criminogenic factors. The hegemony of this narrative frame means that alternative ways of constructing self and experience are rendered unthinkable and thus unspeakable. As a researcher and scholar, I have examined the ways in which criminological and correctional discourses obscure social context and promulgate the subjectivity of women in prison as cognitively deficient, difficult to 'manage' and mentally unstable (Pollack 2007, 2009, 2010, 2012). Reflecting upon this, Tiina Eldridge describes the way she experienced and responded to correctional discursive framings while she was incarcerated. She writes:

> I regurgitated my story over and over and molded my life to fit the shape of the correctional discourse to explain how I was broken and a risk to society but how—by accessing prison programs and education—I was being "fixed" and it would soon be safe to return me to society... Now, having been free for almost two years and having had the opportunity to study and analyze the gendered scripts women prisoners are required to perform, I feel somewhat differently. I actually feel a lot of guilt and shame about being brainwashed into being a correctional puppet. (Pollack and Eldridge 2015, p. 135)

As Eldridge's analysis illustrates, simply providing opportunities for narratives of 'lived experience' to be included in discussions about mental health and prisoners is not sufficient. The dominant framework for how lived experience of mental health problems is narrated is so rigid that it has been called 'patient porn' to signal how personal narratives can be exploited in order to promote and validate a given treatment method or program (Costa et al. 2012).

W2B aims to disrupt 'canned' and official versions of who a criminal 'is' (and other categories such as gender, race, and mental health that rely upon binaries and labels) through several means. Firstly, in class activities designed to facilitate relationships and mutual exploration of course content, a process that 'outside' students attribute to dispelling assumptions and stereotypes about imprisoned people (Pollack 2016). Secondly, if students or instructors are sharing personal experiences, it is done largely within the context of the course material, to shed light on the theoretical or practice concepts being illustrated, rather than as a way to 'tell a story' about crime, addictions or mental health. This helps to mediate the reproduction of dominant discourses in narrations of self. Finally, a number (8 so far) of W2B undergraduate and graduate alumni are contributing to the literature on education and criminal justice (as is the case in this current chapter), thereby redefining the scholarship on criminalised women from the perspective of lived experience of incarceration.[2]

The following section is written by Denise, in first-person narrative form, in keeping with her choices for self-expression. Denise writes about the challenges of growing up in a white settler country that privileges those with white skin and middle-class status and the relationship between feeling excluded and being criminalised. She sets this context to illustrate for the reader the powerful impact of W2B. While in prison, W2B classes reduced her need for psychotherapeutic medications and helped her feel accepted and valued, resulting in feeling a sense of community connection—of belonging—for one of the first times in her life. Since being released from prison, Denise has continued working with W2B to conduct workshops and trainings and to spread the word about this innovative pedagogy. She is also a published fiction writer.

Denise

School began as the place my siblings and peers absolutely had to reach every Monday to Friday between the hours of 8:50 a.m.–3:20 p.m. come sun or snow. It was a trek of four city streets from my front door to the school's main entrance. It was the place we would spend most of our productive hours. At school, we would concentrate on the three Rs even though in essence there was only a single R in the equation. There were thirty of us in my grade three class. Room 303's wooden desks served as our storage for school supplies: pencil crayons, text books, the odd contraband of an assortment of candies and bubble gum, along with empty crinkly wrappers. Life was hard enough at seven, eight, nine, ten eleven years old. In those days, we lived by two universal rules: (One) Try to obey your parents as much as possible as to not have to experience the adage of 'If you can't hear, you will feel'. And trust me, you didn't want to feel whatever that thick brown leather belt felt like on your butt. (Two) Try to obey your teacher as much as possible so as not to warrant them calling your parents; again, so you don't have to experience Rule Number One.

My conscience dramatically shifted early one Saturday morning while I was in the eighth grade. Rather than sleeping in for the weekend I arose early and tiptoed into the kitchen and poured myself a bowl of cornflakes before I settled in front of the television to watch some of my favourite cartoons. I heard the muted echo of my father's trumpet in the den and I made a beeline to greet him. He immediately felt my presence and stopped blowing. The angle of the rising winter morning's sunlight gave him a lift to his six feet two-inch frame.

'It's Saturday morning, remember?'

'Morning', I replied

'Isn't this the day regular teenagers slept in'? he asked sarcastically. We exchanged friendly banter while I ate my breakfast and I then I remembered my cartoons. I was appropriately clad in hunter green flannel pajamas for the fast approaching merriest of seasons and before I had a chance to completely exit in thick woollen socks my father asked me what I thought was a strange question.

'Hey, who's your ultimate hero or heroine? Everyone has at least one person who has challenged them in one way or the next to be the best person they can be. And by the way, your answer can't be an athlete or an entertainer'.

'Hmm'? was my response. My fourteen-year-old brain didn't want to ponder over the question. Besides, the answer was cutting into my cartoon time.

Who do I admire to the extent that I'd like to mirror my life's mission in their shadow? The only person I thought of was getting impatient with me. I watched as his grey eyes shifted from me to his metronome where he adjusted the speed to a slow-paced beat. He was working on the scales to a Chuck Mangione song? *Feels So Good.* It was the instrumental that made me feel as good as the title suggested without any crooning.

'So who is it?' He queried once again.

'What if I was to tell you that its…you?'

'Apart from your mother or I. As a matter of fact, why don't you narrow it down to someone who looks like you and has made a significant positive impact to the world'. *Is there such a person?* He was making it harder for me to answer him every time he opened his mouth. My father removed his bread and butter from the stand and before he brought the instrument to the middle of his lips he looked at me once more and reminded me our conversation would resume at a later day. My father planted a seed in my head that many years later, a stranger by the name of Parker Palmer, would help to fertilise.

***

Innocence lost is never found and some children strive better in a balanced setting of the so-called traditional nuclear family structure or else they test every boundary imagined. I'm not knocking single parenthood or any of the other forms of parenting and making a family. Love is love, period. My family dynamics were changing but so was my body. It started playing some serious tricks on me that I didn't appreciate. Ever the athletic type, my initial resistance to accept(ing) *the* 'achy growing glands' deep in my chest with an odd contraption called a training bra empowered me. Despite taking many a basketball and volleyball assault tossed in with the odd deliberate elbow blows to that danger area, I'd cringe and in true teenage sportswomanship fashion, keep on.

When Mother Nature threw this late bloomer the ultimate dreaded period, I reluctantly threw my hands up in the air. I didn't want to but I had no choice but to surrender. There was no getting around that one. Just when society and church were finally kind enough to allow women of child bearing age control over their reproductive system with the simple act of swallowing a pill daily, why couldn't somebody, any-body, some capital hungry pharmaceutical company, find a tablet to rid me of the biggest interruption at probably the best phase of my life? Accepting the commencement of that era was the hardest part my being had to accept. While other girls I knew were happily jumping around embracing the inevitable inconvenience, I kept my hatred for it to myself. My teenaged world was getting complicated. Despite openly pining away for my father, my trust for him was getting scarcer than my mother's single paycheck's ability to continuously provide for four children the way their combined incomes used to. Ripple effects con-firmed our family fears that 'change was "ah comin"'. First, in a world where cellular phones were still unthinkable, there were the subtle signs when our single stationary landline lacked incoming calls to my popular father. His absence was felt as he came home every few days and then by month to month. The weaning process was obvious. His unpicked-up mail with the deceptive title of *Mr.* typed in bold black letters reinforced our perceptions of societal norms that we might lose *our* ever-important Alpha patriarch. If I was still in denial, a classmate's snide remark proved a reality check: 'How come your father doesn't pick you guys up from school anymore? Where is he? Blah, blah, blah…' Being privy to the growing number of mother-led homes contributed to a bitter burning from deep within because compliance to the lowered notch on the student social totem pole was standard. *The new normal.* I used friends, music, books and for the most part, school to fill my days. '…*someone who looks like you and has made a significant positive impact to the world*'. Still, I missed my father.

It was right around that time in my life when I started processing what I was being taught in school. I was new to high school and a new-found self-awareness sparked questions about my place in the world and the skills necessary for me to successfully navigate that world. By the tenth grade, it was getting harder for me to see a place in the world for myself and the dread of my grades falling further to the rear than my designated seat in the back of the class was real. The disconnection of my intellectual, emotional, physical and spiritual selves was fuelled by the disillusion of memorisation and regurgitating one-dimensional information. But hunger was my cruel taskmaster and since I had acquired a taste for knowledge, I'd forge my own path to find answers to questions not readily available in any textbook I ever opened.

**

Down in the dimly lit basement another world existed. There was fierce competition for available personal space. There was not even any elbow to elbow movements, it was standing room only. The struggle for air, respect and concrete space for our feet to balance intensified as the drum and bass transformed ordinary strangers into a frenzy of tribal camaraderie. The music spoke to us, through us and for us. Of the four walls, three were occupied by couples intertwined and gyrating to precisely timed beats. The fourth wall was specifically reserved for the several turntables and an array of records. Crates of prized forty-fives and thirty-threes were balanced on long banquet style tables awaiting their turn to alter the many moods music was guilty of creating. Once the selector's gifted fingers instinctively plucked a vinyl disc, the patrons showed their approval by slapping any available surface with open hands or pleaded with the appreciative cry of 'Wheel and come again, selector'. It took me no time to realise the phrase was meant as an encore.

It didn't matter that my fresh chemically relaxed hair, European straight only several hours prior, had kinked up in an undesired afro. Nor did it occur to me that the visibly older man who had me pinned against 'our' slice of the wall had managed to rub some of his blue denim dye onto the crotch area of the cream coloured skirt I snuck from my older sister's closet. The cigarette and marijuana scent wafted in the hot, damp air as naturally as if it had all the right to.

Reluctant as I was earlier to sneak out with my best friend Jo-Ann, I didn't want the night to end. And end it did with the threat of two women promising to crack open the others' head with empty Heineken bottles.

The scent of some type of curried stew greeted me before I came to the top of the main level and I would have joined the line-up for a large portion except my dancing partner was intent on getting me out into the fresh morning air for the chance to exchange landline phone numbers. It is still hard to understand how people courted pre-cell phone days.

Several weeks of stimulating conversations with my father-figure lover-man and a mother who couldn't control me led this barely seventeen-year-old to believe I was a grown woman. My West Indian mother was firm and under her roof, her authority was law. My options were limited. They were to listen to my mother or leave her abode. In a heated argument over some trivial matter, I grabbed an overnight bag and headed to notorious Jane and Finch (a low-income neighbourhood in Toronto, Ontario, Canada) where I was sure I'd be the mistress of my own destiny.

The next seventeen years saw me through an array of emotions and experiences I assumed were only privy to people who looked like me. The constant battle with my partner's 'baby momma' drama; witnessing the startled look on strangers' faces whenever I informed them of my undesirable address; the anger of being trailed, monitored and followed in department stores by security and sales clerks regardless of my having more than enough funds to pay for any item I desired. The frustration of letting my mother down for not pursuing every immigrant's dream of their children attaining a higher education. But those feelings paled in comparison to the feeling of not being included in the only country that I knew.

The deep void my heart felt at my father's abandonment fuelled my every justification. When a loved one is lost, there is a void that seems impossible to fill. Yes, I sold drugs. If I didn't, someone else would. I'd purchase stolen goods from anyone skilled enough to get away with it. Those were just the tip of the iceberg of some of the shady things I did. So when the long hand of the law caught up with me and I was sentenced to do a federal bit at Grand Valley Institution for Women, I hunkered down to finding out about myself in a world that I thought considered me invisible.

Blog entry published on December 9, 2014 on the Center for Courage and Renewal website, the organisation run by Parker Palmer (http://www.couragerenewal.org/listening-truth/)

To: Parker Palmer
From: Denise, Grand Valley Institution for Women, Kitchener, ON

Dear Mr. Palmer, you see, I was unsuccessful in my quest for higher education. The conventional classroom/lecture setting did absolutely nothing for me. The deliveries of the teachers were impersonal and sometimes I was strategically seated at the rear of the class. There was such a separation with regards to me, the teacher and the students. I felt disconnected and the experience became too overwhelming for me to enjoy learning. I will confess that I was not successful in acquiring the needed credits to pursue my ultimate dreams of a degree in Sociology or Humanities. So, broken, I dropped out of school.

I am currently incarcerated at a Canadian federal institution for women. The last thing I need is sympathy. What was meant to break me has turned into the biggest blessing of my life.

I was introduced to the Walls to Bridges Program where I learned about you and embraced circle pedagogy. Initially, I avoided your material like the plague but once I did accept it, I was hooked on your concepts. *'No fixing, no saving, no advising, no setting each other straight'*. In this information age we are living in, I could not have imagined that suggestion being passed along, much less adapted.

Stubborn as I am, I did not want to confess that a white upper-middle or upper-class man has impacted my way of life. You have taught me how to trust my inner teacher and most of all to speak my own truth. Black, female, and to further add to my intersectionality, I am a federally incarcerated student at Grand Valley Institution for Women. And I have learned the value and importance of listening to the truth of myself and others like you suggested. Had I been schooled in the circle pedagogy model from the elementary level I know it would have tremendously impacted my life in a positive, holistic way. I feel some unpleasant events I went through in my life might have been eliminated due to lack of support where my opinions were not valued. Because of circle learning, I am more aware of my feelings and fellow world citizens. *We all have a story to tell and we should be allowed to voice our stories without fear of rejection.*

***

Is learning and teaching in a controlled facility-a federal penitentiary-worth any purpose other than the passing of some *time* while tax payers paid the bill? Why should *normal* people waste their time in such an abnormal place? Was it game on for the *othering* techniques to begin since I deliberately set my mind on being in a constant offensive state?

After all, wasn't this one of those very places built for the monsters who should have no part of a functioning society? Well, since the larger portion of citizens apparently looked upon this alien of an *inmate* that way, I was mentally, physically and emotionally prepared to protect my fragile shell. From the very beginning, my first session with the outside students from Walls to Bridges was an interesting mixture of 'me too' and 'really?'. In that sacred space, in the most unlikely of places, a group of ten inside students paired up with the same amount of outside students, realised they had much more in common than not. For the first time in my adult life, I was able to naturally fight off the seasonal misfortune of winter blues. Seasonal Affected Disease (SAD) was as real as my charge but for some reason, this season was not as gloomy as seasons past. Could I place a definite finger as to the diagnosis for the change in my so-called chemical imbalance? Not yet. 'Well, if you'd like, maybe we could place you on another anti-depressant. Stopping cold-turkey is never a good idea and besides, there are other brands on the market'. That was the response I received from one of the nurses at the institution. Actually, that was the same response I got from another nurse, for to get such needed advice from the doctor meant submitting an institutional Request Form and patiently waiting for the doctor's once per month or so visit. My life, my prison sentence forced me to take matters into my own hands. I decided to self-medicate with my weekly blister pack. Instead of popping the prescribed one tablet per day, I'd crack my hope in the form of a tablet in half. Each morning I'd separate two sides of the pill evenly at the score and wash it down with strong, hot, unsweetened black tea.

That winter, despite a severe ice storm and brutal winds enveloping our section of the true, north and free landscape, my moods were chipper. I had my readings to look forward to, my assignments and most of all I had a support system that I was very much a part of. It was at this point that I came to the conclusion that a chain really was as strong as the weakest link. You see, the more I reduced and boiled my observations down to the gravy of it all, I was sandwiched into an interconnectedness of being. There was a simple sharing with my classmates that brought about a profound uniqueness and acceptance.

By the fifth Walls to Bridges class, I was totally weaned off the medications prescribed to me with no sight in the near future of returning to them. Again, I must stress the fact that Walls to Bridges is not a form of therapy nor do I believe they'd want to take on such a monumental mission. There was no denying that my once-per-week class played an integral part in my decision to hop off the normal vs. not-normal, me vs. them, us vs. them mentality. Having the opportunity to teach and learn in a circle pedagogy made a difference. The breaking down of walls where traditional modes of teaching and learning were challenged by interjecting respect for one's whole self, made all the difference. Once one sits in a circle environment and finds it in their heart and head to scrutinise their surroundings by claiming their voice, one will find that there truly is no 'inside' or 'outside'. Once there is a Wall, our combined hearts and heads will move into the construction business of building *bridges.* Midway through my very first Walls to Bridges course, I grudgingly yet gingerly succumbed to the fact that the wonderful plethora of individuals I was blessed with teaching and learning with were in fact just like me. At the end of our magical time I met people I never would have thought experienced marginalisation or hurt. Despite their White privilege, I was privy to the world where cheques didn't seem to balance. Week after week, I found out that despite one's outward appearance, even with the blondest and bluest of some of their privileged eyes, being 'othered' was unavoidable. For the people who shared my weekly sacred circle, their gayness, queerness, dis'*ability*-ness, trans-ness, the sheer *otherness* of it all was reason to come to the conclusion that we were all a part of a mysterious whole and without us, well, we all might as well blend into the bland, grey canvas that dictated the Canadian horizon from September to April. Our uniqueness was an added bonus since we were allowed to embrace it all without fear of shame. We harnessed parts of ourselves that refused to reveal only segmented portions. We sought out to teach each other and in return, to learn from the other. We willingly gave whatever we had and accepted every other gift someone presented us with.

I did return to the institution's Health Services for their assistance but not for any 'head stuff'. By that time, I had successfully rid myself of the little oval tablet that was part of my daily ritual for the better part of a half a century, I was also a half credit closer to the rest of my life. Talk about killing two birds with one stone because that was the closest I'd ever come to whatever rehabilitation Corrections Canada truly had to offer; plus that half a credit opportunity opened doors with 'options to offenders' engraved in gold. I had the choice to continue and add more university credits to my name or chuck the entire Walls to Bridges as an experience while in prison and something to pass *time*. In time, one half a credit led to one full university credit... and then two, and three and so on. The sheer act of building bridges through learning and teaching in any environment, whether controlled or not: priceless!!!

Conclusion

The kind of education and community-building that occurs in W2B is instructive about the role that relationships, destigmatisation and collective critical analysis can play in enhancing well-being and mental health. Plenty of scholarship has documented the fact that a very high percentage of women in prison have histories of childhood sexual abuse and male violence against women (Balfour and Comack 2014). Scholars have also illustrated how prison power dynamics reproduce those inherent in abusive relationships (Pollack and Brezina 2007), and the racist and colonial processes of white settler states (Razack 2015). While there are clearly power differentials between instructor and students, W2B instructors work collaboratively, drawing upon the gifts, knowledge and experiences of students to explore course material and create an equalitarian learning environment.

The integration of circle processes is pivotal in reducing power dynamics, in that group protocols allow for individual perspectives to be shared, drawing upon a 'full self' which includes intellectual, spiritual, emotional and experiential knowledge. Because W2B classes are university-based, they are not part of the correctional apparatus and thus are not required to scrutinise or assess for criminality and risk, thus allowing incarcerated students to just be students. The experience of imprisonment is one in which labels and categorisations pervade daily life, and spaces in which prisoners can interact with non-incarcerated folks as 'themselves', without being diagnosed, assessed, classified or otherwise judged, can be liberating. W2B works towards avoiding conventional dichotomies and labels such as criminal/law abiding, mentally ill/mentally well, addict/not an addict, and abnormal/normal. Fayter (2016) a W2B student who was incarcerated when she published an article on W2B states:

> I have been labelled an 'addict', 'drug dealer', 'criminal', 'inmate' and 'convict', and a 'danger to the community' by guards, parole officers, and others within the criminal justice and correctional system. Many people I know have been called much worse. Eventually, we begin to view ourselves through this lens...the W2B class is the single most humanizing and empowering aspect of my incarceration, replacing these negative labels and stereotypes with positive ones. (p. 59)

W2B's focus on dispelling stigma and stereotypes and developing authentic connections with people on both side of the wall leads to transformation and a sense of belonging (Pollack 2016). As Denise states, in W2B classes:

> there was an honesty about us. Our differences yet our sameness rendered us naked. The kind of stripping away that came with vulnerability, except there was no one to judge our rawness. For the duration of our studies we *reclaimed our whole selves.*

Notes

1. For information on the Inside-Out Prison Exchange Program, see http://www.insideoutcenter.org/.
2. This is similar to the emergence of Convict Criminology (Newbold et al. 2014).

Bibliography

Balfour, G., & Comack, E. (Eds.). (2014). *Criminalizing women: Gender and (in)justice in neoliberal times* (2nd ed.). Halifax: Fernwood Publishing.

Costa, L., Voronka, J., Landry, D., Reid, J., McFarlane, B., Reville, D., & Church, K. (2012). Recovering our stories: A small act of resistance. *Studies in Social Justice, 6*(1), 85–101.

Fayter, R. (2016). Social justice praxis within the Walls to Bridges Program: Pedagogy of oppressed federally sentenced women. *Journal of Prisoners on Prisons, 25*(2), 56–57.

Freire, P. (1970). *The pedagogy of the oppressed.* New York: Continuum International.

Hart, M. A. (2002). *Seeking mino-pimatisiwin: An Aboriginal approach to helping.* Halifax: Fernwood.

Kendall, K., & Pollack, S. (2003). Cognitive behavioralism in women's prisons: A critical analysis of therapeutic assumptions and practices. In B. Bloom (Ed.), *Gendered Justice: Addressing female offenders* (pp. 69–96). North Carolina: Carolina Academic Press.

Newbold, G., Ross, J. I., Jones, R. S., Richards, S., & Lenza, M. (2014). Prison research from the inside: The role of convict autoethnography. *Qualitative Inquiry, 20*(4), 439–448.

Palmer, P. (2014). *A hidden wholeness: The journey towards an undivided life.* San Francisco: Jossey-Bass.

Pollack, S. (2004). Anti-oppressive practice with women in prison: Discursive reconstructions and alternative practices. *British Journal of Social Work, 34*(5), 693–707.

Pollack, S. (2007). "I'm just not good in relationships": Victimization discourses and the gendered regulation of criminalized women. *Feminist Criminology, 2*(2), 158–174.

Pollack, S. (2009). "You can't have it both ways": Punishment and treatment of imprisoned women. *Journal of Progressive Human Services, 20*(2), 112–128.

Pollack, S. (2010). Labeling clients 'risky': Social work and the neo-liberal welfare state. *British Journal of Social Work, 40*(4), 1263–1278.

Pollack, S. (2012). An imprisoning gaze: Practices of gendered, racialized and epistemic violence. *International Review of Victimology, 19*(1), 103–114.

Pollack, S. (2016). Building bridges: Experiential and integrative learning in a Canadian women's prison. *Journal of Teaching in Social Work, 36*(5), 503–518.

Pollack, S., & Brezina, K. (2007). Trauma counseling with women prisoners: Feminist practice in the prison context. *Women & Therapy, 29*(3/4), 117–133.

Pollack, S., & Eldridge, T. (2015). Complicity and redemption: Beyond the insider/outsider research dichotomy. *Social Justice, 42*(2), 132–145.

Pompa, L. (2013). Drawing forth, finding voice, making change: Inside-out learning as transformative pedagogy. In S. Weil Davis & B. Sherr (Eds.), *Turning teaching inside out: A pedagogy of transformation for community-based education* (pp. 13–25). New York, NY: Palgrave.

Razack, S. (2015). *Dying from improvement: Inquests and inquiries into Indigenous deaths in custody.* Toronto: University of Toronto Press.

14

Coping with Incarceration: The Emerging Case for the Utility of Peer-Support Programmes in Prison

Christian Perrin

Introduction

It is now widely acknowledged that punitive prison environments are detrimental to the well-being and mental health of prisoners, and consequently not conducive for constructive rehabilitative work. Indeed, far from reducing recidivism, a body of evidence suggests that some prison environments may actually increase risk of reoffending for some individuals (Cid 2009; Cullen et al. 2011; Gendreau et al. 2014). Such research points to the need to better understand what prisons can do to elicit positive change within prisoners. Much of the research conducted in this area has investigated the opportunities inmates have for personal development and growth (Liebling and Arnold 2004; Reuss, 1999). This relatively new strand of investigation has likely been encouraged

C. Perrin (✉)
Department of Sociology, Social Policy & Criminology,
University of Liverpool, Singapore Campus, Liverpool, UK
e-mail: christian.perrin@liverpool.ac.uk

© The Author(s) 2018
A. Mills and K. Kendall (eds.), *Mental Health in Prisons*, Palgrave Studies in Prisons and Penology, https://doi.org/10.1007/978-3-319-94090-8_14

by the growing reliance on strengths-based approaches such as the Good Lives Model of Offender Rehabilitation (Ward and Brown 2004). It has also been energised by what now appears to be accepted conventional wisdom—that desistance from crime is a personal and subjective process that prisoners themselves should have control over (Maruna 2001; McNeill 2006). Many findings within this ever-emerging field of inquiry point to the importance of reimagining prisons as places for well-being (Helliwell 2011). This shift is supported by the growing optimism surrounding therapeutic communities and rehabilitative climate prisons (see, for example, Blagden et al. 2017; Ware et al. 2010).

As this contextual shift has gathered pace, more and more peer-led programmes in prisons have emerged (Devilly et al. 2005). This has been a response from primarily Western justice systems acknowledging that prison should afford inmates opportunities to source meaning and purpose while serving time. In a UK Prison Reform Trust report, Edgar et al. (2011) emphasise the contribution of 'active citizenship' roles and suggest that peer support offers opportunities for prisoners to prosocially interact with others and engage in personally meaningful activity. Coates (2016) has also emphasised the importance of individualised and person-centred activity in prison, and asserts that prison-based interventions are more successful when they address inmates' personal goals and ambitions. Recent research suggests that peer-support programmes in prison allow inmates to build personally meaningful structures around themselves which rest on mutual helping. This has been the primary source of optimism for peer-led schemes in carceral settings, that they may represent a source of mutually trusted and entirely prisoner-led support.

Peer-led programmes focus on a variety of issues in prisons, such as health education, drug and alcohol abuse, prison orientation, anti-bullying and anti-racism, and suicide prevention. In general, peer support in prison is characterised by reciprocal helping (Parkin and McKeganey 2000). Some research has argued that prisoners who uphold such roles experience profound internal changes and develop a range of skills and attributes that could energise subjective well-being (Foster and Magee 2011; Boothby 2011; Perrin and Blagden 2014). In what follows, this chapter reviews some of the literature based on qualitative data that has contributed to these claims, and makes the argument that peer-led programmes in prisons represent opportunities for prisoners to accumulate meaning and personal agency while serving time. Three mechanisms relating to how inmates are able to cultivate these 'gains' from peer support are discussed. This discussion is informed by recent research from the author of this chapter and a range of others who have explored the utility of peer support in prison.

Defining Peer Support

A review of the literature most commonly depicts peer support as a variation of social and emotional support that rests on the core tenets of mutual reciprocity, shared problem-solving, and empathy (Dennis 2003; Solomon 2004; Devilly et al. 2005). Some scholars have attempted to embed expectations of support into definitions, with the aim of clarifying what constitutes 'mutuality' and 'sharing' for the parties involved in peer support. Consequently, perhaps the most pragmatic yet wholesome conceptualisation is one offered by Mead et al. (2001, p. 135), who have delineated peer support as 'a system of giving and receiving help founded on key principles of respect, shared responsibility, and mutual agreement of what is helpful'. This definition emphasises the importance of balance and equality in peer support-oriented relationships, and highlights that there should be some awareness of directionality in terms of the support given and received. The assumption here is that support is shared, mutually agreed upon, and not unidirectional. Because of this emphasis on shared and mutually useful modes of support, it is broadly accepted that peer supporters must have some joint interest, investment, or prior experience in whatever the context is that enwraps the support being provided (Solomon 2004).

This perhaps presents a need to extend accepted definitions of support, so as to include the notion that peer supporters should be matched in some way in relation to their experiences of personal challenges. So far, this has only been alluded to in descriptions of the core features of peer support, but not interwoven into the boundaries of what constitutes it. For example, Gartner and Riessman (1982) have aligned peer support with 'instrumental support', which they describe as a form of support that requires mutual support of those sharing a similar [mental health] condition. They argue that the mutual closeness to the personal challenge being faced is what makes peer support especially unique and useful for both parties, and is the feature most likely to bring about desired social or personal change (Gartner and Riessman 1982). Although the literature diverges in the factors it includes as paramount to peer support, it converges on several themes. A review of the literature reveals that peer support should be characterised by equality and bidirectionality in support, recurrent sharing of extant and emerging problems, empathising over a mutually experienced challenge or condition, and agreement over and respect for the support that is offered and received (Mead et al. 2001; Parkin and McKeganey 2000; Solomon 2004). These characteristics comprise a novel and uniquely beneficial level of support, illuminate why peer support has been increasingly called upon in health contexts in recent years, and why it may have somewhat of a magnified effect in the prison context.

The Preliminary Case for Peer Support in Carceral Settings

Peer-led programmes in prisons focus on a variety of issues. However, the larger scale peer-support programmes in operation in prisons across the UK focus primarily on the areas of HIV/AIDS and health education, drug and alcohol abuse, sexual assault/offending, prison orientation, anti-bullying and anti-racism, and suicide/violence prevention (Devilly et al. 2005). In general, peer support in prison envelopes a range of different structures and approaches including peer training, peer facilitation, peer counselling, peer modelling, or peer helping (Parkin and McKeganey 2000). Within prison settings, peer programmes have been commonly described as 'Listener[1]', 'befriender', or 'mentor' schemes. A breakdown of the most common prison-based schemes that operate within these broad categories is provided in Table 14.1.

Table 14.1 Peer-support scheme details

Scheme title	Nature of support	Description
Listeners	Emotional	Volunteer Listeners who are trained by the external charity Samaritans provide face-to-face emotional support to prisoners who request help (see Samaritans 2016, for further information)
Buddies	Emotional & practical	Buddies can be paired with new prisoners who may require emotional support and also practical assistance when first adjusting to life in [a new] prison
Helping Hands	Personal care	Helping Hands volunteers care for those less able to do so for themselves. This role can involve personal care duties as well as emotional and practical support
Shannon Trust mentors	Educational	The Shannon Trust is a UK charity that regulates a scheme within which fluent readers are paired with those less able. Through this set up, Shannon Trust mentors help students through a reading programme often over a period of several months (see Shannon Trust 2005, for further information)

The common theme across such schemes is that they are principally founded upon the core tenets of mutual reciprocity, shared problem-solving, empathy, and experiential exchanges. There is evidence to suggest that the presence of these dynamics in prisons may have a somewhat magnified impact for both the recipients and the providers of peer support. Regarding the former, findings are encouraging and many studies have concluded that peer-support schemes are indeed effective in reducing stress and anxiety in prisoners. In an investigation into the Listener scheme, Jaffe (2011) concludes that prisoners who talk to Listeners are able to counter, to some degree, a negative build-up of feelings, heightened by confinement in a cell. Jaffe provides evidence of a cathartic effect resulting from talking to Listeners, as a consequence of the release of burdensome feelings. Prisoners feeling less consumed by their problems as a result of speaking to Listeners are consequently more able to focus on their options in terms of their personal growth and emotional state. Findings from Boothby (2011) endorse the Insiders[2] scheme in the same way. Boothby reports that prisoners who can moderate the stress and anxiety of initially entering the prison system are better prepared to cope with prison. Research exploring other types of peer-support programmes remain consistent in terms of positive findings. For example, Sirdifield's (2006) research into prison health trainers suggests that receiving health-related education in prison may contribute towards removing some of the barriers associated with offending, such as health problems, low self-esteem and self-confidence, low self-worth, and a lack of prosocial interests. More recently, though, research has focused on the potential benefits of being a peer supporter on the supporters themselves.

Research from Foster and Magee (2011), Boothby (2011), and Perrin et al. (2017) has argued that prisoners who uphold peer support roles internalise them and identify with 'being' a 'supporter'. Consequently, findings have been reported of peer-support volunteers experiencing profound internal changes and attitude shifts, and also developing a range of skills and attributes while incarcerated (Perrin and Blagden 2014; Perrin et al. 2017). Other findings have suggested that prisoners find perspective through supporting others who experience despair, and accordingly utilise their work as a coping strategy (Perrin and Blagden 2014).

Some have argued that simple altruism may explain why peer support may provide such internal satisfaction. Proponents of this argument posit that acting out of concern for others can strengthen an individual's social ties and contribute to the fulfilment of basic human needs (Ryan and Deci 2000). This sits in line with some of the early research on peer support in prisons and perspective making, which will be discussed in further detail later in this chapter. Perrin and Blagden (2014), for example, found that prison peer-support volunteers were able to re-story their own worries and concerns and take stock of them, as a consequence of gaining perspective from listening to others. These findings are positive and ultimately indicate that 'doing good' through an active citizenship role in prison might represent a pathway to building subjective well-being in prison. Indicators of subjective well-being have been repeatedly connected to better reintegration outcomes for criminalised individuals (Aresti et al. 2010) and on these grounds, criminologists and others should be optimistic about the utility of peer support in prison. In the interests of encouraging this optimism, and perhaps further research, what follows is a literature review of three clear ways in which peer support appears to benefit the prisoners who uphold these roles.

Three Ways That Peer Support Can Contribute to the Well-Being of Peer Supporters

Countering Boredom

Prison is synonymous with both physical and mental punishment, and is well known to impart significant psychological damage onto those who serve time. Some researchers have argued that the biggest threat to a prisoner's well-being is mundane boredom (Steinmetz et al. 2016). Denborough (1996, 2002) has described the pervasive silence, monolithic lifestyle, and totalised identities that are closely associated with imprisonment's twin dimensions of control and subjugation. In a semi-ethnographic study of a medium-security men's prison in the UK and based on inmate testimony, Crewe (2007) illustrates how various aspects of social order in prison are expressed through a range of adaptations, but also how 'prisoners experience, manage and counteract power in various ways' (p. 273). Many such adaptations appear to revolve around countering purposelessness and the boredom of routine prison life. In the face of prison hegemony, one class of response noted by Crewe is what he refers to as '"dull compulsion"…in which the rules and rituals of prison life generate a pragmatic or fatalistic acceptance of its inalterability' (Crewe 2007, p. 258). Ultimately, prisoners who fail to instil in themselves a sense of personal meaning are forced to accept rituals of 'sameness' and can become overwhelmed by boredom. One prisoner in a study conducted by Steinmetz et al. (2016) articulated this grim reality:

> Well, the hardest thing about being here, to me, is the walk and get my chow. Walkin' to the chow hall, yeah. Anything else, ain't nothing. Bored. Real bored. I mean, there just ain't no activity. I go to yard, work out, I mean, get out of the yard, come on back into the same thing I seen when I went out in the yard. Ain't nothin' changed. (p. 350)

As this participant expressed, boredom appears to be innately woven into prison life. Another participant in Steinmetz et al.'s (2016) findings typified the prison experience as 'about control. It's monotonous, tedious, structured, and full of pettiness – in other words, a constant routine'.

Furthermore, words such as 'lonely', 'isolated', and 'depressing' were amongst those frequently used by participants, and boredom was commonly cited as the most difficult aspect of imprisonment. The authors argue that time, for the majority of prisoners, is either spent dwelling on personal problems, becoming involved in illegitimate activity, or escaping into their own insular routines of purposelessness. These destructive states can be detrimental to prisoners' mental health, and consequently their ability to focus on potentially constructive aspects of a prison sentence (such as education or treatment) (Steinmetz et al. 2016). Perrin and Blagden (2014) called for prisons to afford inmates opportunities to forge meaning and purpose while serving time. Early research suggests that peer-support roles constitute such opportunities. Boothby (2011), for example, found that 'rep jobs' in therapeutic community (TC) prisons (where prisoners adopt roles as policy representatives and speak on behalf of prisoners) afforded inmates opportunities to invest in something meaningful and legitimate. In turn, this enabled basic needs such as autonomy and connectedness (Ward and Brown 2004) to be fulfilled, and ultimately for imprisonment to become more psychologically manageable.

Only recently has research explored this claimed link between enacting peer-led roles in prison and enhanced subjective well-being. Perrin and Blagden (2014) interviewed 15 prisoners serving medium-term (average 6 years) sentences for violent offences. All prisoners held a position in one of the peer-support roles listed in Table 14.1 and the interviews explored what having such a purpose meant to the participants and whether or not it influenced their experience of prison. With striking resemblance, participants recounted how their roles allowed them to discover a sense of purpose and direction as they served their time. Most commonly, however, participants expressed the importance of simply having something mindfully taxing to do in a context of sheer pointlessness. One participant's account represented the theme of countering boredom well:

> While you're in prison, there are other things that punish you at the same time, and the first thing is mental pressure...you've got to keep yourself occupied or do something. There are times when you don't just wanna watch TV, don't wanna play a video game, don't wanna read a book...so what do you do with yourself? And that's why I decided it's important to try and find something to occupy my mind. Men need purpose. My roles as an advisory sort of person in prison is that – I just try and pass things on to others. (Perrin and Blagden 2014)

The data from this study suggested that peer support plays an important role in keeping prisoners occupied and engaged in something constructive and legitimate.

This is not an entirely new finding; in an earlier study solely exploring the roles of prison Listeners, Perrin and Blagden (2014) found that most of the participants described the lure of getting involved in negative or illegal activity in the prison. However, they articulated being able to counter these temptations because they had a rewarding role and purpose to focus on. Indeed, the prison environment has been known for increased drug usage (Carpentier et al. 2012), a high presence of violent gangs (Fleisher and Decker 2001; Griffin 2007) and a variety of other antagonistic conditions (Dye 2010). Combined with the pressure to conform to prison 'norms' and achieve social identity, the prison environment can encourage destructive behaviours (Haslam and Reicher 2007). Much of this has been attributed to boredom and a desire to belong to some notion of a network (ibid., 2007). However, peer supporters appear able to resist illegitimate and harmful responses to prison boredom. One participant (Perrin and Blagden 2014) seemed to suggest that this was mainly a consequence of becoming bonded to something prosocial and internally satisfying:

> [my time] would've been harder and I would've obviously learned less and, I don't know what my attention would have gone on to then… so it kind of taught me to just be content with what I've got, and like I said again just be patient, behave myself…it's not about letting down the (Listener) team. (p. 914)

This notion of maintaining purpose and 'having something to lose' was recurrent across the data presented by Perrin and Blagden (2014), but has also been alluded to in research from Foster and Magee (2011), Boothby (2011), Sirdifield (2006), and recently, Perrin et al. (2017). Peer support at the very least appears to alleviate boredom and the ritualistic mundane reality of prison life for inmates who adopt roles. Moreover, the challenge of 'keeping sane' throughout incarceration appears to be heavily influenced by having a meaningful role. When reviewing the qualitative data available, peer-support schemes appear to provide such roles, and may therefore unearth important implications for well-being in prison, and potentially for within- and post-prison outcomes.

Shielding from Deprivation

While Sykes (1958) originally detected five core deprivations of prison (loss of: freedom, autonomy, security, goods and services, and heterosexual relationships), scholars have since expanded the model to include a broader spectrum of adverse constructs that fundamentally attack well-being (see for e.g. Irwin 2008; Johnson and McGunigall-Smith 2008; Maitland and Sluder 1998). Wright et al. (2017), for example, recently discussed 'entry shock', 'temporal vertigo' (a state of physical or mental anxiety in response to the feeling of time vanishing) and 'intrusive recollections' (repeated and vivid flash-backs and unwanted thoughts about a traumatic event). The authors discuss how prisoners develop defence mechanisms (suppression, denial, and sublimation) in response to these destructive states, which also have implications in terms of the trajectories of prisoners' mental health. In terms of what prisoners themselves report, the consequences of not overcoming prison deprivations have been spoken about in terms such as 'losing your mind', 'going mad', being consumed with 'negative thoughts', and so on (Blagden and Perrin 2016; Kerley and Copes 2009; Perrin et al. 2017). There is now a broad body of research supporting the detrimental impact of the 'pains of imprisonment' (Sykes 1958), and thus it is crucial to identify ways in which prisoners can maintain better mental health while inside.

In a study by Rocheleau (2013) exploring a number of factors potentially affecting prison misconduct, the removal of autonomy and the consequent purposelessness of prison life were amongst those most strongly correlated to increased conflicts with staff and serious misconduct and violence. In contrast, Steiner and Wooldredge (2008) found that prisoners who underwent programmes and who upheld prison jobs were less likely to be involved in prison assaults, substance abuse, and other types of prison misconduct. Furthermore, the likelihood of misconduct decreased as employment hours increased. These findings testify to the importance of prisoners being able to source meaning and purpose not just for their own well-being, but for the encouragement of behaviours that are socially acceptable. The types of 'purpose' that prisoners are able to cultivate also appears to be important, with Duggleby (2016) identifying that roles characterised by caring for others can be especially meaningful. This is consistent with emerging research exploring peer support; those who uphold peer-led roles reportedly express how they are able to shield themselves from some of the deprivations of incarceration through focusing on purposive objective to help others.

In describing self-determination theory, Ryan and Deci (2000) have argued that humans not only need to establish a sense of autonomy and purpose in their lives, but need also to feel needed by others and by their surrounding environment. Fulfilling this basic need is one of many factors that can enhance an individual's human and social capital and thus their connectivity to the prosocial bonds around them (Lochner 2004; Wolff and Draine 2004). Researchers have argued that enabling prisoners to secure states and traits that attach them to socially constructive outlets is the key to enhanced subjective well-being but also effective reintegration (Mills and Codd 2008; Rose and Clear 2003).

Research from Foster and Magee (2011) on the prison Listener scheme found that participants felt needed and developed a sense of liberty as a consequence of their helping roles. Perrin and Blagden (2014) delved deeper into this notion, uncovering that 'being a Listener' in prison enabled participants to consider themselves as 'better selves' (of increased self-worth and more at peace with their present self-concepts). Such self-perceptions are not common amongst prisoners, with research consistently noting that prison populations are typically highly anxious, long-term depressed, depleted of hope and subjective well-being, and low in self-esteem (Beijersbergen et al. 2014; Castellano and Soderstrom 1997; Fichtler et al. 1973; Fazel and Danesh 2002). These states and traits are commonly associated with failed reintegration attempts and increased (re)offending (Beech et al. 2002; Gendreau et al. 1996). However, instead of becoming consumed with the shock and despair of having found themselves in prison, succumbing to the pains of imprisonment (Crewe 2011), and allowing their perceptions of hope, self-worth, and personal value to plummet, peer supporters appear to fuel a positive forward momentum that keeps them optimistic and from feeling that they are doomed to deviance (McCulloch and McNeill 2008).

While this apparent protective element of being a peer supporter could in fact be undermined by reverse causality/selection bias mechanics (the prisoners that opt to become peer supporters might already be 'well'), many participants have reported that their roles had a direct influence on how they experienced prison and themselves. Perrin et al. (2017), for example, noted recurrent extracts affirming how peer supporters felt more like humans, and less like simply prisoners:

> it just brings it back to normality that, you're not a prisoner in a sense, although you are a prisoner, to be able to have that trust, it's something

that can only be earned, you don't just get it…but it kinda just makes you feel, "OK, I'm not as much of a prisoner". (p. 14)

One participant described earning something of an elevated status within the prison, as a result of enacting a helpful role, earning trust, and consequently forging a more normative work and social life in prison:

> the other Insiders, I wouldn't have known them like I do, the safer custody department… I wouldn't have known them, as well as kind of higher ranking governors and that, when I go to the meetings… I know all the governors and they kind of know me and, whenever I see them in the corridor they'll ask me how I am…so to have that kind of rapport in the place… [I can] kind of be proud that I'm, in that kind of position. (Perrin et al. 2017, p. 11)

Ultimately, peer-support role holders in prison speak of the protective elements their work affords them; it keeps them focused on something constructive, and provides a sense of autonomy, mastery, and connectedness. These constructive outputs appeared to better equip prisoners to maintain more positive mental health. While these findings are in their infancy and require further exploration, the available qualitative data in this emerging field recurrently point to a number of significant benefits that peer support appears to offer.

Finding Perspective

Along with enabling prisoners to instil a sense of meaning, counter boredom, and garner more constructive inputs from incarceration, another consistent finding amongst research on prison peer support relates to perspective finding. It is well known that the strain of complete institutionalisation brings about despair, suicidal feelings, self-injurious behaviours, prison misconduct, and a loss of hope amongst those incarcerated (Sykes 1958; Dye 2010; Morris et al. 2012). In Perrin and Blagden's (2014) study, prison Listener participants expressed how they were able to counter this level of strain to a degree, through enacting their roles as 'active citizens'. Participants expressed that through supporting others, they came to realise that their own situations were not uniquely traumatic, but that others were also going through great personal struggles. The realisation that others were suffering appeared to counter feelings of extreme loneliness and isolation and enabled participants the 'headspace' to take stock of their position. One participant recounted:

> because I'm serving an IPP sentence[3]... I don't know when I'm gonna get out...and I remember I said to myself "boy, how am I gonna cope with this?". So when I started listening to other people's prison problems, I thought my problem was nothing... As I started listening to their problems I thought 'wow, I thought I was the only one. (p. 913)

Becoming a Listener for many participants seemed to allow for continual perspective finding, which in turn contributed to better adaptation to the realities of imprisonment (Dye 2010). This was recently supported in a repeat study from Perrin et al. (2017) which explored the impact of a wider range of peer-support roles with a sample of sexual offenders. As with the earlier study, participants spoke about how helping others acted as a buffer for their own stressors.

These consistent findings sit in line with theories of generative helping and altruism. Indeed, a broad range of research has found that behaving selflessly and carrying out 'acts of kindness' for others enhances self-esteem, lowers morbidity, increases perceptions of social support, produces better health and mental health outcomes, and extends people's social networks (Schwartz 2003; Brown et al. 2005; Post 2005). In exploring why altruistic acts bring such benefits to those who carry them out, Schwartz (2003) applies Erikson's notion of generativity. Schwartz argued that acting on concern for those other than the self brings about internal satisfaction, a feeling of autonomy, and an assurance that the individual is making a difference in the world (Schwartz 2003). Conversely, those who fail to contribute in generative ways are more prone to 'stagnation', which is characterised by feelings of low self-worth and social disconnect (Slate 2003). In essence then, those who behave altruistically and out of concern for others strengthen their bond to the society around them, and, in doing so, satisfy an array of basic human needs such as commitment to other people, maintenance of intimate and familial relationships, and a sense of social belonging and high self-worth (Ryan and Deci 2000).

Additionally, scholars have argued that simply the act of giving, and thereby focusing on something external, enables people to counter the anxiety and depression associated with obsessing over the self (Schwartz and Sendor 1999). This phenomenon is said to stem from a process of 'response shift', whereby intrapersonal values, beliefs, and perspectives of life are disempowered and become more flexible due to the adoption of a more outer-directed stance (Visser et al. 2013). In this respect, by adopting a volunteer position such as those akin to peer-support roles, individuals may be empowered to reorganise and reconceptualise their viewpoints regarding life stressors and what is truly important (Sprangers and Schwartz 1999). This could be crucial not only for mental well-being, but also for the recovery and reintegration of offenders. Indeed, Dhami et al. (2007) have proposed that in order for prisoners to adjust to imprisonment, they need to be afforded some sense of personal agency to counter feelings of hopelessness. Peer support seems to offer this to those who volunteer, and this seems largely attributable to meaning making, purpose building, perspective finding, and the enhanced adaptability to prison life that these afford.

Concluding Comments

Peer-support schemes have existed in prisons for decades, yet have only recently garnered attention from investigators seeking answers regarding how prisons can better support their inhabitants. This chapter has reviewed a body of qualitative data recently made available within this emerging and promising topic of research. Encouragingly, participants across recent research studies have spoken about their peer-support work constructively, and alluded to cultivating indicators of subjective well-being. Through upholding personally meaningful roles, prison peer supporters inject a sense of purpose into their prison lives. In turn, this enables them to counter boredom and to resist becoming consumed by the deprivations of imprisonment. There is some evidence to suggest that these dynamics may afford prisoners the headspace and personal agency to take stock of their own circumstances and begin to build personal resilience. This is also supported by the perspective finding that peer supporters have articulated across recent qualitative studies. Considering these early themes, there should be optimism and interest from policy-makers and researchers regarding its potential influence.

Notes

1. Listeners are prisoners who are selected and trained by the Samaritans, a UK-based emotional health charity, to provide emotional support to their peers.
2. Insiders are prisoners who are also peer-support mentors for fellow prisoners. They assist their peers in dealing with bullying issues and provide emotional support for other issues such as entry shock.
3. Indeterminate sentence for Public Protection. This category of sentence was introduced in England and Wales in the Criminal Justice Act 2003. It meant that courts could sentence individuals considered high risk to indeterminate prison terms. Individuals sentenced indeterminately needed to demonstrate reduced risk to psychology staff before being considered for release. IPP sentences were abolished in 2012 as a result of human rights concerns.

Bibliography

Aresti, A., Eatough, V., & Brooks-Gordon, B. (2010). Doing time after time: An Interpretative Phenomenological Analysis of reformed ex-prisoners' experiences of self-change, identity and career opportunities. *Psychology, Crime & Law, 16*(3), 169–190.

Beech, A., Friendship, C., Erikson, M., & Hanson, R. K. (2002). The relationship between static and dynamic risk factors and reconviction in a sample of UK child abusers. *Sexual Abuse: A Journal of Research and Treatment, 14*(2), 155–167.

Beijersbergen, K. A., Dirkzwager, A. J., Eichelsheim, V. I., Laan, P. H., & Nieuwbeerta, P. (2014). Procedural justice and prisoners' mental health problems: A longitudinal study. *Criminal Behaviour and Mental Health, 24*(2), 100–112.

Blagden, N., & Perrin, C. (2016). 'Relax lads, you're in safe hands here': Experiences of a sexual offender treatment prison. In C. Reeves (Ed.), *Experiencing imprisonment: Research on the experience of living and working in carceral institutions* (pp. 27–45). UK: Routledge.

Blagden, N., Perrin, C., Smith, S., Gleeson, F., & Gillies, L. (2017). "A different world": Exploring and understanding the climate of a recently re-rolled sexual offender prison. *Journal of Sexual Aggression, 23*(2), 151–166.

Boothby, M. R. (2011). Insiders' views of their role: Toward their training. *Canadian Journal of Criminology and Criminal Justice, 53*(4), 424–448.

Brown, W. M., Consedine, N. S., & Magai, C. (2005). Altruism relates to health in an ethnically diverse sample of older adults. *The Journals of Gerontology: Series B: Psychological Sciences and Social Sciences, 60*(3), P143–P152.

Carpentier, C., Royuela, L., Noor, A., & Hedrich, D. (2012). Ten years of monitoring illicit drug use in prison populations in Europe: Issues and challenges. *The Howard Journal of Crime and Justice, 51*(1), 37–66.

Castellano, T. C., & Soderstrom, I. R. (1997). Self-esteem, depression, and anxiety evidenced by a prison inmate sample: Interrelationships and consequences for prison programming. *The Prison Journal, 77*(3), 259–280.

Cid, J. (2009). Is imprisonment criminogenic? A comparative study of recidivism rates between prison and suspended prison sanctions. *European Journal of Criminology, 6*(6), 459–480.

Coates, S. (2016). *Unlocking potential: A review of education in prison.* Ministry of Justice. Available at: http://dera.ioe.ac.uk/26435/1/education-review-report.pdf. Accessed 8 July 2016.

Crewe, B. (2007). Power, adaptation and resistance in a late-modern men's prison. *British Journal of Criminology, 47*(2), 256–275.

Crewe, B. (2011). Depth, weight, tightness: Revisiting the pains of imprisonment. *Punishment & Society, 13*(5), 509–529.

Cullen, F. T., Jonson, C. L., & Nagin, D. S. (2011). Prisons do not reduce recidivism: The high cost of ignoring science. *The Prison Journal, 91*(3 suppl), 48S–65S.

Denborough, D. (Ed.). (1996). *Beyond the prison: Gathering dreams of freedom.* Adelaide: Dulwich Publications.

Denborough, D. (2002). Prisons and the question of forgiveness. *The International Journal of Narrative Therapy and Community Work, 1*, 75.

Dennis, C. L. (2003). Peer support within a health care context: A concept analysis. *International Journal of Nursing Studies, 40*(3), 321–332.

Devilly, G. J., Sorbello, L., Eccleston, L., & Ward, T. (2005). Prison-based peer-education schemes. *Aggression and Violent Behavior, 10*(2), 219–240.

Dhami, M. K., Ayton, P., & Loewenstein, G. (2007). Adaptation to imprisonment: Indigenous or imported? *Criminal Justice and Behavior, 34*(8), 1085–1100.

Duggleby, W. (2016). Fostering hope in incarcerated older adults. *Journal of Psychosocial Nursing and Mental Health Services, 43*(9), 15–20.

Dye, M. H. (2010). Deprivation, importation, and prison suicide: Combined effects of institutional conditions and inmate composition. *Journal of Criminal Justice, 38*(4), 796–806.

Edgar, K., Jacobson, J., & Biggar, K. (2011). *Time well spent: A practical guide to active citizenship and volunteering in prison.* Prison Reform Trust. Available at: www.prisonreformtrust.org.uk/Portals/0/Documents/Time%20Well%20Spent%20report%20lo.pdf. Accessed 21 July 2017.

Fazel, S., & Danesh, J. (2002). Serious mental disorder in 23,000 prisoners: A systematic review of 62 surveys. *The Lancet, 359*(9306), 545–550.

Fichtler, H., Zimmermann, R. R., & Moore, R. T. (1973). Comparison of self-esteem of prison and non-prison groups. *Perceptual and Motor Skills, 36*(1), 39–44.

Fleisher, M. S., & Decker, S. H. (2001). An overview of the challenge of prison gangs. *Corrections Management Quarterly, 5,* 1–9.

Foster, J., & Magee, H. (2011). *Peer support in prison health care: An investigation into the Listener Scheme in one adult male prison.* Samaritans. Available at: http://gala.gre.ac.uk/7767/1/helenDraft_Listener_report_27_091_doc-finalversion2.pdf. Accessed 12 July 2017.

Gartner, A. J., & Riessman, F. (1982). Self-help and mental health. *Psychiatric Services, 33*(8), 631–635.

Gendreau, P., Listwan, S. J., Kuhns, J. B., & Exum, M. L. (2014). Making prisoners accountable: Are contingency Management programs the answer? *Criminal Justice and Behavior, 41*(9), 1079–1102.

Gendreau, P., Little, T., & Goggin, C. (1996). A meta-analysis of the predictors of adult offender recidivism: What works! *Criminology, 34*(4), 575–608.

Griffin, M. (2007). Prison gang policy and recidivism: Short-term management benefits, long-term consequences. *Criminology & Public Policy, 6*(2), 223–230.

Haslam, S. A., & Reicher, S. (2007). Beyond the banality of evil: Three dynamics of an interactionist social psychology of tyranny. *Personality and Social Psychology Bulletin, 33*(5), 615–622.

Helliwell, J. F. (2011). Institutions as enablers of wellbeing: The Singapore prison case study. *International Journal of Wellbeing, 1*(2), 255–265.

Irwin, T. (2008). The "inside" story: Practitioner perspectives on teaching in prison. *The Howard Journal of Crime and Justice, 47*(5), 512–528.

Jaffe, M. (2011). *A Listener lives here: The development of Samaritans' prison listener scheme.* Samaritans. Available at: http://www.samaritans.org/pdf/listener_scheme_12pp_web.pdf. Accessed 23 Nov 2017.

Johnson, R., & McGunigall-Smith, S. (2008). Life without parole, America's other death penalty: Notes on life under sentence of death by incarceration. *The Prison Journal, 88*(2), 328–346.

Kerley, K. R., & Copes, H. (2009). "Keepin' my mind right": Identity maintenance and religious social support in the prison context. *International Journal of Offender Therapy and Comparative Criminology, 53*(2), 228–244.

Liebling, A., & Arnold, H. (2004). *Prisons and their moral performance: A study of values, quality and prison life.* Oxford: Oxford University Press.

Lochner, L. (2004). Education, work, and crime: A human capital approach. *International Economic Review, 45*(3), 811–843.

Losel, F. (2007). The prison overcrowding crisis and some constructive perspectives for crime policy. *The Howard Journal of Criminal Justice, 46*, 512–519.

Maitland, A. S., & Sluder, R. D. (1998). Victimization and youthful prison inmates: An empirical analysis. *The Prison Journal, 78*(1), 55–73.

Maruna, S. (2001). *Making good: How ex-convicts reform and rebuild their lives.* Washington, DC: American Psychological Association.

McCulloch, T., & McNeill, F. (2008). Desistance-focused approaches. In S. Green, E. Lancaster, & S. Feasy (Eds.), *Addressing offending behaviour: Context, practice and values* (pp. 154–171). Cullompton: Willan.

McNeill, F. (2006). A desistance paradigm for offender management. *Criminology & Criminal Justice, 6*(1), 39–62.

Mead, S., Hilton, D., & Curtis, L. (2001). Peer support: A theoretical perspective. *Psychiatric Rehabilitation Journal, 25*(2), 134.

Mills, A., & Codd, H. (2008). Prisoners' families and offender management: Mobilizing social capital. *Probation Journal, 55*(1), 9–24.

Morris, R. G., Carriaga, M. L., Diamond, B., Piquero, N. L., & Piquero, A. R. (2012). Does prison strain lead to prison misbehavior? An application of general strain theory to inmate misconduct. *Journal of Criminal Justice, 40*(3), 194–201.

Parkin, S., & McKeganey, N. (2000). The rise and rise of peer education approaches. *Drugs: Education Prevention and Policy, 7*(3), 293–310.

Perrin, C., & Blagden, N. (2014). Accumulating meaning, purpose and opportunities to change "drip by drip": The impact of being a listener in prison. *Psychology, Crime & Law, 20*(9), 902–920.

Perrin, C., Blagden, N., Winder, B., & Dillon, G. (2017). "It's sort of reaffirmed to me that I'm not a Monster, I'm not a terrible person": Sex offenders' movements toward desistance via peer-support roles in prison. *Sexual Abuse,* 1–22, https://doi.org/10.1177/1079063217697133.

Post, S. G. (2005). Altruism, happiness, and health: It's good to be good. *International Journal of Behavioral Medicine, 12*(2), 66–77.

Reuss, A. (1999). Prison(er) education. *The Howard Journal of Crime and Justice, 38*(2), 113–127.

Rocheleau, A. M. (2013). An empirical exploration of the "pains of imprisonment" and the level of prison misconduct and violence. *Criminal Justice Review, 38*(3), 354–374.

Rose, D. R., & Clear, T. R. (2003). Incarceration, reentry, and social capital. In J. Travis & M. Waul (Eds.), *Prisoners once removed: The impact of incarceration and reentry on children, families, and communities* (pp. 189–232). Washington, DC: The Urban Institute.

Ryan, R. M., & Deci, E. L. (2000). Self-determination theory and the facilitation of intrinsic motivation, social development, and well-being. *American Psychologist, 55*(1), 68.

Samaritans. (2016). *The Listener Scheme.* Samaritans. Available at: https://www.samaritans.org/your-community/our-work-prisons/listener-scheme. Accessed 18 Aug 2017.

Schwartz, B. K. (2003). *Correctional psychology: Practice, programming, and administration.* Kingston, NJ: Civic Research Institute Inc.

Schwartz, C. E., & Sendor, R. M. (1999). Helping others helps oneself: Response shift effects in peer support. *Social Science and Medicine, 48*(11), 1563–1575.

Shannon Trust. (2005). *For Mentors.* Shannon Trust. Available at: http://www.shannontrust.org.uk/our-work/for-mentors. Accessed 14 July 2017.

Sirdifield, C. (2006). Piloting a new role in mental health-prison based health trainers. *Journal of Mental Health Training, Education and Practice, 1*(4), 15–22.

Slater, C. L. (2003). Generativity versus stagnation: An elaboration of Erikson's adult stage of human development. *Journal of Adult Development, 10*(1), 53–65.

Solomon, P. (2004). Peer support/peer provided services underlying processes, benefits, and critical ingredients. *Psychiatric Rehabilitation Journal, 27*(4), 392.

Sprangers, M. A., & Schwartz, C. E. (1999). Integrating response shift into health-related quality of life research: A theoretical model. *Social Science and Medicine, 48*(11), 1507–1515.

Steiner, B., & Wooldredge, J. (2008). Inmate versus environmental effects on prison rule violations. *Criminal Justice and Behavior, 35*(4), 438–456.

Steinmetz, K. F., Schaefer, B. P., & Green, E. L. (2016). Anything but boring: A cultural criminological exploration of boredom. *Theoretical Criminology, 21*(3), 342–360.

Sykes, G. (1958). *The society of captives*. Princeton, NJ: Princeton University.

Visser, M. R., Oort, F. J., Lanschot, J. J. B., Velden, J., Kloek, J. J., Gouma, D. J., et al. (2013). The role of recalibration response shift in explaining bodily pain in cancer patients undergoing invasive surgery: An empirical investigation of the Sprangers and Schwartz model. *Psycho-Oncology, 22*(3), 515–522.

Ward, T., & Brown, M. (2004). The good lives model and conceptual issues in offender rehabilitation. *Psychology, Crime & Law, 10*(3), 243–257.

Ware, J., Frost, A., & Hoy, A. (2010). A review of the use of therapeutic communities with sexual offenders. *International Journal of Offender Therapy and Comparative Criminology, 54*(5), 721–742.

Wolff, N., & Draine, J. (2004). Dynamics of social capital of prisoners and community reentry: Ties that bind? *Journal of Correctional Health Care, 10*(3), 457–490.

Wright, S., Crewe, B., & Hulley, S. (2017). Suppression, denial, sublimation: Defending against the initial pains of very long life sentences. *Theoretical Criminology, 21*(2), 225–246.

Part V

Mental Health in Prisons: Key Messages and Strategies from Critical Perspectives

15

Conclusion

Kathleen Kendall and Alice Mills

Mental Health in Prison: Key Messages from Critical Perspectives

Sociologist David Garland (1985) wrote that critical analyses have the potential to alter and strengthen our understanding of punishment and inform more progressive and tenable policies and practices for the future. Following his vision, the aim of this collection was to provide critical perspectives on mental health and imprisonment which, among other things, challenge the dominant narratives of individualism and pathology. Representing a range of professional backgrounds and personal experiences, as well as a diversity of critical lenses, the contributors have achieved this in a number of key ways.

K. Kendall (✉)
University of Southampton, Southampton, UK
e-mail: K.A.Kendall@soton.ac.uk

A. Mills
University of Auckland, Auckland, New Zealand
e-mail: a.mills@auckland.ac.nz

A. Mills and K. Kendall (eds.), *Mental Health in Prisons*, Palgrave Studies in Prisons and Penology, https://doi.org/10.1007/978-3-319-94090-8_15

First, the chapters collectively demonstrate that the people most likely to experience mental health problems and imprisonment are from marginalised communities including the poor, racialised, colonised, disabled and queer and trans people; and that although proportionally smaller numbers of women are incarcerated, they face particular deprivations and hardship. As Denise Edwards highlights in Chapter 13, when describing her own situation as a Black incarcerated female, imprisoned persons occupy several marginal positions. Critical race theorists employ the term 'intersectionality' to highlight how different power structures interact and overlap so that individuals who belong to several oppressed groups experience compound forms of oppression *and* a unique oppression stemming from the way their own positions in each of these marginalised groups overlap. For example, Crenshaw (1989) notes that Black women experience not only racial and gender discrimination, but also a specific form of discrimination based on their dual identity. However, in their study of Aboriginal and Torres Strait Islander women with mental and cognitive disability in Australian prisons, McCausland, McEntyre and Baldry (Chapter 8, p. 185–210) find the notion of intersectionality insufficient and instead adopt the framework of 'cumulative and compounding disability and disadvantage' to account for 'the negative synergistic effects of multiple and often coinciding events and factors that create more than the sum of these parts'. This work provides us with an important means of understanding the complexity of marginality and it reminds us that imprisonment is itself an oppression that interacts with other oppressions to shape experience and identity in complex and harmful ways.

Second, a number of chapters in this book draw attention to the ways in which the dominant discourses and technologies of governance locate troubling issues associated with mental health and incarceration within individual prisoners. The effect of this is to obfuscate the role of oppressive structures and relationships in the creation, maintenance and exacerbation of problems and to render alternative understandings unimaginable. As such, prisoners are identified as both the source of, and solution to, problems. Norton-Hawk and Sered (Chapter 11), for example, show how formerly incarcerated women in Massachusetts are encircled by a grand narrative of personal choice which depicts them as inherently flawed. While this discourse recognises that the women are victims, it also holds them responsible for their own victimhood. Sim (Chapter 10) demonstrates that this process of individualisation occurs even in cases of prisoner suicide, where deaths are explained officially solely as the result of the deceased's supposed pathology. In such a way, attention is deflected away from the vital role of the prison and the state in creating conditions of violence and terror leading to suicide.

Arrigo and Sellers (Chapter 4) expose how correctional deficit and desistance models conceptualise prisoners as faulty 'others' in ways that negate their shared humanity, including with those who work inside carceral regimes. Consequently, the authors argue that prisoners and those who treat, manage and keep them are governed by correctional discourses and technologies that not only obscure the social context, but also prevent the possibility of genuine human connection. They conclude that strategies to expose and replace the dominant discourses must be underpinned by a care ethic of relational virtue. Their analysis and recommendation for action are illustrated in practice by Pollack and Edwards (Chapter 13) who recount how both incarcerated and non-incarcerated students enrolled in the Canadian Walls to Bridges (W2B) university educational programme learn together to disrupt the correctional discursive framings they have internalised, to value difference and recognise their shared humanity. The importance of incorporating relational elements into scholarship and of fostering mutually reciprocal relationships in practice is thus highlighted here.

Third, rather than identifying the problem of mental health and imprisonment as residing within socially excluded individuals or groups, the contributors to this book illustrate how structural inequalities and violence contribute to poor mental health and create social problems which are then managed through confinement and other exclusionary and controlling practices. As Mills and Kendall (Chapter 5) note, during the writing of this book, UK news headlines announced that there was a prison mental health crisis. While composing their own chapters, other contributors are likely to have observed similar media reports from the USA (*New York Times* Editorial Board 2017), Australia (Whitbourn 2017), New Zealand (Wesley-Smith 2017) and Canada (Solomon 2017). The critical histories of imprisonment by Cox and Marland (Chapter 2) and Cross and Jewkes (Chapter 3), however, provide a crucial context for these stories. Fundamentally, they demonstrate that there have always been mental health crises within prisons. That is, prisons have permanently contained persons with mental health problems and they have continually created or exacerbated poor mental health. Such a conclusion suggests that the crises are not caused by individual pathologies but rather by social forces. This position aligns with Seddon's (2007) argument, as outlined in the introduction to this book, that the existence of mental health problems within prisons are predictable because they are an inherent feature of a system of confinement designed to remove, contain, manage and punish those deemed troublesome, non-conforming, unproductive, vulnerable, unwanted and/or dangerous—overwhelmingly individuals who are marginalised.

Although prisons have served as repositories for marginalised individuals since their construction, several authors note that the current neoliberal political climate has increased inequalities, contributed to harsher penal policies and practices, led to mass incarceration and expanded the carceral regime into varied spaces including within the community. For example, Norton-Hawk and Sered (Chapter 11) demonstrate how the women in their study became trapped in and dependent upon a circuit comprised of numerous and varied institutions such as prisons, probation, social services, hospitals, shelters, and rehabilitation facilities. The boundary between punishing and 'helping' institutions was porous so that the same kinds of mental health services, underpinned by a neoliberal trope of individual choice and responsibility, operated in both. Their chapter also serves as a reminder to employ caution when engaging with services within the community as a means of improving mental health and as an alternative to imprisonment. Dainius Pūras (2017), a United Nations Special Rapporteur, recently argued that a reductionist biomedical model, which neglects the social context and frames people with mental health problems as violent, dominates mental health services in both communities and institutions, leading to coercive practices and the violation of human rights. Pūras (2017, p. 19) concludes that the seemingly global crisis in mental health should be addressed 'not as a crisis of individual conditions, but as a crisis of social obstacles'.

Daley and Radford (Chapter 12) also challenge psychocentric discourse and practice in demonstrating how it pathologises and individualises the reactions of queer and trans people to structural inequalities and violence. They do so by reframing distress as a 'normal' response to the transphobia, homophobia, racism, sexism and classism queer and trans people encounter inside and outside of prisons. Such a model reflects the growing scholarship and activism within critical disability studies (Ben-Moshe et al. 2014) and mad studies (LeFrançois et al. 2013). Drawing on this work, Johnstone and Boyle (2018) propose an alternative to psychiatric classification and diagnosis called the 'power threat meaning framework' (PTM), which is summarised as follows:

> You are experiencing a normal reaction to abnormal circumstances. Anyone else who had been through the same events might well have ended up reacting in the same way. However, these survival strategies may no longer be needed or useful. With the right kind of support, you may be able to leave them behind. (Johnstone and Boyle 2018, pp. 17–18)

The authors note that rather than imposing a Western lens, the PTM recognises the existence of diverse cultural experiences and expressions. Cavney and Hatters Friedman (Chapter 9) likewise draw attention to the importance of acknowledging cultural differences as they highlight how diagnoses of mental illness may be considered ethnocentric social constructions rooted in Western medicine. They illustrate this with the example of how, for many Māori, seeing visions and hearing voices is considered to be a spiritual experience, and acknowledge that treatment from a tohunga or traditional healer, may be most appropriate. Their chapter thus brings attention to the importance of recognising Western biases and acknowledging cultural contexts when addressing mental health. In such ways, this volume not only deconstructs the dominant biomedical discourse, but also provides alternative means of understanding and treating mental and emotional distress. It furthermore alerts us to the reach of carceral systems and practices into a range of community facilities and programmes, including mental health services, so that medicalisation and criminalisation operate as two sides of the same coin.

Fourth, the critiques in this collection reveal the emotional and mental devastation caused by imprisonment. For example, Mills and Kendall's (Chapter 5) study of a mental health in-reach team (MHIRT) in an English prison, demonstrates how security and control consistently took priority over care. Consequently, the MHIRT often found it difficult to even see prisoners and, rather than providing treatment or even listening to prisoners, they primarily carried out a variety of activities associated with penal governance and risk management. Prisoners spent inordinate amounts of time 'banged up' in their cells with a lack of purposeful activity leading to boredom and mental and emotional distress. In her chapter on New Psychoactive Substances (NPS), Moyes (Chapter 6) argues that these conditions of boredom and distress are key reasons why prisoners use NPS. However, she notes that these drugs frequently worsen mental health and make prisons still more dangerous places by facilitating violence and even leading to death. Jablonska and Meek (Chapter 7) further demonstrate the pains of imprisonment by exposing the 'double punishment' experienced by English women prisoners with disabilities and serious physical health conditions; these women are punished for being convicted of a crime and by being kept in an environment inappropriately designed or adapted for their needs. The harms caused by the unsuitable built environment are compounded by the lack of care and kindness from others, which substantially affects their mental health, even contributing to suicide attempts. Citing Foucault, Sim (Chapter 10) makes the stark assertion that in creating brutal conditions leading to self-inflicted deaths, prisons can be conceptualised as 'death machines'. These chapters strengthen the case made by other contributors that mental health problems are an inherent feature of prisons and, therefore, this book challenges the notion that prisons can ever be healthy places. Such a critique is particularly important in light of the current healthy prisons agenda in the UK and elsewhere.

Mental Health in Prison: Key Strategies from Critical Perspectives

This collection ultimately leads to the conclusion that we must address social inequalities which are at the root of the mental health problem in prison and look towards alternatives to incarceration. A classic public health parable illustrates this point. Although told in different guises, the story generally unfolds as follows: imagine that you are sitting by a river. All of a sudden, a drowning child floats by. You immediately jump in, grab hold of her and swim to shore. Just as you are about to call for help, another child drifts by so you save him too. Soon you see another child. Then another. And another. You are getting very tired and cannot keep up with the number of children floating by so you decide to climb out of the river and follow it upstream to find out why so many children have fallen into the water. After ten minutes of running along the bank, you see a man throwing the children into the water and stop him from doing so. Had you not changed the focus of your actions to head upstream, the problem would have continued. However, as Seddon (2007, p. 163) notes in his recounting of Cohen's version of this tale, a number of children will have drowned while you were running along the riverbank. The point here is that we need to tackle the fundamental causes of social problems but while we do so, we must not neglect the anguish of those who remain incarcerated.

In this regard, the essays included here provide solid examples of how we might address both the immediate concern to alleviate the pains of imprisonment and begin to establish longer term strategies directed at the root of the problem. With respect to the former, Perrin (Chapter 14) demonstrates how peer-support schemes, built on the principles of empathy, mutual reciprocity and emotional support, help improve the mental health of both those providing support and those receiving it. Indeed, a key feature of these programmes is that support is bi-directional, that is, mutually agreed upon and shared. This guiding philosophy coincides with the W2B programme outlined by Pollack and Edwards (Chapter 13), which similarly emphasises collaboration; values lived experience and knowledge of both 'inside' and 'outside' students; and attempts to reduce power dynamics. The success of this programme is demonstrated by the fact that it has created communities wherein authentic connections and belonging thrive, thus benefiting mental health. Both peer support and the W2B programme foster mutually reciprocal relationships and embody a care ethic of relational virtue of the kind called for by Arrigo and Sellers (Chapter 4) and discussed above. Sim (Chapter 10) moreover argues that while prisons remain open, we must hold them democratically accountable through the establishment of transparent systems. Although such systems are currently absent, the interventionist activism of grassroots organisations and the families of prisoners who have died in prison have held prisons to account by exposing the failure of the prisons to follow their own guidelines for the care and protection of inmates.

Longer term, radical strategies were identified by a number of contributors calling for alternatives to prison. For example, Daley and Radford (Chapter 12) advocate for a mad queer abolitionist strategy and Sim champions abolitionist praxis. While, as noted in the book's introduction, abolition is often criticised as idealistic and unrealistic, it provides us with an objective to which we can aspire. The late activist Rose Braz expressed this sentiment in an interview as follows: '[a] prerequisite to seeking any social change is the naming of it. In other words, unless we name it and fight for it today, it will never come' (Bennett 2008). In the same discussion, she describes abolition as the creation of a world that does not rely on prisons and other carceral practices as the answer to problems that are social, political and economic in nature. To reach such an end, she states that it is necessary to create healthy, sustainable communities rooted in accountability so that harm is reduced in the first place. She furthermore maintains that when harm does occur, it should be addressed in a non-punitive manner.

In efforts towards the creation of such communities, it is helpful to demonstrate, as widely as possible, that our personal struggles are in fact tied to those of others. For example, we can publicise recent research that shows while those on the bottom socio-economic rung have the worst mental and physical health and life expectancy, there is a gradient that runs from the top to the bottom of the spectrum affecting everyone (see, for example, Smith et al. 2016; Wilkinson and Pickett 2009). That is, those at the top of the ladder have better health and live longer than those on the rung just below them, who, in turn, have better health and live longer than those on the rung just below them and so on, in a downward incline, until the bottom of the ladder is reached. The more unequal a society is, the greater is the scale of difference between the top and bottom and all the rungs in between, and the poorer the mental and physical health of its citizens overall. The better health of more equal societies reflects the fact that they have stronger connected communities, greater interpersonal trust and lower levels of violence. In such a way, our mental health and freedom are ultimately bound to one another.

Future work on mental health and imprisonment can embody this observation by adopting the abolitionist praxis identified by Sim (Chapter 10) as a mixing of interventionist activism and the tools of scholarship. In a similar fashion, Daley and Radford (Chapter 12) note that theory can be a facilitator of social justice and work lived in practice. Taken together, the critical analyses within these pages suggest that we can best address the problem of mental distress within prisons through the creation of alliances among a diverse collection of academics, activists, prisoners and other criminalised persons, individuals with lived experience of mental health issues and critical practitioners. Such coalitions would strive to build knowledge intended to alleviate the immediate suffering of prisoners by improving their current circumstances and to create equal societies in order to pave the way for better mental health for all and imprisonment for none. Towards this end, we can be guided by the following words: 'If you have come here to help me, you are wasting your time. If you have come because your liberation is bound with mine, then let us work together' (Lilla Watson, cited in Pate 2013, p. 205).

Bibliography

Ben-Moshe, L., Chapman, C., & Carey, A. (Eds.). (2014). *Disability incarcerated*. Houndmills, Basingstoke: Palgrave Macmillan.

Bennett, H. (2008, July 11). Critical resistance: Organizing to abolish the prison industrial complex. *Dissident Voice*. Available at: https://dissident-voice.org/2008/07/organizing-to-abolish-the-prison-industrial-complex/. Accessed 9 Apr 2018.

Crenshaw, K. (1989). Demarginalizing the intersection of race and sex: A black feminist critique of antidiscrimination doctrine, feminist theory and antiracist politics. *University of Chicago Legal Forum, 1989*(1), 138–167.

Garland, D. (1985). *Punishment and welfare: A history of penal strategies*. Aldershot: Gower.

Johnstone, L., & Boyle, M. with Cromby, J., Dillon, J., Harper, D., Kinderman, P., Longden, E., Pilgrim, D., & Read, J. (2018). *The power threat meaning framework: Towards the identification of patterns in emotional distress, unusual experiences and troubled or troubling behaviour, as an alternative to functional psychiatric diagnosis.* Leicester: British Psychological Society.

LeFrançois, B. A., Menzies, R., & Reaume, G. (Eds.). (2013). *Mad matters.* Toronto: Canadian Scholars' Press Inc.

New York Times Editorial Board. (2017, February 27). Mental illness, untreated behind bars. *The New York Times.* Available at: https://www.nytimes.com/2017/02/27/opinion/mental-illness-untreated-behind-bars.html. Accessed 7 Jan 2018.

Pate, K. (2013). Women, punishment and social justice: Why you should care. In M. Malloch & G. McIvor (Eds.), *Women, punishment and social justice* (pp. 197–205). London: Routledge.

Pūras, D. (2017). *Report of the special rapporteur on the right of everyone to the enjoyment of the highest attainable standard of physical and mental health.* United Nations General Assembly. A/HRC/35/21. Available at: http://ap.ohchr.org/documents/dpage_e.aspx?si=A/HRC/35/21. Accessed 2 Apr 2018.

Seddon, T. (2007). *Punishment and madness: Governing prisoners with mental health problems.* Abingdon: Glasshouse.

Smith, K., Hill, S., & Bambra, C. (Eds.). (2016). *Health inequalities: Critical perspectives.* Oxford: Oxford University Press.

Solomon, E. (2017, March 3). The mental health crisis in Canadian prisons. *Maclean's.* Available at: http://www.macleans.ca/news/canada/the-mental-health-crisis-in-canadian-prisons/. Accessed 7 Jan 2018.

Wesley-Smith, M. (2017, May 6). Prisons or hospitals? *Newshub.* Available at: http://www.newshub.co.nz/home/shows/2017/05/prisons-or-hospitals.html. Accessed 7 Jan 2018.

Whitbourn, M. (2017, August 10). Mental illness and cognitive disability the "norm" among prisoners: Report. *The Sydney Morning Herald.* Available at: https://www.smh.com.au/national/nsw/mental-illness-and-cognitive-disability-the-norm-among-prisoners-report-20170810-gxtf9y.html. Accessed 7 Jan 2018.

Wilkinson, R. G., & Pickett, K. E. (2009). *The spirit level. Why equality is better for everyone.* London: Penguin Books.

Index

© The Editor(s) (if applicable) and The Author(s) 2018
A. Mills and K. Kendall (eds.), *Mental Health in Prisons*, Palgrave Studies in Prisons
and Penology, https://doi.org/10.1007/978-3-319-94090-8

Printed by Printforce, the Netherlands